MEMORY QUEST

TRAUMA AND THE SEARCH FOR PERSONAL HISTORY

Elizabeth A. Waites

W. W. NORTON & COMPANY, INC. • NEW YORK • LONDON

Quotes from *Everything in Its Path* by Kai Erikson reprinted with permission of Simon & Schuster. Copyright © 1976 by Kai T. Erikson.

The line from "love is more thicker than forget", copyright 1939, © 1967, 1991 by the Trustees for the E. E. Cummings Trust, from *Complete Poems: 1904–1962* by E. E. Cummings, Edited by George J. Firmage. Reprinted by permission of Live-right Publishing Corporation.

Copyright © 1997 by Elizabeth A. Waites

Printed in the United States of America

First Edition

Composition by Bytheway Typesetting Services, Inc.
Manufacturing by Haddon Craftsmen, Inc.

For information about permission to reproduce selections from this book, write to Permissions, W. W. Norton & Company, Inc., 500 Fifth Avenue, New York, NY 10110.

Library of Congress Cataloging-in-Publication Data

Waites, Elizabeth A.
    Memory quest : trauma and the search for personal history / Elizabeth A. Waites.
        p.   cm.
    "A Norton professional book"
    Includes bibliographical references and index.
    ISBN 0-393-70234-0
    1. False memory syndrome.   2. Recovered memory.   I. Title.
RC455.2.F35W34   1997
616.89 – dc20   96-32288   CIP

W. W. Norton & Company, Inc., 500 Fifth Avenue, New York, N.Y. 10110
http://www.wwnorton.com
W. W. Norton & Company, Ltd., 10 Coptic Street, London WC1A 1PU

1 2 3 4 5 6 7 8 9 0

To
Nicholas and Gina
and
Emily and Lund

Contents

Preface

WRITING A BOOK, even the most factual in focus, is inevitably an exercise in autobiographical memory. It is not just that all writing depends on memory. It is, rather, that the process of writing transforms even as it informs. This is especially so when the subject is personal history.

I grew up in an extended family of storytellers who enshrined the past, not just as a nostalgic diversion, but as one long cautionary tale. The Great Depression and two world wars, as well as more ordinary accidents and illnesses and deaths, were endlessly recounted and interpreted. It was as if, through constant repetition, we might finally "get it right." As I listened, I became intrigued by the ways in which general calamities are comprehended and memorialized in terms of particular ones. I learned to look for the pattern in the weave. It was a first step toward a systematic study of memory.

At school, too, memory was hallowed. Rote repetition was still a pedagogical mainstay, and children were praised for accurate recall. Oblivious to the deeper structures of mathematics, my generation repeated the multiplication table *ad nauseam*. Unaware of the inherent ambiguity of texts and the suspect status of sources, we memorized history as a vast compendium of names and dates and facts. Unperplexed by the search for underlying meaning, we proudly recited a standard repertory of poetry and patriotic speeches—Mark Antony's eulogy over Caesar, the verses of Edgar Allan Poe, the Gettysburg address. This mass of memorized material was considered important in itself, of course. But it was not inculcated simply for that reason. Memorizing was supposed to train the mind.

As a child, I had a vividly accurate auditory memory that stood me in good stead scholastically. Yet a clever parrot, however amusing, is not an original thinker, and I sensed, even then, the distinction between received and original ideas. Fortunately, in spite of the official emphasis on memorizing, I was also encouraged to think for myself and question hoary authorities.

Eventually, after I began my training in psychology, I continued to be lucky in my teachers, and the ideas they stimulated have been much on my mind as I wrote this book. From Edward Walker, I learned to view memory as an evolving process rather than a static entity. As he shared his store of anecdotes on the history of psychology, I was delighted to discover that scientific discourse can be rigorous without being stuffy. From Gerald Blum, I learned how inextricably cognitive processes are joined to emotional and motivational states. State-dependent memory, which became my dissertation topic, was a novel concept in the early 1960s when he introduced me to it.

It was from clinical mentors, most notably Frederick Wyatt and David Gutmann, that I learned to listen to stories in a new way and to carefully negotiate the fine line between cynicism and gullibility. I discovered that human memory is always distinctly and inescapably human, that unconscious dynamics exert a powerful influence on social as well as personal history, and that there are more things in heaven and earth than are dreamt of in laboratories. And I learned to learn from clients, lessons that continue to guide my writing as well as my practice.

Clinical practice, finally, helped me comprehend and continually refine what I had learned as a student. Over the years, I have had the opportunity to witness many dimensions of memory, abnormal as well as normal. I have observed victims of dementia cut loose from the past that once anchored them in reality, hospitalized patients whose manufactured memories can be glib as they are false, strangers who seemed to remember me from their childhood, and well-known acquaintances who seemed to have forgotten me entirely. I have talked with people who claim to have been privy to visitations from God and people tormented by remembered encounters with Satan. Although I constantly question as I listen, covertly if not overtly, and although I never underestimate the power of fantasy, I pay respectful attention to what I hear. The skepticism or faith I bring to what people tell me is tempered not only by the nature of the recollections themselves, but by their impact, for good or ill, on individual lives.

I began my career in an age of anxiety in which the subversion of memory was becoming a matter of accepted social policy as well as an individual defense. Yet it was also an age of revelation and confrontation. Psychology — indeed, the world itself — was increasingly being transformed by discoveries and rediscoveries long overdue: the prevalence of child physical and sexual abuse, the lasting effects of trauma, the intricate evasions that can be managed by minds in flight from unbearable experiences.

Having lived through the heyday of psychoanalytic influence, I appreciate recent reactions against Freudian orthodoxies, especially those that have impeded the study of real-life trauma. Nevertheless, as simplistic inferences about childhood memories have increasingly come into vogue, I have been dismayed to see the baby thrown out with the bathwater. Many aspects of Freud's legacy remain timely and valid, and an informed sensitivity to the dynamic tensions and creative compromises that shape overt behavior is still to be recommended.

In recent years, I have also been saddened by the extent to which political agendas and either-or mindsets have sometimes overshadowed rational debates about memory. The effect on victims of intentional abuse has been especially disturbing. It was concern with all these troubling issues that provided the immediate impetus for writing this book.

During the actual writing, input from several sources proved especially helpful. Charlotte Doyle enriched my understanding of how children come to think about and narrate the past, and Margery Franklin provided a valuable lead on the same topic. Ronald Kessler and William Cunningham responded graciously to my inquiries concerning the epidemiology of trauma reactions. Marita-Constance Supan, a fellow psychotherapist, offered valuable perspectives on such phenomena as dissociation, the uses of metaphor, and the significance of readiness as a factor in remembering.

Throughout the project, the editorial assistance and ongoing encouragement of Susan Barrows Munro have helped me stay the course. And the support and technical assistance of Sonya Kennedy has, once again, been invaluable.

I am keenly aware that the subject of personal memory is altogether too broad to be encompassed by a single book and that new research is constantly modifying our understanding of what we know. As part of a quest, this book is, in any case, a starting point rather than a destination. I hope it may lead to unexpected places.

CHAPTER 1

Interrogating Memory

> We walked down the path to the well-house, attracted by the fragrance of the honeysuckle with which it was covered. Someone was drawing water and my teacher placed my hand under the spout. As the cool stream gushed over one hand she spelled into the other the word *water*, first slowly, then rapidly. . . . Suddenly I felt a misty consciousness as of something forgotten—a thrill of returning thought; and somehow the mystery of language was revealed to me. I knew then that "w-a-t-e-r" meant the wonderful cool something that was flowing over my hand.
>
> —Helen Keller, 1902/1988, p. 16

HELEN KELLER was nineteen months old when an illness, never definitively diagnosed, deprived her of sight and hearing. At the time she was stricken, she was already beginning to use a few words. One of these she remembered afterward—the word *water*, which she continued to pronounce "wa-wa." But without the ability to hear, she lost the ability to learn new words. The connection between verbal language and thought, which had probably been developing rapidly in the precocious nineteen-month-old, was broken. Not until she was almost seven years old was it restored to her.

Helen Keller's discovery at the well house was so remarkable that it was hailed as a miracle and Anne Sullivan, the teacher who led her to it, was called a "miracle worker" (Gibson, 1975). Helen's life bears witness to the miracle; no one can detract from it. Yet her own account of what happened attests not simply to a brand-new discovery, but to the integrative power of memory. The insight that suddenly illumined her darkness was "a thrill of returning thought." And once thought returned, there was no stopping her. A world opened to her that eventually included an education at Radcliffe College, authorship of numerous articles and books, and an inspiring career as lecturer and advocate for the blind and deaf.

Memory was a remarkable ally in all these achievements, and her exceptional memory, not only for language but for facts, was acknowledged by many who knew Helen. She could, for example, remember for months the names of people encountered only once (Lash, 1980). After she became a student at Perkins Institution for the Blind, one of her teachers there remarked that she seldom showed any failures of memory and did not need to review her lessons (Lash, 1980).

Yet it was memory that betrayed her. When she was only eleven years old, she was accused of plagiarism and, subsequently, was called to defend herself at a formal hearing. She had written a story called "The Frost King" which, following publication, was found to resemble in many details a story previously published by a famous children's author, Margaret Canby. However unintentional the mistake, many were quick to blame her for it. She was severely interrogated and publicly humiliated.

Helen was dismayed, having no clear idea of her offense. Yet, as traumatic as this experience was for her, it was a significant part of her education. The power of unconscious thought was brought home to her as surely as the power of language had been revealed to her at the well house.

But the Frost King incident was not merely a lesson in the psychology of memory. It was also a lesson in politics. Her inadvertent mistake reflected badly on a powerful man, Michael Anagnos, the director of the Perkins Institution for the Blind. Before the incident, he had sung her praises and gloried in her accomplishments. He took the Frost King incident as a personal affront and continued to discredit her for years thereafter (Lash, 1980).

The aftermath of the incident dampened Helen's refound joy in language: "I have never played with words again for the mere pleasure of the game," she remarked in her autobiography (Keller, 1902/1988, p. 50). During the following months, she became depressed and withdrawn and notes that, without her teacher's dogged encouragement, she would have given up writing altogether.

MEMORY ON TRIAL

Unconscious plagiarism still stands as a cautionary signpost for anyone who confronts the mysteries of memory. The insidiously deceptive trick of the mind that betrayed Helen Keller is technically called *cryptomnesia*, a phenomenon characterized by high-fidelity accuracy for factual details accompanied by amnesia for the source of the information. The source amnesia associated with unconscious plagiarism is taken as an example of how treacherous the mind can be (Bowers & Hilgard, 1988). Like Helen, so the argument goes, the rest of us who consider ourselves the authors of our own thoughts may be suffering from a failure of memory; perhaps our thoughts, including our reported memories, are just received stories suggested to us.

In fact, memory on trial is easy to discredit. Anyone can give examples of the vagaries of memory, and a century permeated with psychoanalytic discourse has taught us to smile knowingly when childhood dims in memory, dreams disappear, or a routine appointment with the dentist is forgotten. The well-known imperfections of memory are an obvious target for anyone who wants to challenge the authority, credibility, or competence of another person. And the less familiar ones give an aura of scientific authority to the challengers.

Yet, in spite of all disclaimers, most people rely constantly on veridical memory. It is not, after all, the treacherous nature, but instead the usual dependability of ordinary memory that makes the errors that do occur so noteworthy. We find our way to work without a map. On cue, we reel off strings of numbers — telephone numbers, social security numbers, zip codes — that have no intrinsic meaning. Even the lists we devise are typically elliptical notations: "shampoo" is shorthand for an easily recalled brand name. And although we grumble about minor lapses and make anxious quips about the onslaughts of age, any major memory lapse is an eerily unnerving experience, like quicksand underfoot. An encounter with a severe organic impairment, such as Alzheimer's disease or senile dementia, brings home forcefully how closely meaningful existence is connected with veridical memory. Watching the light of memory flicker and go out, we know that something real and essential is gone indeed and forever.

A PLURALITY OF STANDARDS

In everyday life, however, although people habitually depend on memory, they do not necessarily give careful thought to the criteria they employ in evaluating it. Newspaper readers, juries, psychotherapists, and research scientists, for example, may apply very different standards of accuracy or truth. Given this plurality of standards, it is scarcely surprising that the debates about memory that capture public attention from time to time often shed more heat than light on the subject.

The situation is even more confusing when there are deliberate attempts to subvert memory. Information that might be contrary to the interests of particular individuals or groups may be systematically suppressed, denied, or distorted. And when controversy arises and debate becomes strident, truth does not merely get lost. It can become a confusing buzzword in a battle of words.

Historically, the subversion of memory has been a typical instrument of political control. Totalitarian governments censor documents and restrict access to the media. In ancient Egypt, the names of figures out of favor were even erased from public monuments. In the twentieth century, President Nixon tried to suppress tape recordings that incriminated him. Self-styled guardians of memory are constantly at work to revise history. Even well documented events like the Holocaust have become targets of organized campaigns of denial (Lipstadt, 1993).

The supposedly objective and impartial scientific arena is by no means exempt from such campaigns. On the contrary, it is often a major battleground. Any piece of scientific evidence is subject to dispute, and attempts to discredit particular discoveries can always be buttressed by pointing to imperfections in the process of gathering or analyzing data. Or, an opposite tack, issues that are still unsettled may be discussed as matters of established scientific fact.

In an adversarial climate, it is difficult to avoid the extremes that sometimes polarize debate. But the complexities of memory need not be lost in a barrage of sound bites. Since the early 1900s, when Helen Keller was assailed for her "false memory," the scientific study of memory has produced a vast body of theory and research. Much of this has focused on the cognitive dimension of memory. Some efforts have even attempted to develop models of memory based on the workings of computers. Those who work in the laboratory usually consider their methods of inquiry superior and privileged, more scientific than case histories or anecdotal reports. The quantitative analyses to which their data are subjected seem to confirm this appraisal. Textbooks on memory typically describe research that averages data across many subjects.

Distinct personal histories are not only irrelevant to most such approaches; they are frequently completely overlooked or discounted. As a result, much remains to be studied about how individual histories and competencies impact on memory. Unusual memory feats, such as Mozart's memorization of a long score after one hearing or the astonishing demonstrations of Luria's subject S (1968), are mentioned in textbooks, to be sure. But for the most part, when "memory" as a general concept is discussed, or when controversies about the reliability of given memories arise, individual differences are scarcely considered.

There is, however, another form of scientific inquiry that involves a methodical consideration of individual differences. Clinical psychologists, as distinct from experimental psychologists, are especially trained to view clients from this perspective. And although their knowledge base is as limited as any other, trained clinicians have a body of useful professional experience as well as experimental research to offer to the individual in search of personal history.

Those well trained in particular methods of inquiry, such as forensic investigation or clinical evaluation, have both a knowledge base and special techniques of inquiry at their disposal. A skilled clinician, for example, may learn a great deal not just from accurate responses to questions but also from a consistent pattern of inaccuracies. Clinicians are well aware that individual styles of information-processing can have a great impact on what is later reported as a memory. Some people, for example, are quick to move beyond an external stimulus to their own encoded meanings of it or fantasies about it. Others are more careful about checking and recheck-ing what they have encountered in the external world. Some people are easily influenced or persuaded by other people. Others are steadfast, even defiant, in not being moved from an initial opinion.

A major factor contributing to individual differences in memory is how people confront and cope with traumatic events not just at the time such events occur but at later points of recall as well. Emergency reactions (Cannon, 1953; Selye, 1956) affect information-processing by restricting the range and focus of attention and by psychobiological responses ranging from changes in cerebral blood flow to variations in the turnover of neuro-transmitters (Axelrod & Reisine, 1984; Rose, 1980). While such reactions are related to stress responses that can be observed across individuals, and even across species, these responses may be also shaped and modified by personal histories (Waites, 1993).

Controlling access to specific memories is a common way of coping with stress and trauma. This control may be a simple matter of avoiding external reminders or a complex pattern of psychological avoidance that includes deliberate strategies of distraction. The troubling stimulus mem-ory may be ignored, denied, distorted, or selectively interpreted. These psychological operations may occur at the time an event occurs or later, when it is for any reason recalled.

Differential responses to trauma have traditionally been studied as de-fensive reactions. Several clinical theories have been devised to explain them, among the most influential of which have been the psychoanalytic theories derived from Freud. The controversy associated with clinical the-ories, however, should not detract from an empirical finding that is by now generally accepted. People differ in how they cope with stressful events, and the uses they make of memory are among the notable ways in which they differ.

From a clinical perspective, discussions of Helen Keller that draw gen-eral inferences about the unreliability of memory are especially ironic. By almost any measure, Helen Keller was a very unusual person. Yet, the argument can be made after all that each of us is unique.

Clinical experience also continually illustrates the extent to which stud-ies of memory as a cognitive process, however important, tell only part of the story. Human memory is more than a cognitive competence. It is a social achievement. Because of this inherently social aspect, many of the controversies that continue to vex students of the subject can only be clarified by a consideration of social dynamics. From a purely cognitive standpoint, for example, accuracy appears to be a defining attribute of memory. But in everyday life, as Helen Keller discovered to her sorrow, an exceptionally accurate memory may be a blessing or a curse. Whether it stands praised or condemned depends on how it is integrated with the adaptive requirements of situational and social contexts.

In a different social context, for example, Helen's high-fidelity memory might have been praised in spite of her amnesia for source. If she had been memorizing factual information for a test that did not question sources, she might have made an A+. If she had been giving an oral rendition of a properly attributed story, she might have been applauded. Some people recognized the significance of these social issues. Margaret Canby, the author of the purloined story, chose to emphasize the positive rather than the negative aspects of Helen's memory, praising her extraordinarily retentive mind. Mark Twain, a friend of Helen and Anne Sullivan, also chose to accentuate the positive. He wrote a humorous commentary on the ubiquity of unconscious plagiarism, recounting instances of his own literary thefts: "As if there was much of anything in any human utterance, oral or written, *except* plagiarism" (quoted in Lash, 1980, p. 154).

MEMORY AS SOCIAL COMPETENCE

David, who greeted me at Winnebago my first day on the unit, had memorized the entire bus system of the city of Milwaukee. Leslie, with his repertoire of thousands of songs has a tremendous memory. George remembers what the weather was on *every day of his adult life*. Prodigious memory seems to be characteristic of every savant, but for some, hypermnesis itself is their special ability. (Treffert, 1989, p. 95)

In his book, *Extraordinary People,* Darold Treffert describes numerous cases of exceptional memory in a group of individuals he calls "autistic savants." He employs the term "savant syndrome" to describe a configuration of special gifts and defects; high-fidelity memory in some particular subject area, such as music or mathematics, is accompanied by a usually profound mental retardation. Like cryptomnesia, the extraordinary memory of the savant is a striking illustration of the paradox that veridical memory, in and of itself, cannot be simply equated with useful memory.

Social withdrawal is a diagnostic feature of autism, and social skills are typically as lacking as memory skills are sometimes striking. In spite of their extraordinary memory feats, autistic savants are often so intellectually and socially impaired that they cannot care for themselves outside an institutional setting.

However spectacular, then, savant memory is limited by two important constraints. First, it has an automatic and inflexible quality that makes its application unselective and indiscriminate. And second, it is not integrated with social intelligence. Because of these limitations, it is commonly manifest as a compulsive but uncritical parroting of facts and is relatively impervious to direction from other people. It resembles the rote performance of a machine with fixed programming.

The socially unintegrated memories of the savant stand out like isolated islands in the stream of their ongoing behavior. They are marveled at as intriguing and novel displays, but are seldom a means of facilitating every-day coping. With guidance from other people, some savants are able to use their phenomenal memory for adapted achievements. But this need for an external guide in itself highlights a basic characteristic of normal human adaptation: for most people, memory itself is a guide.

Treffert (1989) believes that the exceptional memory that characterizes savant syndrome is a result of special forms of neural organization. In normal people, the hippocampus, a subcortical brain structure in the limbic system, is richly connected with the cortex; the cortico-limbic system, as this organization is called, is critical for transfer of short-term memory into long-term storage. Because of damage to limbic structures, Treffert believes, the savant develops an alternative memory network, the cortico-striatal system. This network is associated with automatic rather than volitional memory functions, nonsymbolic cognition, and a lack of emotional tone.

Whatever the validity of this hypothesis, it points to the possibility that it is not just *what* is remembered, but *how* it is remembered, that characterizes exceptional memories; that is, special forms of neural organization and processing may distinguish some extraordinary kinds of memory. Other researchers (Alkon, 1992; Restak, 1994) have suggested that even in normal people special mechanisms and processes of organization may be involved in the formation of traumatic memories.

From a functional perspective, too, the peculiarities of savant memory suggest important insights into both autism as a syndrome and memory in general. In adaptive contexts, it is not just what or how much people remember but the integration of memories into the fabric of social life and personal identity that matters. A compulsive recall of exact details of bus schedules or long strings of numbers provides evidence of how accurate memory *can* be. But much more than accuracy is required for adaptive memory.

Helen Keller's cryptomnesia makes a similar point. As an example of how much the mind can accurately retain, her reproduction of Canby's story was almost as remarkable as the memory feats of a savant. But as a human achievement, it was just as maladaptive.

CONSIDER THE PERSON

The contrasting histories of Helen Keller and autistic savants with prodigious memories illustrate how one observable phenomenon, high-fidelity memory for detail, may have quite different origins and manifestations. In respect to memory, as with many other psychological processes, competencies and deficits that appear superficially similar may arise from very different causes. People possessing different capabilities, guided by different habits, motivated by different needs, and confronting different tasks develop different ways of using memory to help them cope. Close examination of behavioral patterns often reveals specific signs and symptoms that are diagnostically significant.

In spite of some superficial similarities, for example, the high-fidelity memory of the savant differs in crucial respects from the unusual memory displayed by Helen Keller. One important distinction, the problem that got her into trouble, was that Helen's memory was implicit; she was not conscious that her story was a memory and so mistook it for original thought. David, in contrast, knew that he remembered. Helen also acquired her high-fidelity memory through mechanisms quite different from those that characterize savant memory. In contrast to the savant, who is abnormally insensitive to social influence, Helen got in trouble because she was especially vulnerable to social influence, particularly that of her teacher, Anne Sullivan.

This vulnerability to influence was related to Helen's unusual dependency on others. Although normal children have gained considerable autonomy by the age of eleven, when Helen was interrogated concerning her plagiarism, Helen's dependency had been prolonged by her disabilities. As a result, the boundaries between her developing self and the person of her teacher were especially permeable, and she was late in achieving the autonomy to think for herself. Comparatively isolated from input from other sources, she was hypersensitive to whatever Teacher tapped into her hand.

After she regained the use of language when she was almost seven, Helen faced the formidable task of learning as much as possible about the world as soon as she could; she was making up for lost time. The extent of her need made it adaptive for her memory to cast a wide net. And the sharpness of her retentive mind meant that an amazing array of information got caught in that net. Usually, too, the more she remembered, the more she was praised. But before the Frost King incident, the task of interrogating her memory critically had not been taught her. Thus she continued to face obstacles in discriminating between information from the inanimate world and information she was merely told about.

Anne Sullivan's teaching style may have contributed to Helen's difficulties in that respect. In contrast to those who subscribed to traditional forms of didactic instruction, Teacher consciously emphasized the casual, oral style of information transmission more characteristic of preschool experience (Lash, 1980). She deliberately sought to teach Helen in the way normal children learn language and other basic information about the world, through constant social interactions in natural settings. Thus, a walk though the garden became an opportunity for learning not only language, but botany, geography, and meteorology.

When Teacher told Helen stories and read to her, amusing anecdotes were often presented in the most offhand way, mixed in with conversations about surrounding scenes. The Frost King imagery, for example, was probably used to illustrate what happened to nature as the seasons changed (Lash, 1980). Anne Sullivan's teaching style may thus have contributed to Helen's unconscious plagiarism; many suspected, in fact, that Anne Sullivan herself may have been the original source of the Frost King story.

Helen was also different from other children in that she was taught to read as she was still being taught spoken language. Plagiarism, conscious or unconscious, is a textual offense only comprehensible in a literate culture. Learning to pay attention to textual sources and to discriminate between authoritative accounts and hearsay is an important and carefully practiced aspect of formal education. Texts typically have authors, and authorship is a proprietary right that children learn in school to acknowledge and value.

But these distinctions were blurred for Helen; the discontinuities between the typical modes of information transmission in early childhood and the textual culture of later childhood and adult life were not as sharp for her as for most children. She probably had no understanding of what "plagiarism" was all about. As a result, she was quick to display what she excelled at, including her imagination and memory, but failed to appreciate the significance of her sources. When "The Frost King" was originally read to her—and "reading," like talking, meant that a series of symbols was tapped into her hand—she may not even have attended to the fact that the words came from a book. She could not, after all, see the source for herself.

Helen might have been more discriminating, however, if she had been more familiar with certain social conventions. Freeman (1993) suggests that perhaps Helen did not experience stories as a normal child might; she was merely taking in and remembering sequences of words. In any case, she did not understand conventional standards of storytelling well enough to guard against offending against them.

But harsh as the lesson was, she eventually learned it, perhaps even too well. From that point on, she became conscious, even anxious, about the task of questioning the accuracy of her memories. By the time she wrote *The Story of My Life*, she remarked rather apologetically, "When I try to classify my earliest impressions, I find that fact and fancy look alike across the years that link the past with the present" (Keller, 1902/1988). Even so, what a valuable ally her veridical memory turned out to be in the achievement of her remarkable life!

CONSIDER THE TASK

Helen Keller's cryptomnesia highlights the distinction between failures of memory per se and failures to integrate memory with social tasks and contexts. She remembered very much very clearly, but forgot what other people considered a crucial task, remembering where she got the information. And she had not initially focused on that detail because she did not comprehend the high value placed on attribution of authorship by those around her. Lash (1980) contends that even Anne Sullivan did not really comprehend what plagiarism was.

From a purely cognitive perspective, the key to the paradox of unconscious plagiarism lies in the simple fact that even a remarkably detailed memory can never be perfect. The processes underlying the formation and retrieval of memories — ranging from attention and perception, to recognition and recollection — are necessarily selective. Memory must be true enough to be useful, but in order to be really useful, it must be more than true. It must be relevant to the task or tasks at hand.

Practically speaking, this means, too, that sometimes a useful memory must be less than true; it must be pragmatically evaluative in the selections it encodes or retrieves, ignoring details that seem to be irrelevant in order to focus on those judged important. A memory that includes too much makes it hard to see the forest for the trees. In infrahuman species, certain stimuli automatically preempt attention. In human beings, however, selectivity is seldom preprogrammed; it is usually a function of individual needs and motives as well as external events. And it is acquired in the context of systematic socialization. In order, then, to understand a phenomenon like Helen Keller's inattention to the source of her story, it is necessary to understand not only how memory works as a process, but how young children learn to make use of it.

Childhood is devoted to the acquisition not only of stores of specific information about the world but also of schemas and strategies for organizing information (Bartlett, 1932/1995). From the beginning, too, memory is Janus-faced; it has a prospective as well as a retrospective dimension. In order to be adaptively useful, what reflects the past must anticipate the future. Learning to anticipate one's future needs, however, is as complex a process as learning to remember (Kreutzer et al., 1975).

Early in life, sensation captures memory; the world is a pictured place, a vividly immediate presence. Gradually, however, conventional categories of coding and organizing experience begin to modify, even replace entirely, the "raw" data of immediate sensory perception. And as the child develops, practical memory is increasingly facilitated by being able to move from the particular to the general, from the specifics of single episodes to the categorical mappings and schemas that organize day-to-day interactions. As the specific is increasingly subordinated to the general, more and more information is stored in what Tulving (1983) describes as *semantic* form. The development of language, which begins in infancy and blossoms profusely after the first year, greatly accelerates this process (Bloom, 1993).

Normally in childhood, cognitive and social competencies develop in tandem and mutually enrich each other. But although all these develop-ments are made possible by innate capacities such as brain structure, they do not unfold automatically and are not acquired in isolation. In normal development, such competencies bear the stamp of the particular cultures and families in which they are acquired (Vansina, 1985). And social depri-vation, whether as a function of early neurological damage or of deliberate neglect, can interfere with normally expectable integrations (Emde & Sameroff, 1989).

From birth, individual memory is socially regulated by ongoing dia-logues. Even before the child has language, he or she is acquiring the habits of observation, thinking, and behavior that will shape not only a repertory of memories but also a remembering self who will orchestrate these memories.

Prior to the maturation of the child's autonomous self, it is the acknowl-edged role of family and culture to guide and teach these acquisitions. In all cultures, much of what young children learn at first is necessarily transmitted by word of mouth in casual interactions with caregivers. In literate societies, written texts and the influence of the media are never far away, but early childhood is, in many respects, an oral culture (Ong, 1982).

In most cultures, the vital but casual dialogues of early childhood are also eventually supplemented by formal systems of instruction. While these vary, schooling is typically organized around the study of written texts. The world of early childhood, rich in sensory experience and typi-cally centered in the family, is not eclipsed by the wider world of school, but it is to some extent superseded. Memory will reflect both worlds and the transitions between them.

In school, tasks are explicit and standards of achieving them are speci-fied. Source is, in many instances, highlighted as a valued fact. Dialogues multiply; the child is attuned to an expanding world. The very nature of texts facilitates these changes. By framing events in a linear narrative in which past, present, and future are clearly demarcated, texts also become a major tool for organizing memory (Ong, 1982). As verbal symbols, words are abstract, but as printed words on a page they have a concrete character that tends to freeze memory into definite and durable forms. Because they are accorded objective authority, texts are commonly taken as reliable reference points for what "really" happened in the past. True or false, the written word easily becomes a guarantor of correct memory.

Throughout all these developments, informally guided or formally schooled, learning is integrated with individuation. In any human being, the development of memory over the lifespan will reflect the typicalities and aberrations, the continuities and discontinuities of several stages of socialization. From the reciprocal patterns of regulation characteristic of infancy, to the increasingly articulated competencies of the toddler, to the systematic instructions of schooling, the child continually learns the complex matches between fact and task that make memory useful as well as true.

Stages, of course, are not always strictly bounded or discontinuous. They may overlap and merge. Guided transitions allow the child to move back and forth between contexts and modes of experiencing. At any stage of development, some personal memories may be primarily visual or auditory or verbal, the vestiges of specific events that persist as unchanged images, like fossils in the mind. Many memories, however — perhaps most — are multimodal, refined and transformed as they are repeatedly accessed over time. In this respect, the concept of episodic memory as distinct from semantic memory (Tulving, 1983) is less useful than it may appear at first glance. After infancy, a remembered episode is usually a mix of the general and the particular. Even the most graphic images are labeled. Even the most objectively clear events are structured by narrative forms. In many respects, too, the development of memory, like development generally, is a continuous process; integration of distinct modes of experiencing and definable stages of maturation is the norm.

TRAUMA AND MEMORY

Sometimes, however, life changes abruptly, with no intermediate stages to ease the transition. Such an abrupt change is commonly experienced in connection with a traumatic event and involves integrating experiences of physical as well as psychological injury. Even in the absence of observable injury, sudden and extreme change can be traumatic, overtaxing the capacity of the individual to cope with changed circumstances and integrate disparate experiences.

Memory evolved to help organisms cope with change as well as sameness. But change that is too sudden and severe may seriously interfere with adaptive coping. Any abrupt change may produce a disjunction in memory systems. For reasons that will be subsequently discussed, traumatic disruptions are especially likely to do so.

Some transitions and disjunctions are so commonplace that their significance for the development of memory is easily overlooked. Traumatic changes may be so commonplace or widespread that they are taken for granted. Some special but stressful events, such as initiation rites, may be a social tradition, expectable for every child in the culture. Or a natural disaster, such as a hurricane that destroys a community, may be an experience shared by all children there. Sometimes, too, continuous or repeated trauma is the norm of everyday experience. For children who grow up in contexts of ever-present danger and deprivation, trauma itself may be the thread of continuity that binds developmental stages and systems of memories together.

Representation is a major mechanism for coping with trauma. The personal histories remembered by individuals are a function not simply of what has happened to them, but also of the complexities of cognitive and social development. How any specific event, including a traumatic one, is woven into the fabric of memory will vary with the nature of the event itself and with how the individual learns to represent and interpret it. Representation, in turn, is not only a facilitating factor in communication, but also a consequence of the dialogues that have molded individuation. The self who consults personal history will almost inevitably discover a chorus of voices, each with stories to tell or silence, each with interests and perspectives to foster.

The significance of the connections among individuation, representation, self-representation, and memory have not always been appreciated by researchers investigating memory. It is commonly observed, for example, that people have difficulty remembering episodes from their early childhood. This phenomenon, labeled "infantile amnesia," has been given several explanations, ranging from Freud's (1899) theory that it results from repression of infantile conflicts, to Schachtel's (1947) explanation that it is related to language codes, to modern theories that it may be a function of biological as well as psychological factors. The possibility that infantile amnesia is not a loss of memory per se but results primarily from an inability to access existing memories has also received some support (see Kail, 1990).

The loss of early episodic memory may in many instances be an expectable consequence of discontinuities between social contexts or disjunctions of personal history. At any rate, such discontinuities could interact with more basic cognitive processes to create dissociations between life stages and the memories associated with particular stages. In dissociative disorders, for example, there may be extensive amnesia even for periods beyond early childhood (Putnam, 1989). The year in school when one learned the multiplication table may be missing, or the period following a chaotic disruption of family life.

IN SEARCH OF THE PAST

At every stage of memory development, from the earliest perceptual encodings to the latest recollections, from the earliest impressions of infancy to the latest revisions of age, most people are involved in matching their individual actions to the preferences or demands of other people. As a result of this social agenda, the search for personal memory is often a search for the authentic voice of the self amidst the din of competing voices. The search for personal history is, in this respect, an ongoing aspect of individuation. Anyone who undertakes it confronts the task of separating self from other not only in the present but also at earlier stages of development. And the self itself is not a static entity but an ongoing transformation. Both the voices of other people and those of previous selves shape the dialogues out of which a coherent and meaningful past is constructed.

The search for the past is in many instances a private endeavor. Whether it involves a trip to an old hometown, the unpacking of a trunk, reading an old journal, or attempting to write an autobiography, the quest confronts the self with the complexities and mysteries of memory. How strange the difference between what one remembered and what one now discovers! How remarkable the accuracy of a particular recollection! How curious the loss of a significant detail or episode! The discovery of transformations and discontinuities can be disquieting as well as difficult to comprehend. And disputes that arise between self-now and self-then can be as contentious, even painful, as disputes between self and other.

The self can also be impeded in its search — sometimes stymied — by the uniqueness of personal experience. The scientific study of memory has traditionally focused on general processes and group norms. The individual who, for whatever reason, differs from the norm is mentioned as an unusual aberration rather than studied as an instructive example. Unfortunately, to those in search of their personal past, the complexities of memory not only as a process but as a social achievement are often a source of dismay rather than reassurance. It would be so much easier if memory were a simple stored entity, like a keepsake in a box. It would be so convenient if some grand authority, the definitive arbiter of memory, could step forward to attest to the truth or falsity of any particular recollection. It might be reassuring, too, to be told that memory is always there for the finding. Or that it most definitely is not. Or even that it doesn't matter.

Questions about important personal issues cannot be resolved by simple appeals to authority, however. Nor can debates about the truth be resolved by simple appeals to relativism. Certain facts are as inescapable as they are hard to interpret. However doubtful a memory, the distinction between memory and fantasy is so significant for most people that it continues to guide the process of search. And even when definitive answers are not and may never be available, the persistence of the question cannot be ignored. The self must come to terms with it, in all its ambiguity. Such internal conflicts or disputes are commonly the reason people consult psychotherapists. Psychotherapy offers the prospect of exploration, clarification, and integration in a safe, nonadversarial context.

Psychotherapy should always be distinguished from forensic investigation or diagnostic evaluation. The investigator explores the accuracy or reliability of memory in the context of tasks defined by other people, commonly a social agency or a court. The psychotherapist, in contrast, is engaged to work for and with the client. Anything that compromises the client-therapist relationship, including intrusions of third parties or a subordination of the interest of the client to the interest of third parties, can be expected to impact adversely on the therapeutic process.

Whether the exploration of memory arises in an investigative or a therapeutic context, however, it is always important to approach issues about memory on the basis of knowledge and training, rather than mere opinion. Caution is especially in order when some important decision, such as the guilt or innocence of an accused person, hangs on an evaluation. Certainly, anyone who embarks on a search for his or her personal past is in quest of a unique set of experiences. The assumption that there is some greater authority than the one who had the experiences is inherently suspect. Whatever the limitations and distortions of personal memory, there is often no measure that is more reliable.

The fact that some investigators or therapists are poorly trained or even unethical does not negate the validity of the inferences of those who are. It merely requires attention to the particular abilities and experience of any so-called "expert."

As a guide in the quest for memory, the competent investigator or therapist can be expected to be familiar with scientific research on memory, including research on the impact of trauma on memory, as well as aware of factors that can compromise memory. A discerning investigator does not take at face value everything a client says. But anyone who understands the infinite variety of human experiences and the individual variations in memory will also be cautious in making inferential leaps from group data obtained in laboratory settings. A remarkable individual can sometimes do what most normal people cannot. And under unusual conditions, even the memory of normal people may perform more — or less — efficiently than usual.

It is also useful to keep in mind that reliability and usefulness of a memory do not require that either a memory or the person reporting a memory be perfect. As Terr (1994) has emphasized, in many instances when memory matters, a miss is not nearly as bad as a mile. Neisser (1982) emphasizes the same point in discussing the testimony of John Dean about the Watergate incident. In spite of provable inaccuracies, it told an important truth: Richard Nixon had committed a crime. Suppressing Dean's testimony as unreliable evidence might have been a disservice to the country.

Fortunately, most people who embark on the search for their personal past do not do so in an adversarial climate. The task before them is not proving the accuracy of their memories to the satisfaction of other people, but, rather, coming to terms with what they remember or what they don't. Autobiographical memory, like the self who bears witness to it, is a lifelong construction. When the search for the past becomes explicit or urgent, it may lead to troubling ambiguities and undecided questions. But it can also lead to satisfying insights.

The role of the therapist in such a search is not to function as an authoritarian arbiter or controlling decision maker. It is, rather, to supplement the skills and assets of the client with a specialized body of skills and training. The role of the therapist is not to tell the client what certainly happened in the past. It is, rather, to make it safe for the client to remember.

In practice, reliable or accurate memory is only a part of a successful psychotherapy. Compulsive remembering, however accurate, can disrupt adaptation as much as compulsive forgetting. The past can be a prison as well as a guidepost. Whatever the client's stated goal, an overriding therapeutic consideration is the integrity and autonomy of the client. In therapy as in life, the measure of memory is not just what it reveals about the past but also how it paves the way toward the future.

Beyond the endless debates and citations of sometimes conflicting data, the mind is neither a laboratory nor a courtroom. It is, rather, a home to a passionately partisan self. Memory guards and defends it, helps keep it tidy, even, on occasion, makes it a hospitable and entertaining place. When threatened, the mind and all its resources, including memory, may become a fortress under siege. And when that happens, survival may take precedence over truth. If it does, however, the truth the self asserts, like any other truth, deserves a hearing. Only those who are willing to listen to it can stand as credible witnesses to other standards.

Most important, however, the partisan self, for all its biases, is not usually a delusional self. The adaptive and integrative function of memory lies in the amazing capacity of the mind to *re*-present and *re*-collect real experiences. However these are embellished or amended, veridical memory remains a cornerstone of human adaptation.

PART I

The Integrative Function of Memory

CHAPTER 2

Getting Past the Present

O joy! that in our embers
Is something that doth live,
That Nature yet remembers
What was so fugitive!

—William Wordsworth, "Ode on Intimations of Immortality
from Recollections of Early Childhood"

M EMORY IS THE persistence of the familiar in a sea of change. It is the
organization of discrete and coherently connected events out of an
endless flux of sometimes chaotic happenings. In the absence of memory,
the world would seem forever new. But, of course, the concept of "new"
would have no meaning.

As we scan the world, we seem to move imperceptibly but inexorably
through time. Yet the only perspective from which we actually view any
particular event is that which William James called "the 'specious' present,
a sort of saddle-back of time with a certain length of its own, on which we
sit perched" (1892/1985, p. 147). Magically, though confined to this perch,
we are time-travelers, anticipating the future and revisiting the past. The
future, however predictable, is recognizably a fantasy trip, but the past
seems more of a sure bet, finished and knowable. Memory bears witness
to it.

Yet when we look back, the line from the present through the past is
not continuous, and some regions of it stand out more clearly than others.
We encounter the past as a connected or disconnected series of episodes,
organized sequences that typically have a beginning, middle, and end and
are often given temporal tags: Last week, I put up the storm windows.
Yesterday, I went to a movie. Such episodes, trivial or significant, are a
large part of what we access when we consciously consult memory as
personal history.

Episodes are only a small part of what we remember, however. Much of what we store and use consists of skills, habits, and general information about the world. Some of this store is accessible to the conscious mind. Other aspects cannot be subjected to conscious reflection but form an implicit background to ongoing behavior.

Those who study memory as a cognitive process have, in fact, devised numerous classifications, distinguishing between declarative and procedural memory (Cohen, 1984; Cohen & Squire, 1980), between implicit and explicit memory (Graf & Masson, 1993), between semantic memory and episodic memory (Tulving, 1983), etc. Other classifications that have sometimes guided approaches to memory include the distinction between unconscious and conscious memories (Freud, 1899), and that between repressed and dissociated memories (Ellenberger, 1970; van der Kolk & van der Hart, 1989). These classifications are useful in devising studies of how people remember. Nevertheless, although, with clever experimental techniques, the categories may be studied in their specificity, they are not always mutually exclusive. Explicit or declarative memory, for example, which usually involves accessing verbal representations of the past, is a typical though not essential aspect of memory for episodes. And the distinction between semantic and episodic memory (Tulving, 1983) turns out, on close examination, to be less clear-cut than appears at first glance.

Sometimes differences in types of memory point to differences in how different kinds of information are acquired and retained. We need no words to acquire skills like learning to ride a bicycle, for example. But words are indispensable for narratives about the past. We study for a test that will measure concepts differently from the way we learn lines to a play. We observe and remember the world differently when it challenges survival than we do when we are casually going about the business of daily living.

Different types of memory, such as procedural or skill memory, emotional memory, and declarative or stated memory, are not only based on different mechanisms of learning but may be mediated by distinct regions or structures in the brain. Such distinctions help explain the common observation that someone with an excellent memory for words may perform poorly on tests of visual recall or that someone who never forgets a face may often be at a loss for names. They help clarify why, following brain disease or damage, some memory functions may be retained while others are lost. All these considerations illustrate the broad referential base of the term *memory*. What is casually described as "remembering" is usually a complex and multifaceted process.

In spite of these distinctions, the human mind normally works as an integrated system; integration, facilitating harmonious transactions between parts of the self or between self and world, is a major function of memory. Sometimes what is observed superficially as a failure in memory turns out, on closer examination, to be primarily a failure in integration. When integration fails or is suspended, whether because of organic or functional factors, different types of memory may even function independently. Such unintegrated processes are called *dissociations* (Feyereisen, 1991; Hellige, 1983; Kinsbourne & Hiscock, 1983; Putnam, 1989).

The more complex a particular recollection, the more memory systems it involves, the more vulnerable it is likely to be to failures of integration at one or more levels of processing. For example, anything that disrupts basic neural mechanisms, such as brain disease or extreme psychological trauma, may affect not only circumscribed memory functions but also the apprehension of episodes and the organization of personal history. On the other hand, complex developments like autobiographical memory may be marked by failures of integration even when there has been no disruption of basic underlying memory mechanisms.

Autobiographical memory, a major focus of this book, is an especially complex organization of cognitive systems. It is likely to include numerous episodes as well as factual data defining who and what one is. It is closely allied to the experience of identity and the recognition of the individual self as a coherent and consistent pattern of thinking and an agent of action (Barclay & DeCooke, 1988; Barsalou, 1988; Brewer, 1988).

Autobiographical memory is typically accessed through the narrative of personal history and is marked by the implicit or explicit affirmation, "I remember." Memory for skills and facts makes possible everyday coping, but it is autobiographical memory that guarantees any given memory as personal experience and can promise to tell the truth about it.

Perhaps because of the complexities involved and the emphasis in psychological research on the study of the basic mechanisms and general parameters of memory, the study of both episodic and autobiographical memory has only recently come to the fore of scientific investigation. As a result of this lag in experimental observation, much about how personal memories are constructed and accessed still remains mysterious. In recent years, however, there have been many attempts to make sense of the mystery. An understanding of how several memory systems working in tandem organize personal history requires a consideration of numerous facets of mental functioning, ranging from the biological structure of cells and neural networks to the development and transformation of personal identity over the lifespan. A survey of this domain reveals both our kinship with animals and our uniquely human acquisitions.

The integrative function of memory is a useful guide in this endeavor. As useful as it is to understand the basic mechanisms of memory and our evolutionary heritage, it is memory as an emergent function that helps make humans unique. We are more than the simple sum of our memory traces. At any given moment, it is not just the encoding, storage, and retrieval of information, but also the interplay of personal needs, motives, and abilities that determines our recollections of things past. In approaching such questions as how any particular individual can distinguish between what is true and what is false in memory, it is always important to keep in mind what is human and what is personally relevant as well as what is possible.

COPYING THE WORLD

How memory allows us to travel back in time is a problem that has intrigued people from their earliest ventures in self-reflective thought. Explaining how memory works is not simply a matter of satisfying curiosity but a practical concern that facilitates teaching the young, keeping track of business, and making sense of history. Not surprisingly, the models of memory proposed during particular epochs reflect modes of thought characteristic of those periods.

Internal images of past events intuitively suggest that a memory is a copy. But a copy of what? The naive mind says *things* or *real* occurrences; a real world outside us is somehow copied and carried inside the mind and can be re-presented (presented again) in the absence of the actual entities that were copied. But this notion immediately raises questions about specifics of what, how, and why. And attempts to be specific lead not only to theories about memory but far-ranging speculations about what *things* are and what *mind* is. Before the development of psychology as an empirical science, such speculations were subjects of endless philosophical debate.

One way of solving the problem of how the outside gets inside is by doing away with the dichotomy. If the distinction between the world and the mind is declared to be mere illusion, the contents of the mind, including memories, can be seen as given and perhaps eternal rather than made over time. This point of view has perennially appealed to mystics and some philosophers; however, perhaps because it is counterintuitive, it has always inspired skepticism. The notion that the mind really copies something real is powerfully appealing. The unresolved questions of what gets copied and how it does so eventually inspired more scientific forms of inquiry.

Even in antiquity, memory was recognized—perhaps it would be more accurate to say *defined*—as a matching process. One method of enhancing memory, the method of loci, explicitly instructed people in how to make this match most usefully. This method envisioned the process of remembering as a stroll through a familiar place where every object of memory was located, like furnishings in a room. Finding a particular memory was then a matter of placing it in space rather than time (Schwartz & Reisberg, 1991). This approach to memory may seem odd to modern minds. But metaphors that reflect it are still in use. We sometimes speak of "losing track" of thoughts as if we had meandered from a chosen path. And the loss of a memory is sometimes compared with the misplacing of an object. There is actually some experimental support for the notion that memory capabilities evolved in tandem with the ability to perform spatial mappings (Neisser, 1988).

The invention of writing and the increasing reliance on texts as memory aids called attention to a special kind of matching process, that between things and words. The ancient Greeks had compared memory to the imprinting of a stylus on clay. By the eighteenthth century, the widespread dissemination of texts increased the appeal of this analogy. John Locke, for example, concluded that at birth the mind is a *tabula rasa*, a blank sheet on which experience is literally imprinted. But although it was tempting, especially after Locke, to view memory as a concrete imprint of experience on the mind, this metaphor has proved a source of confusion rather than clarification for students of memory.

One problem with the printing metaphor is that it sometimes encourages people to treat the words that represent objects as the objects they represent. But words are not things. And memories are neither words nor things. Words point to and represent objects, and memories point to and represent events. But it is important to distinguish between such pointers and their referents.

When the names of objects are not differentiated from the referents to which they point, the result is called *reification*. Reification is a logical fallacy that has frequently muddied debate on controversial issues, particularly those concerned with how the mind works. Reification tends to treat hypothetical constructs, like "the memory trace" or "repression," as if they were concrete entities or physical events. As a result of such traditional ways of thinking and powerful tendencies toward reification, even after the development of scientific traditions, the mind continued to be envisioned as a repository of *things*, a kind of museum where artifacts were stored or a library of literal texts.

MINDS AS MACHINES

In the nineteenth century, philosophical speculations about the mind were increasingly supplemented by empirical investigations of the brain and nervous system. Yet copy theories of memory continued to hold sway; as the brain was mapped and measured, it continued to be envisioned as a special kind of copying device.

As Rose (1992) has reviewed the history of this research, much of it was based on an analogy that remains very popular today, the view of biological organisms as machines. In the seventeenth and eighteenth centuries, civilized life began to be transformed by technology. As increasingly wonderful machines were invented, human beings began to be viewed as the most wonderful machines of all. Not surprisingly, the temptation to think of the brain itself as a machine eventually proved irresistible. In the search for the mechanics of memory, the brain began to be viewed as a kind of factory where engrams were assembled and warehoused.

The most amazing and influential machine in our own day is probably the computer, and computer models are now among the most influential explanations of human learning and memory. The logic of the computer analogy is undeniably compelling: if we can understand how, by punching a few keys, anyone can call up on the screen a whole library of information, surely we can eventually make sense of how our brains store and access the massive archive that seems to comprise human memory.

Computer models of mental activities, sometimes called models of artificial intelligence (AI), represent the world as a source of information that is subjected to various stages of processing (Charniak & McDermott, 1985). Prior to processing, information must be encoded into a form congenial to the machine, in the case of human beings, the functioning nervous system. Once encoded, information is supposedly stored in organized ways, like files in the computer, from which it can subsequently be accessed by processes of retrieval. Retrieval, the end-product we typically call "remembering," depends on being able to produce the relevant access codes (Humphreys, Wiles, & Dennis, 1994).

A large part of our continuing fascination with computer models seems to derive from their heuristic utility. Breaking down the processes of learning and memory into distinct linearly related components — encoding, storage, and retrieval — provides a useful framework not only for devising laboratory studies of learning and remembering, but for exploring the nervous system as a organization of structural and functional modules.

Yet critics from many perspectives, ranging from those involved with mapping neural processes to students of autobiographical memory, have begun to emphasize the inadequacies of the mind-as-computer analogy. It is not simply the complexity of neural structures or the difficulties in mapping them that has led to such doubts. A more fundamental difficulty lies in the differences between living organisms and even the most complicated machines. Computers are essentially slave systems. But even in autocratic societies, an individual mind is not simply a slave system, obeying the command inputs of supraordinate controllers. Nor is the brain, or the mind associated with it, a static structure or even a network of fixed structures. It is rather a set of self-regulating and mutually facilitating systems that function together to organize coherent adaptations.

Memory, as one identifiable outcome of these systems, is not even merely a function of mind, particularly not in the restrictive sense that mind is commonly viewed as a correlate of brain structures. When we focus on *remembering* as a process rather than *memory* as an entity, it quickly becomes apparent how this process involves the whole organism.

In human beings, especially, it is obvious that the mind and its memories are not merely reactive products, but active creators. Both in structure and function, the human nervous system has evolved to both adapt to environmental contexts and modify them according to its own needs. As a consequence of such adaptations, the plasticity of the nervous system is associated with an indeterminacy and flexibility of functioning that contrasts markedly with the functioning of computers.

In humans, this flexible functioning is orchestrated by overreaching goals and priorities. These are typically associated with thoughts, feelings, and actions conceptualized under the rubric of the "self." We need not view this self as a homunculus in the brain who directs everything in order to acknowledge its role in autobiographical memory. The memories organized as the self, however generated as a process, have empirically demonstrated motivational implications. They direct attention, encode observations, and play a powerful part in those encoding-retrieval interactions typically labeled "remembering." The self, in turn, is a system only comprehensible in terms of its links to a network of external systems, particularly social systems — families, institutions, cultures — with which it is interconnected. In order to remember effectively, the self needs more than a brain. It needs other selves. From this perspective, even the brain as a biological entity is not just a warehouse. It is a mediator between self and self and between self and others.

Many of the persisting conundrums about memory arise not just from the complexities of memory as mechanism, but from the complexities of memory as a set of integrated processes. Although the basic mechanisms of memory are part of an ancient evolutionary heritage, it is the integration of these with more specifically human developments, such as the evolution of social minds, that gives human memory its characteristic stamp.

Failures of integration, at whatever level, may be disruptive, or even tragic, but they are also instructive. Memory without the capacity for self-reflection or explicit recall, as occurs in some instances of brain damage, highlights the structural origins of memory systems in the survival contingencies that challenge all animals. But memory integrations that fail in spite of a structurally intact nervous system indicate that, in the uses of memory, integration is often as consequential as structures.

THE REMEMBERING BRAIN

One problem with the computer analogy is the complexity of the brain as an integrated modular system. It is relatively easy to measure information inputs and outputs, to map forgetting curves, to demonstrate that different retrieval strategies produce different amounts of remembering. But the more we learn about the brain, the clearer it becomes that it is made and wired differently from any computer with which we are familiar. Certainly, it handles information differently. This aspect of the brain is evidently an outgrowth of fundamental properties of brain cells and systems.

"Structurally the properties of chips AND/OR gates, logic circuits, or whatever, do not at all resemble those of neurons" (Rose, 1992, p. 88). Brain cells and the systems they comprise are, as Rose notes, "radically indeterminate." Human cognition is characterized by nonlinear processes and dynamics; the parallel distributed processing of information by the brain stands in marked contrast to the serial processing typical of computers and enables human beings to accomplish operations that are beyond the capability of existing computers (Heath, 1994).

The variety of processing states of which the brain is capable is thus strikingly different from the workings of computers. Brains, in contrast to computers, carry out linear computations relatively slowly, but find judgmental functions quite easy (Rose, 1992). If the brain can be characterized as a computer at all, it is more adequately described by the mathematics of chaos theory than that of linear models.

The emerging understanding of the complexities of brain functioning has greatly complicated the search for the structural basis of the memory trace or engram. We are confronted with a paradox. It has long been recognized that intact memory is correlated with the intactness of specific neural structures. And in recent years, much has been learned about these structural underpinnings. But structure tells only part of the story.

The functional coherence of the brain was dramatically revealed in a series of experiments by Lashley (1929, 1950), who investigated changes in the brains of rats trained to run mazes. He discovered that it was not the specific parts of the brain removed that affected learning and memory, but the *amount* removed. Brain functioning is equipotential. From the beginning, however, the notion of equipotentiality seemed in conflict with clinical findings about the specificity of losses following brain damage. And subsequent research has, indeed, modified interpretations of Lashley's original findings (Squire, 1987). The brain is plastic in the sense that it can structurally adapt to damage and insults. But it is not infinitely plastic. In many instances, the limits of neural plasticity make the difference between whether or how much recovery there is from injury.

Some failures in memory are recognized hallmarks of particular kinds of damage to particular areas of the brain. In organically-based amnesias, for example, such as those that result from lesions to the hippocampus, declarative memory can be impaired while skill memory remains intact. Patients with lesions in the diencephalic or medial temporal regions of the brain have characteristic impairments of memory, as do patients with the kinds of damage associated with Korsakoff's syndrome (Parkin, 1987).

Much modern research has also supported the idea that the brain has numerous specialized functional areas, some of them quite small. For example, the human brain has many processing systems that deal with distinct tasks, such as language comprehension and recognition of faces (Squire, 1987). The organization of brain systems is such that discrete subcortical regions can exert widespread modulatory effects on neocortical structures (Squire, 1987). Multiple areas of neocortex, activated through limbic structures, are involved in representing what we usually identify as discrete memories.

The complex relation between neural structure and function has been clarified in recent years by considerable research on the basic biochemical, physiological, and morphological changes associated with memory. Information is stored by alterations in synaptic strength in interconnecting webs of neurons. Even at the cellular level, learning has been shown to produce structural alterations that can be measured through an electron microscope. Dynamically, it is marked by localized, transient changes in blood flow and oxygen uptake by the nerve cells. Biochemical changes in cell synthesis and physiological changes in the electrical properties of cell membrane structures are also observable (Rose, 1992). But although structural changes are observable, research also clearly reveals that the memory trace is not simply a static structure, but a dynamic process, the outcome of the topography of a neural wiring diagram and the dynamics of neural functioning. It can only be adequately conceptualized as a functional outcome of the whole system.

As a result, any complex memory is not simply contained in localized engrams; rather, it involves the flow of information between different regions of the brain. Pathways that are not themselves the site of change can affect those that are (Krasne, 1978; Squire, 1987), and memory storage can be amplified or dampened by neural events that occur after the original learning experience. Drugs, hormones, or other agents given after a training experience, for example, have been shown to facilitate or disrupt memory.

Alkon (1992) has described memory at any given instant as "like a tidal wave of associations" involving hosts of brain regions. Specific structures may be activated, but the role of any given structure may be that of a relay station rather than a simple repository of memory.

Squire (1987) considers the seemingly conflicting findings that memory is, on the one hand, distributed across many brain systems and, on the other, localized in specific structures a matter of emphasis. He concludes that memory is both distributed and localized. Representation is highly localized, yet memory for whole events is widely distributed and different loci store different aspects of a whole memory.

Much research indicates that there are critical periods of development in both lower animals and humans that affect the structure and maturation of the nervous system itself. Alkon speculates that during such critical periods experience adjusts synaptic weights and actually determines which synapses survive. "Memories in childhood then, would become doubly imprinted in the brain. They would not only be stored in networks already present in a child, they would actually be stored in the network *designs* they helped to create and structure" (1992, p. 159).

As we have learned more about the brain, it has been increasingly appealing to view it as the locus of what was traditionally called "the soul." The brain can be shown to be the locus of most of those functions we characterize as mental: thinking, wishing, imagining, and evaluating. Cessation of brain function is now often considered the defining feature of death.

Yet as essential as the brain may be for memory, we never observe it or the functions associated with it in isolation. At every stage of development and at many levels of functioning, the brain is embodied. And although the brain may tell the body what to do, the body is not simply a silent or passive recipient of commands. It is, rather, an active partner in an ongoing dialogue.

THE REMEMBERING BODY

In a humorous scene from the movie *Dances with Wolves*, Kevin Costner attempts to communicate with Indians concerning his interest in buffalos. Having no common language with them, he pantomimes the behavior of the animal. By producing an easily recognizable but nonverbal schema, he gets his point across.

Gestures like mime are commonly thought of as forms of communication, and it is in order to communicate that people consciously employ them. But they can also have a more fundamental representational function. The "presenting again" that serves as a foundation of memory is a function of the body as well as the brain, and the retention of motor responses is a basic form of memory (Zajonc & Markus, 1984). By coding events in terms that make sense to both body and brain, gesture bridges the gap between somatic and conceptual responses to events. It thus facilitates the integration of meaningful behavior.

Normally, for example, gesture is an integral part of social interaction. Encountering another person, we shift our gaze and posture and change facial expression. Our explicit verbal communications are accompanied by variations in rate and tone of speech and physical movements that convey important meanings (Mehrabian, 1981). Although many nonverbal cues are implicit, they can have a powerful influence on others.

As a form of language, gesture evolves developmentally in tandem with verbalization (Rimé & Schiaratura, 1991). During the first few years of life, conceptual re-presentation based on language radically changes our transactions with the past. However, although eventually overshadowed by spoken words, nonverbal modes of presenting and re-presenting are never simply replaced by verbal ones. Throughout life, gesture continues to function as a major factor in the embodiment of conceptualization as well as memory.

As Rimé and Schiaratura (1991) point out, for example, the spiraling movement is latent in our representation of a spiraling staircase. When we have difficulty remembering the name of an object, we can still sometimes facilitate memory of it by accessing motor codes associated with it. To researchers who study memory, however, the role of gesture in encoding and retrieving experience is easily overlooked. This is one respect in which computer analogies can obscure basic features of human memory. Computers have no gestures of their own. They are only the recipients of ours.

Mimicry, an imitative response with infrahuman roots, is closely related to gesture. Piaget (1950/1981, 1962) has described how representation evolves over the first eighteen months of life as an "interior imitation" based on sensorimotor schemas. The infant is not a passive recipient of sensations or impinging stimuli; he or she actively constructs the world. In the beginning, sensorimotor imitation by the infant requires the actual presence of an external model. Eventually, however, it develops as memory: external objects no longer immediately in view can be evoked as internal images. As maturation proceeds and experiences multiply, this imaginative evocation of the past in the present continues to be mediated by behavioral responses as well as by cognitive processes.

Imitation and gestures are not the only somatic forms in which memories are embodied. Other systems, such as the autonomic, glandular, and visceral, are intimately involved in representational functions (Zajonc & Markus, 1984). Even reflexive or involuntary bodily responses, such as orienting responses, often have specific representational functions that facilitate the encoding and retrieval of information about external events and can thus enable us to make useful inferences about the past.

Conditioned Somatic Responses

The specific cognitive representations that comprise memory in higher animals are sometimes contrasted with conditioning. Emotional, expressive, and deliberate motor responses can be conditioned without any explicit awareness on the part of the subject. In everyday life, such conditioned somatic responses are normally integrated with other memory systems, such as the verbal memories that typically structure narratives about the personal past. Such "gut-level" responses are what people are perhaps most likely to recognize as the embodiment of memory. Stressful or traumatic events, for example, produce an array of physical responses ranging from heightened arousal to reflexive avoidance.

Conditioned gut-level responses do not necessarily have a representational function, however. Nor are they always integrated with cognitive representational processes. And even when such integrations have been present at some point, the connections may have been disrupted, with the result that conditioned somatic responses become dissociated from verbally encoded memories. These distinctions may make so-called "body memories" difficult to interpret. In any case, conditioned somatic responses do not in themselves substantiate interpretations about how they came about. Inferences about their origin and meaning can be treacherous. The exact nature of a stressor cannot be determined from either the intensity or nature of a conditioned stress response. We can only infer that a stress response has been evoked.

Clinicians, for example, are commonly asked to evaluate and interpret symptoms of stress or trauma, such as heightened startle reflexes or somatic tensions. A specific configuration of responses involving increased emotional arousal alternating with emotional blunting has been described as characteristic of posttraumatic stress disorder (van der Kolk & Greenberg, 1987). Yet the presence of this configuration only informs us *that—* not *how—*the individual has been traumatized. Somatic stress symptoms cannot be meaningfully interpreted without other kinds of information, such as knowledge of the circumstances in which they arose or were first observed.

Even in the absence of specific cognitive elaboration, however, gut-level responses do commonly encode intensities of stress and general information about the nature of the threat posed by stimuli—for example, whether a noxious event is controllable or uncontrollable (van der Kolk, Greenberg, Boyd, & Krystal, 1985). Memory systems designed for effective processing of such events evolved early in lower animals. An extensive research literature describes the conditioning in animals of somatic and behavioral responses, as well as the neurological substrates of such processes.

But the elaboration of these ancient stress responses is another way in which people differ from other animals. In human beings, stress responses are commonly subjected to extensive cognitive processing at the time that they occur. As part of an original episodic gestalt, many observations and responses are initially connected in perception, even though they may not be connected in subsequent retrievals of the event. These cognitive correlates can include veridical encodings of the nature of the stressor, interpretations about its significance and meaning, and conscious strategies for coping with it.

So-called simple conditioning, in any case, is not always so simple. In experimental settings, the conditioning of emotional reactions is not restricted to some particular response under study, such as limb flexion or eye blink, but typically involves many response systems (Squire, 1987). Any conditioned response would thus be likely to involve many neural systems.

In natural settings, emotion and arousal level might be expected to become a typical part of the encoded pattern of events that constitutes a memory episode. High levels of arousal may strengthen cognitive responses even while somatic responses are being conditioned. Because of these expectable integrations, internal somatic cues, even though nonspecific, might facilitate subsequent recall. Some internal states, such as the release of neurotransmitters, could also be expected to affect storage.

Cognitive memories may become functionally dissociated from somatic ones. But, although only accessible in particular states or if triggered by specific contextual cues, they may nevertheless remain as veridical memory markers for a stressful or traumatic experience. Sometimes the emotional and the cognitive fragments of an episodic gestalt can be reconnected. It is important to keep in mind, in any case, that conditioned somatic responses may be, but are not necessarily, isolated from veridical cognitive representations.

Encoding, Expression, and Representation

The embodiment of memory is constantly effected by the integration of cognitive processes with internal states and their expression. Expressive responses are often an intrinsic part of the meaningful encoding of events. "The scream, the laugh, the shedding of tears, the rapid withdrawal of a burned finger, are, *in themselves,* all representations of the affective states" (Zajonc & Markus, 1984, p. 79). The motor activity that accompanies cognitive processes, such as raising the eyebrows or smiling or wincing becomes a contextual feature of what is being encoded and remembered.

This is scarcely surprising if we consider the role of memory in adaptation. Adaptation requires more than mere apprehension of external events. It necessitates a comprehension of their significance and value. This comprehension, in turn, depends not just on the coding of external events but also on the processing of affective and behavioral responses to events. Representations of affective states thus become a significant part of the representational configurations that comprise useful memories.

Zajonc and Markus (1984) view certain state-dependent learning effects in terms of the interface between affective and cognitive systems. State-dependent effects are observed whenever accuracy is increased by the matching between the state in which learning occurred and the state in which memory is retrieved. Such effects have been typically studied in connection with alcohol and drug use. But it may be that the most common and significant state-dependent effects are tied to internal states regulated by internal processes, such as arousal and sleep cycles or the release of stress hormones.

As we explore the affective complexities of representational as well as mnemonic processes, it becomes obvious that the information-processing model that divides memory into sequences of encoding, storage, and retrieval, however useful for some purposes, is incomplete and sometimes even misleading. Rimé and Schiaratura (1991) put it succinctly:

> Transactions between individual and external reality are such that in terms of collected information, "responses" generally cannot be dissociated from "stimuli." Represented stimuli would probably have no adaptive meaning if they were not made up of response elements that contributed to their being built up in the subject's mind. (p. 266)

Although the role of somatic and motor responses in representation has sometimes been eclipsed by a research emphasis on the role of language in memory, language itself is normally closely bound up with nonverbal behaviors. A linguistic representation is not simply an encoding of a verbal stimulus; it is an encoded configuration of many stimulus-response contingencies.

Motor coding may function in the retrieval of verbal information, although it is not altogether clear how this process works. Rand and Wapner (1987), for example, instructed subjects to assume different postures while learning nonsense syllables. Subsequently, when required to relearn the syllables, subjects' performance was facilitated by their assuming the postures associated with the original learning. A study by Saltz and Dixon (1962), however, found that motor enactment was not a specific cue for retrieval, although it did facilitate memory in both children and adults. But whether the facilitation effected by motor coding is general or specific, the re-presenting that is so intimately bound up with memory can seldom be simply equated with verbal encodings. Laboratory studies that measure simple verbal responses or even complex narratives ignore an important dimension of episodic memory: memory, even as a merely cognitive function, is always embodied.

THE REMEMBERING SELF

Human beings represent and remember much more than facts and happenings. In contrast to animals, they link their representations of objective events with representations of themselves as the experiencing observers of events. They organize personal histories, repositories of past events and knowledge that are shaped by the motives and experiences of the self. Memory as a repository of individual history that can be explicitly recalled is a specifically human development of great consequence for our species. Because self-reference is a characteristic, though not essential, feature of many aspects of human memory, much of what any person recalls at a given point in time involves not just representations of events but also connections between external events and a complex pattern of self-representations.

Brewer (1988) has defined the self as "a complex mental structure that includes the ego, the self-schema, and portions of long-term memory related to the ego-self (e.g., personal memories, generic personal memories, and autobiographical facts)" (p. 27). Many of the most salient schemas and scripts that affect the formation and retention of memories involve the self, and the self-schema is both a consequence and cause of memory organization.

Barsalou (1988) describes the reciprocal relation between memory organization and self organization in terms of extended-event time lines. In the development of such time lines, events are summarized as being representative of one's personal history. The development of autobiographical memory in children may be closely tied to their perception and organization of extended events, which in turn are tied to the child's understanding of how events are repeated and related over time.

An event is not necessarily a continuous temporal unit; it is, rather, a coherent activity or situation in which an individual is involved over time (Neisser, 1982a). Recalling an experienced event involves moving among nested levels of event structure. Some memories, which Neisser (1988) labels *repisodic*, are representative or symbolic, in the sense that they refer not to specific occurrences but to summarized or classified events. These are likely to be greatly influenced by self-perception and personal values.

Self-recollection as a dimension of event memory is not only important to an ongoing sense of personal integrity, but also an important personal guarantor of the accuracy and reality of a given memory (Brewer, 1988). When a courtroom witness swears to tell the truth, the whole truth, and nothing but the truth, this does not necessarily guarantee that the truth will follow. But it affirms how much the integrity of the self is at stake in the process of telling.

Yet, the relation between the self and its memories may also be a source of distortion. Greenwald (1980), for example, has shown that the self-schema may be strongly biased in the direction of positive self-evaluation. Some studies have reported that information consistent with one's self-concept may be remembered more accurately than inconsistent information (Markus & Sentis, 1980; Rogers, 1980).

One way self-interest distorts memories is through the motivational effect of emotions and evaluations. Linton (1986), who monitored her own personal memories over the course of twelve years, found that, even when she remembered negative events, she did not typically note them in her protocols. And, with repeated samplings of particular memories, she noted shifts in emphasis as well as deletions from recall that reflected her changed evaluations of the significance of specific events.

The tendency of the self to construct and reconstruct memories on the basis of personal needs and values does not necessarily result in inaccuracy and distortion, however. Reality-monitoring (Johnson, 1988; Johnson & Raye, 1981) is a necessary aspect of ongoing adaptation reflected in the organization of memory as well as other human activities. Normally, fantasy does not substitute for memory. It is integrated with memory. The integration of fantasy with memory safeguards reality-testing. In this respect, failures of integration are often more consequential than failures of memory per se. Memory need not be perfect to be useful, but delusional thinking, the inability to distinguish between imagined and real events, is a hallmark of psychosis (Oltmanns & Maher, 1988).

On the other hand, even proven distortions are not necessarily inconsistent with important truths. As Neisser (1982a) observes, John Dean's testimony about Nixon's behavior during the Watergate scandal was inaccurate in many particulars, but correct in essentials. Although as a record of what really happened it might have been easily disputed in a courtroom, it told a truth the country needed to hear.

Because of the pervasive self-referential organization of human memory, anything that disrupts the representation of the self may affect what is forwarded as memory. An extreme discontinuity in the development of personal identity, for example, may result in the loss of broad categories of knowledge, such as the first language one learned as a child, or the mathematics one learned during a traumatic period. And the phenomenon labeled "infantile amnesia," which involves an inability to recall specifics of what happened in the first few years of life, may be as closely related to changes in self organization as to any fundamental aspects of memory as a process.

Sometimes developmental changes reflect failures of integration or dissociations rather than loss of memory per se. For example, the role of nonverbal experience in the development and organization of the self may be gradually subordinated to the ascendance of self-reflective verbal memory (Schachtel, 1947). But it does not necessarily follow that other kinds of memory fade away entirely. Normally, the remembering *I* and the remembering body are integrated; the one confirms the other. When this integration is lacking, the consistency and the authority of the self as witness to experience are compromised. In such instances, body and self, self and self, or self and other may function like confusing adversaries rather than coherent allies (Putnam, 1989).

These confusions can be a major source of self-doubt and of uncertainty about the status of particular memories. The self may have no conscious idea of why the body acts as if some external cue were associated with danger. Or why perplexing images, unconnected with personal memory, suddenly flood the mind. It may be tempting in such instances to dismiss the significance of the somatic responses or internal images, even to emphatically deny that they could be connected with real events in the past. After all, imagination plays a major role in human adaptation as well as in pathology; also, under some conditions, imagination *can* confound memory.

Even a minor failure of memory and self integration invites explanation. But when body and self give confusing or conflicting testimonies about the past, the observer who seeks objectivity cannot find it by simply taking sides, by simply accepting one of the partisans to the quarrel. To make sense of what has happened, one must focus of the integrative function of normal memory and how integration has gone awry.

A FUNCTIONAL VIEW
OF REMEMBERING

Historically, the study of memory has been fragmented by the tendency of individual investigators to focus on one type of memory or one experimental paradigm to the exclusion of others. The remembering brain has been detached from its body. The self has been viewed as a composite of verbal units. The integrative function of memory has come under scrutiny, if at all, only when it has been disrupted by brain injury or disease. Yet, after all, the fundamental function of memory is not copying the world or storing information or unpacking a box of mementos. It is the adaptive integration of past with present, self with self, and self with others. Normally, we neither experience a world in pieces nor behave piecemeal. We perceive and remember meaningful events and stories. And we do so not as disembodied minds but as embodied selves.

This functional view of remembering as a process involves a radical shift in the way we conceptualize what a memory is. A memory is not a thing, a copy, an entity we retrieve from the brain like a stored item in a trunk. It is not even an anatomical structure, although it obviously depends on the intactness of certain neural structures. A memory is a composite event, a reinstatement of a dynamic process that occurred in the past in the context of dynamic processes occurring in the present.

The recognition that memory is an ongoing constructive process does not imply that memories are arbitrary inventions like fantasies. Schemas and scripts are pragmatic summations, and reality-monitoring is an intrinsic feature of information-processing observable from infancy. The structural configurations of the nervous system and their functional outcomes have evolved to be adaptively veridical, however imperfect. Memory as a constructive process is a matter of surviving and thriving in the real world.

The integrative function of memory at any given moment reflects present motives, tasks, and competencies and a complex personal history. If the individual is very disturbed or impaired, memory may be a very unreliable guide to much reality. But even severely impaired individuals, such as those with organic amnesias, usually retain some accurate memories. And even when memory is entirely implicit, that is, inaccessible to self-reflective consciousness, it may be veridical.

In any case, the evaluation of any particular report labeled *memory* can be facilitated by a functional perspective that is not restricted to one class of observations—verbal statements, conditioned responses, or self-referential narratives. It is the connections between these different representations of the past that usually prove essential for coping.

Nor can memory be adequately judged on the basis of simple dichotomies like true or false. Counting accurate details, like counting beans, may provide a comforting illusion of scientific rigor, but outside the laboratory this endeavor is likely to be more confusing than helpful. The search for meaningful memory in everyday life is a search for pattern and coherence.

As time-travelers we cannot escape the limitations of memory. We can never revisit every place we have been. Any revisitation at all is something of a trick; we can only discover the past in the present. Yet life depends on this trick, and we need not be intimidated by it. The past in the present is as real as any reality the mind *can* know, and the quest for this reality is one of the most consequential endeavors the mind can embark on.

CHAPTER 3

Selective Processes in Memory

Better by far you should forget and smile
Than that you should remember and be sad.
— Christina Rossetti, "Remember"

L ONG BEFORE the complexities of conscious thought, long before there was even a brain to think with, creatures developed the capacity to carry the past into the future. In infrahuman species, memory may be simple, but it is adaptively veridical. And for any animal, memory is shaped by the needs and capabilities characteristic of the species, as well as those of the individual remembering.

For example, although the nervous system of the chick is inherently adapted to connect pecking with particular kinds of foodstuff, specific connections are not necessarily instinctive; instead, they are based on experience. A single noxious experience enables the chick, many hours later, to avoid potentially poisonous substances. Rose (1992), who has measured the neural correlates of such avoidance learning in chicks, contends that what is acquired is not just a stimulus-response connection but an internal *representation* of experience. Representation, in this sense of reinstating not only past events but their significance, is an essential component of adaptation.

Representations are not merely copies; they are constructs. The process of constructing them from the raw materials of external stimuli and internal states highlights the role of selective processes in memory. What is new and different stands out, arrests attention. But what we know already and what we need to know shapes how we respond to it.

Even encounters with the world that seem strictly determined by physical parameters can be found, on close inspection, to involve selective internal processes. It is tempting, for example, to think that the beginning of memory is an objective physical event, such as light rays impinging on the retina. Our sense organs are structurally adapted to respond to particular classes of stimuli with specific reactions, and immediate sensations *are* basic building blocks of memories. But they are merely a beginning.

From a very early age, perhaps even before birth, sensations are organized by classificatory habits. The eye as a sensory organ reacts to specific wavelengths of light, while the perceiving mind identifies blue, or sunshine, or the face of a friend. The ear responds to sound waves, but the developing infant, perhaps even in utero, recognizes a familiar voice that will eventually be labeled "mother" (DeCasper & Fifer, 1980).

In human beings, selective processes in memory are complicated by the complexity of our needs and capabilities. In contrast to machines that may know a great deal but do not care, we organize knowledge in terms of values. And in contrast to animals, we value many things that are only tangentially related to survival.

Our uniquely human predicament also introduces considerations that operate against our being too narrowly selective or too quick to foreclose possibilities. Humans bring to the present an ever-expanding view of the future. Any observation, however irrelevant at the moment, may eventually turn out to be relevant. Yet time travel, like space travel, is more than a survival mechanism; it is an adventure. Whether it is useful or not, we visit the past just because it is there, and even the most familiar memory may suddenly, in the light of a new discovery, be transformed by new meaning.

In spite of our selective habits, this perspective often makes indiscriminate collectors of us. Like squirrels foraging for nuts, we gather from every source available. In the mind, rumor is thrown in alongside fact and gossip may be hoarded as zealously as truth. A characteristically human rule of thumb seems to be "gather now, sort out later." Many of our most valued memories spring from this gathering and hoarding. While exploratory behavior is common in other primates too, it assumes a central place in human adaptation, so much so that the sheer volume of information stored up not only in human minds but also in our archives and libraries is staggering.

Many of the items in this expanding array of information seem impersonal, factual, given. As pragmatists, we value facts and make careful distinctions between the factual and the fantastic. Yet this attitude should not obscure the inescapable fact that every record, internal or external, is the outcome of personal choices. There is no avoiding the significance of selective factors in what is dryly termed "information-processing." Subjectivity haunts the most sterile laboratory, the most objective compilation of data.

Selective processes are as important in the retrieval of records as in their initial construction. As time travelers, we can only access the past by highlighting a present rendering of it. Recognition and recall are necessarily contingent on what was initially noticed and recorded. But our view of the past is also always contingent on what we are noticing and recording in the present.

Evaluating a particular record, then, inevitably becomes a process of constructing and reconstructing representations as we attempt to back-track from a present rendering to a set of past encodings, decodings, and transformations. Whether we are reconstructing the path of a subatomic particle, the birth of the universe, the evolution of a species, or the creation of a memory, reconstuction is as close to reality as we can expect to get.

There are, even so, constraints on the process of reconstruction. Not just any story will do. Quarks may be difficult to observe, but they are more reliably observable than leprechauns. The far-flung reaches of the universe may be beyond our ken, but it is safe to say that no heavenly body will ever be found to be made of green cheese. Dinosaurs once roamed the earth, but centaurs never did.

The tension between the wish to explore widely and the need to be selective molds what will, at any given moment, be forwarded as memory. Yet our limitations need not discourgage us. In tracking back to the past, we are not only limited by what we can no longer see, but also continually enlightened by what we can now see more clearly.

STAGES IN THE
DEVELOPMENT OF MEMORY

We now know that, at any stage, the process of remembering involves constantly flitting back and forth between external sources of information and internal ones. The brain that makes this possible is constantly engaged in the parallel distributed processing of information. The body that gathers information is usually in motion, even if the motion consists of little more than eye movements. And the self who emerges as an organizing reference point is constantly being constructed and reconstructed.

In studying these processes, it is often useful to break down complex patterns into simpler ones. One of the most useful models for doing so conceptualizes memory from the standpoint of information-processing stages like those that govern machines. From this perspective, what we observe as memory is the outcome of a linear sequence, the encoding, storage, and retrieval of information.

Whatever its limitations, this model has enabled researchers to reduce vast complexities to manageable units of observation. Whether a so-called memory consists of a conditioned response, a memorized item of information, or a complicated narrative, the processes underlying its construction and eventual utilization may become more accessible to study when approached as a series of discrete stages. However, in focusing on these discrete stages, it is always important to keep in mind that they are heuristic devices to help us make sense of data rather than inherent features of the data. It bears repeating, too, that a memory is not just a record but an ongoing construction. What is retrieved at any given point may be a composite of reactions and transformations at several points in time. Immediate accounts may be revised or amended, even after long delays, to produce a new story about an old event.

Different versions of a memory may or may not be integrated with one another. Stressful events, in particular, may create memory fragments before, during, and after the fact that make narratives seem disjointed or inconsistent. Whether the mind integrates such fragments with those self-referential narratives that comprise autobiographical memory will depend on motives as well as abilities.

PAYING ATTENTION

How does the mind perceive and evaluate the "recurrence and typification" that, according to Hundeide (1985), is the basis for meaningful and ordered experience? How does it know when the present has slipped away? How does it impose the boundaries that define the beginnings and endings of episodes?

Attention is the gateway to memory. For the most part, we remember what we notice. And it is what captures attention that is likely to be subjected to further cognitive processing.

Episodes are commonly marked in memory because they become distinct; something sets them apart from the ongoing flow of life. A sudden disruption of routine—tripping in the course of a walk, observing a bolt of lightning—is a blip in time that may be more easily remembered than the routines that preceded or followed it. A frequently repeated experience, on the other hand, such as eating breakfast or driving home from work, may scarcely be noted at all and, consequently, may fade from memory as a specific event.

Whether during an initial encounter with an event in the external world or reviewing internal representations of the world, we also necessarily focus on particulars. Some details are noted. Others escape observation. After being noted, some are rehearsed, while others are ignored or even actively avoided.

Attention regulates adaptive behavior through complex, recursively evaluative action sequences. The startle response, an alerting reaction, is reflexive and is closely related to orienting behavior that points the organism in the direction of incoming stimuli. Startled, we snap to attention, look and listen, decide that the input was not really important, relax, and proceed with business as usual. Or, in an alternative scenario, we decide that some input requires immediate action and behave accordingly.

The startle that jolts attention is also closely linked to energizing processes that prepare the organism for action. It is prudently adaptive that both the sudden shift of attention and the energizing of preparatory responses occurs automatically and immediately—better to be safe than sorry. As a result, self-protective action sequences are set in motion before there is even time to think about them. If the cognitive processing that is also triggered indicates that there is no need for alarm, the startled individual can calm down. Theoretically, anyway.

Attentional processes are regulated by neural mechanisms that are among the oldest from an evolutionary standpoint and that reflect basic survival contingencies. Selection, focusing, and referencing of both internal and external events is an ongoing process that continues even during sleep (Ross, Ball, Sullivan, & Caroff, 1989).

Attentional mechanisms evolved in tandem with motivational and emotional dynamics, as well as with memory mechanisms. They are mediated by the reticular activating system (RAS), a group of brain structures that have extensive connections with subcortical as well as cortical systems. The RAS helps coordinate cycles of continuous alerting, such as REM mechanisms during sleep, that serve a basic survival function (Antrobus, 1990; Moorcroft, 1989).

Although attentional mechanisms are closely connected with such reflexive behaviors as startle reactions and orienting reflexes, the voluntary deployment of attention is learned early in life. After birth, the infant increasingly refines an ability to bring the peripheral into focus. Over the course of development, focusing is supplemented by increasingly complicated forms of cognitive processing that may help seal in memories (Derryberry & Rothbart, 1984).

In the organization of behavior, attentional processes continually coordinate both what is noticed and explored and what is avoided. In animals, flight at a sign of threat is a basic survival mechanism that may be instigated immediately at the first sign of danger. In human beings, not only flight but more subtle patterns of avoidance may be learned as a means of controlling both general levels of stimulation and specific stimulus selection. Such intentional behavior plays an important role in self-regulation across the lifespan.

We also learn to selectively avoid subjecting certain perceptions to repeated observation and more careful processing. When a memory is overstimulating or noxious, for example, it may be treated the way an external stimulus would be, as a threat to be avoided. This defensive avoidance can be effected by focusing attention away from the memory whenever it is activated and away from any external cue that tends to activate it. Although such defensive responses may initially be a matter of intentional strategies, they can, with practice, become so habitual that they appear automatic.

Arousal, Attention, and Memory

Biologically, the structures and mechanisms that regulate attentional processes are closely allied to those that regulate levels of arousal. An event that captures attention is exciting. Excitement, in turn, produces internal changes ranging from increased cerebral blood flow to the release of powerful neurotransmitters and hormones. The combination of heightened arousal and focused attention associated with novel or threatening situations may facilitate the storage and encoding of memories (Searleman & Herrmann, 1994). Emergency situations and the reactions they trigger are often particularly memorable.

Many investigators have theorized that there is an optimal level of arousal for information-processing. The Yerkes-Dodson Law, a famous maxim in memory research, states that optimal performance is associated with moderate levels of arousal. The *Easterbrook hypothesis* clarifies some of the specifics of the interaction between arousal and learning in terms of attentional effects. According to this view, increasing levels of arousal narrow the focus of attention. At low levels, distracting and irrelevant as well as relevant information is taken in, whereas at extremely high levels performance may be impaired because not enough information is encoded. The Easterbrook hypothesis, sometimes called the "weapon focus hypothesis," is well supported by research on animal learning (Schwartz & Reisberg, 1991; Searleman & Herrmann, 1994), as well as experiments involving human subjects (Christianson & Loftus, 1987).

Another set of experimental observations complicates the picture, however. According to *action-decrement theory*, arousal affects not only encoding but also the consolidation of the memory trace, the process by which it is made relatively permanent through neural restructuring (Walker, 1958). According to this view, which also has considerable experimental support (Searleman & Herrmann, 1994), high arousal is associated with high levels of inhibition. The inhibitory process makes it more difficult to retrieve a memory trace shortly after it is formed, but facilitates retrieval after a longer delay.

Such conflicting experimental data point to the complexities of encoding-retrieval interactions. Arousal and emotional responses may produce different effects at different stages of learning and remembering. Some instances of delayed recall may be related to such basic processes as the consolidation of memory traces. Others may arise from more complicated dynamics, such as a lack of integration or a functional dissociation between memory systems. In general, however, considerable evidence supports the idea that the health and stability of organisms are related to the moderation of extreme levels of under- and over-arousal. This moderation, in turn, is effected not only through behavioral responses to stimuli, such as exploratory behavior and stimulus selection, but by the modulation of attentional and emotional responses associated with thoughts and memories.

Clinically, it is well established that extreme overstimulation, particularly if persistent and unmoderated, may constitute a form of stress and can even impact detrimentally on physical health (Kiecolt-Glaser, Garner, Speicher, Penn, Holliday, & Glaser, 1984; Krystal, 1990; Selye, 1956). Remembering that produces extreme arousal may in itself have detrimental effects. Such effects can serve as powerful motivation to avoid and forget.

Subliminal Perception and Implicit Memory

Some forms of memory are not much accessible through narratives about the past. One may tell an interesting story about learning to ride a bicycle, but actually remembering and riding it is just a matter of trusting the body to know. Such phenomena have led researchers to distinguish not only between *procedural* and *episodic* memory, but also between remembering that is *explicit* and that which is *implicit*. Explicit and implicit memory are evidently mediated by different neural mechanisms. In certain forms of brain damage involving amnesia for recent events, implicit memory is spared (Parkin, 1987; Squire, 1987).

The distinction between explicit and implicit memory is tied not only to the question of underlying neural mechanisms, but also to the still-mysterious phenomenon of consciousness. Perception and memory, as well as attention, often seem intimately related to consciousness. Intentional learning is facilitated by consciously directed attention and rehearsal. So is recollection. Communicable memories are usually both explicit and conscious; we are self-reflectively aware of them.

The whole issue of what constitutes "consciousness" has always been controversial and continues to be the subject of considerable ongoing debate among philosophers and psychologists (Gazzaniga, 1985; Jaynes, 1976). It is commonly acknowledged, however, that consciousness is closely bound up with self-referential processes that have emerged only in higher primates and can only be measured in human beings.

The connection between consciousness, attention, and information-processing is a complicated and vexing one that has been rendered even more confusing by popular notions about the Freudian unconscious. It is tempting, for example, to assume that implicit memories are unconscious. From one standpoint this is true; they cannot be accessed by the narrative forms we use to access consciousness. But it is a mistake to assume that such memories reside in a place, the unconscious, from which they might potentially be retrieved. Again, a memory is not a keepsake stored in a place but an ongoing integration of dynamic processes. Humans learn a great deal that is never in consciousness as that term is usually conceptualized. Basic forms of associative learning, such as conditioning, can occur without awareness and, once in awareness, may or may not be subject to voluntary control.

Emotional responses are easily conditioned in humans as well as in animals and, as anyone who has ever developed an irrational fear or aversion is well aware, are not easily modified by simply paying attention and behaving differently. Adults react to unexpected signals, for example, with physiological and behavioral responses, such as cardiac deceleration, eye blinks, or pupil dilation, which they do not necessarily detect, and such responses can be conditioned (Schwartz & Reisberg, 1991).

When we examine the problem of consciousness and implicit memory for episodes from an empirical perspective, the role of attention stands out sharply. In the formation of episodic memories, it is possible to attend to an event without noticing that one has attended. It is possible to make and act on inferences about information on the periphery of awareness without engaging in complicated narratives. As a result of the variable deployment of attention, small details or peripheral events may be noted in some way, although they seem altogether out of mind. Little noticed and unfocused details may then hover about consciousness as a vague presence.

Sometimes, too, information that is at one point in the center of attention is pushed to the side; a startling cue may reflexively turn heads, for example, but a shocked observer may also immediately turn away.

Whatever the relation between attention and subliminal perception or implicit memory, the importance of attention for explicit, conscious recollection cannot be overestimated. No matter how clearly a memory has been initially formed, no matter how well it has been stored, it cannot be accessed as a personal memory if it cannot be clearly focused in attention.

Attention Regulation and Memory

Learning to regulate attention has important effects on many aspects of life, especially learning and memory. The child who cannot pay attention in class misses out on important learning. The adult who ruminates obsessively on particular ideas and cannot shift attention may be socially or occupationally handicapped. If the events obsessively thought about are associated with negative emotions—anxiety or depression—perseveration of attention on such noxious thoughts may be debilitating.

Whenever remembering is a matter of practical adaptation, it can be facilitated or discouraged by paying careful attention to the significance of attention. Techniques ranging from self-distraction to hypnotic focusing are based on the voluntary deployment of attention as a means of regulating perception and recall. And it should be noted that such techniques, while sometimes utilized by trained professionals, are also discovered and used by untrained people in the course of daily living.

Whether perceptions and memories are implicit or explicit is often a matter of how attention is directed and focused in encoding as well as in retrieval. In this respect, the clarity and availability of specific memories are closely allied to how attention is deployed at several stages of processing. Delayed recall, for example, may sometimes be just a matter of delayed attention.

Avoidance can be conditioned and implicit, and thus never in awareness at all. Avoidance of specific cues can also be voluntarily used to regulate both the contents of accessed memories and the intensity of emotional reactions to specific recollections.

Through selective attention or inattention, a specific memory may also be detached from the contexts that typically reference it, particularly contexts of self-reference. It may be disconnected from the emotional responses that accompanied its formation. Or it may be reinterpreted. Subsequent to such defensive modifications, a cognitive representation of a disturbing event can become, in effect, recontextualized. It becomes just a detached narrative instead of something problematic or painful. Once the memory has been safely modified or the need to avoid it has diminished, a less troublesome version of it may become available for conscious recall.

If once-clear memories are repeatedly banished from awareness by acts of avoidance, they are effectively excluded from rehearsal and conscious retrieval. For this reason, they may gradually fade from recollection even after they are no longer threatening. In any case, once learned, defenses structure both encounters with external events and access to internal representations of those events.

Control over attention and incoming information enables individuals to avoid unpleasant inputs and the conflict that results from ambivalence about how to respond to inputs and to information that contradicts other information. A simple strategy for avoiding internal conflict and the anxiety associated with it is the systematic avoidance of situations that might disconfirm one's existing ideas (Festinger, 1957). The possibility of defensive avoidance is one reason that explicit recognition or recall is not necessarily a measure of memory per se. Even a clearly encoded and previously overlearned memory may be banished from awareness. Nor is this banishing necessarily accomplished by special mysterious mechanisms, such as "repression." It can be achieved by the carefully orchestrated deployment of attention.

ENCODING:
INTERNALIZING THE WORLD

In addition to attention deployment, certain other habitual patterns of information-processing have a powerful selective effect on perception and memory. Many of these have to do with the way inputs are coded and classified by the mind. These codes and classifications, rather than the inputs themselves, often become the basic forms in which memories are cast.

Classification reduces overwhelming arrays of information to manageable units. In this process, some information may be lost: a memory of seeing an animal is less specific than a memory of seeing a dog. But classification is, in the long run, useful. There is considerable redundancy in the environment, and many details are not only repetitive but irrelevant to the needs and tasks at hand. Schematic encoding and remembering allow us to glean significant general information from such redundancies and to maximize the way in which we store and utilize data.

In discussions about memory, the initial translation of external stimuli into existing codes is termed *encoding,* a term familiar from computer models of information-processing. Tulving (1983) has defined encoding as "the process that converts information about an experienced event, in a particular setting and at a particular time, into an engram or memory trace" (p. 11). This trace may be almost immediately subjected to more extensive processing, and what is eventually retrieved as a memory will depend on such factors as storage and synergistic interactions between the memory trace and retrieval cues.

Encoding is necessarily selective. As a feature of stimulus selection and perception, encoding functions as an important determinant of what details are retained in episodic memory as well as how easily details may be retrieved. Encoding strategies can greatly increase our capacities for storing information. Short-term memory, as measured in laboratory experiments, holds about plus or minus two packages of information. This holding capacity can be expanded by a process called chunking, grouping the packages into larger meaningful units (Miller, 1956). A long sequence of numbers, for example, may be hard to memorize if studied as individual numbers but easier to recall as a sequence of larger units, such as two familiar telephone numbers linked together.

An important principle of learning, which has been criticized but has been cogently defended by Tulving (1983), is the *encoding specificity hypothesis.* According to this hypothesis, recollection involves matching past events to current cues, and so in order for remembering to occur, encoding traces and retrieval cues must be compatible. Memory effects always involve encoding-retrieval interactions (Jacoby, 1988), and variations in either or both influence the products ultimately identified as "memories."

Even apparently simple forms of encoding involve processes of judgment and organizational habits. As Swartz and Reisberg (1991) have succinctly stated the problem, a physical stimulus is different from a psychological stimulus. After an initial (and possibly unconscious) reaction to what is "out there," the mind busily transforms sense data into cognitive data. In this respect, encoding, storage, and retrieval are not independent processes that can be located on a time line, but reciprocally modifying processes in which feedback from internal as well as external sources continually regulates inputs and outputs. Any act of remembering becomes itself a memory and affects the content of what is subsequently remembered.

In everyday life as distinct from the laboratory, encoding as information-processing always involves interplays between new events and existing response repertoires. From the moment an event captures attention, processes of classification are set in motion. In humans, many of these involve verbal categories and inferences. A sudden explosive sound is labeled thunder or explosion or gunshot. This almost immediate attribution is in many respects a function of habitual experiences: if the sky has darkened suddenly, thunder is an expectable sound; if a road crew is blasting nearby, sudden explosions may have become predictable.

One of the most consequential factors in encoding is language. Even prior to language learning, infants are learning to perceive similarities and categories of experience that will determine how inputs will be grouped together conceptually as well as perceptually. But increasingly, what is remembered and how it is remembered involves verbal processing. To a great extent, the significance of language is related to the importance of social attachment and social schemas in human life. Perception, memory, and thought generally develop in tandem with communicational skills. Over the course of development, as language skills are honed, linguistic codings and schemas exercise increasing influence on stimulus selection. They organize memory from the earliest stages of processing to the latest retrievals.

Many contextual factors affect encoding and, by implication, encoding-retrieval interactions. The internal state associated with experienced events may affect both attentional and perceptual processes. Such internal variables as emotional responses, the presence of drugs or alcohol, and mood disorders such as depression have been observed to lead to state-dependent effects on memory (Bower, 1981; Eich, 1977, 1980, 1989); that is, retrieval is facilitated when the state in which the original encoding occurred is reinstated.

One aspect of encoding that is especially significant for memory is the tendency to collapse similar events categorically and across time. Once noticed, an event repeated tends to become less remarkable, less attention-grabbing and exciting. If often repeated, it may become so routine that it is scarcely noticed at all as a unique occurrence. In memory, separate instances of such oft-repeated events will blur together. The seemingly episodic event is then remembered, not just as a single episode, but as a *repisode*, as Neisser (1982a,b) contends. The repisode is a composite exemplar of a class of similar experiences. Although repisodic remembering may involve deletions and distortion, it should be emphasized again that such transformations do not necessarily imply that a composite experience is a fantastic fabrication. On the contrary, information that is judged as most salient or essential may be preserved intact in a repisodic memory.

Schemas and Scripts

A major selective factor in memory, one that may affect both initial encoding and later encoding-retrieval interactions, is the set of schemas typical of particular contexts (Bartlett, 1932/1995). Schemas that organize action sequences are sometimes called scripts. Both schemas and scripts allow us to make inferences on the basis of limited information. A memory that something happened in the kitchen, for example, implies that it probably occurred in the vicinity of a stove and refrigerator. Remembering a trip to a restaurant implies, for most people, that one was attended by a waiter (Mandler, 1984; Schank & Abelson, 1977). A film depicting a pie thrown in someone's face that might be labeled an assaultive action by the proverbial visitor from Mars is interpreted by knowledgable audiences as an example of slapstick comedy. Schemas and scripts reflecting typical organizations of experiences and events can be viewed as implicit encoding strategies that allow us to infer a great deal on the basis of general categories. Although the process of schematization does not necessarily preserve the particulars of individual episodes, it facilitates plausible hypotheses.

Schemas interact with repetitions of common events to produce some paradoxical memory effects. The more often a routine event is repeated, the more strongly it is likely to be remembered. Yet, because of schematic effects, particulars may be lost in general typicalities. It may be hard to remember what one had for breakfast on a given day of childhood, but if having breakfast was a routine event, the report that one did so is likely to be accurate. And if one almost always had the same thing—say bacon and eggs—inferences about what one had on a particular morning may be quite reliable. But, if one ever varied from the routine, there will be instances in which inferences based on schemas and scripts will be inaccurate.

When it comes to retrieving specific episodes, these schemas and scripts can be deceptive. Remembering a trip to a particular restaurant on Friday night, one may easily infer that a waiter was present, that food was served, that a bill was paid. Yet the very typicality of the events that are part of most scripts involving "going to a restaurant" may make it difficult to recall particulars. Unless there was something remarkable about particular details, it might be difficult to recollect which of several typical menu selections one ordered.

Typically, schematic habits orchestrate perception as well as memory (Schwartz & Reisberg, 1991). We attend to aspects of a situation that are relevant to our schemas and filter out or distort inputs that are not. As long as such overlearned and automatic encoding habits work, there is little incentive for modifying them. Long-ingrained patterns, in fact, may be extremely difficult to modify. Yet, because they are originally learned schemas, many such patterns can be changed with careful and deliberate practice. Learning to live in a new environment or culture provides numerous instances in which, by deliberately shifting old habits, one learns to adapt to new contingencies.

REHEARSAL

One factor that focuses both attention and consciousness on a given event and that helps "seal" the event in memory is rehearsal. Rehearsal can affect recall of an event not only immediately afterward but much later. Each new accurate rehearsal constitutes a retrieval that helps forge linkages between encoding and retrieval cues. A given recollection is seldom simply a matter of what happened at one point in time; it reflects a history of repeated rehearsals.

Rehearsal is normally an organized and intentional process that involves selectively bringing into focus relevant details of an event or episode. But it can also involve a more complicated and lengthy process of narrative encoding. When rehearsals are modified by elaborations of remembered material or by adding details or interpretations, these additions will determine the final shape of the "memory."

At the simplest level, rehearsal may involve a rote repetition of some salient item of information, as when one repeats several times to oneself, "The car is in lot 19. Nineteen. Nineteen." Careful repetition of specific material, such as learning one's lines in a play, is one of the most common ways people deliberately try to remember and can, undeniably, lead to long-lasting, high-fidelity memories.

Rehearsal is not necessarily a verbal or narrative process. People hum melodies to themselves or engage in deliberate acts of visualization. But because nonverbal forms of rehearsal are not easily observed or measured, they are difficult to study in the laboratory. To study them, experimenters must usually rely on self-reports or cleverly contrived observations, such as lip reading.

Many aspects of deliberate remembering or forgetting are orchestrated by rehearsal. Directed rehearsal is one way people commonly influence each other. Teachers specifically suggest which items should be studied for a test. Parents or anyone else who admonishes "Remember!" are implicitly suggesting that the child rehearse some item of information. Habitual forms of directed rehearsal are eventually internalized by the self, which learns to instruct itself explicitly about what to repeat and remember in particular situations.

Directed rehearsal works both ways, of course — the suggestion, "These dates are not important; they won't appear on the test," is an invitation to ignore information as irrelevant and, by implication, not to bother rehearsing it. Sometimes suggestions not to think or talk repetitively about something are more forceful, as when a parent insists that a child stop talking about some disturbing topic. And sometimes the self directs itself to stop thinking or talking about an event that arouses distress or conflict.

Directed rehearsals may affect not only what details of an event are attended to in the first place but also the narrative gloss that is given a story. One effect that especially concerns memory researchers is that of post-event information. When suggestive information is given through leading questions about an event or when someone else's story is narrated, it may be difficult for an individual, particularly a child, to disentangle what she initially experienced from what someone else said about it (Ceci, Ross, & Toglia, 1987). If post-event information is incorporated into subsequent rehearsals, memory for the event in question may be organized to deviate considerably from initial experience.

Several factors associated with the effects of post-event information have come under recent scrutiny. One of the most often mentioned is suggestibility. Suggestibility is connected with social factors like attachment and authority and is especially strong in children. This is scarcely surprising, since much of what goes on in socializing children involves suggestions and guidance from adults.

Individuals, including children, differ in how suggestible they are (Hilgard, 1979). Not only the authority or persuasiveness of the person making a suggestion, but the tendency of the individual to comply with authority affect whether a suggestion will be followed or ignored (Ellenberger, 1970). Even among people who are not particularly suggestible, the impact of directed rehearsals is to a great extent a function of the authority of the person who gives an instruction. What a teacher says about studying is more likely to be taken to heart than what a peer thinks might be important. A parent's statement that something is irrelevant and should not be talked about gives permission to avoid rehearsal.

Responses to coercion should also be distinguished from suggestibility. When one person has power over the well-being of another, that power also typically confers the ability to direct the organization and repetition of a particular narrative. In such instances, suppressing one's story and rehearsing an alternative story that fits with another person's directives may be a matter of survival. Cult mind control, for example, typically involves the directed repetition of slogans (Singer, 1995); eventually, these rote repetitions may come to replace independent thought.

Rehearsal may be overt or covert. Practicing one's part in a play typically involves repeating lines aloud over and over. But much of the repetitive talking to oneself that goes on is subvocal and never made public. The possibility of covert behavior is a problem in experiments that try to measure and control for rehearsal.

The possibility that covert rehearsal may differ from an overt narrative also influences how differing recollections of the same event may be constructed. A famous anecdote about Galileo, for example, is that, after he publicly complied with the demand of the Inquisition to recant his theory that the earth moved around the sun, he muttered under his breath, "But it moves." As a scientist he could presumably keep track of distinctions between his public and private statements. But an immature or unsure individual might easily become confused.

Rehearsal is thus one point in the process of organizing and consolidating memories where two or more versions of a particular event may be formed in memory. Under strong suggestion or coercion, a person may change what she says or does while continuing to rehearse covertly a very different version of the story. The covert story and the "official" story become divergent narratives. Although both may be forwarded in memory, for the sake of consistency the self may eventually focus attention on one to the exclusion of the other.

One possible response to inconsistent narratives is dissociation; on different occasions, attention may shift from a socially desirable story to the more covert, perhaps forbidden version, and back again, and the discrepancies may be tuned out. The right hand, in effect, does not know what the left hand is doing. Dissociation is facilitated by selective patterns of attention deployment and rehearsal. By focusing now on one detail of a memory, such as an emotional response, then again repeating a narrative that ignores that detail, the self moves back and forth between distinct versions of reality. In individuals who develop self-induced trance states, trance logic (Orne, 1959) facilitates this toleration for inconsistency.

Rehearsal may produce shifts in emphasis that bring certain details into focus and blur others. Ordinarily, the self-referent organization of memories includes references to internal physiological states. But the remembering self that observes and rehearses may choose to acknowledge a bodily response as part of itself or to repudiate it. The complexities of such acknowledgment or repudiation complicate the relation between the body and its memories.

If fear is an unacceptable emotion, for example, either the fact or the intensity of the fear may be deleted from subsequent rehearsals about a particular event. An injury that initially involved fear and pain may then be reported and subsequently recollected as one in which the injured person responded stoically. The memory of the original fear and pain may persist; however, in the absence of a rehearsed narrative that acknowledges it, it may gradually become unavailable to self-referent recall.

Other aspects of an event may be omitted from narration and rehearsal because they are unacceptable to the self. The experience of sexual abuse as a child, for example, may include experiences of pleasure that are reprehensible to the self and are subsequently tuned out for that reason. The fact of the abuse may be clearly recollected, but the associated feelings will be selectively avoided.

STORAGE: THE
PERSISTENCE OF THE PAST

Traditionally, searching for the memory trace involved looking for some place or structure in the brain where memories were permanently warehoused. As researchers became more knowledgable about the brain and nervous system, they realized that there is no simple correlation between structure and function. In part the difficulty derives from the behavioral processes, such as schematization, narration, and rehearsal, that transform memories over time; in part, it is a function of how the nervous system itself is organized.

Observing these distinctions, some memory researchers have postulated that memory consists of several kinds of stores. The distinction between *short-term* and *long-term* memories has proven especially useful in the laboratory as well as in everyday life. This distinction makes intuitive sense. Much information—once-used telephone numbers, the traffic jam on the way to work—remains only briefly in the mind. Other experiences, typically those given special attention and thought, may pass out of immediate awareness but can be recalled at a later time if needed.

The type of memory store that seems most closely to resemble the literal replicas of stimuli imagined by copy theorists is a sensory store (Sperling, 1960, 1963) or a sensory register (Atkinson & Shriffrin, 1968). Closely matched to sensory inputs, this register faithfully represents stimuli impinging on receptors at a given moment. After a couple of seconds, most of this information decays, but that selected for more extensive processing enters a short-term store that persists for up to 30 seconds.

From an evolutionary standpoint, sensory memory will obviously vary with the sensory capacities of a given organism, as well as other features of the nervous system.

Although sensory memory is a rapid, seemingly almost instantaneous process, it does take time. Raw material must be attended to long enough for basic sensory encodings to be made. Other kinds of encoding, such as concept formation and stimulus categorization, also occur in the earliest stages of perception. The observation that, in animals as well as in humans, the longer a stimulus is presented, the longer it is likely to be retained, provides some support for the idea that a memory is laid down as a trace (Schwartz & Reisberg, 1991), even though that trace may undergo considerable transformation over time.

Moreover, although sensory stores may be faithful replications of sensory events, what is eventually retrieved as a memory has usually been subjected to considerable processing. Sensory memories are integrated with complex processes of recoding as well as storage transformations. According to Baddeley (1990), for example, short-term memory is associated with processing functions he has termed a visuo-spatial sketchpad and a phonological loop.

Sperling (1963) spoke of sensory memories as icons, very transient copies of inputs. Neisser (1967) distinguished between iconic or visually based sensory memories and echoic ones based on auditory processes. Olfactory cues may also be retained in sensory memory.

One concept that has received considerable attention in memory research is that of the *consolidation* of the memory trace. Whatever processes underlie the neural development of memory, much data support the notion that storage develops over time. Consolidation may involve several stages. Such factors as electroshock therapy and drug effects may interfere with it (Parkin, 1987). The action-decrement hypothesis, which has considerable experimental support, indicates that consolidation is a process that impedes short-term recall but enhances long-term memory. The assumption that during the interim structural changes are occurring in the nervous system is supported both by learning experiments and by investigations of physiological, biochemical, and anatomical changes in the brain (Rose, 1992).

RETRIEVAL: REINSTATING THE PAST

The end product of recollecting or reinstating the past is sometimes called *retrieval*. Information-processing models of memory typically conceptualize retrieval as an associational linkage between memory traces and cues (Tulving, 1983). This process need not be explicit; the existence of implicit memory has been extensively studied (Graf & Masson, 1993).

In everyday contexts, the word *retrieval* brings to mind the image of a dog fetching a bone. And this prosaic image may, in fact, be as relevant to what commonly takes place as the notion of a computer conducting matching processes. Intuitively, for example, most people associate retrieval not with implicit or automatic connections but with intention and effort. We search until we find.

The tip of the tongue phenomenon, in which one knows that one knows something but cannot state it explicitly, is a common example of this distinction between memories as stored information and memories as intentional recollections. A recollection on the tip of the tongue can be quite annoying, but most people do not simply acquiesce passively to the experience. On the contrary, it motivates active search strategies. In the absence of effective cues, we seek out cues that will jog memory.

The word *retrieval* also suggests bringing back some specific item of information. In laboratory experiments, it is commonly studied in terms of individual responses. Ebbinghaus, who was the first to plot a forgetting

curve as a function of time, counted his accurate recall of nonsense syllables at particular intervals. A long history in this tradition has elucidated
how memories for simple stimuli are formed, preserved, and lost (Searleman & Herrmann, 1994).

In natural contexts, however, people typically recollect not isolated associations but episodic gestalts. Nor is the retrieval of episodic memory a
matter of reinstating one set of representations. It is usually a process of
coordinating representations that have been encoded in several modalities,
of integrating different types of representations, and of utilizing these
integrations for the task at hand.

Representations are not just images or words. Throughout the animal
kingdom, even in humans, motor movements serve basic signaling functions. Conditioned response patterns can also come to function as signals.
Zajonc and Markus (1984) call the representations provided by the motor
system *hard* representations. Verbal, iconic, or analog representations, in
contrast, are called *soft*.

Hard representations based on motor responses as well as autonomic,
glandular, and visceral processes underlie the representation of memory
for emotions. Emotions, in turn, have a vital role to play in initiating,
maintaining, and integrating adaptive behaviors, including memory. The
emotional context in which a personally relevant memory is encoded and
eventually retrieved is usually quite different from the neutral or artifi-
cially imposed emotional contexts that characterize laboratory experiments.

In everyday life, different systems of representing the same event may be
incongruent. Conflicts resulting from incongruent representational systems
can produce very physical effects—behavioral oscillations between approach
and avoidance, muscular states of tension that belie verbal statements.

Episodic memory as observed in the search for personal history is thus
not a simple process involving one modality of functioning or one encoding of information. It depends, rather, on encoding-retrieval interactions
(Jacoby, 1988) that potentially involve several representational systems.
The complexities of such interactions can result in the dissociation of
functions.

Awareness is variably associated with remembering; people do not necessarily know how they are utilizing memory. What Jacoby calls the "stage-
setting" function of memory enables us to use the past to plan for the
future. But the practical use of a memory for prior experience is not
necessarily accompanied by self-referential processes.

STATE-DEPENDENT MEMORY

One of the most intriguing concepts in the study of how selective
processes affect learning and memory is that of state-dependent memory

(Eich, 1989; Goodwin, Powell, Bremer, Hoine, & Stern, 1969). Much of the relevant research on this topic has involved observing the effects of alcohol and drugs (Eich, 1977; Swanson & Kinsbourne, 1979). Some studies have also reported that mood may produce state-dependent memory effects (Bower, 1981). Experimental studies of state-dependent memory effects, however, particularly those involving moods, are limited by procedures used to cue recall and the intensity of the moods involved (Searleman & Herrman, 1994). After reviewing the literature on the relationship between mood and memory, Blaney (1986) concluded that the phenomenon observed is really that of mood congruence; that is, a mood has selective effects on encoding as well as on the retrieval stage of memory.

One of the problems in studying state-dependent memory effects is confounding encoding and recall congruency (Singer & Salovey, 1988). To avoid this confounding, mood must be controlled during both encoding and retrieval. There may also be differential effects between positive and negative moods. Happy people may be more likely to encode or retrieve pleasant memories but this effect is not reversed by reversing mood; unhappy people are *not* more likely to encode or retrieve unpleasant memories (Blaney, 1986).

The concept of state-dependent memory has proved especially useful in the study of dissociative disorders, pathological reactions that sometimes occur in the wake of extreme stress or trauma (Putnam, 1989). Theoretically, memories organized during traumatic states are more accessible if such states are revived, cued by reminders that elicit the psychobiological responses produced by the original trauma. Because the states of arousal produced by trauma are sometimes quite intense, associated biochemical and neurological responses in the organism may, like the effects of drugs or alcohol, produce stronger state-dependent effects than might be ordinarily observable in less intense experiences.

THE ARTICULATION OF MEMORY

The complexities of episodic memory call into question the utility of textbook categories that have become so popular in modern explications of memory. Arguing for a functionalist perspective in the study of memory, Jacoby (1988) has stressed that the ongoing interaction between perception and memory dooms attempts to locate any reported memory on a simple timeline. The past always sets the stage for the present, and encoding-retrieval interactions are more useful predictors of many of our observations about memory than hypotheses about concretely defined inputs and fixed stores.

The complexities involved even at early stages of processing complicate the integrations that eventually emerge as autobiographical memory. The articulation of personal memory at any point in a life is invariably compli-

cated not only by what can be recollected at that point but by how repeated past retrievals, reconstructions, and elaborations have modified
recollections for any specific episode. Personal history, like cultural history, is not just a fabrication. In normal people, it is constrained by facts
and actualities. Like cultural history, however, it is constantly being revised in the light of new information.

Equally important, episodic memories, particularly self-relevant ones,
are constantly being mined for new meanings. Again, this interpretive
process is not merely a fantasy trip; rather, it is a pragmatic tool for coping
in the present and planning the future. Only when we understand the
significance of a particular memory can we move from automatic, unre-
flective responses to intentional transformations of the remembering I.

In the study of personal history, experimental research offers important
suggestive guidelines but leaves many questions unanswered. Such research is limited by the kinds of conditions that can be manipulated in the
laboratory. It is difficult, for example, to elicit the intensities of emotion
that typically accompany extremely salient life events. Certain situations,
such as the effects of trauma on memory, cannot be experimentally manipulated at all. They can be studied only in natural settings.

The study of autobiographical memory is complicated, too, by the very
mass of material that has usually accumulated by the time an individual
reaches adulthood. The number of constructions and reconstructions that
may have modified a particular salient memory may be numerous and
inconsistent. In evaluating these, however, simple dichotomies like true
and false can be as misleading as they are simplistic. Unlike laboratory
settings, where standards about what constitutes a correct or incorrect
response are determined in advance of an experiment, real-world evaluations are constantly modified by changing tasks and needs as well as by
changing facts.

The articulation of memory in human beings is thus not only a function
of biological reactions and sequential factors in information-processing,
but also an aspect of developing competence. From birth until death,
remembering is both a matter of encoding, storing, and retrieving information and of making sense of the world and the evolving self.

CHAPTER 4

Memory as Competence

Love is more thicker than forget.
— e. e. cummings

F IVE CHILDREN stand side by side several yards from the front porch of
a house. From the top of the porch steps, another child who is "it"
dispenses commands. The object of the game is for the other children to
advance, bit by bit, to the porch and the privilege of being "it."

"Kirsten, take three baby steps," the leader orders. And the child addressed hesitates or moves forward impulsively. If she simply hurries ahead
in her eagerness to reach the porch, the leader will shout triumphantly,
"Go all the way back! You forgot to say, 'May I?'"

"May I?" (or "Mother, May I?") is one of those children's games that
seem to be about the fun of giving orders. Obviously, too, it is a game
about remembering. "Go all the way back" is a harsh penalty for forgetting
to ask permission.

On close examination, though, the game is more complicated than it
immediately appears. What really makes it fun is the tension between
obeying impulsively, like a dog answering a whistle, and interpolating a
social rule into the sequence. "May I?" the child who is ordered asks
politely. "Yes, you may" or "No, you may not," replies the autocratic leader.
The point of the game, then, is, "Remember! Don't just follow orders.
Follow rules. And think before you act."

Things get still more complicated if one observes the behavior of the
other four children while the leader is busy ordering Kirsten about. If they
can move without being noticed, they can sneak closer to the porch. This
sneakiness is not a matter of cheating, as it would be in, say, a game of
checkers. It is, rather, part of the way in which rules about obedience have
been embedded in this particular game. In the long run, the winner of the

game will be the child who manages the right mix of polite "May I's" and surreptitious initiative.

The tensions around which games like "May I?" revolve are those that constantly occupy the minds of growing children. Who gives the orders? What are the rules? How much autonomy may one safely exercise at any given moment? The pleasure grade-school children take in such games reflects their appreciation of their own developing skills and savvy. By this point, they have learned to remember the rule about asking permission. But they have also achieved a degree of autonomy that allows them to move beyond the boundaries set by parental authority, to exercise independent initiative and even to engage in crafty deceit.

Children who play "May I?" are also implicitly acknowledging something of their understanding of how memory must be deployed in order to be socially adaptive. Obeying commands is an almost reflexive behavior, an acquiescence to the control of another person learned by toddlers. In contrast, choosing to follow or break rules is the act of a more consciously controlled self. It demands more differentiated appraisals; recalling what the rules are must be supplemented by an understanding of how they function to facilitate particular outcomes. Winning a game fairly is carefully demarcated from cheating. Impulsive behavior is distinguished from planned initiative. And lying is differentiated from keeping secrets.

Useful memory, in other words, involves integrating knowledge about facts and rules with task requirements, social demands, and personal needs. As they grow, children practice these integrations over and over, not only in the contexts organized by formal training but also in their own games. Their delight in doing so reflects their recognition of the competence they are achieving in negotiating a complex world.

THE SOCIAL MATRIX

Such developments in children depend on competencies that have been unfolding since birth. The independent initiatives exercised by five- or six-year-olds emerge out of a history of sheltered dependency and organized attachment. The school-age child can increasingly escape the controlling confines of "Mother, may I?" because, earlier in life, mother and other caregivers had provided a safe "holding environment" (Winnicott, 1971).

Attachment is the social matrix of memory. In infrahuman species, many necessary adaptations may be hard-wired into the neonate, whose rapid maturation leads quickly to independence. With the evolution of social species, the development of memory, as well as that of other capacities, reflects the contingencies of longer neonatal dependency and complex social interchanges. The autonomous self who eventually emerges from this matrix is both a repository of individual memories and an ongoing carrier of relationships that continue to organize shared memories across the lifespan.

Some theorists have conceptualized human infancy as a period of symbiosis in which awareness of the distinction between self and mother is only gradually differentiated (Mahler, Pine, & Bergman, 1975). Attachment, as indexed by behavioral interactions, evolves through a series of stages. The earliest form of connection may involve clinging to the mother's body and cues associated with it. As the child achieves locomotion and is able to move away from the mother, attachment is manifest in close checks with her. Her input about the relevance or safety of external events continues to influence where and how far the child will go in exploring the environmental surround.

The major function of attachment behavior in infancy, according to John Bowlby (1982), who was among the first to study it carefully, is the maintenance or restoration of proximity between an immature animal and a specific caregiver. Attachment ensures that the helpless neonate is protected by the full repertory of adaptive responses available to the mature members of the species. Most importantly, it serves to protect immature offspring from predators by making sure they are never far from the watchful eyes of parents.

In both animals and humans, the separation cry is a distinctive alarm reaction that occurs whenever a helpless neonate becomes isolated from caregivers. Some researchers (see van der Kolk, 1987) view this reaction as an antecedent of trauma responses that may have important implications for subsequent stress sensitivities and coping behavior.

One of the most striking attachment mechanisms is that of imprinting, commonly observed in birds. The imprinted hatchling follows its mother confidently and enjoys her protection in precarious circumstances. The imprinted songbird learns to mimic the parent's songs. Such primitive forms of memory function automatically to ensure survival by structuring relationships in which subsequent patterns of learning can unfold (Hinde, 1982).

Researchers have pointed to the time-sensitive aspect of early attachment behaviors. In both puppies and rhesus monkeys, for example, it becomes progressively more difficult to become attached to a new object after an early sensitive period (Bowlby, 1982).

Although social attachments in human babies are more complex than imprinting, they are nevertheless facilitated by innate mechanisms, such as the orienting reflex, which helps fix the infant's attention on the mother's face, and early attunement, possibly developed in utero, to the mother's voice (DeCasper & Fifer, 1980). From the beginning of life, basic processes of stimulus selection, encoding, rehearsal, and retrieval are guided by caregivers, typically in face-to-face interactions with the child (Brown, 1991). The newborn infant also has built-in capacities for facilitating social interactions (Donaldson, 1978; Emde, 1989). The social smile, which appears around the age of two or three months, is an important example.

Early attachment behavior depends on the availability of accurate recognition memory in both mothers and neonates (Bowlby, 1982). In all species of mammal, the mother recognizes her own offspring within hours or days of its birth and restricts her caretaking behavior to that specific individual; mothers and neonates respond selectively to one another. Early in life, empathic emotional responses are conditioned in the human infant in response to the mother's affective states. The mother's bodily states of tension and feelings of anxiety are communicated by the way she holds and talks to her child (Hoffman, 1984; Sullivan, 1953).

The empathic responsiveness of caregivers facilitates an interpersonal matching of regulatory systems between themselves and the infant (Bruner, 1975; Emde, 1989). Thus, even basic physiological processes in the infant are socially synchronized. As they are elaborated in complex patterns of mutual cuing between infant and caregiver, sequences of self-regulation and interpersonal interaction come to resemble the mutuality of a social dance.

Bowlby (1982) conceptualized human attachment as a process that, like imprinting, is stage-specific. According to his observations, human infants, during the second quarter of the first year of life, are ready to make a "discriminated attachment." After the age of about six months, specific affiliative ties become especially prominent. Between seven and nine months, substitutes for familiar caregivers are not easily accepted. Memory has developed to the extent that infants can demonstrate anticipatory responses to impending departures. Typically, attachment is strongly exhibited from the age of nine months until about the end of the third year, after which, although it persists, it may be expressed less urgently.

Once attached, an infant shows anxiety at being separated from the caregiver. Normally, however, children become increasingly tolerant of such separations during the first three years of life. Although the toddler shows increasing autonomy during the period between eighteen and twenty-one months, for example, he or she still clings, especially when tired or ill.

Although some researchers have disputed the stage-specific nature of this process, almost all agree that early attachment lays an important foundation for subsequent social development and perhaps for competence in such important social areas as peer relationships, impulse control, and interpersonal conduct.

In most discussions of attachment, the early role of the mother is strongly emphasized. But infants can and do become attached to other caregivers. Fathers, in particular, become the objects, sometimes even the primary objects, of discriminated attachments. And even when the first attachment is primarily to the mother, fathers become more and more important as the child develops.

> No form of behavior is accompanied by stronger feeling than is attachment behavior. The figures toward whom it is directed are loved and their advent is greeted with joy. . . . A threat of loss creates anxiety, and actual loss sorrow; both, moreover, are likely to arouse anger. (Bowlby, 1982, p. 209)

DISORDERED ATTACHMENT

Security of early attachment varies. Inconsistent or insensitive care leads to patterns of attachment behavior that affect not only social interactions but also cognitive development. Ainsworth (1973, 1978) found, for example, that infants with such a history are wary about exploring the environment. They tend to develop patterns of attachment characterized by anxiety and/or avoidance that persist beyond infancy and can be observed in nursery or school settings.

Such patterns can in turn produce repetitive experiences that function as schemas for organizing memories. Sroufe (1989) describes how frequently children with avoidant attachment relationships behave in ways that confirm their preexisting models and expectations. Thus, children with anxious, resistant attachment have been found to be controlled more by teachers, shown less warmth, and treated with lower expectations of compliance.

Disordered attachment behavior as a consequence of stress has been studied in both animals and humans. Attachment behavior tends to become more intense when an infant is alarmed. It thus has a regulatory effect on exploratory behavior, since the novel properties that invite exploration also tend to elicit alarm and withdrawal. Harlow and Harlow (1971) found, for example, that infant monkeys who have become attached to nonfeeding cloth models will seek out and cling to such models if alarmed. Having done so, they may then begin to explore the alarming object.

In infant monkeys as well as humans, attachment is also intensified by maltreatment (Seay, Alexander, & Harlow, 1964). The more punishment a juvenile receives, the stronger it becomes attached to the punishing figure (Bowlby, 1982). Bowlby contends that increased clinging to an abusive caretaker, which seems paradoxical, is an inevitable result of the tendency of any alarming stimulus to elicit attachment behavior.

Relationship disturbances in early childhood can have profound effects on subsequent development. Basic patterns of interaction and affect regulation laid down from infancy persist across the lifespan. And since attachment is the social matrix of memory, not only the form but the content of memories will be profoundly affected by individual histories of attachment.

ATTACHMENT, MEMORY, AND
COGNITIVE DEVELOPMENT

The relationship between memory and attachment is reciprocal. Even in babies, memory is necessary for attachment. And across the lifespan, attachment organizes and regulates memory. By facilitating the communication of learned behaviors, it makes possible the transmission of adaptive skills from one generation to the next. Attachment is thus not only the social matrix of memory but also the facilitating context of culture.

Although cognitive appraisals of the world depend on the maturation of neural mechanisms and processes, they are increasingly differentiated and modified through social interaction. For example, the appraisal that a situation, such as an impending inoculation, is threatening depends on the ability to recognize familiar cues. After experience with such events, avoidance and protest may appear as conditioned responses to any signal that suggests a visit to the doctor. Even pets may recognize and react to an impending trip to the vet. In human children, such reactions can be socially modified by interpretations about the unpleasant experience (Brown, O'Keeffe, Sanders, & Baker, 1986). Protest may give way to acquiescence and even pride in being "big" enough to cooperate.

In infancy, cognitive developments occur in tandem with changes in patterns of sleep-wake organization. As the infant is awake more, she shows an increasing interest in prolonging interesting events (Emde, 1989). Research by Bauer and Hertsgaard (1993) indicates that children thirteen and sixteen months of age can maintain over time information about the temporal order of some events.

The first social context of memory is the family, and within the family, the mother, who is usually the primary caregiver, functions as the first organizer of memory. A basic aspect of this organization is the infant's experience of bodily contact with her. There is some evidence that human infants in the womb can discriminate their mother's voice; within a few days after birth, they can distinguish the smell and voices of different people (DeCasper & Fifer, 1980).

Infants and young children encode memories in terms of sensory features (Ackerman, 1981; Owings & Baumeister, 1979). Visual cues probably function somewhat later than olfactory, tactile, and auditory ones, but become increasingly important during the first year. Wolff (1969) found that, as early as the fifth week, many babies begin crying when the person they are looking at leaves the visual field and stop crying when the person reappears. However, the visual specificity of the stimulus figure only becomes important later, from about the age of five months.

Catherwood (1993) found experimental evidence that supports the widely held view that infants learn and retain much information on the basis of haptic (touch) exploration. Eight-month-old infants were capable of sustaining haptic memory over a brief delay, despite intervening exposure to other tactile information.

Integrating memories across modalities develops with the capacity for categorical and semantic processing, which in turn evolves with repeated exposures to similar occurrences.

From birth, face to face interactions between mother and child establish mutual patterns of attunement. The mother's posture and affect are communicated to the infant, and babies respond empathically to parental emotions (Sullivan, 1953). Parents also differentiate the emotional implications of their baby's signals. Social smiling develops around two months and social vocalization soon after that; these developments facilitate the articulation of an increasingly complex dialogue.

Although recognitory memory develops from birth, recall as a specific competence is more difficult to measure (Kail, 1990). Part of the problem is that, prior to language, recognition and recall can only be studied as aspects of motor behavior. Imitation and a search for hidden objects are indirect measures of recall that have been employed in many studies (Kail, 1990).

Experiments by Rovee-Collier and her colleagues, using an ingenious conjugate reinforcement paradigm in which infants are trained to kick a mobile, have revealed the progressive development of retention in infants. Even in infancy, contextual factors play an important role in recall. Following two days of training, two-month-olds exhibit retention for about one to three days (Greco, Rovee-Collier, Hayne, Griesler, & Earley, 1986). By the age of three months, the retention interval has increased to six to eight days (Sullivan, Rovee-Collier, & Tynes, 1979), and six-month-olds have been shown to exhibit retention for fifteen to sixteen days (Hill, Borovsky, & Rovee-Collier, 1988).

Hayne and Rovee-Collier (1995) studied encoding-retrieval interactions in three-month-old infants. Their findings are consistent with other experimental observations that, following periods of delay, effective reminders (in this case a moving training mobile) can reinstate specific memories. They conclude that their results support the encoding specificity hypothesis; that is, memory retrieval during infancy is highly specific to the conditions of the original encoding.

Perris, Myers, and Clifton (1990), replicating an earlier experiment by Myers and her colleagues (Myers, Clifton, & Clarkson, 1987), found evidence that, given original contextual cues, it is possible to retrieve memory processes that occurred during the first year of life. In this experiment, children who were almost three years old had retained some memory of a single experience studied in an identical laboratory condition two years previously.

EMOTION AND MEMORY

Affective responses are a major factor in the organization of memories. From birth, emotional interchanges between infant and caregivers orchestrate cognitive and social competencies. There are neural substrates in the limbic system common to emotion and cognition, and the maturation of neural structures is related to emotional as well as cognitive development in childhood (Izard, 1984).

Throughout development, emotion plays an important role in the encoding, storage, and retrieval of specific memories. Level of arousal is closely associated with the deployment of attention, which, in turn, organizes encoding and rehearsal and may even affect the consolidation of memory traces (Izard, Kagan, & Zajonc, 1984). Shifts in affect, level of arousal, cognition, and action structure the boundaries of episodes as these become distinctly represented. "An episode appears to enter memory as an indivisible unit — a singular moment of experience — and it is recalled from memory as a single indivisible unit, although that is not to say that one cannot access the memory via one of its attributes alone" (Stern, 1989, p. 57).

The emotions of interest, distress, and disgust, as evidenced by motor expression, appear to be present at birth. The social smile, observed in one-and-a-half to five-month-old infants, is at first displayed indiscriminately, but over the first year comes to be elicited by specific caregivers. Izard (1984) considers the smile to be a form of affective information-processing and cites experiments on adult subjects in which the interpersonal induction of emotion has been shown to affect selective perception and recall.

Anger emerges around four months in response to arm-restraint, but over the course of the first year becomes associated with the social experience of separation from the mother (Izard, 1984). Fear is observable at seven or eight months, and there is some evidence that the fear mechanism becomes functional earlier than usual in abused infants (Gaensbauer, 1980). Fear of strangers, which typically becomes prominent around eight months, seems to be related to the development of attachment to a specific caregiver (Izard, 1984).

Although emotions serve a vital expressive and communicative function from the beginning of life, there is evidence that as early as three months of age infants may begin to be socialized to dissociate internal emotional states from outward expressions (Malatesta & Haviland, 1982). By late childhood, individual and cultural display rules play a decisive role in emotional expression (Ekman, 1992).

REPRESENTATION AND
INTERNALIZATION

Over the first two years, attachment provides basic interactional schemas for organizing memories about self and others: It regulates the focus of attention and perception (Izard, 1984); it provides the emotional context that makes certain experiences memorable (Izard et al., 1984); it provides the conceptual and linguistic categories into which experience is encoded (Bloom, 1993); and it prescribes the evaluations that help the child differentiate between what should be remembered and what should be forgotten (Kagan, 1984). The forms into which memories are cast continually evolve through relationship experiences, constantly repeated and recreated, as the infant develops representations not just of events but of interactive patterns. As a result, infant development is organized by the memories of two or more individuals (Stern, 1989). As it is increasingly internalized, this coordination of repertories between infant and caregivers gives continuity and coherence to individual experience.

Reviewing research on infant memory, Stern (1989) concludes that infants develop prototypes, abstractions of reality, based on averaging experiences across time. But some memories, such as those that are traumatic, may resist assimilation into prototypes. Such unassimilated memories may be associated with actions that differ from actions associated with assimilated memories.

According to Bloom (1993), the earliest representational memories can be observed in behavioral patterns Piaget (1950/1981) called "circular reactions." These involve the infant's acting intentionally to repeat results that originally happened by chance.

The earliest representations are sensorimotor patterns that rely on immediately accessible connections between stimuli and responses. Gradually, the child extends the range of what can be held in mind and is able to organize representations in problem-solving tasks, such as the search for absent objects. After the first six to eight months of life, for example, infants are able to find objects that have been completely hidden behind obstacles (Diamond, 1985). By ten months, they can find the hidden object after delays of as long as eight seconds, and by sixteen to eighteen months, after delays of twenty to thirty seconds (Daehler, Bukatko, Benson, & Myers, 1976).

By seven months, the infant has internalized the caregiving context (Sroufe, 1989). He has developed working models of the world that are organized around "who his attachment figures are, where they may be found, and how they may be expected to respond" (Bowlby, 1982, p. 203). These models are resistant to change, according to Sroufe (1989), because they are constantly reinforced through repetitive enactments. They affect not only what information is accepted and assimilated, but how it is utilized in social interactions.

Even after the child is able to crawl or walk away from her, the mother's face continues to be used to facilitate appraisal of cues about the safety of the environment. Experiments of social referencing have demonstrated, for example, how the infant uses the mother's smile as a signal that it is safe to cross a visual cliff (Campos & Stenberg, 1982; Feinman & Lewis, 1983). Her postures and emotional cues also affect how the child behaves in the presence of strangers.

Implicitly as well as explicitly, early caregivers shape the content and form of memories. What others notice, react to, talk about, or ignore offers cues to the child developing his or her own capacities to think. Even prior to language, the child is being taught how, why, and what to remember. The memories of caregivers themselves are explicitly or implicitly transmitted as part of this early instruction (Engel, 1995). And the memories spontaneously created by the child are confirmed, amended, or denied.

Halford, Mayberry, O'Hare, and Grant (1994) contend that increased cognitive efficiency is a major factor in cognitive development associated with the differentiation of representations. The limits of short-term memory as a neural process may not change much with age, but such factors as faster and more efficient rehearsal and coding can greatly facilitate the deployment of memory.

Research by Farrar and Goodman (1992) supports the hypothesis that memory development in children is related to schema development. Four- and seven-year-olds differed in their ability to recall details of an event that deviate from a standard procedure employed during event acquisition. The younger children tended to merge two types of event into a generalized event representation and became confused about details. Seven-year-olds, in contrast, were able to keep their memories for the two types of event separate.

Throughout development, the social matrix of memory is as significant to what is eventually internalized psychologically as those neural mechanisms that are our basic biological heritage. By orchestrating attention and establishing the schemas that organize encoding and retrieval, social interactions eventually evolve into personal history. After infancy, even private experience is usually articulated by the self talking to itself. And when this articulation is lacking, as seems to be the case in autistic children, reflective self-awareness is lacking, too.

Integrating Language

In humans, the attachments that organize representational processes are initially mediated by emotional and nonverbal forms of communication. From the first, however, these are supplemented by verbal communications from adults and the symbolic forms valued by the family. Long before the infant says a word, babbling is shaped by the typical patterns of language and the rhythms of interpersonal dialogue.

During the second year of life, the infant moves from early dependency on emotional signals and nonverbal forms of communication to an increasing reliance on words. Typically, by the end of the second year, she has acquired a vocabulary and may even have begun to say simple sentences (Bloom, 1993). Language integrates developing cognitive competencies with social behavior. "Children learn language in the first place because they strive to maintain intersubjectivity with other persons — to *share* what they and other persons are feeling and thinking" (Bloom, 1993, p. 245). Intellectual and social competence thus develop in tandem.

Bloom (1993) contends that expression is a basic function of language. By the time they begin to talk, children realize that their speech must be interpreted by others in order to be effective. Expressive acts, including speech, translate internal, personal representations of events into public representations. The communicative function of language determines mental meanings. Another major function of language, according to Bloom, is to represent and communicate intentional states. "Acts of expression and interpretation require plans, just like other acts that we do" (1993, p. 21). Plans, in turn, depend on and facilitate the development of memory.

Early words are context-bound. Initially, a child's spoken utterance involves what Bloom terms a "word-image representation," a fusion of form and content. Recalling the word is interdependent with recalling the particularities of an episode, and reencounters with events serve as perceptual cues for speech.

Language has an important schematizing function. As it develops, representation is gradually freed from immediate perceptual contexts. Remembered episodes become increasingly independent of immediate stimuli. Gradually, language development facilitates the decontextualization of representations (Donaldson, 1978). Over time, words become associated with generalized concepts and, eventually, with other words. Representation proceeds from episodes, to concepts, to semantic thought. Bloom (1993) contends that this sequence is empirically as well as logically invariant.

Towards the end of the second year, when words increasingly begin to cue recall not only of perceived events but of other words, there is typically a vocabulary spurt. According to Bloom, this spurt constitutes a discontinuity in development. It is associated with developments in object permanence and in the ability to sort objects into categories.

As language develops, it increasingly organizes memory in semantic forms and facilitates the integration of verbal with nonverbal information. In a series of experiments involving children from several age levels, from first grade through college, Duncan and his colleagues (1982) found that verbal information influenced both recognition and recall of visual material at every age level. Incorrect verbal information, in contrast, decreased performance on both recognition and recall tasks.

In infancy and childhood, memory is increasingly organized by not only by verbal competence but by communication. Language, like attachment, develops in a context of mutual dialogue and is guided by the intentions and memories of the self in relation to other people (Hermans & Kempen, 1993). The early acquisition of language is carefully shaped by explicit instructions and guidance that are a natural consequence of earlier, preverbal interactions. Words begin to function as tools both for representing one's own experiences and for effecting representations in the minds of others.

Language facilitates rehearsal. In an experiment by Flavell, Beach, and Chinsky (1966) children were shown a series of pictures and asked to remember a selected subset. An experimenter trained as a lip reader observed the children's behavior prior to their being asked to recall what they had seen. Rehearsal was first regularly observed at approximately seven years. By the age of ten, 85 percent of the children rehearsed the material. Children's rehearsal often consists of rote repetitions of words (Kail, 1990). Younger children use strategies like looking, pointing, and touching in their attempts to remember. Older children become more sophisticated in their use of external aids. Instructions to remember make a difference and are likely to affect which material is rehearsed.

There is some evidence for asymmetries in acquisition and retrieval processes during childhood. In an attempt to extricate storage-based forgetting from retrieval-based forgetting, Brainerd, Kingma, and Howe (1985) concluded that both storage and retrieval processes improve steadily during childhood, but that the greatest improvements in storage occur in the preschool years while the greatest improvements in retention occur during the later elementary school years. The data from their experiments indicate that the declines in long-term memory during childhood are largely specific to retrieval.

As language develops, it is organized into increasingly complex narratives, and these, too, are jointly constructed with others. Babies are surrounded by the stories family members tell one another, and by the age of two or three toddlers begin to tell their own (Engel, 1995). By the time they are three, they typically describe their experiences in story form; many of their stories will have a beginning, a middle, and an end. By the age of five, they have developed distinctive narrative styles and can accurately relate complex events.

It is important to keep in mind, however, that language does not simply replace other representational behaviors; rather, it is normally integrated with expressive and gestural forms. Nonverbal signals continue to cue recall, and over the lifespan nonverbal schemas continue to be integrated with verbal ones.

For this reason, it is misleading to equate nonverbal memory with preverbal memory; the tendency to do so confuses many discussions about memory. Memory that develops prior to language is only part of the nonverbal repertory, which includes much procedural memory and perhaps pictorial and auditory representations of episodes. It may be predictably and routinely organized on the basis of sensorimotor schemas, but to the extent that it has never been integrated with language it is not available for narrative recall.

SCRIPTS

One concept that has proved useful in understanding how people organize episodic memory and generalize it across time is that of scripts (Schank & Abelson, 1977). Scripts consist of patterns of associations that allow us to infer typicalities: at a restaurant, one is usually served by a waiter; going to a movie involves buying a ticket, etc. Because of these predictable patterns, which in some instances resemble rituals, people do not need to focus on and store every detail of an experience in order to make plausible inferences about it after it occurs. Integration of experiences across time allows us to extract the *gist* of an experience (Neisser, 1982a,c).

Nelson and Gruendel (1981) found that children as young as three or four can articulate their understanding of typical scripts for recurrent events such as having lunch. The difficulty children experienced in recalling specific episodes from the previous day led them to hypothesize that episodic memories are contingent on the establishment of general scripts. Repeated exposure is necessary for the construction of scripts, and children learn them as part of their ongoing socialization. While scripts are obviously adaptive in many respects and facilitate smooth negotiations of routines, because they consist of generalizations they can potentially distort memory for specific episodes. Children may forget events that do not conform to the script or may remember them as having done so (Hudson & Nelson, 1983, 1986).

Novel events are less likely than familiar ones to be distorted in memory. The first instance of an event, such as a trip to the beach, may be more accurately recalled than later ones, for example (Hudson & Nelson, 1986; Nelson, 1989). In part, this effect may be due to the tendency of novel happenings to preempt attention, to be processed more completely, and perhaps, to be rehearsed more frequently. In part, too, it may result from the simple fact that having no category in which to place an event makes the event stand out and calls for special efforts of comprehension. The routinization that goes along with scripting, in contrast, glosses over details and may not encode or rehearse more than a few prototypical ones.

Some scripts have special meanings, are overlearned, and are repeated with comparatively little variation. They have a ritualistic component that in itself may attest to their importance as memory markers. Social rituals associated with special occasions or events are commonly structured in this way. Paradoxically, they stand out in memory because of their specialness but may seem timeless and difficult to recall in terms of particulars. One Thanksgiving Day blurs with another. Birthday cakes are remembered generically.

THE EMERGENT SELF

One outcome of social development is an increasingly individualized self (Sroufe, 1989). Donaldson (1978) believes that the sense of self develops early and is closely related to the experience of the body as a distinct source of cues. She notes that bodily experience is typically more continuous than information from external sources.

This early *sense* of self, which is probably organized around recognitions of consistencies in bodily states and behavioral competencies, only gradually evolves into a *concept* of self. Repeated experiences in state regulation and growing realization of how one's own behavior contributes to outcomes are eventually organized into self-recognitory patterns. Around eighteen months the infant recognizes her own mirror image (Mans, Cicchetti, & Sroufe, 1978). Around that time, too, children start to be able to talk about themselves and by the end of the second year they can think about themselves (Donaldson, 1978). The flowering of symbolic thinking between eighteen and thirty-six months facilitates not only the articulation of cognition and behavior, but also the emergence of the self as a coherent agency. Attachment, which continues to be an important organizing matrix, is increasingly integrated with self-awareness and autonomy.

Throughout early development, cognitive processes are increasingly organized by verbal development. The differentiation of the self as a point of reference occurs simultaneously with other cognitive developments, such as the capacity to represent and symbolize. As language skills improve, memory, like other dimensions of life, is increasingly organized by narrative structures that bear a cultural as well as an idiosyncratic stamp (Fentress & Wickham, 1992; Vansina, 1985). The integration of nonverbal with verbal schemas, including narratives about the self and others that are labeled "memories," is an ongoing process.

Awareness of the past as a time distinct from the present and future is increasingly articulated after the second birthday. At that point, children can talk about things that have already happened or that they expect to happen. Speech about the personal past does not usually occur, however, until the beginning of the third year (Donaldson, 1978). By the age of four, children have a sense of relative distances in the past and are accurate in judging the location of events with respect to time of day (Friedman, 1991). It is about the age of four, too, that children develop an understanding that the words *remember* and *forget* refer to prior knowledge (Lyon & Flavell, 1994).

Once the self becomes an organizing context for episodic memory, specific episodic memories can be valued not only for the pleasures with which they are associated but also for their meaning for the emerging self. After this development, ideas and feelings about the self become major determinants of what is recalled and how it is interpreted. As the self evolves, it becomes an important focus of internal dialogue. Positive self-talk, for example, is an important coping strategy (Brown et al., 1986).

Social requirements and evaluations shape the development of the self and self-referential memories at every stage. Parental references to the child are eventually internalized as self-references. Later, particularly after the child goes to school, referential statements by other authorities, especially teachers, continue to modify the emerging self and its memories.

Evidence suggests that the retrieval of self-relevant memories in childhood is also closely tied to peer evaluations. Cole and Jordan (1995), for example, found a significant relation between peer nominations of competence and incidental recall of self-referential information in fourth-through eighth-grade students. Children who received positive evaluations from peers appeared to have enhanced recall of positive self-relevant information, but children who were devalued by peers showed a *reduced* capacity for negative recall. The authors consider the possibility that self-schemas facilitate the storage, organization, and retrieval of positive self-relevant informations, but that a lack of positive feedback from peers may inhibit the very formation of self-relevant memories, including negative ones. Also in this study, self-reported symptoms of depression were related to peer estimations of competence; the most depressed subjects were regarded by peers as the lowest in competence.

At any point in development, the deletion of references to a particular version of the self is likely to be connected to the avoidance or revision of particular episodic memories. This avoidance may be quite explicit and deliberate (Cottle, 1980). When it becomes habitual, the unaccepted version of the self and the memories with which it is associated are effectively sequestered from the accepted self and its memories.

Although the consistency of external references is an important source of self-consistency, the cohesion of the self is also affected by such internal variables as the capacity to integrate conflicting and disparate experiences, including shifting internal states (Stern, 1989). Extreme states of arousal and associated emotions may be difficult to integrate with more typical states. Chaotic experiences are not easily organized into coherent patterns of feeling and thought. Some experiences do not lend themselves to narration, and thus cannot be communicated. The result may be a fragmentation of experience that is reflected in the referencing of memory and the integration of the self.

Adolescence is a significant period in the articulation and consolidation of identity (Erikson, 1968). Around this time, behavior and self-reference are increasingly organized in terms of ideals and life plans. References to the self by peers continue to be highly salient, and there may be intentional, socially orchestrated attempts to differentiate the childhood self from the adolescent or adult self. In some societies these differentiations are guided by social rituals, rites of passage that demarcate the boundary between childhood and adult identity (Van Gennep, 1960). Such rites may include the giving of a new name to the individual.

Symbolic rituals thus make the sequestering of the childhood self a public act. Henceforth, others will react differently to the child, sponsoring not only new kinds of experiences, but also new narratives about the self and the relation of the self to the community. Special salient memories, such as those associated with rites of passage, also become a focus of public as well as private attention. These are the memories that matter, that become the defining marks of identity. Whatever does not fit this identity may no longer be noticed.

Attitudes about the childhood self may be crucial in determining if or when or how early memories are rehearsed. If childhood versions of the self are explicitly devalued, such devaluations will function as admonitions to forget the past, particularly any story about the past that seems not to fit with one's present identity. In the face of acknowledged adult achievements, the fears and failings of childhood may fade from the awareness of the self as well as others. On the other hand, memories of childhood that remain may be modified to fit current conceptions of who the self is and should be.

Throughout development, perhaps even before birth, communal myths sponsor personal myths. Whenever the self continues to remember what others have forgotten or devalue, the result may be a split between public and private self. This split may itself be internalized, so that the internal self is divided into a socially validated persona and a hidden self. These variable versions of the self can function as organizing contexts for the retrieval of specific memories. In the dissociative disorders, for example, one part of the person may consciously remember one set of experiences unavailable to another part (Putnam, 1989).

Even normal people develop personas, typically demarcated in terms of salient social or occupational roles: soldier, priest, judge, farmer, teacher. Where a life history has been chaotic, the public self structured in terms of well-demarcated roles can offer a refuge from the inconsistency and confusion associated with more private experiences. A carefully maintained public persona may help one avoid troubling kinds of self-reference, such as memories associated with pain, shame, guilt, or confusion.

INFANTILE AMNESIA

Some researchers have attributed the inaccessibility of early memory, including preverbal memory, to "infantile amnesia" (Freud, 1899). Although psychoanalytic explanations for the phenomenon pointed to repression, a dynamic exclusion of ideas from conscious awareness, other theorists have attributed it to maturational timetables and the social orchestration of memory (Kail, 1990).

Obviously, children retain a great deal of what happens to them early in life, including the knowledge structures they will use over the course of a lifetime. It is only memory for episodes that is usually in question. Salaman (1970) has described early memory as like "an island without a background" (p. 62). Schachtel (1947) ascribes the problem to the differences in schemata employed by adults and children.

Estimates concerning the period shrouded by infantile amnesia vary. A study by Waldfogel (1948) reported that relatively few experiences are recalled from the time preceding the third year. Nelson (1988) notes that a memory block for events prior to the age of three or four years has been found consistently by many researchers. But the age of the first memory reported varies widely among individuals.

Theories about infantile amnesia emphasize that encoding, storage, or retrieval mechanisms may be involved. Encoding in childhood, for example, involves selective attentional factors and schemas that are different from those typical of adults.

Others have found evidence that infantile amnesia results from retrieval failures rather than inadequate storage. An experiment by Myers, Clifton, and Clarkson (1987), for example, demonstrated that children who returned to a laboratory setting two years after being tested extensively there showed signs that the setting was familiar to them.

Infantile amnesia may be related to the possibilities or difficulties involved in reinstating contextual cues associated with early memories. As Hayne and Rovee-Collier (1995) noted, developmental changes in attention, perception, schematic encodings and generalizations would over time greatly decrease the matching of early events to later experiences. These observations are consistent with those that emphasize the effects of schematic and linguistic encodings on the subsequent retrieval of early memories (Schachtel, 1947).

In this respect, narrative schemas may be especially consequential for the recall of early episodes. When experience has never been encoded in a reference system that can be articulated to self or others, it may remain restricted to nonverbal contexts that either are unavailable in later life or are specifically avoided. Such memories may also be elaborated as part of an idiosyncratic and private memory system that, however real and vivid, has never been communicated and socially validated and may, as a result, seem isolated or dream-like to the remembering self.

Studies in which infantile amnesia is assessed after childhood can be methodologically difficult; without an independent measure of the target experiences to be recalled, their existence and accuracy in recall are open to question. And as Kail (1990) notes, subjects' estimations of their age at the time of remembered episodes may be incorrect. Thus, even correctly remembered incidents may be given incorrect time tags.

Again, when studying a phenomenon like infantile amnesia, nonverbal memory should be distinguished from preverbal memory. Sometimes verbal and nonverbal experiences together form an original episodic gestalt, the components of which only became dissociated at a later point in time. When that happens, making the nonverbal memory explicit is primarily a matter of reintegrating contexts. The original episodic gestalt can then be deliberately focused in attention and connected with meaningful self-reflective narratives.

FANTASY

The common observation that young children often misinterpret events, as well as their delight at certain stages in making up preposterous stories, sometimes leads to misunderstandings about the relation between fantasy and memory in childhood. The observation that children make statements contrary to fact or that their interpretations of experience may differ markedly from those of adults can lead to a hasty dismissal of their reports, particularly when they say something contrary to what adults believe or want to believe. In such instances, adults may conclude that it is the child's memory that is a problem. On close consideration, however, what appears to be memory is often more a matter of social compliance or the wish to please.

As a form of cognitive construction, too, fantasy is based on processes that may be related to but are distinct from memory. Ontogenetically as well as phylogenetically, memory develops prior to fantasy; the evolutionary antecedents of memory can be traced far back, but fantasy depends on complex cognitive developments that are probably unique to humans and that are only well articulated in children after the development of language.

Children acquire the conceptual distinctions between memory and fantasy in social interchanges that communicate values about truth-telling and about acceptable playful departures from reality. They learn to make complex, memory-based discriminations long before they can talk about what they are doing; eventually, however, after language develops, they learn to use the concept "memory" to refer to a real event that happened in the past to an observing self. They also learn that, in order to be consciously recognized as a piece of personal history, a memory must usually be explicit and self-referential.

Although it may refer to an external event, a memory is also recognizably an internal event. It belongs in the special class of internal or mental experiences considered "real" and is commonly distinguished from "make-believe," "dreaming," and "lying."

From the time they learn to talk, children are told explicitly about remembering: "You remember, yesterday you went to the circus." "You remember Uncle John." They also learn to differentiate between memory and fantasy. "No, that never happened" or "What a wild imagination you have!" may become cues to label an experience "not a memory" or even to banish it from the mind altogether.

Experimental studies of children's memory reveal that, in spite of imperfections and limitations, it is essentially adaptive. Even the development of pretend play in children reflects their growing understanding of reality. Pretense, in fact, requires an ability to move beyond literal encodings of reality and to construct nonliteral representations (Harris & Kavannaugh, 1993).

The emergence of the human ability to construct fantasies adds a new dimension to everyday adaptation. Effective coping requires an ability to distinguish between real external events and those that are merely imaginary. Although the internal processes that make this distinction reliable are not fully understood, the practical uses of memory—recognition and recall of actually encountered events—can be observed in infants long before there are clear indications of fantasy. And although fantasy may intrude into memory, anyone who cannot practically discriminate between the two functions is likely to be seriously handicapped. Clinicians commonly consider such a disability to be a diagnostic sign of psychosis (Oltmanns & Maher, 1988).

Fantasy play evolves in a social context; it is augmented by the involvement of the mother (Harris & Kavannaugh, 1993). Like realistic skills, it is often developed through imitation of adult models (Piaget, 1962). Many childhood fantasies are, in fact, received from other people or the media. Shared fantasies, like shared memories, are a legacy of culture as well as of individual history.

A major impact of attachment history is reflected in the fantasy play of children. Sroufe (1989), citing research by Rosenberg (1984), finds it most significant that children with avoidant attachment histories do not engage much in fantasy play involving people. When injury or illness became a focus of play, securely attached children could fantasize a positive resolution, but avoidantly attached children less frequently did so.

The ability to engage in pretense may be facilitated by the growth of language and the capacity to construct narrative sequences (Harris & Kavannaugh, 1993). Fenson (1984) reported that two-year-olds sometimes referred to imaginary objects or events in terms of their make-believe status. Bretherton (1984) found a sharp increment in pretend language between twenty and twenty-eight months. Harris and Kavannaugh (1993) found that two-year-olds can respond appropriately to adults' make-believe stipulations and can understand adults' nonliteral references. They can describe what is happening in a fictitious world and can coordinate the successive parts of pretend episodes.

Other experimental studies have revealed that three- to five-year-old children understand the distinction between real and make-believe entities; imaginary constructions cannot be touched or seen (Harris & Kavannaugh, 1993; Wellman & Estes, 1986).

Harris and Kavannaugh (1993) note that there is no general agreement about just when collaborative role play between children develops. Once it emerges, however, partners in play can not only stipulate the existence of a make-believe entity but produce actions appropriate to the agreed-upon pretense.

Fantasy play, even so, develops in tandem with an understanding of real-world contingencies. Once they can represent how the world works, children can substitute props in realistic sequences; in fact, many pretend scripts are quite clearly representational of real-life happenings. In pretend play, for example, a banana may be used as a telephone; the prop sustains a recognizable action sequence. It is the realistic *use* of the prop that makes the pretense understandable.

When the action sequences of pretend play are realistic, an adult can easily interpret what is being represented. And, because the action involves make-believe entities and, in addition, is often stylized, the behavior being observed can clearly be recognized as play. A pretend tea party or trip to the store, for example, is organized around conventions of everyday experience as well as conventions of make-believe. Children raise cups to their lips but do not expect to really swallow pretend tea. They enact the roles of storekeeper and shopper, but do not expect play money to buy real candy.

Pretend play, in other words, depends on an adaptive integration of memory with fantasy. And, in spite of their growing ability to distinguish between fantasy and reality, children's fantasies are nevertheless typically limited and shaped by their memories. They may combine objects and events to form patterns contrary to reality, but the building blocks of these inventions, the objects and events they combine, are usually taken from real life.

Combining recognizable entities characterizes human creativity in general, whether it emerges as a feature of childhood play or as an aspect of adult invention. Even the most clearly imaginary entities and objects typically involve recognizable components from the real world. Fairies, dragons, fanciful creatures from outer space appear with fantastic but recognizable body parts—heads, bodies, legs. Any science fiction fan can attest to the difficulty of inventing an object or story that has no connection at all with life on earth as we know it.

Fantasy is often based on a deliberate attempt to escape the confines of reality, to create things unreal or even impossible. And even young children can invent preposterous entities and objects. But they are not clairvoyant; they cannot give realistic accounts of objects and events they have never encountered. A child who has never experienced a particular medical procedure, for example, may use her toy doctor set to perform all sorts of imaginary operations. But she cannot describe a real operation with any degree of accuracy. A would-be astronaut may envision flying to the moon, but without prior instruction he cannot tell what the inside of a space shuttle looks like or how moon rocks differ from earthly ones.

Specialists familiar with children's level of knowledge at particular ages, as well as with the forms and functions of their fantasies, can make plausible and reliable distinctions between fantasy and reality in certain reports. A child who has never actually experienced certain sexual acts, for example, cannot accurately describe them.

At a certain point in development, after a child has a reliable knowledge base about many subjects, preposterous departures from reality may become quite amusing. Nonsense, for example, is a specific genre that even young children recognize and appreciate as such. It involves a deliberate suspension of rules and unrestricted forms of combinatorial play. The more contrary to fact—or even possibility—nonsense is, the more fun. The clown with windshield wipers on his glasses is funny because everyone knows real glasses are not made like that. Going to sea in a sieve (as the creatures in Edward Lear's poem did) is silly; it cannot really be done. Wearing one's shoes on one's head is ridiculous.

Some nonsense forms, like jokes, are conventional. The social conventions of play are, in fact, an important part of what children learn to remember. Convention is such an expectable part of children's fantasies that something really novel or unusual stands out. The assumption that the child just "made it up" is not necessarily incorrect, but a trained observer will examine it carefully.

Similarly, fantasies may be unconscious, in the sense that they are vaguely elaborated or persistently excluded from attention. But since fantasy, too, is commonly self-referential, fantasy is usually, at some point, a conscious and explicit elaboration.

Distinctions

Misunderstandings about the origin and development of fantasy in childhood have had unfortunate effects both on the study of children's thinking and on psychotherapy. An influential psychoanalytic theory first proposed by Melanie Klein, for example, traced the origins of psychopathology to infantile fantasies supposedly operative from birth. Other psychoanalytic theories, such as those of Freud and Jung, have assumed that certain fantasies are inherited and universal. The Oedipus complex, for example, which is a keystone of Freudian theory, was considered to be a universal instinctive development.

In experimentally-based discussions of the topic, the relationship between memory and fantasy has frequently been obscured by a failure to distinguish between error, interpretation, and invention. Fantasy is logically and observably distinct from errors or omissions of memory. Since memory is imperfect, mistakes are an expected aspect of remembered episodes. A report that a car driving away from the scene of an accident was green when, in fact, it was blue is usually just a mistake, although potentially a consequential one. On the other hand, a report that the car was driven away by an enemy alien who planned the accident, though not necessarily in error, would be more suspect; that kind of interpretive elaboration is characteristic of a class of fantasies clinicians call paranoid and pathological.

The problem of discriminating fantasy from reality in narratives about events is further complicated by the way inferences about reality are sometimes incorporated into fantasies. Although mistaken interpretations or inferences may be labeled fantasies, there are important reasons for differentiating them from pure inventions. Inferences are commonly the result of thinking that is tied to both experience and logic. Even distorted inferences often represent attempts to make sense out of the world, to discover and adapt to reality. Interpretative elaborations, however, may extend far beyond logical inferences to wild flights of fancy.

After the development of the ability to construct fantasy, fantasies become part of the repertory of what is remembered. At that point one confronts the task of discriminating memory from fantasy. In many instances, as when fantasy involves very obvious departures from reality, these discriminations are easy enough. But there are instances when fantasies are realistic enough to pose problems unless they have been in some way clearly demarcated from reality. When that happens, people usually make inferences about the reality status of a perception or memory on the basis of their knowledge of the real world.

A woman who dreamed that she was in her kitchen cooking, for example, realized she was dreaming when she noticed that water was boiling but the stove had not been turned on. Even in her dream, she realized that these discrepant images indicated a fantasy construction as distinct from a piece of reality. But her accurate inference depended on knowledge that might not be available to a very young child.

Johnson and Raye (1981) view the process of discriminating real from imaginary events in terms of *reality-monitoring*. Reviewing experimental work on this topic, Johnson (1988) concludes that the more sensory overlap there is between memories derived from perception and those based on imagination, the greater the tendency to confuse them.

False memories are logically distinct from false beliefs, which may also provide important schemas for processing and retrieving information. Many beliefs that serve as guides to thinking and conduct are received from other people as true and incontrovertible; in this respect, the social matrix of memory is often as consequential a determinant of what is accepted as reality as direct experience with events and objects.

One way of transmitting and perpetuating beliefs is through the restriction of access to information or experience that might disconfirm the beliefs (Singer, 1995). In this respect, enforced dependency and isolation in childhood can become powerful determinants of what is forwarded as correct information about the world. Children who present ideas and beliefs that differ from social norms are not necessarily out of touch with reality; in some cases, they have simply learned to survive in atypical environments.

SUGGESTIBILITY AND AUTHORITY

The relation between memory and fantasy in childhood is sometimes complicated by what is typically referred to as *suggestibility*. In recent years, children's suggestibility as a factor in reported abuse has come in for considerable attention. This issue is particularly relevant to forensic investigations and judicial proceedings (Doris, 1991; McGough, 1994).

Adults as well as children can be quite suggestible, but children have long been considered especially so (Lindberg, 1991). This is scarcely surprising given their dependency on adults. After all, openness to the suggestions of other people is what makes a child educable. The negative dimension of this tendency, of course, is that the child may be shaped in erroneous or distorted modes of information-processing or schooled in antisocial beliefs and behavior.

Suggestion, in any case, is not limited to the invention of fantasy. It frequently operates to substitute an unacceptable narrative for a more desirable one or to silence truthful reports (Cottle, 1980). In many instances, too, it operates subtly rather than globally to delete disturbing details from an otherwise accurate account. Children learn to amend facts in terms of interpretations, to place emphasis in such a way that they will be approved of as well as believed.

Suggestibility has sometimes been explained in terms of the impairment of an original memory trace by post-event information or by misinformation (Bekerian & Bowers, 1983; Christiaansen & Ochalek, 1983; Loftus & Loftus, 1980). However, though it is empirically well established that manipulation of information at the time of encoding and storage may alter subsequent recollections for events (Lindberg, 1991), there is controversy concerning the underlying causes of these effects. Since the effects may differ with age—they are more noticeable in young children, for example, than in college students—they may be a consequence of several developmental factors rather than of some underlying biological process.

As some investigators have emphasized (Flin, 1991; Zaragoza, 1991), many effects attributed to suggestibility may not be a function of memory at all, but merely a result of compliance. Compliance, in turn, varies in individuals, even among children, and in many experimental studies, it is difficult to differentiate the effects of acquiescence from such variables as encoding, storage, and retrieval.

In a series of studies investigating children's suggestibility to leading questions, for example, Goodman and her colleagues (Goodman & Clarke-Stewart, 1991) have shown that children *can* give very accurate though limited accounts of events simulating abuse, but that inaccuracy tends to increase when an interrogator makes strong suggestions. Yet children differ in their susceptibility to influence. Some are more suggestible than others.

In everyday life, compliant behavior is often a matter of obedience to authority. Even adults have been shown to comply with commands that may be quite contrary to their expressed values (Milgram, 1974). Given the emphasis placed on obedience in some families and the power of adults to enforce compliance in children, it is scarcely surprising that children are likely to be especially susceptible to influence.

Throughout life, authority, external or internal, is a powerful gate-keeper of memory. It may function as a reminder or a censor. Authority also serves as an arbiter of source; nonauthoritative sources of information may be simply unnoticed or dismissed. At the same time, paradoxically, authority can contribute to confusion about the origins of memories and beliefs. When authority is absolute, it may serve as an incontrovertible source. And when a source is unquestioned, it may be simply identified as basic reality, like the sun coming up every morning.

Authority is associated with power. Authority permits or forbids, praises or blames. It may be absolute or provisional, rigid or flexible. Typically, it supplies narratives to the developing child that rationalize or justify its decisions. Many such narratives explicitly or implicitly shape memory.

Even in nonauthoritarian families, the dependency of young children makes the authority of adults an expectable dimension of attachment. Until the child has a reliable store of memories to guide his or her behavior, the memories of caretakers are vital to survival. Until personal memories can be integrated with skilled adaptations, social memories function as guides to appropriate conduct.

The internalization of authority is a normal part of development that enables the child eventually to separate safely from caretakers and to move into the wider world as an independent person (Erikson, 1959/1980). This internalization can be either facilitated or impeded by external authorities, and the facilitation or interference itself is likely to be internalized by the growing child. One dimension of this development is observable in the child's growing confidence in exploring the world and negotiating skilled adaptations. Another is the development of conscience, a set of internal moral evaluations that govern behavior even in the absence of external constraints.

In childhood, the programming and control of memories may be orches-trated by authorities who simultaneously insist that their word is unargu-able and prevent contact with other sources of authority (Waites, 1993). This development tends to simplify and solidify the internalization of the caretaker as authority, with the result that the caretaker is incorporated into the emerging self like an internal tyrant.

Caught in conflict, the child may obey under protest; emotional avoid-ance is then matched with behavioral compliance. This is easier to accom-plish if the authority of the adult who demands compliance has been internalized. Compliance is also facilitated by fragmenting the memory of pain, detaching it from reference to the self, or depriving it of the narrative form that connects feeling with the self. The memory forbidden by author-ity is, in effect, dissociated.

Internalizations of authority play an important role in the internal or-ganization of episodic memories. One of the most common forms of social programming is the inhibition of a child's responses to an event the adult considers necessary or desirable. For example, the child may be told that a nurse's injection will not hurt and may be scolded for expressing fear or pain. The authority of the caretaker's admonition is encoded along with the painful experience. Yet the conditioned physiological and emotional concomitants of the experience continue to be cued by reminders of it, so that the memory of the reality of pain may be strong enough to continue to affect the child's behavior in spite of valiant efforts to be "good" and uncomplaining.

As an internalized feature of self-development, authority organizes be-havioral, cognitive, and affective schemas. When the word of authority conflicts with other schemas, overriding the rule of authority may require the institution of a new or higher authority. Instituting the self as a distinct authority who can override other authorities is a complex aspect of individ-uation that is typically not fully achieved until adulthood and, in some individuals, never achieved at all.

LYING

The notion that children lie, particularly in accusing adults of abusive behavior, has long influenced approaches to children's testimony (Arm-strong, 1994; Masson, 1986; McGough, 1994). Cautionary tales, such as that of "The Boy Who Cried Wolf," are a familiar part of the folklore in which children are schooled. At the same time, of course, they are con-stantly being schooled in the lighter side of lying—the exaggerations and "big fish" stories that enliven reports of events, the tall tales that entertain family gatherings.

The ability to invent a deliberate lie is an aspect of developing compe-tence. In order to distort the truth intentionally, one must know what it is. And in order to fabricate a convincing lie, one must know how to manipu-

late another's view of reality. Intentional lying thus requires the development of complex cognitive skills.

A study by Bussey (1992) indicated that even preschoolers can differentiate between lying and telling the truth; with age, their accuracy in this
regard increases. The basis for discriminations also changes with development. Initially, moral judgments are likely to be based on fear of punishment, but gradually children come to rely on their own internal evaluations and to take pride in truthfulness.

Strichartz and Burton (1990) review studies that shed further light on
age trends. By the age of four, children distinguish whether statements are
factual, and until somewhere between six and ten years of age, they tend
to match truth and factuality. By age nine, they more clearly discriminate
intentional lying from objectively false statements, although older children
and even adults do not always make this distinction clearly.

Learning to make these discriminations involves acquiring some understanding of distinctions between different kind of mental representations,
such as the distinction between factuality, pretense, and deceit. These
discriminations are related to an evolving theory of mind (Perner, 1993).
Studies by Lillard (1993) suggest that only around the sixth year do children come to understand pretense as a mental representational act. The
ability to use deception can be viewed as one index of the child's developing theory of mind (Chandler, Fritz, & Hala, 1989).

In childhood, fantasy is increasingly structured by the narrative forms
characteristic of the family or culture. Story-making is a pleasurable activity shared by children and their caregivers (Engel, 1995) as well as a solitary
game. The very process of inventing narratives can develop an impetus of
its own that leads to nonfactual embellishments, and as they explore the
story-making process children may get carried away by the fun they are
having. The excitement of invention can be contagious; adults as well as
children like to entertain others, and a responsive audience can exert a
powerful influence on the construction of tall tales. This pleasure in inventing and showing off stories does not, in itself, prove that the child
cannot distinguish between lying and make-believe or has lost touch with
reality. In fact, a firm hold on reality enables a normal child to enjoy
fantasy in a way a disturbed child cannot. It does indicate, however, that
the motives of any storyteller become more comprehensible in light of the
motives of the audience. Children learn early in life to be sensitive to what
adults want to hear. Adults *can* suggest, even insist on, certain narrative
reports in children.

The distinction between lying and truthfulness, moreover, is not absolute. Over the course of development, children learn to distinguish between several different kinds of departures from truth-telling. A made-up
story is just for fun. A lie, in contrast, is a deliberate departure from the
truth that is likely to draw censure or punishment. But there are "little

white lies" that are considered harmless or even socially desirable, such as giving compliments to people and hiding critical thoughts. Learning to be tactful may be valued as much as learning to be truthful. Children thus learn directly from adults not only about what constitutes lying, but how and when to avoid telling the truth. At home and school, as well as through individual experimentation, they learn how to use deception to advantage and to avoid getting caught.

Children also observe that adults quite commonly lie — about important issues as well as minor ones (Ekman, 1992). Adult deceptions can be a strong factor in the development of disillusionment and cynicism in children (Cottle, 1980). When they are internalized by the child, they can also contribute to confusion and inconsistency. A parent who denies an important piece of reality, for example, subverts memory in ways that can contribute to the formation of divergent narratives about the same event. The child often learns, in effect, that although the "official" story is quite different from the real story, it is the only story that can — or must — be told.

Lying is an important dimension of family secrets. A child may get the impression that, although deliberate lying is undesirable, it is quite acceptable or desirable to avoid the truth by omissions. Silence then becomes an important component of memories that may eventually be sequestered in the self as well as in the family.

Although socially orchestrated narratives become privileged in public discourse, they do not necessarily obliterate unacceptable private memories. They may merely give rise to contrasting accounts of the same event, one of which is sequestered in silence. But at any point in life, social validation or devaluation can be a significant contextual factor in the retrievability of self-relevant memories. By discouraging or even forbidding rehearsal, an audience can have a profound effect not only on the organization but on the persistence of particular recollections. Over time, the memory either never shared or explicitly devalued may simply disappear from conscious retrieval.

COMMEMORATION: REMEMBERING TOGETHER

Learning to sort out fact from fantasy, lying from truth-telling, myth from reality is a dimension of individual competence constantly articulated in social contexts. The orchestration of personal history occurs in tandem not only with specific cognitive acquisitions but also with the internalization of social reality. People remember together. Throughout life, both individual memories and socially significant ones are commemorated in ongoing rituals and dialogues. This form of remembering may depart from what modern observers might label as accuracy, but it is the very substance of what cultures consider truth (Fentress & Wickham, 1992).

Traumatic memories are among those that are sometimes subjected to special forms of commemoration and may be institutionalized in political or religious observances. In such cases, it is not trauma but triumph over trauma that often becomes the focus of ritual (Volkan, 1988). Memorial Day becomes an occasion for honoring living heros and laying wreaths on the graves of the dead. Monuments are erected in public squares to remind everyone of a decisive battle or a natural disaster. The speeches typical of such occasions remind assembled audiences of triumphs and tragedies and exhort them to emulate the heroes who came before them.

Sometimes, too, specific or individual traumas are explicated in terms of symbolic representations common to everyone in a community. The Jewish observance of Passover, for example, commemorates not only the particularities of the flight from Egypt but the persistence of Jewish culture. The Christian commemoration of Easter interprets personal failings and adversities in the context of a death and resurrection story common to many religions but specifically embodied in the life of Jesus.

Traumas that affect many people, such as earthquakes or wars, are also commonly represented in social memory by commemorative practices. Individuals who experienced a given trauma, such as being struck by lightning, may come together to share experiences and to support one another (Ehrlich, 1994).

Remembering together is such an important dimension of life that a deliberate refusal to do so can operate as a powerful constraint on an individual's behavior. This refusal does not necessarily deny the individual's reality. It may simply withhold validation in a way that makes the individual feel isolated. Such isolation can be so uncomfortable that an individual replaces a true but unvalidated personal story with a false or distorted but socially acceptable one. When both accounts are forwarded in memory, the inconsistency may be a source of conflict or discomfort. It is often easier, however, to capitulate to a shared story than to persist in a private but unacknowledged or disputed one. The narrative that deviates from the prescribed story may be carefully suppressed. Unnoticed and unrehearsed, it may eventually disappear from conscious recollection.

Throughout life, then, memory as competence is not merely a cognitive development but a social achievement. Although rooted in reality, it may branch out in divergent directions. The individual who can resist the subversion of memory may be in touch with reality but paradoxically out of sync with family or society. Anyone who cannot learn to lie may discover that, in some contexts, the truth is not simply inconvenient or embarrassing but dangerous.

The effect of these social contingencies on the construction of personal history is multifaceted. When personal history is especially traumatic or systematically invalidated, the influence of social memory on individual memory can be decisive.

CHAPTER 5
Representation and the Self

I celebrate myself, and sing myself
And what I assume you shall assume.
— Walt Whitman, "Song of Myself"

A S FAR BACK as I can remember," said Avery, "I've known I was going to be a doctor. It wasn't so much talked about. It was just sort of in the air. My father was a doctor. My mother had been a nurse. I liked science in high school. But now that I'm getting ready to start medical school next year, I'm not sure I want to go."

In his growing uncertainty about his choice of a vocation, Avery was not so different from many college students. What made him somewhat different was that he had always been so sure of himself before. While his peers had tried on different fantasies about their future, Avery's choice of a medical career had seemed like a ready-made uniform preselected for him. He had only to grow into it.

"As far back as I can remember," said Avery. And yet, as he began to explore that remembering, no particular moment of knowing came to him. There were relevant memories, to be sure: being taken as a small child on a tour of the hospital where his father worked, rescuing an injured bird after a storm, trying to make sense of some of the difficult books in his father's library. But it was hard to explain his pervasive sense that his destiny had always been "in the air."

Many of the most significant scripts that guide the evolving self are like that. Sometimes a decisive event can be found as a starting point for them. But often they are rooted in less specific experiences; implicitly, if not explicitly, they simply organize ongoing existence. As he thought about his own life plan, for example, Avery discovered that his parents, especially his father, had always expected him to be a physician and must have communicated that all along. This supposition was confirmed when Avery announced to his family that he had decided not to go to medical school after all. His decision precipitated a family crisis, and his father's disappointment and anger were strong and clear.

Avery's change of plans might be viewed as a matter of finding himself. But the self he was finding had not really been there before. The habitual representation of himself as a future doctor had always been based less on his personal commitment than on his acquiescence to a ready-made identity defined by his parents. In that respect, deciding to become something else was not so much a matter of finding himself as of becoming himself.

Becoming himself, in turn, required thinking about issues he had always taken for granted, questioning scripts he had previously followed unquestioningly, confronting his history from a new perspective. Doing so, he revised both his idea of who he was and his relation to some of the self-defining memories of his childhood.

He remembered, for example, that he had always wanted to build things and that he was a mechanical whiz. He remembered a time when his hero had been Thomas Edison and he had envisioned being an inventor or an engineer. But he had never seriously considered going to a vocational or technical school or even majoring in engineering in college. And he now began to get in touch with the simple fact that he was tired of going to any school and wanted to take some time off to travel around the country on his own.

This new self Avery began to discover dismayed the family who thought they knew him. They defined his change of plans as a serious problem, a sign there was something seriously wrong with him. They hoped psychotherapy would help him get back on what they considered "the right track."

Avery himself, on the other hand, was beginning to feel excited about the person he was becoming and did not feel crazy at all. He was upset by his parents' reaction, but firm in his decision not to go to medical school. "Being a doctor is just not me," he said. As he asserted this, his memory of how his original plan had come about shifted accordingly. "It was always their idea," he said, "not mine."

But how accurate was this new memory? Who could say that Avery's decision to be a doctor was always merely "their idea" instead of his own? He had certainly at one point presented it as his idea. In doing so, however, he had left competing ideas out of the picture for fear that they would not be acceptable to other people. It was easier to do what was expected than to sort out his misgivings.

For Avery, remembering who he had been and what he had thought was turning out to be more complicated than simply retrieving specific memories from the past. It was not just a matter of finding events, moments when he or his parents said or did something. It was instead a matter of exploring how the awareness of himself as a person had been, over his lifetime, slowly articulated through constant external appraisals and self-reflections. And although he was beginning to discover that many of his own appraisals of himself did not match those of his parents, for many years they had seemed to do so.

Avery began to discover discrepancies between what he remembered about certain aspects of his own history and what his parents seemed to remember. They said, for example, that he had always hated sports. But as he remembered it, they were the ones who had discouraged him from playing football in high school, and when he made the team, they did not come to see him play. They said he had chosen the college he wanted to attend, but that, too, seemed predestined; his father had gone there.

It was not so much that his parents remembered things wrong. It was, rather, that their memories did not encompass the whole of Avery's history in the way his own memories did. At this point, he could no longer accept their version of his history because even his inaccurate or distorted memories were a part of a self that was now intent on asserting separateness from them.

As he moved increasingly away from the path his parents had planned for him, Avery was also still in the process of constructing and revising self-defining memories with which his parents were unfamiliar. Since he had left home, he had had a life of his own that they really knew little about. Their idea of him was fixed in a way his idea of himself was not. While he had been evolving into a still-undecided future, they had imagined him a finished product.

When he said, "It was always their idea, not mine," then, Avery was right but not entirely so. He had not always been this particular self. Yet growing up is not an event or an episode. The self is, rather, a discovery one makes while in the very process of moving beyond it.

THE SELF AS WITNESS TO MEMORY

It is often more reassuring to think of a memory as a concrete thing or a neural structure or a measured test response than as the changing creation of a constantly evolving self. For a long time, in fact, the study of memory was guided by the search for the memory trace and the plotting of learning and forgetting curves. It was only after Bartlett (1932/1995) emphasized the schematic and reconstructive character of remembering that this focus started to change And even then, memory as a phenomenon occurring in natural settings was mostly left out of the picture (Neisser, 1982c).

The study of autobiographical memory, which inevitably leads back to how the self evolves, is still not well integrated with what we know about the basic biological and developmental processes of memory formation. Yet, particularly in matters of episodic memory, confronting the significance of the self is unavoidable and the history of the self is a major determining factor.

Most episodic memories, in contrast to general stores of knowledge, are implicitly if not explicitly self-referential. It is the self who experienced the event. And it is the self as actor or observer who usually stands as the authoritative source of an episodic memory and as guarantor of its accuracy.

In the twentieth century, the relation between the self and its memories has increasingly come under scrutiny from psychologists, historians, literary critics, and artists. Our interest in these issues reflects entrenched cultural tendencies and values, particularly Western values, as well as intellectual trends. In some cultures (Tonkin, 1992), memory is viewed as a collective process. But the American heritage stresses rugged individualism. Whether we celebrate and sing the self or denigrate and deny it, the self is very much at the center of what is remembered.

For better or worse, then, much of what we know about the past consists of the personal memories of individual selves who lived through it. Historical documents are seldom as available and complete as the firsthand accounts of people who were there. Even written archives and diaries are typically removed in time, by minutes, days, or years, from the events they record; no matter how objective in intention, the selective focus they reveal is that of a self-interested observer. The limitations of seemingly objective records, such as photographs and tape recordings, are familiar to us all from famous instances of tampering and forgery.

The authority and honesty of the investigator are as important in warranting the accuracy of experimental data as in evaluating the credibility of anecdotal reports. Like anyone else, experimental researchers must contend with the inherent limitations of records. Their notations and measurements reflect the choices of informed but imperfect and sometimes biased individuals. Their data are typically based on processes of averaging across subjects that indicate little or nothing about the reliability, accuracy, and credibility of any particular individual.

What we can know about the past at any point inevitably boils down to what individuals say about it. The self is the ultimate arbiter of memory.

THE SELF AS A
PSYCHOLOGICAL STRUCTURE

As a psychological phenomenon, the self is typically encountered as an integrated pattern of habits of remembering, knowing, and behaving. One does not need to treat this self as a homunculus—a little person inside the mind—in order to acknowledge the significance of the self as a supraordinate structure organizing the welter of episodic gestalts that comprise personal history. From one perspective, the overall organization of events, subjected to self-referential patterns of observation and reflection, *is* the self.

As memories of a personal past are viewed and reviewed, some become the object of special focus and are elaborated as self-defining. Others are experienced as atypical or alien; "I was not myself," one says on recalling them. Yet the very experience of self-alienation may be a vivid memory the self continually confronts and tries to understand.

Self-representations elicit confirming or disconfirming responses from other people; these, in turn, play a vital role in the evolving organization of the self. George Herbert Mead (1934) was one of the first social scientists to emphasize that social evaluations are at the very heart of self-evaluations.

From infancy, attachment, the social matrix of memory, functions as an organizing context of evolving self-representations. Attunement to the mother coordinates not only the understanding of external events, but also attunement to internal feeling states. The mother's face, reflecting a changing but increasingly predictable array of emotional responses to the infant, becomes a guide to desirable and undesirable behavior. The mother's voice is a reference point that confirms not only the fact but the significance and value of what the self is doing.

In recent years, many psychologists have studied the development of the self as a process of gradual differentiation and individuation (Mahler et al., 1975). The psychoanalyst Heinz Kohut (1971) conceptualized the early representations of significant people in the infant's life as selfobjects. Experienced as external yet part of the self, selfobjects are like the transitional objects conceptualized by Winnicott (1971). Psychologically, they occupy a kind of intermediate space between self and other and facilitate self-regulation as the individual gradually separates from early caregivers.

Even after the differentiation of an individuated self, social referencing continues to guide the interactions and dialogues around which self-referential memories are organized. Throughout life, knowing what a valued other will say and do becomes a cue to what the self should or will say and do and what the self is like. Statements about the self that are confirmed reinforce existing self-representations. Statements that are ignored or disconfirmed may lead to unintegrated representations of self and other and to divergent narratives about the past.

Constructing and differentiating representations of self and other is a process normally integrated with feelings and values. Representational systems, including memory systems, facilitate and regulate one another. As episodic memories are organized in self-referential configurations of affect, behavior, and thought, statements about the self and about others are continually monitored and revised in the light of confirming or disconfirming information.

Normally, in the course of this development, the self learns to monitor personal representations in terms of external appraisals: the statement, "I am trustworthy," if disputed, may lead to behavioral change to bring it into line with reality. Or the statement, "My mother is a witch," may be revised in the light of changing interactions with her. But pleasing others has limits; normally, too, the self develops independent, stable internal standards and learns to resist the ever-changing winds of opinion and fashion.

According to Singer and Salovey (1993), the wish for consistency is a major determining factor in self-definition. Memories about the past may be mustered explicitly to demonstrate that the past self and the present self are one and the same. Over time, they may be systematically transformed to reinforce self-consistency and the coherent narrative structure of personal history.

One factor in the integration of representations and behavior is cognitive dissonance (Festinger, 1957). When cognitive representations do not match up consistently, the inconsistency itself may motivate efforts to make them consistent. Having expressed a favorable attitude toward another person, for example, one may be more likely to bring behavior into line with that attitude. Having described an intention, one may be motivated to carry it out.

Such motives to think and behave consistently can distort memories. But it is not necessarily correct to assume that the distortions have fundamentally altered the memory by, say, changing a memory trace. The compliant self may have simply followed a path of least resistance, acquiescing to what other people say. Sometimes, too, an overt narrative diverges from a covert one. At some point in time, the self is quite aware of discrepant versions of a story, although over time the story never told and acknowledged may fade from memory.

The remembering self motivated to do so can sometimes track divergent narratives to the point of divergence: "I remember now. At first I rebelled against what was happening, but when I realized that I could not change it, I decided to live with the situation and make the most of it."

The relation between self-consistency and a consistent set of memories about the past is obvious. From a pragmatic perspective, it is undeniable that a self who fails to achieve some degree of consistency is likely to be handicapped in everyday life. No matter how many social roles we play, they must be coherently orchestrated in order to avoid chaos.

Yet the status of the self as a unitary phenomenon, even in normal people, has been extensively debated over the last few years. Some critics contend that the complexity of modern life precludes such unity. And some emphasize that multiplicity rather than unity typifies the organization of consciousness and personality and of the brain patterns presumed to underlie such phenomenal structures (Beahrs, 1982; Gazzaniga, 1985). According to such perspectives, the self is more adequately characterized as a confederation or partnership than as a monolithic agency.

A pathological multiplicity of self-structure is most strikingly evident in what clinicians term "dissociative disorders." Of these, dissociative identity disorder (formerly multiple personality disorder) has received the most attention (Putnam, 1989). Dissociative disorders typically involve disturbances not only in the sense of personal identity and self-presentation but in memory. Characteristic memory disturbances are, in fact, a major diagnostic indicator of dissociative identity disorder.

REPRESENTATIONAL ACTS
AND THE EVOLVING SELF

Self-referential memories are typically organized in social interactions that are based on the schemas and narrative structures valued by family and culture (Freeman, 1993; Stone, 1988; Tonkin, 1992). Personal histories are molded by these shared patterns. And the evolving self learns to use them to tag specific memories.

Pivotal events in an individual life are commonly marked by prescribed rituals and narratives, for example. Before the child can organize them as personal memories, they exist as patterns into which representations of the self will eventually be molded. "You were an easy baby" and "You cried all the time" are social reflections that may turn out to be self-fulfilling prophecies. Or the reputation of a child may follow him so persistently from grade to grade in school that it molds not only self-referential thinking but also social validation or lack thereof, which in turn shapes individual history.

The behavior pattern Erikson (1968) described as a "negative identity" is an example of how such patterns shape an individual life. It typically develops in contexts that reinforce the idea that one is bad or a problem to others. In this respect, attachment or relational difficulties can be self-perpetuating. Children who are insecurely attached, for example, have been shown to elicit more negative evaluations from teachers than those who are securely attached.

Throughout development, the role of language in structuring self-reflection and social interaction can be easily elevated to centrality in self-definition. Yet, although the importance of language is undeniable, certain patterns that are prior to and variably integrated with language are fundamental to the organization of the self and its memories. Social rituals, for example, are at the heart of many of the most fundamental self-defining memories.

IDENTITY

The achievement of a coherent identity is often considered a hallmark of mature personality development (Erikson, 1968). Identity is not a static entity, however; it is, rather, a dynamic achievement of the evolving self. Identity consolidation is an ongoing process that involves the integration of representational and self-representational structures across the lifespan. This integration is often contingent on both favorable circumstances and competence. Developmental arrests and discontinuities may impede it. Trauma may prevent or disorganize it. It is in any case shaped by the expectations and demands of other people, as well as by individual motives and goals.

Certain developmental periods are especially important to identity consolidation. As Erikson (1959/1980) has illustrated, the integration of a coherent idea of who one was, who one is, and where one is going is a major issue during adolescence. At that point, the imagined relation between past and present can have a profound impact on such life tasks as choosing a vocation or a mate. The adolescent is also maturing cognitively (Piaget, 1950/1981) in ways that facilitate understanding and interpreting his or her personal history.

Many adolescents become preoccupied with self-definition, a process often associated both with introspection and with attention-getting behaviors that broadcast choices about belief and style to others. The process of self-definition also extends to deliberate explorations of the past and conscious — even self-conscious — attempts to rework memories in the context of current identity concerns. In this construction of the self, the construction and reconstruction of the past serve to bolster a sense of continuity and control. Given the maturational transformations and discontinuities characteristic of adolescent development, a coherent story about the past can be reassuring as well as stabilizing.

Adolescents, for example, frequently become very interested in the process of constructing autobiography. In journals and diaries, they recount their reflections on childhood and their hopes for adulthood. They engage in endless discussions with peers about who they have been, who they are now, and who they are becoming. They carefully contrive images that announce identity through dress, hair style, and makeup.

Adolescents are often intent on sorting out reality from fantasy, so much so that they become critical of any perceived lapses in truth-telling on the part of adults. They may demand honesty and accuracy to the point of tactlessness. They question official stories and privileged narratives about life and are often triumphant in exposing cover-ups and euphemisms. In this process, they may become brash and confrontational. They challenge adult secrecy even while they are stridently asserting their own rights to privacy.

The pressures of adolescent life occur in a context of physical changes, including hormonal pressures, that can lend a sense of urgency to the developing self. Adolescents are notoriously self-reflective. Yet they are also notoriously impulsive, impatient, and given to active confrontations. This action orientation may be the major mode in which memories are experienced and transformed. Particularly when there is a conscious flight from childhood, the conflicts and traumas of childhood may be banished from narrative, only to be enacted in ritualistic behaviors that, on the surface, appear cryptic or unrelated to the past.

Adolescents who, for whatever reason, cannot manage the integration of a coherent self are sometimes said to be suffering from identity diffusion. They flounder in inconsistency, unable to settle on who they are or want to be. Until the diffusion is replaced by stable, reality-based integrations, it is difficult for the maturing individual to achieve the major tasks of adult life. He or she may seem stuck in a perpetual adolescence, cut off from both childhood and the future.

Sometimes this arrested development involves a compulsive flight from the past. Drug and alcohol abuse during adolescence, for example, may enable the adolescent to avoid confronting either a traumatic history or adult challenges and commitments.

Sometimes, as in the case of Avery, adolescence is in a sense extended; major decisions about identity are postponed until early adulthood. Eventually confronting what can no longer be postponed, the person may engage in extensive exploration and revision of self-defining memories and received stories about the past. Whether this process is a private odyssey or occurs in an organized context like psychotherapy, it often constitutes a major divergence from a previously followed path. The coming-of-age narratives that describe the point of divergence, like more formal initiation rites, may assume a kind of mythical status in the personal history of the individual.

RITUALS

At every stage in the development of the self, memories are shaped not only by what happens but by who one is. Who one is, in turn, is as much a matter of what one does as of what one says. In the definition of the self as well as in life generally, actions often speak louder than words.

Certain actions, because they are repetitive, help formalize and stabilize remembering. Ritualistic behavior in particular is a major form in which memories, ordinary as well as traumatic, are carried forward by the self.

The repetitive rhythms of daily life include many behavior patterns that can be described as ritualistic, in the sense that they are relatively invariant as well as automatic and are taken for granted rather than subjected to logical analysis. Rituals range from the familiar routines of the breakfast table to the stylized sequences prescribed for special occasions.

At the simplest level, social rituals reflect the convenient arrangements of daily life. From birth, the repetitions that comprise them are a basic component of the social matrix of memory, and throughout life they serve as basic memory aids by embedding memory for events in predictable routines. In their sameness and predictability, they serve as a buffer against the unexpected; in learning them, the child is reassured about his own ability to control life.

From early childhood, rituals smooth transitions between contrasting external events and internal states. Bedtime rituals facilitate the transition from waking to sleep. Seasonal rituals may facilitate changes in adaptation required by natural events. When tied to biological states or cyclical changes in nature, rituals come to reflect the rhythms implicit in such phenomena.

In addition to patterns they share with the culture at large, families have their own customs, rituals, schemas, and scripts. These are transmitted explicitly or implicitly, often with the implication that they are a necessary acquisition for anyone who "belongs" to the family. Such transmissions become part of the fabric of individual and social identity.

Reiss (1989) has described several features of family rituals. They are generally practiced by the whole family and are consciously acknowledged. They are marked by stages of preparation and, at the point of enactment, take precedence over other sequences of behavior. He notes that many such rituals have an initiatory or corrective function and align the practices of individuals not only within the family but also with the larger social group.

Many repetitive aspects of family life have a ritualistic flavor, teaching children the conventions of family and culture (Roberts, 1988). The interactive rhythms that organize life in a particular family are sometimes as stylized and predictable as the patterns of a carefully choreographed dance. Although many such rituals are implicit, some are carefully prescribed and elaborated. These often have a commemorative function; that is, ritual enactment is a way of remembering and of transmitting memories from one generation to the next (Stone, 1988). In this respect, remembering is structured as a carefully prescribed process. The verbalized memories that are forwarded as social history are embedded in celebratory routines. The story of how an ancestor emigrated to America, or how two parents met and married, is repeated time after time, sometimes verbatim. The menu eaten on special occasions, such as Thanksgiving, is the same from year to year.

The effect of such rituals on memory is to provide a set of nonverbal as well as verbal scripts that are so familiar and consistent that they may offer highly veridical sources of information about the past. And yet, ritualized memories are not necessarily episodic; they are more like semantic knowledge structures. Indeed, *departures* from ritual are what tend to stand out as specific episodic memories: the Christmas Eve spent in the airport; the fortieth birthday party when the decorations were black.

Some commemorative rituals do stand out especially, however, because they mark unique or relatively infrequent events. A funeral, for example, is often especially memorable because the death of a significant person is a turning point in the life of the survivor. But the rituals prescribed for the occasion may make it even more memorable. They commonly involve explicit and formal efforts to state and forward memories about the deceased. The life story that is ended is fixed in a narrative that memorializes it as officially and as definitely as the commemorative monument that marks the grave.

The force of ritual is more than the force of habit. Many who have studied the development and function of rituals have viewed ritualization as a form of social control and communication (Bell, 1992). By defining and prescribing social behaviors, rituals function to maintain power relationships. Some have a carefully guarded privileged status in families and communities. This privilege is particularly apparent in religious practices, which may define departures from ritual structure as sacrilege. However, even nonreligious rituals can have a peremptory directive force, so that failing to perform them may result in sanctions ranging from stated disapproval to outright shunning.

Bell (1992) notes that ritualization typically avoids explicit speech and narrative. Ritual acts, in fact, have their own structure, which may or may not be congruent with narratives about the acts performed. The function of ritual speech is not necessarily to communicate rational concepts (ritual words may in fact be cryptic); nevertheless, even ritual speeches that are incomprehensible can have the power to cue and control behavior.

It is not necessary to understand a ritual in order to perform it and to be controlled by it. Many rituals, in fact, seem incomprehensible when subjected to logical analysis. Their power derives from the emotions to which they are connected and these, in turn, derive from the role of ritual in social connectedness. In this respect, rituals are often a means of structuring nonverbal as well as verbal dialogues that are fundamental to social integration. Being integrated into a group means participating in rituals valued by the group; initiation rites, for example, make this contingency explicit.

Refusing to comply with accepted rituals is a form of rebellion that may be punished by sanctions ranging from subtle forms of disapproval to ostracism. When rituals include the recitation of official stories and memories, anyone who deviates from the prescribed form may be confronted with an organized social sanction that discredits the authority of the merely personal memory. Anyone who defies socially valued rituals is apt to discover that an isolated witness to history, however accurate, is not considered credible.

In childhood, the rationalization of familiar rituals is one aspect of language development. Many rituals are given a special narrative gloss, an authoritative interpretation that explains their importance. This story is sometimes incorporated into the ritual itself; even when the factual truth of the story is suspect, it is valued for the emotional or symbolic meaning it represents.

Rituals that are primarily nonverbal may never become explicit at all or, although initially explicit, may become dissociated from self-referential recollections. When such rituals continue to persist as somatic and behavioral habits, they may seem mysterious to the person who performs them. As memory tags, such behavioral rituals can provide clues to experiences that have been an important part of personal history but that are disconnected from consciously organized narratives.

A twelve-year-old girl, for example, invented a private ritual of riding her bicycle to an old, abandoned cemetery where she then sat quietly, as if keeping vigil. As she later remembered it, she had thought of nothing in particular during these peaceful interludes, but had found the ritual somehow soothing, almost hypnotic. Recollecting this behavior as an adult, she found it a bit morbid, though not really disturbing, and seemingly meaningless. As she explored her thoughts about it, however, she became increasingly convinced that it was connected with several losses in her life, particularly the loss of a significant caretaker when she was two. The connecting link between earlier losses and the later ritual was a powerful though unarticulated emotional response to disrupted attachments. Haunted by seemingly forgotten events, she unconsciously memorialized them by haunting the abandoned cemetery.

DIALOGUES

The influence of rituals on the self and its memories illustrates the extent to which even nonverbal modes of representation are orchestrated by social agendas. From the beginning of life, interactive rituals organize individual memory systems. Nonverbal as well as verbal "dialogues" are internalized as the building blocks of personal identity. The resulting internal representations, including those that shape autobiographical memory, are commonly composites of personal experiences and social directives. Dialogues between the self and other people focus attention, supply narration, and orchestrate interpretation. They permit utterance and action or command silence and immobility. They create official stories that are forwarded as historical truth even when the self covertly knows otherwise.

According to Hermans and Kempen (1993), "Dialogue is at the heart of every form of thought" (p. 43). From birth, the infant "converses" with the mother. By the age of two or three, the evolution of language has greatly expanded the range of possible conversations. Whether a particular narrative is a private recounting to the self or a public interchange, it is typically structured in the form of dialogue and reflects the imagined voice of an audience as well as the voice of the speaker who bears witness (see Bakhtin, 1929/1973).

Although we customarily think of dialogue as a verbal conversation, it is much more than that. It consists of the gestures, emotional expressions, and behaviors that accompany and clarify speech. Hermans and Kempen

(1993) have argued persuasively for the role of the body both in self-knowing and in communication. Dialogues are structured by actual and imagined interactions with others who feel and move as well as speak.

Yet the special role of speech and language in human communication has a powerful effect on which dialogues eventually become privileged and which stories about the past become "official." The body can engage in nonverbal dialogues that are structured by predictable sequences of action and reaction. But from birth, the importance of the voice in parent-child interactions reflects the increasing significance of language in human adaptation; consequently, though a reciprocal interplay between remembered sensory images or somatic responses may be structured like a dialogue, dialogues are most commonly experienced as voices.

As the child grows, a widening world of social interaction confronts the evolving self with a multiplicity of voices, some of which are in harmony, some in conflict. The child engages in dialogues not only with parents and siblings, but also with imagined interlocutors. Evolving dialogues impart an integrative or a disruptive tension to self-development. When one voice in a dialogue is disturbing, there may be an attempt to silence it. When one voice is especially powerful or persuasive, it may drown out competing voices.

The ubiquitous role of dialogue in development makes dialogue intrinsic to self-reflection; self-talk, in fact, is often the internalization of dialogues that were once external. Even a singular and cohesive self commonly learns to speak to itself in a dialogue that includes two voices, two perspectives, two possible statements or narratives. The self in dialogue with itself also commonly constructs a third voice, the mediator who chooses between one perspective and another or decides, on the basis of either-or arguments, what to do.

Dialogue is thus one of the major factors complicating the construction of memory. Whether it is internal or between the self and other people, whether it is faithful to essential information or effects blatant distortions, dialogue tends to create departures from simple facts. Some facts or details usually become privileged over others. Other details are ignored. Interpretations are added to the recounting of events. Everything may be integrated to make the story more coherent or consistent or communicable than the events themselves were originally.

Vivid images, gut-level feelings, and action sequences are not always easily articulated in verbal communications; as a result, they are not easily integrated with dialogues. Consequently, such nonverbal experiences or memories may seem insignificant or unreal to other people, even to the reflective self.

Dialogues have powerful effects on how memories are forwarded over time. Where two internal voices echo each other, the effect can strongly reinforce a recollection. If voices are in disagreement, however, the conflict itself can have either a clarifying or a distorting effect. When there is an intentional attempt by one voice to subvert memory, the wish of the other voice to appease or defy may shape what is forwarded in memory.

Such internalized dialogues and narratives are often as important in the building of personal identity as veridical self-defining memories. In this respect, even the most solitary self is a social being. From the earliest interactional dialogues to the latest verbal narratives, self-perception and identity consolidation are shaped by the memories of other people as well as those that are strictly private. It is this social dimension of the self that makes it possible for personal memory to be subverted by other people for their own ends. It is not simply that human beings are suggestible, although some are. It is, rather, that they care about approval and acceptance and will sometimes compromise veridical memory to please other people. In this respect, they stand in marked contrast to autistic savants. One dimension of the remarkably accurate and consistent memories of savants is the savant's indifference to influence.

When memory is intentionally subverted by other people, the self does not necessarily forget. But a compliant self will learn to accentuate the official story at the expense of what is covertly remembered but socially unacceptable. When actual threats or intimidation are involved, the self has a strong motive for hiding unacceptable memories. One of the simplest evasions is saying, "I don't remember."

The subversion of individual memory is not always based on sinister motives, however. Groups as well as individuals have identities to be consolidated and maintained. Shared history is an important dimension of group identity and includes both stories of triumph and joy and histories of failure and ignominy. Whether it is a matter of family stories or national rituals, the individual self internalizes such official stories in order to belong. And gradually, over time, the self becomes a witness to cultural history as well as to its own past.

Though shared history contributes to schematic and imperfect encodings of personal experience, it does not always and necessarily run counter to the truth. What people remember together may be highly veridical. And the social orchestration of memory may include ways of learning to remember that foster accuracy and veridicality. Much formal schooling, for example, is designed not only to help people remember correctly, but also to organize their searches for the past in ways that maximize efficiency and accuracy. In this process, identity as a pattern of individual integration is necessarily a pattern of social integration. Memories that cannot be shared are isolating. Private narratives that cannot be voiced in dialogue with others can trap the self in ruminative self-talk.

As any particular dialogue is internalized, the self may claim it as personal invention. Or it may be carried alongside other dialogues and narratives that tell a very different story. One result is a set of multiple representations and divergent narratives about a single event.

Even when there is no intrinsic motive to distort a story, the need to make the story comprehensible or acceptable to the self and to others sometimes overrides the wish to give an accurate rendering. And when an event is, in fact, confusing and incomprehensible, the need not only to make sense of it but to communicate it can become a major, but distorting, factor in how it is reported.

NARRATIVES

As language skills improve, memory is increasingly organized by narrative structures that bear a cultural as well as an idiosyncratic stamp. The integration of nonverbal with verbal schemas, including narratives about the self and others that are labeled "memories," is an ongoing process.

Developmentally, dialogue is prior to narrative. But as nonverbal dialogue is increasingly supplemented by verbal exchanges, narrative structures become a major organizing factor in communication and thought. These narratives tend to structure events in linear sequences and to establish time lines and time tags that help stabilize memories.

Verbal narratives facilitate rehearsal. Saying something over and over stabilizes the form as well as the content of the repeated statement. In the course of narration, the distinction between what happened and the *story* of what happened often fades, as the story becomes identified with the memory for the original event.

The narratives children eventually construct, as well as the narratives of the adults who teach them, may come to have a ritualistic or stylized character. Acquiring forms of storytelling and specific stories typical of a family or culture is an important way of schematizing memories about the past, since the encoding of experience in language greatly facilitates the social orchestration of memory. The learning of basic schemas, especially linguistic ones, is not simply left to chance; it is carefully taught. From birth, encoding processes are shaped to match narrative conventions (Engel, 1995). Overt forms of recollection are differentiated from covert ones; children learn what they can talk about in public, what can be discussed only in the family, and what must remain unspoken. They also learn that, although some narratives are taboo, they cannot easily be dismissed from mind.

Certain scripts are carefully inculcated, too, yet the ways in which this occurs are not necessarily explicit. Scripts that, in childhood, are painstakingly acquired but that eventually become habitual may even be composed long before the child is even born. The expectation that Avery would become a doctor, for example, was an important part of the fantasies that his parents had about him from the beginning of his life, and their fantasies, even when unspoken, shaped many of their interactions with him. As a result, Avery felt predestined to become a doctor, although he could not recall ever being explicitly instructed to do so.

The broader social context, though not immediately obvious to the young child, influences from the beginning what parents transmit. As Sameroff (1989) has emphasized, the regulatory behavior of the parent is itself embedded in culturally specific regulatory contexts. Cultures prescribe ideals for the bringing up of children; many of these are implicit but some are written down or legally encoded. The episodic gestalts typical of the culture shape how time itself is structured and organized.

Social schemas typically value certain forms of remembering and particular kinds of memories while devaluing others. In Western culture, for example, written texts are highly valued, oral forms of narrative somewhat less so. Nonverbal forms are not necessarily devalued — art and music have an honored place — but that place is commonly subordinate.

Social rituals and stories sometimes include deliberate, carefully organized rehearsals of desirable memories. Even those shared memories that are casually transmitted are often guided by implicit or explicit forms of social editing. As a result, the version of a story produced for public consumption may be quite different from that originally experienced or privately elaborated. This process is complicated not only by the encoding schemas that transform information inputs but also by narrative conventions that are typical for the individual, the family, or the culture (Schank & Abelson, 1977). These in turn are influenced by such factors as display rules (Ekman, 1992), expressive styles, and taboos.

Emotion plays an important role in the development of stories. Engel (1995) believes that the very process of narration helps children to master feelings and gain some distance from events. The urge to communicate a particular content combines with the wish to communicate with a particular audience. These interacting motives shape the structure and style of the story produced.

Over time, after several repetitions, an individual's story of a significant shared event may become both personally stylized and socially shaped, an almost mythic structure. Retelling becomes a repetition of a habit, as distinct from the retrieval of a specific memory. But unless subjected to careful observation, this acquired narrative habit is easily mistaken for an original memory.

Culturally, the rehearsal of significant events often has a history marked by periods of frequent repetition, periods of elaboration and/or condensation, and periods of comparative silence or avoidance. Each of these periods is likely to be guided by social cues and conventions. Thus, after a shared trauma, such as the assassination of a president, people tend to repeat their personal stories and compare notes with their cohorts. The elaboration of another's story may lead one to elaborate one's own story.

After an initial period of shock, during which the story of the trauma is constantly repeated and exposure to many narrations of it is high, the focus of awareness shifts; it becomes an old story and is no longer in the public spotlight. Shorthand references to it may be developed, and these references, whether public or private, come to serve as tags for the memory. These shorthand memory markers, like other narrative habits, easily come to substitute for a more detailed encoding of an event.

Similarly, the rehearsal of memories for privately significant experiences may have a history of intense focus and repetitive review followed by habituation and a shift of focus to something else. A traumatized child, for example, may independently shift focus, perhaps guided by developing defensive strategies such as the internal command, "Don't think about it." Once-public memories may be privatized and relabeled as a shift of focus is actively guided by others who urge, "Please, not that story again!" or "Stop making things up."

The avoidance of narration shapes memory not only by destabilizing the form of what is remembered, but by facilitating the avoidance of emotional cues associated with narration. Avoidance of narration leaves even a strong memory more shapeless and inchoate than a clearly verbalized story. This shapelessness in itself facilitates avoidance and the fading of memory. Thus, avoiding is a kind of circular process; the more persistently one avoids, the easier it is to avoid; the longer a story is untold, the harder it may be to tell.

If there are social directions, explicit or implicit, to avoid telling a story, it cannot be overtly rehearsed. And even a well-known story, repetitively rehearsed over a period of time, once familiar not only to the self but to other people, may fade from recall once the story stops being rehearsed. When official stories conflict with personal memories, the "official" version may eventually drive the discrepant memories from consciousness or, at least, from any public acknowledgment.

FAMILY STORIES

The importance of certain narratives to the needs and beliefs of parents plays a strong role in shaping what children eventually learn to label as their own memories. From an early age, they may be coached in which statements count as acceptable memories and which do not. And once told about an experience, the imaginative child may incorporate it into his or her repertory of personal memories.

Family stories prescribe memorial structures and provide narrative glosses of events that are consistent with the family's image of itself, its history, or its ideals of conduct (Stone, 1988). Some stories are cautionary, intended to warn those in the younger generation against repeating the mistakes of their elders. Some are explanatory, structuring a rationale for how and why things came to be the way they are. Some are nostalgic, enshrining a lost past and, through the retelling of it, momentarily resurrecting its pleasures.

Family stories may have ritualistic characteristics. Citing the work of Zeitlin, Kotkin, and Baker (1982) on a family folklore project at the Smithsonian Institution, Reiss (1989) notes several functions such stories serve: they commonly highlight conspicuous heroes or rogues in the family's history; they dramatize and demarcate significant family transitions or events, such as migrations, fortunes made or lost, courtships, and weddings; and they enshrine valued family customs. Rituals and stories thus embed the emerging self in the family's version of history. Over time, certain memories acquire an "official" status and a prescriptive force. In this respect, they become important elements of individual identity, confirming the integration and continuity of the self over time and extending the boundaries of the self beyond the limits of personal memory.

Children are not simply programmed automata, however. Social convention and direction is only one contributing factor in the development of personal memory. During childhood, the self is constantly transformed by internal developments as well as by external events, and the stories that narrate these changes are amended, elaborated, removed from focus, or integrated according to many needs and capabilities. The self is not a static or unitary development, and the memories that help structure the self, especially narratives, are multifaceted and variable.

DIVERGENT NARRATIVES

The social programming of memory may be a powerful source of inconsistency in self-referential memory. Conflict and inconsistency, in turn, are powerful motivational variables that continually guide both the internal and external elaboration of memories. The matching of self-consistency to social consistency is part of learning to live in a family, a neighborhood, or a culture.

Because such conflicts can be uncomfortable, it may be easier for the child to stop rehearsing a strictly personal version of events altogether and to acquiesce to someone else's version. This behavior is associated with suggestibility and, undeniably, some people, children especially, are very suggestible. But suggestibility should not be confused with being overwhelmed by the will of another person.

Coercion may involve violence or threats or violence. But much coercion is more subtly achieved, through psychological forms of intimidation. Family loyalty is a strong controlling motive. The child who tells a family secret, for example, may be emotionally outcast even if not physically punished. Withdrawal of affection or approval by needed caregivers is a powerful means of shaping conformity in any dependent person. As a control tactic, it is used in totalitarian forms of brainwashing; a captor may treat a captive kindly just in order to gain the power of being able to withhold kindness (Lifton, 1961).

A common scenario in the family involves shaming; the child is led to believe that failing to keep a particular family secret would be disgraceful to everyone concerned. Where the secret involves wrongdoing on the part of a family member, such as physical or sexual abuse, the self-blaming child may be unable to discriminate between shameful acts by the perpetrator and shameful acts by the self.

As an emotional experience, shame involves recognizing a discrepancy between a true story and an ideal story. A real event has been inconsistent with social expectations or personal integrity. The individual may blush with shame whenever the event is recalled. Shame, then, becomes one motive for banishing the event from memory.

Guilt, too, leads people to avoid remembering and to silence the telling of stories. Guilt, however, often involves more cognitive elaborations than shame. Memories associated with guilt may be amended to supply a narrative gloss that rationalizes and excuses one's behavior. Shame is not so easily rationalized away.

In any case, however, neither guilt nor shame is necessarily rational. Children are commonly shamed and blamed for events over which they have no real control at all, and this practice is especially typical of abusive family contexts. Moreover, feelings of guilt and shame, even if irrational, are not always differentiated by children. Instead, a painful memory may be associated with diffuse, poorly articulated feelings of being out of control and flooded with powerful but socially forbidden emotions — rage, fear, hatred.

Shame and guilt, then, play an important role in structuring divergent narratives about disturbing events. The reworking of a memory over time often involves an increased distancing of the self from such painful feelings. And distancing from feelings is more easily managed when one can distance oneself from memories. When other people, too, are in flight from shame and guilt, every such distancing is likely to be socially reinforced, if not actually demanded.

Divergent narratives are expectable whenever an event reflects badly on the self or on those the self is attached to. The true but disturbing story is defensively transformed to make it less disturbing. Since being out of control of memory is itself disturbing, these transformations may restore a sense of control. Every time the amended story is repeated, it reassures the self that overwhelming events did not really occur or, if they did, that the self is no longer overwhelmed by them.

Divergent narratives can distort memory at any stage of processing. If they occur early in the process of encoding an experience, many details of the experience may never be noticed or rehearsed at all. An alternative story may almost immediately replace a true one. In many cases, however, divergent narratives are created at some point or even several points after an initial experience. When an event is traumatic, for example, the shock it produces may delay narrative construction. The striking images and intense emotions accompanying the trauma may be recorded as images, feelings, and reactions rather than as verbal responses. Even if the traumatic event is accompanied by narrative self-talk, as usually happens when the trauma is extended in time, the self-talk may not be integrated with the nonverbal components of the experience.

Divergent narratives, recalled, are usually a source of discomfort. The self recognizes its own inconsistency. This inconsistency, in turn, leads to attempts to integrate or reconcile the divergent stories. But doing so is not always possible, especially if there is now no objective evidence that favors one story over the other. It may be tempting to give up trying to remember which version of a story is true and to acquiesce to the explanation, "I really can't remember." This response to the conflict may be socially encouraged. "Of course you can't or don't remember," says anyone who stands to lose by the recall.

In some cases, though, one version of a story merely goes underground; it persists in memory alongside a publicly stated story. Depending on the level of development the child has reached, he or she may speak the unspeakable subvocally. This suppression of a taboo memory may help structure a split between a public persona and a private self.

Social orchestrations can also result in the fragmentation of a particular episodic memory into verbal and nonverbal components. In some instances, the boundaries within a compartmentalized memory may be permeable; one *can* talk about the memory but hesitates to do so because one knows it is taboo. In other cases, the functional boundaries detach a memory from all verbal narratives about it, even from self-referent components that were initially encoded with the memory.

Sometimes the self learns to tolerate divergent narratives by dissociating them from one another. At one point, one story is remembered or told. At another, a contrasting version is produced. Other people may or may not notice the inconsistency. If they do, they may be astonished at the inconsistent behavior, discount the credibility of the narrator, and dismiss both stories as mere fabrications.

Historically, for example, women diagnosed as "hysterical" were sometimes described as displaying "la belle indifference." They blandly told terrible stories or displayed inappropriate feelings about them. They changed their stories from one day to the next. It was easy to dismiss such stories as fantasies. Until late in the twentieth century, the actual abuse that shaped the lives of these women was discounted or minimized.

When discrepant identity configurations are organized around divergent narratives, the fragmentations associated with dissociative identity disorders are sometimes the result. Such discrepancies are sometimes used to discredit the memories of abuse reported by one or more of the dissociated identities. The inconsistent individual may be diagnosed instead as having a factitious disorder. Once anyone has been discredited as out of touch with reality, suffering from factitious disorder, or lying outright, the veridicality of any of that person's memories may be called into question. Internalizing the skeptical evaluations of others, the confused self may acquiesce in the notion that memory cannot be trusted.

Veridical memory, however, is not so easily dismissed from internal dialogues. Even when narrative is silenced, it may continue to insert itself into everyday life. When the memory involves trauma, flashbacks and nightmares as well as somatic symptoms may substitute for missing or silenced narratives. Unfortunately, these too may be dismissed as mere fantasy constructions.

But the self, even silent, may know the truth. And the integrity of the self may depend on telling it.

CHAPTER 6

The Impact of Trauma

Things just wasn't connected. Like I couldn't remember my telephone number. I couldn't remember my brother's or sister's telephone numbers. I couldn't remember where I lived. It's just—I don't know how to express it. I was just standing there and it seemed like I really didn't have anything on my mind at the time. Just everything disappeared.

It was a horrible thing, I'll tell you it was. A man will never forget it. If I live to be a hundred years old, I will never forget it.

— Buffalo Creek survivors, quoted in Erikson, 1976

Two years after the Buffalo Creek flood roared down a mountain hollow in Logan County, West Virginia, destroying everything in its path, Kai Erikson, a sociologist, interviewed survivors. Every one of them was suffering from symptoms of anxiety, depression, apathy, disorientation, and/or social disconnection. Medical examinations confirmed this observation. When six hundred fifteen survivors were examined by psychiatrists, 93 percent were found to be suffering from an identifiable emotional disorder (Erikson, 1976).

Memory problems were prominent. The problems described included two common but seemingly paradoxical posttraumatic symptoms: being unable to remember and being unable to forget. In some survivors, one or the other symptom seemed to predominate, but others were plagued both by losses of reliable memory function and by intrusive recall, particularly during sleep.

To the experimental purist, accounts by survivors of the Buffalo Creek trauma might be suspect as anecdotal. They are the dramatic articulations of a few individuals rather than the controlled responses of subjects in carefully selected samples. They are constructed after the event and thus possibly affected by post-event occurrences. It should be noted, however, that the descriptions of the effects of this disaster could not have been influenced by modern controversies about trauma and memory. In the 1970s, neither the effects of civil disasters nor the sequelae of other traumas, such as war, had been much discussed in the media. Survivors of this coal-mining community in Appalachia would have had little if any access to published reports about posttraumatic syndromes.

To be sure, they were seeking damages from the coal company that they held responsible for the flood. But mental anguish was not a primary basis for their claims; they had lost many family members and friends, all their personal possessions, even the land they had once lived on. The whole community, normally a support to the recovery of trauma victims, had been destroyed.

Thus, the descriptions given to Erikson were spontaneous attempts to convey the indescribable. The flood and its aftermath was simply more than the mind could manage. The integrative function of memory failed.

MEMORY GONE HAYWIRE

The reports of these survivors are convincing not only because of the immediacy and vividness with which they tell a particular story, but also because of their consistency with what we now know about survivors of many different kinds of trauma—natural disasters, war, interpersonal violence, and child abuse. As Lifton and Olson (1976) have observed, extreme stress produces similar disturbances in all victims. Van der Kolk (1987a) concurs: "... the human response to overwhelming and uncontrollable life events is remarkably consistent" (p. 2). Posttraumatic remembering dramatizes the breakdown of complex coherences characteristic of normal functioning. Normally integrated functions can be disarticulated. Response patterns that are normally connected can be dissociated.

The anecdotal reports of these survivors are also consistent with a growing body of careful research. In spite of research limitations—we cannot manipulate trauma experimentally—we have, during the last century, accumulated a great deal of information about the psychobiological and social effects of trauma. These characteristic effects include cycles of extreme arousal alternating with numbing and behavioral avoidance. Cognitive disturbances include intrusive reexperiencing of the trauma, sleep disturbances, and, in some instances, psychogenic amnesia. Depersonalization is a common response to trauma (Shilony & Grossman, 1993), as are dissociative symptoms both at the time of trauma and in the aftermath (Cardena & Spiegel, 1993; Chu & Dill, 1990; Koopman, Classen, & Spiegel, 1994). In addition, survivors commonly exhibit guilt, shame, behavioral constriction, interpersonal isolation, and alterations in self-esteem. Physical illness or injury is also a common sequela; trauma has negative effects on the immune system as well as on behavior associated with self-care (Figley, 1985; McCann & Pearlman, 1990; Ochberg, 1988; Waites, 1993; van der Kolk, 1987b).

The cognitive difficulties, which are in part mediated by the psychobiology of trauma, seem always to be closely intertwined with more complex emotional and motivational ones. Uncontrollable disruptions of memory are compounded by the conscious wish to escape memory and deliberate strategies of avoidance. The inability to forget is complicated by the wish to remember, to integrate the past with the present, the self who existed before the calamity with the one who survived it. Both memory loss and intrusive flashbacks can be frightening in themselves, precipitating defensive coping behavior to help the survivor reestablish control. This sometimes confusing admix of disturbances and motives, ranging from the automatic to the carefully contrived, has become a hallmark of posttraumatic memory.

Although the variability of posttraumatic memory effects can be confusing, they are consistent not only with what we know about trauma, but with what we know about memory in general. A wide array of neurological and psychological processes are involved in what is eventually observed as normal episodic memory. The special biological and psychological effects of trauma modify normal responses; thus, episodic memories of trauma may be characterized by distinctive processing patterns (Kolb, 1987).

Flashbacks, vivid intrusive recollections of the traumatic event, are an especially strong indication of such special forms of processing. During a crisis, attentional processes, always a significant factor in memory, alter normal forms of scanning and stimulus selection. Some details of the terrible event — not necessarily those a calm observer might choose as most important — are encoded with vivid clarity. And after the crisis is over, these may spring to mind quite suddenly, commanding attention.

The fact that not only flashbacks but also other memories not immediately retrievable may intrude into consciousness many years after occurrence indicates that posttraumatic storage can be remarkably durable. Yet retrieval of traumatic memories is frequently uncontrollable and inconsistent. Deliberate attempts to forget or distract oneself may work intermittently. Even after they have been seemingly effectively suppressed, memories may leap forth without warning. In this respect they resemble the spontaneous recoveries sometimes observable in conditioned responses.

These intrusive recollections can interfere with many aspects of posttraumatic adaptation, including new learning. Replayed repetitively, they can preempt attention, overshadow present external input, disrupt sleep, and wreck havoc on the victim's life. When they trigger avoidance reactions, these have the effect of isolating the victim from exposure to information and the practicing of coping behaviors that might facilitate recovery.

In some instances, traumatic memories are apparently forgotten for long periods, only to resurface with troublesome intensity and persistence years later. In one case, a World War II veteran had not been troubled by memories of his war experiences until, thirty years after combat, they were reactivated by the stresses associated with deteriorating health and loss of his job (Van Dyke, Zilberg, & McKinnon, 1985). In another WWII veteran, who had experienced psychogenic amnesia for thirty-seven years following his war experience, traumatic memories began to surface following a cerebral vascular accident (Cassiday & Lyons, 1992).

Several Holocaust survivors interviewed forty years later reported that experiences they had avoided thinking about in the past had recently returned with a painful vividness (Mazor, Gampel, Enright, & Orenstein, 1990). The reactivation of these previously avoided memories evoked feelings ranging from anger, sadness, fear, alienation, and wishes for revenge to a sense of relief. Yet the authors report that "The most salient characteristic [of survivors' responses] is the individuals' awareness of the importance of memories and the intentional effort to remember some aspects of their past which may create a sense of sequence and cohesion in their personal history" (p. 11).

POSTTRAUMATIC STRESS DISORDER

In recent years, contrasting posttraumatic memory effects have increasingly been understood as a component of a typical syndrome commonly observed in trauma survivors. Currently, they are considered among the diagnostic signs of posttraumatic stress disorder (PTSD) (American Psychiatric Association, 1994).

Posttraumatic stress disorder may occur shortly after a traumatic event or after a period of delay. Symptoms may be acute and temporary or chronic and persisting. PTSD occurs in children as well as in adults, and may adversely affect developmental processes or interfere with stage-specific achievements (Eth & Pynoos, 1985).

Many of the symptoms now associated with PTSD were first systematically studied as a consequence of war (Trimble, 1985). Since the first world war, psychiatrists have recognized that memory disturbances are a frequently reported symptom of battle fatigue (Grinker & Spiegel, 1945). Follow-up studies of World War II veterans were consistent with these earlier reports (Archibald & Tuddenham, 1965; Christenson, Walker, Ross, & Maltbie, 1981; Van Dyke et al., 1985; Yehuda, Keefe, Harvey, Levengood, Gerber, Geni, & Siever, 1995).

Characteristic memory disturbances, ranging from flashbacks to psychogenic amnesias, have also been found in Vietnam veterans (Bremmer et al., 1993; Laufer, Frey-Wouters, & Gallops, 1985; Marmar et al., 1994), former prisoners of war (Sutker, Winstead, Galina, & Allain, 1991), Cambodian refugees (Carlson & Rosser-Hogan, 1991), and Holocaust survivors

(Mazor et al., 1990; Rosen, Reynolds, Yeager, Houck, & Hurwitz, 1991). Similar trauma-related symptoms have also been observed in veterans of Operation Desert Storm (Southwick et al., 1993).

In recent years, PTSD as a syndrome has proved useful in clarifying responses to other forms of interpersonal violence and victimization, including child physical and sexual abuse (Green, 1985; Rowen & Foy, 1993), rape (Burge, 1988), and battering (Waites, 1993). Increasingly, too, the concept is shedding light on the high incidence of previous trauma and abuse experiences reported in those hospitalized for psychiatric illness (Briere & Zaidi, 1989; Carmen, Ricker, & Mills, 1984; Goodwin, Attias, McCarty, Chandler, & Romanik, 1988; Husain & Chapel, 1983; Mullen, Martin, Anderson, Romans, & Herbison, 1993). Although survivors of sexual abuse typically claim to have always remembered that the abuse occurred (Loftus, Polansky, & Fullilove, 1994), the retrospective nature of clinical reports of earlier abuse in hospitalized psychiatric patients has led to controversy over the accuracy of delayed reports of such memories. A study by Herman and Schatzow (1987), however, found that it was often possible to verify recovered memories of early sexual trauma through independent sources. In a study of women with a history of addiction (Loftus et al., 1994), just under a fifth of the subjects claimed that they forgot for a period but later recalled the memory of abuse.

Briere and Conte (1993) found that partial or complete amnesia for sexual abuse was common in their sample of survivors of sexual abuse; 59 percent of abused subjects reported a time period before the age of eighteen during which they were unable to recall their first experience of molestation. Abuse-specific amnesia was especially associated with violent abuse, multiple perpetrators, and fears of death if the abuse were disclosed; it was also associated with greater current symptomatology.

Painful medical procedures are also a documented source of trauma that may affect subsequent behavior, whether or not the procedures are recalled (Shopper, 1995). In children, the impact of such procedures interacts with phase-specific developmental acquisitions (Gomes-Schwartz, Horowitz, & Sauzier, 1985; Nader, Pynoos, Fairbanks, & Frederick, 1990; Rowen & Foy, 1993). Life-threatening physical illness or injury is especially stressful and is often associated with intrusive recollections and obsessive memories. How an individual copes with such stress may have an important effect on the medical outcome (Nir, 1985).

Witnesses to a violent event who themselves experience no physical injury may nevertheless develop posttraumatic symptoms, as was indicated in a study of individuals who witnessed or were close to a school shooting (Schwarz, Kowalski, & McNally, 1993) and in a study of eyewitnesses to an execution (Freinkel, Koopman, & Spiegel, 1994).

Pynoos and Eth (1985) studied children exposed to homicide, rape, or suicide. They reported that witnesses of violent events experience intense perceptions of vivid external events and of internal responses such as autonomic arousal. Images related to the traumatic events are subsequently present in drawings, storytelling tasks, and play. Certain specific details are commonly imbued with special meanings; one teenage girl, for example, became preoccupied with the fact that her mother had been wearing one of the daughter's dresses when she was murdered.

Posttraumatic Memory Effects

General as well as specific posttraumatic memory deficits have been noted in PTSD. Bremner and his colleagues (1993) reported that PTSD patients scored significantly lower than comparison subjects on both immediate and delayed measures of verbal memory on the Wechsler Memory Scale. Retention for the figural memory component of the Wechsler scale was negatively correlated with PTSD symptom severity. These authors conclude that the memory impairments shown by PTSD patients in their sample are comparable to those in clinical populations with clearly documented temporal lobe damage, a finding suggesting that neurological damage may underlie some of the memory disturbances associated with PTSD.

Research has also indicated that, although combat veterans with PTSD may show normal abilities in immediate memory functions, they seem to have a circumscribed cognitive deficit revealed by significant retention decrements following exposure to an intervening, potentially confusing word list (Yehuda, Keefe, et al., 1995). The authors suggest that, in PTSD, the intermingling of past with current experiences, as occurs in intrusive thoughts and flashbacks, leads to specific deficits in memory regulation.

The psychobiological underpinnings of PTSD indicate that it is not simply a "mental" disorder, but a problem that affects the whole person. While remembering past combat experiences, affected individuals showed increases in heart rate, skin conductance, and facial electromyogram (EMG) levels (Orr, Pitman, Lasko, & Herz, 1993; Pitman, Orr, Forgue, deJong, & Claiborn, 1987; Shalev, Orr, & Pitman, 1993). A study extending these findings to civilian subjects with histories of noncombat-related trauma led the authors to conclude that psychophysiologic assessment, particularly heart rate response during trauma-related imagery, is a promising tool for diagnosing PTSD (Shalev et al., 1993).

Some findings suggest that the basic neurological effects of trauma on memory may be mediated by irregularities in the functioning of the hypothalamic-pituitary-adrenal (HPA) axis, one of the major hormonal systems involved in stress reactions. These effects include the release of stress hormones and neurotransmitters (Yehuda, Giller, Southwick, Lowy, & Mason, 1991) that varies with the duration of the stress; initial overactivation following acute stress is followed by adaptation to chronic stress, which results in underactivation and reduced sensitivity.

Reduced levels of urinary cortisol excretion, an index of these HPA axis abnormalities, has been found to characterize individuals diagnosed as suffering from PTSD (Yehuda et al., 1991). In Holocaust survivors, severity of avoidance symptoms correlated especially highly with reduced cortisol levels (Yehuda, Kahana, Binder-Byrnes, Southwick, Mason, & Giller, 1995). The authors note that the latter study represents the first report of HPA axis abnormalities in woman with chronic PTSD.

Prior stress, especially family system stressors, can be a predisposing factor in the development of PTSD (Emery, Emery, Shama, Quiana, & Jassani, 1991; Koopman, Classen, & Spiegel, 1994). A history of severe physical punishment in childhood has been found to be correlated with severity of combat-related PTSD symptomatology (Zaidi & Foy, 1994).

Active coping styles have also consistently been found to be associated with recovery from traumatic stress, although avoidance may also be adaptive at some points in the process of coping and recovery (Gibbs, 1989). Perceived social support may mitigate posttraumatic symptoms (Perry, Difede, Musngi, Frances, & Jacobsberg, 1992).

A study of survivors of a firestorm in California (Koopman et al., 1994) suggests that dissociative symptoms as an immediate response to trauma are a major mediating factor in the later development of posttraumatic stress disorder. This study corroborates earlier findings by Lindemann (1944) that trauma survivors who initially showed little emotional response were at greatest risk for later problems such as suicidality and depression. The authors also conclude that their findings support Janet's theory that dissociation, as a defense against the pain of immediate trauma, may lead to subsequent pathology (see also van der Kolk, Brown, & van der Hart, 1989).

Biphasic Patterns in PTSD

Some of the confusion and contradictions that emerge in studies of trauma and memory are clarified by consideration of the biphasic nature of the trauma response, which seems to result from the deregulation of psychobiological processes and attempts to restore homeostasis (van der Kolk & Greenberg, 1987). The diagnostic criteria for PTSD recognize these contrasting effects. On the one hand, intrusive reexperiencing of the trauma is associated with high levels of anxiety and agitation; on the other, emotional constriction and avoidance behavior lead to an apparent unawareness of or unresponsiveness to traumatic events. In PTSD, these contrasting response patterns typically alternate.

The biphasic character of PTSD contributes to the disorganizing effects of trauma. Radical extremes of feeling and behavior disrupt behavioral and psychological integration. As a result, the behavior of the traumatized individual may appear to observers to be quite inconsistent and erratic.

Hyperarousal and numbing are associated with measurably distinct physiological as well as behavioral responses, which may produce contrasting effects on memory. In this respect, the literature on state-dependent learning is suggestive (Parkin, 1987). States of arousal and states of numbing produce different effects on attentional processes and, possibly, on storage. Hyperarousal may be associated with such effects as a constriction in the range of attention accompanied by a heightened awareness of (and memory for) particular stimulus details (the Easterbrook or "weapon focus" hypothesis). Hyperarousal also typically motivates actions, such as flight or fight behaviors, that may make a situation more controllable and thus less traumatic.

Numbing, in contrast, is behaviorally characterized by underactivity or even immobility. It constricts behavior and commonly blunts awareness. Although the defensive function of numbing has sometimes been viewed in terms of deliberate attempts to avoid traumatic reminders, it may have the more basic psychobiological function of conserving the overtaxed body and its depleted energy resources. It is often phenomenologically described as resembling anesthetization and may be biologically mediated by endogenous opioids (van der Kolk et al., 1985).

Numbing and effortful avoidance are distinct response patterns (Foa, Riggs, & Gershuny, 1995) and are evidently based on different mechanisms. Numbing, for example, is part of the psychobiological response to extreme activation. High levels of stress lead to an overactivation of the HPA axis, but chronic stress leads to underactivation as a physiological adaptation (Yehuda et al., 1991). After initial trauma effects have subsided, however, the individual typically institutes active patterns of avoidance designed to prevent their being triggered again.

States of extreme numbing may resemble a loss of consciousness and, in certain susceptible individuals, may be accompanied by trance. Some trance states are characterized by a kind of psychogenic autism (Waites, 1993). This autistic trance should be distinguished from the socially mediated trance states usually associated with hypnosis. Although autistic trance states may have some features of hypnotic trances, they are characterized by extreme withdrawal from external stimulation and social contact and are not necessarily accompanied by imagery or fantasies.

Different kinds of trance may be expected to have contrasting effects on memory. Whereas individuals under hypnosis are commonly extremely suggestible, a phenomenon that may be associated with confabulated memories (Pettinati, 1988), autistically withdrawn individuals may be relatively impervious to outside influence (Waites, 1993). When trance is also combined with anesthetic effects, the victim of trauma can effectively shut out potentially overwhelming stimulation. The most extreme example of this imperviousness and immobility is observable in catatonic states.

The inaccessibility of the autistically withdrawn individual may make it difficult to discover just what is happening mentally. The individual may function like an automaton and may follow orders, for example, not because he or she is suggestible, but because what one does no longer matters. Anesthetized to pain, he may calmly recount horrific details of a trauma with no apparent concern. And when memory falters, there is no particular motivation to retrieve it even when it has not really been forgotten. Yet even hospitalized catatonic patients who appear completely unresponsive are sometimes acutely aware of what is happening around them.

However, automatic forms of numbing and autistic trance states, though temporarily self-protective, leave the traumatized individual vulnerable and out of control. Intentional patterns of avoidance are likely to appear, superficially at least, to be more adaptive. Effortful avoidance strategies, which are mediated by complex cognitive processes and may include complicated sequences of behavior, appear later than immediate psychobiological responses to trauma, but are woven into more reflexive avoidance patterns. It is these complex strategies that most clearly resemble what clinicians have conceptualized as "defenses."

For example, the biphasic pattern typical of PTSD tends to lead to inconsistencies of behavior as well as internal experience. Sometimes these inconsistencies are reduced by the evolution of a cognitive or behavioral style that emphasizes one or the other pole of the biphasic response pattern. Two typical styles are monitoring, in which the person constantly seeks and attends to information related to threat, and blunting, in which information is avoided and attention is focused on distracting stimuli (Solomon, Mikulincer, & Arad, 1991).

Different styles of information processing may have extensive effects on adaptive coping. Solomon and his colleagues (1991) report, for example, that the use of blunting strategies was associated with more widespread combat-related PTSD than the use of monitoring strategies, and that the external orientation of high monitors/low blunters may contribute to post-trauma adjustment.

Both numbing and effortful avoidance can have significant consequences for interpersonal relations. In the process of trying to control uncontrollable levels of stimulation, the traumatized individual may become quite isolated from social support systems. Isolation, in turn, removes the opportunity for external validation of memories and may increase feelings of depersonalization and derealization.

Neural Circuitry and Posttraumatic Memory

Posttraumatic memory may involve a special organization of brain circuitry that evolved to maximize chances of survival in challenging contexts. As Richard Restak states succinctly:

A sound in the brush of the Serengeti Plain may indicate a lion or merely the play of the wind. But a response is called for prior to a full determination of these alternatives. It is the thalamoamygdalar pathway [in the brain] that does this. Moments later the fear response may be further increased when the presence of the lion is confirmed on the basis of more complete information reaching the amygdala from the cortex (the corticoamygdalar pathway). (1991, p. 147)

The ability to respond in an emergency situation on the basis of neural circuitry that bypasses the cortex is a pattern humans share with other animals. Humans, too, need have no conscious perspective on these immediate anxiety or fear responses. But since the nature of the subcortical responses involved is nonspecific to the danger or trauma, autonomic symptoms by themselves cannot be used as a source of information about the specifics of the traumatic context.

These considerations highlight the characteristics of implicit forms of information-processing that have been described as "the cognitive unconscious," a concept quite distinct from Freudian perspectives (Epstein, 1994; Kihlstrom, 1990). As Restak (1991), who conceptualizes consciousness as an emergent property of parallel interacting modules, emphasizes, most of the brain's activities do not involve consciousness. The absence or disruption of consciousness, whether normal, as in sleep, or abnormal, as in pathological dissociative states, obviously affects how we process information. But as research on implicit memory amply illustrates, information never in consciousness may nevertheless be encoded, stored, and, although not necessarily accessible through verbal or self-referential narratives, in some instances retrieved (Graf & Masson, 1993; Jacoby, 1988).

The fact that posttraumatic autonomic response patterns are nonspecific and that some learning may be implicit does not necessarily indicate that traumatized individuals have no specific veridical memories, however. Subcortical processing may precede, but is not necessarily permanently disconnected from, cortical processing. The dissociation between conscious and reflexive or somatic responses that sometimes occurs illustrates the complexities of posttraumatic memory.

For example, even if the individual experiencing trauma is responding almost automatically, the self may, at the same time, be observing itself and making inferences about what is going on. Experiences of derealization and depersonalization often include the inference that "I left my body." The adaptive advantage of this response is noted in a study by Shilony and Grossman (1993), who found that victims who experienced depersonalization during a trauma were less symptomatic than those who experienced trauma without depersonalization.

After the trauma, too, persisting cycles of hyperarousal and constriction or persisting reflexive responses are not only observed but interpreted by the self. Even when these observations and interpretations involve cognitive processing at a different level than that accompanying immediate trauma, they may involve constant attempts to integrate disparate response patterns. Thus, considerable rehearsal as well as interpretive narration of memories may occur both at the time of trauma and during subsequent recollections.

Sometimes, in contrast, there are intentional efforts to effect dissociations and achieve detachment or distance from a trauma. In this respect, the significance of encoding-retrieval interactions (Jacoby, 1988) in what we usually observe as episodic memory is important. By blunting somatic responses or selectively avoiding attending to them, one may escape cognitive associations to which such responses would be naturally tied. Yet, when the self does for some reason focus attention on them, somatic responses may point the way to more specific, and possibly retrievable, conscious memories.

The psychobiological underpinnings of such posttraumatic responses as hyperarousal and numbing suggest specific avenues for research. Unfortunately, studies of psychophysiological changes in PTSD have not yet been systematically related to symptoms like amnesia and intrusive recollections. The research that does exist is nevertheless highly suggestive.

One study has provided tantalizing evidence that extreme stress may result in physical changes in neural structures known to be important to memory. An investigation employing MRI (magnetic resonance imaging) measurements found an 8.0 percent smaller right hippocampal volume in PTSD patients in relation to comparison subjects (Bremner et al., 1995). These findings persisted after controlling for alcohol and drug abuse; although they may represent a premorbid risk factor for PTSD, it is also quite possible that they are an outcome of psychophysiological events, such as kindling and changes in neurotransmitter release associated with traumatic stress. While not conclusive, these data are thus consistent with those reported following specific damage to the hippocampus, a structure recognized to be significant in memory formation.

One problem with studies attempting to relate memory function and neural or psychophysiological responses lies in the measures of memory typically chosen. Standardized tests of memory, such as the Wechsler Memory Scale, tap into general features of short- and long-term memory, but do not reveal much about individual anomalies such as repetitive flashbacks. Clearly, it is misleading to view deficits on such tests simply in terms of loss of memory function. Victims of PTSD typically remember too much too vividly as well as too little too vaguely. It may well be, in fact, that the persistence of intrusive memories is a distractor that interferes with attention to new information or with the formation of new memories. To the extent that this is true, at least some observations of memory deficits may be artifactual.

Sleep Disturbances, PTSD, and Memory

In my dreams, I run from water all the time, all the time. The whole thing just happens over and over again. . . . (Buffalo Creek survivor, in Erikson, 1976, pp. 143-144).

My daughter, who was four years old at the time of the flood, has really had a time . . . We have to sleep with her because she tries to run out and tries to climb the walls. (Buffalo Creek survivor, Erikson, 1976, p. 237)

Sigmund W. . . . insists that after coming to America in 1948, he put his [concentration] camp experiences in a time capsule and decided not to think about them. . . . Yet, he admits, his wife tells him that for the first *ten* years of their life together, he woke up *every night* screaming. (Langer, 1991, p. 142)

The repetitive reexperiencing characteristic of PTSD includes not only daytime recollections and flashbacks but also vivid dreams and sleep disturbances in which victims behave as if enacting terrifying experiences. Patients with chronic, combat-related PTSD also complain of recurrent awakenings and excessive body movement during sleep; aroused states and behaviors intrude into states of diminished arousal (Mellman, Kulik-Bell, Ashlock, & Nolan, 1995). Difficulties in maintaining nighttime sleep may contribute to daytime symptoms, such as irritability and poor concentration.

These disrupted sleep patterns may be, from an evolutionary standpoint, among the oldest and most basic features of the trauma response. Sleep cycles are one aspect of the biorhythms that characterize normal adaptation. Periods of heightened activity typically alternate with periods of recuperative rest. Sometimes, however, rest, even when needed, can be dangerous. An adaptive solution to the need for continuous monitoring of the external world is the evolution of sleep states that include periods of increased alerting as well as reduced quiescence. REM cycles have been interpreted as an instance of such continuous alerting (Ross, Ball, Sullivan, & Caroff, 1989).

Ross and his colleagues (1989) have suggested that the central nervous system mechanisms involved in PTSD are related to biological disruptions of normal sleep patterns, particularly states of REM sleep. This sleep pattern is characterized by a desynchronized EEG similar to that of waking, although it is distinguished from waking arousal by an absence of muscle tone and may represent a state of continuous alerting with obvious adaptive advantages in animals as well as humans.

Ironically, in patients with chronic delayed posttraumatic stress disorder, the threshold of arousal from sleep seems to be increased (Schoen, Kramer, & Kinney, 1984). While, in comparison to normal subjects, they have more physiological systems, especially respiratory and motor, activated in REM sleep during the first part of the night, they report less awareness of the source of the arousal (Kinney & Kramer, 1984). Kramer (1990) concludes that such traumatized subjects are vigilant to internal rather than external stimuli. A once-external threat has been internalized and the memory of it has become a focus that preempts attention.

The disruption of normal sleep patterns may have direct but complicated effects on memory. On the one hand, flashbacks and nightmares are memorable replays that may reinforce recollections of original trauma; they can be viewed as uncontrollable forms of rehearsal. On the other hand, some research indicates that normal sleep patterns may be intimately involved in the consolidation of the memory trace itself (Badia, 1990; Horne, 1988). To the extent that normal sleep is required for the consolidation of long-term memories, sleep deprivation and disruption may result in structural memory deficits.

Although the results of sleep studies are inconsistent, there is substantial evidence that veterans suffering from PTSD have disordered patterns of REM sleep. Data from pharmacological studies support the hypothesis that a reduction in REM sleep is therapeutic in cases of PTSD (Ross et al., 1989). Sleep disturbances have also been found to be characteristic of Holocaust survivors, even forty-five years after the end of the war (Rosen et al., 1991). The severity and profile of sleep problems distinguished the survivor group in this study from a group of the elderly depressed and from healthy subjects. Sleep problems were also related to the degree of trauma; the group of survivors who reported frequent nightmares had spent comparatively more time in concentration camps.

The impact of disturbed sleep patterns on memory is complicated by the fact that flashbacks and nightmares are themselves so traumatic that they sometimes lead to deliberate but equally dysfunctional forms of avoidance, such as the abuse of alcohol and drugs. Studies of PTSD and memory need to control for any such effects as well as for such obvious confounding variables as head injury.

BEYOND PTSD:
COMPLEX PATTERNS OF COPING

The uncontrollable, sometimes seemingly automatic responses to trauma that are a definitive aspect of PTSD are complicated by a host of responses related to the prior history and personality of the survivor. Both awareness that something terrible has happened and awareness of how one has been affected by it must be integrated subsequent to trauma. Such integrations can severely tax the adaptive capabilities of the individual, particularly if integration was precarious or incomplete to begin with. Traumatized children, especially those repetitively traumatized, may never achieve stable integrations of important mental organizations, such as those involved in the consolidation of a stable identity. They may, instead, develop fragmentary patterns of integration, such as dissociated identity constellations. Even adults who were previously well adapted can, in the wake of extreme traumas, feel estranged from the self that used to be.

Some deliberate avoidance strategies, such as attempts to ensure that one never reencounters a painful external reminder, can profoundly alter many aspects of the survivor's life. Survivors often move away from the scene of the trauma and attempt to divest themselves of all reminders. They may break social ties with others who know about, and thus remind them of, the trauma. They may adopt a radically new style of living or even deliberately construct a new identity.

Life changes can have complicated effects on memory. One who never revisits a painful scene escapes being repetitively overwhelmed by it but, at the same time, loses the opportunity to correct mistaken views of it. In a study of Holocaust survivors, for example (Mazor et al., 1990), it was reported that the most helpful coping mechanism immediately after the war was psychic numbing. The pragmatic tasks of building a new life helped survivors focus away from the traumatic past. It was only much later, after the new life had been created, that they stopped fighting memories and attempted to become reconnected with the previously dissociated past.

Some deliberate avoidance strategies are designed to directly moderate the psychobiology of continuing posttraumatic symptoms. As automatic numbing wears off or becomes an unreliable protector, survivors may seek to anesthetize themselves by chemical substances. In addition to street drugs and alcohol, many develop dependencies on medications prescribed to help them cope with some aspect of trauma, such as sleeping medications or tranquilizers. The effects of substance abuse on memory vary with the chemical involved.

Dissociation as an immediate response to trauma can subsequently be employed as a habitual coping mechanism. Dissociation functions as a buffer against overwhelming emotions and may have profound effects on memory, compartmentalizing traumatic memories and fostering narrative accounts that emphasize or delete particular details of the trauma. Individuals prone to dissociation may avoid normal responses to trauma that would be adaptive or restorative, such as grieving for a lost loved one or anger at an assailant. Deliberate avoidance may extend not only to external cues but also to any internal ones that might stimulate recall. When recollections spring to mind, they may be immediately countered by distracting thoughts or behavior. Because rehearsals are systematically nipped in the bud, certain memories may never be consolidated.

The most extreme dissociative responses are employed by individuals who develop dissociative identity disorder (multiple personality disorder).

In such individuals, distinct alter personality configurations may remember and respond to particular traumas for which other alters are amnesic (Putnam, 1989; Waites, 1993.)

The Divided Self

I am just not the same person I was before. . . . (Buffalo Creek survivor, in Erikson, 1976, p. 136)

I felt like all the clocks in the world stopped and time went back to the beginning. All of us had to start all over again. It was like I was a new me. (Willie Fryer, in Cottle, 1980, p. 36)

The uncontrollable stress typical of traumatic events disrupts coping systems and integrative processes, producing extensive physical, psychological, and behavioral disorganization. This disorganization, which may persist long after the traumatic precipitant passes, has profound effects on self-perception, self-concept, and self-esteem. It may contribute to feelings of helplessness and hopelessness and a sense that the old self has been irretrievably lost.

Disorganization is usually followed by attempts to repair the damage and reinstate integration. How one relates to the past has a powerful effect on the outcome of such attempts. Continual confrontations with the trauma may retraumatize the individual, producing prolonged states of helplessness and disorganization. Refusing to confront the past, in contrast, may result in encapsulating or dissociating it. The result may be an apparent integration that is continually threatened by the breakthough of dissociated ideas or feelings and the disorganizing effects of such breakthroughs.

Sometimes the memory that divides the self is a single overwhelming trauma. Stable recovery involves a gradual reorganization of the self that acknowledges the trauma and its impact but is sufficiently distanced from it to avoid being overwhelmed by retraumatizing reactions. Many individuals manage this recovery on their own or with the help of a reliable support system. Others cannot. Or they manage in ways that cause new problems.

The reorganizations instituted in the wake of trauma may differ radically from prior ones. Sometimes a recovering individual feels like and appears to others, as well as the self, to be a "new person." The traumatized individual may be dismayed to remember two distinct versions of existence, one in which life was normal and the self felt in control, another in which nothing was normal and the self felt miserable and out of control. If the dividing line between these two modes of existence—normal life and a traumatic event or series of events—is clearly recalled, the traumatic moment and the posttraumatic state may be interpreted as a kind of death and resurrection. The new identity may even be set apart from the old by being given a new name.

Consider the life of Fyodor Dostoevsky. When he was 28, he was arrested for illegal political activity and sentenced to die. The preliminaries of the execution were actually carried out. At the last minute, as he stood on the scaffold believing himself minutes away from death, the sentence was commuted and he was taken to prison.

Dostoevsky experienced his reprieve as a rebirth. This view of it was no mere metaphor; it was based on a powerful sense of mystical transformation. Though his prison experiences, which he compared to living in a coffin, were dehumanizing, he was able to hold onto the sense of hope and transcendence that had followed his brush with death on the scaffold. He spent the rest of his life integrating both that encounter with death and his subsequent transformation; it became a recurring theme in his greatest literary creations (Mochulsky, 1967).

The psychological relation between trauma and transformation is recognized in numerous social rituals. It is institutionalized in the specified "ordeals" of initiation rites (Van Gennep, 1960). In any instance when suffering is rationalized as a "test," survival may be viewed as passing an exam or graduating to a higher rank.

Conversion and rebirth, a well-recognized psychological phenomenon, does not necessarily result from trauma; it may instead represent a solution to a longstanding internal or social conflict. The conversion experience resolves the question of ambivalence about who to be with a firm declaration: the old self is dead. In such instances, the transformation is often cast in a positive, even idealized, light, and the new self is asserted to be in some important respect "better."

Conversion experiences are a common aspect of integration into new social groups, such as religious sects. In some societies, they are a recognized part of initiation rites that permit the entry of the initiate into some special category—those recognized as "adult," those privileged to special kinds of knowledge and power, etc. Whether one is "flying up" as a Girl Scout brownie, or advancing to a higher degree in a male secret society, or being admitted into an elite priesthood, such rites formalize and substantiate the idea of personal transformation. Initiation rites commonly include real or symbolic ordeals that enact trauma or death and transcendence.

The emphasis on traumatic incidents as opportunities for transformation can facilitate posttraumatic adaptations in some people. Adversity sometimes does bring out the best in people, and focusing on one's strengths can sometimes be an important positive step toward recovery. But this focus can also become an escape from dissociated pieces of personal history. It can distort memories of trauma, effectively erasing details that do not confirm the idea that the experience was helpful or positively transformative.

Unfortunately, too, the notion that survival can be strengthening easily becomes a rationalization for minimizing the impact of trauma or refusing help to victims. It can even be used as a transparent rationalization for inflicting pain. In such instances, individual distortions of memory are compounded by social ones: "That didn't really hurt, did it?"

Such rationalizations are an example of how even the most destructive traumas can be altered by representational and self-referential processes. Like other aspects of experience, trauma is schematized in terms of social categories. One of the challenges of trauma, in fact, is to locate such categories.

SOCIAL DISCONNECTION

I couldn't remember nobody. I didn't want nobody around me. I didn't want nobody to speak to me or even to look at me. I wanted nobody even ten miles around me to call my name. (Buffalo Creek survivor, quoted in Erikson, 1976, p. 217)

I had to stop talking. (Angelou, 1970, p. 73)

The articulation of the self is an ongoing social phenomenon, mediated not only by what the individual does but also by dialogues and interactional patterns. Trauma, too, even if restricted to one individual, always occurs in a social context. When the context is supportive, the individual may maximize personal resources for recovery. But even in a supportive context, the traumatized individual may experience a rupture in the fabric of social connectedness.

Social disconnection decontextualizes traumatic memory. The terrible thing that happened simply does not fit anywhere and, when confronted, may contribute to a sense that the one who remembers is a misfit. And when the community itself is damaged by trauma, it cannot continue to function reliably as an arbiter of memory and reality. It cannot foster the continuance of habits and rituals that tend to preserve memory. It cannot validate the value of remembering.

Sometimes the breach between self and other is effected by the impact of psychobiological posttraumatic symptoms on social integration. Trauma can disinhibit social controls and precipitate antisocial behaviors — rage, aggressive outbursts, revengeful attitudes — that lead others to be wary around the victim. Then, too, trauma-induced changes may be obvious to others, who begin to treat the survivor differently; the survivor becomes a stranger to other people as well as himself.

Posttraumatic adaptations also typically include increased defensiveness, which may isolate the survivor from social contact. And finally, there is simply the issue of trust. Trauma is typically experienced as a fundamental breakdown in the protective function of the social milieu.

Some of these difficulties are reflected in the inability of survivors to communicate about the trauma. What happened may be indescribable and inexpressible. Langer (1991) describes the chronic frustration of Holocaust survivors, who doubt the audience's ability to comprehend their testimony. Current narrative structures and the normal context of *now* cannot contain and communicate the abnormal *then*. Survivors often describe their own difficulty in believing their own stories, in spite of the undeniable accuracy of their accounts.

Even when it is possible to communicate, communicating may feel unsafe. Speaking may trigger flashbacks and other posttraumatic reactions in the victim. It may cause the audience to withdraw in discomfort or horror. It may lead to actual admonitions — well-meaning or malevolent — to keep silent.

Silencing of victims, of course, is a common sequel to deliberate acts of abuse or violence. Maya Angelou (1970) describes how in childhood, following a violent rape and the subsequent death of the perpetrator, she stopped talking to everyone except her beloved brother, Bailey. The perpetrator had commanded her to keep silent, and she feared her failure to do so had caused his death: "if I talked to anyone else, that person might die too" (p. 73).

Even those who had no part in the creation of a trauma may attempt to escape being confronted with it. Confrontation, especially if vividly experienced, can lead to vicarious traumatization. Acknowledging the impact of trauma may lead to uncomfortable, though irrational, feelings of helplessness or guilt that one did not prevent it.

All these variables may result in a disruption of dialogue between the survivor and others. Sometimes, however, the disruption is more comprehensive. Sometimes a trauma is a collective experience that destroys a whole community physically and/or psychologically. When this happens, there may, literally, be no one to pick up the pieces (Erikson, 1976).

The destruction of community that occurs in the wake of natural disasters or war is an added shock that impedes recovery from other individual shocks. As Erikson (1976) emphasizes, one of the functions of culture is to form a protective barrier between the individual and certain harsh realities. In this sense, culture is an extension of the personal "stimulus barrier" (Freud, 1920). It helps protect psychic reality by making physical reality bearable.

All these dislocations and disruptions impinge on memory. The inability to articulate traumatic experience deprives the self of those durable verbal structures so fundamental to personal memory. Silencing, too, prevents such structuralization and, in addition, inhibits all rehearsals that might stabilize memory.

When silence or an accurate account is replaced by an alternative narrative, this story may effectively supplant the accurate one. Yet the degree to which alternative narratives distort or replace original responses varies. Children may be especially vulnerable to suggested distortions, but there are individual differences in suggestibility in children as well as in adults.

In a study of five-year-old children's reactions to inoculations, for example, suggestive feedback about how much the shot hurt did not influence their reports about how they acted a week later. But a second study, which examined the influence of multiple suggestive interviews many months after the inoculation, found some of the children susceptible to the influence of misleading information about such variables as the gender of the person who administered the shot. Children who were suggestible in this experiment took longer to calm after the initial inoculation than children who resisted suggestions, indicating that stress may be one of the factors that makes individuals vulnerable to influence (Bruck, Ceci, Francoeur, & Barr, 1995).

Against these distorting or disruptive influences, however, there are powerful social as well as individual motives to foster the persistence of accurate memory. In this respect, the importance of memory for social as well as intrapsychic integration frequently outweighs obstacles to remembering. The amending of memory that goes on in adult life is often not simply an unconscious and self-serving revision of the past, but an active search for facts and authenticity.

This need to remember in spite of the wish to forget is sometimes an attempt to restore social connections. As was observed in one study of Holocaust survivors, "The survivors' memories become a heritage that they leave to the following generations as well as a memorial to their lost families . . . " (Mazor et al., 1990).

POSTTRAUMATIC REMEMBERING

The recollection of trauma can be a sudden unwanted intrusion or a slowly achieved reconstruction. It may involve mysterious bodily feelings, inexplicable emotions, or disconnected images. It may be automatic and uncontrollable or intentional and careful. It may be experienced as self-destructive or self-saving. Because of the nature of trauma responses, it is often fragmentary and inconsistent. Integrating such memory into a coherent life story usually requires patience and effort.

Often, particularly immediately following trauma, the integrative effort seems too much to manage. The overwhelmed victim craves respite, oblivion. The trauma is like a foreign body, a not-me experience that the self wants to throw off. Forgetting is felt to be a blessing rather than a problem. Comfortable forgetting is seldom easily managed, however. Even when there are amnesias or loss of memory for details of an experience, recollections may intrude unbidden. Even when the waking self forgets, the sleeping self may be overwhelmed by remembering. And the sense that the integrity of the self has been compromised is a powerful factor motivating attempts to remember and to make sense of what one remembers.

The wish to remember often collides not only with the wish to forget but also with the lack of established modes for thinking about a shocking, unusual, indescribable event. In the absence of available categories for describing and communicating, the trauma becomes harder to grasp and hold onto; no wonder it sometimes slips from conscious memory like a bad dream.

When forgetting cannot be reliably or consistently managed following trauma, self-protective defenses are usually instituted. The deliberate strategies of avoidance sometimes developed to seal off intrusions can result in the dissociation of the traumatized self. The division of the self before and after trauma, however, does not necessarily involve a conscious recollection of the traumatic moment or any social acknowledgment of it at all. In some instances, the trauma itself fades from conscious, self-referential memory and only contrasting states of being remain in view. The perplexed individual may then complain, "I don't know why, but I am just not myself" or "I don't know what's wrong, but nothing works right anymore." Even this degree of self-awareness may be missing; the report that something has changed may come only from other people.

Yet human beings value conscious memory. Being able to remember is commonly perceived as a form of control; not being able to remember can make one feel out of control, continually retraumatized by one's own limitations. And memory is vital to the integrity of the self. When an awareness that one is different is disconnected from important memories that might explain why, the self may seem mysteriously and uncomfortably alien. When self-defining contexts change, the self may become almost unrecognizable. This self-alienation has deep roots in the relation between the self and its memories. Remembering, which is always an important component of identity development and consolidation, has become a potentially painful and disruptive process.

Sometimes two sets of memories — "before" and "after" — just do not fit well together. It is easier to keep them separated than to attempt to integrate them. This separation can be enhanced by focusing on the differences between the way things used to be and the way they are now. It can be facilitated by special narratives that describe and rationalize change as a meaningful event rather than a disorganizing catastrophe.

Asserting that everything has changed and that one is completely different may simply provide reassurance that the trauma is all over, a part of ancient history. The past as finished history may be continually invoked to rationalize present-day existence or to excuse current problems and failings. Or it may be acknowledged to magically reinforce the illusion that "all that horror is in the past and can never hurt me again."

Conditioned Responses and Flashbacks

Every time it rains, every time it storms, I just can't take it. I walk the floor. I get so nervous I break out in a rash. (Buffalo Creek survivor, quoted in Erikson, 1976, p. 143)

I feel my head is filled with garbage: all these images, you know, and sounds, and my nostrils are filled with the stench of burning flesh. And it's . . . you can't excise it, it's like—like there's another skin beneath this skin and that skin is called Auschwitz, and you cannot shed it, you know. . . . And it's a constant accompaniment. (Holocaust survivor, in Langer, 1991, p. 53)

Conditioned somatic responses are among the most persistent form of posttraumatic remembering. Whether they are verbalized or narrated depends on the specifics of the traumatic context and the capabilities of the victim at the time. Before a child has language to describe external events or to label her own emotions, fear may be conditioned as a state of autonomic arousal and somatic tension. And even in people who can verbalize and explain, self-referential narratives may be suppressed or disconnected from somatic responses.

Sensory images originally associated with trauma can recur with hallucinatory intensity as flashbacks. Such flashbacks may happen spontaneously, in the absence of discernible cues, but are often cued by specific reminders (McCaffrey, Lorig, Pendrey, McCutcheon, & Garrett, 1993). Somatic and behavioral responses, too, may subsequently be triggered by sensory cues that seemingly lack context or meaning. An odor associated with fear or pain may precipitate panic. Having one's body touched a certain way may elicit flight tendencies. In spite of their effects on behavior, these decontextualized responses may be puzzling to the individual who experiences but does not understand them. They are likely to be construed as symptoms of some mysterious malady; sometimes they will motivate the person to seek help.

Conditioned avoidance may function as an anticipatory defense that prevents the individual from coming in contact with stimuli that might be frightening or painful. Like other reflexive responses, avoidance patterns may have no conscious context. If they succeed in protecting the individual from frightening or painful encounters, they may be scarcely noticed at all or considered symptomatic of any problem.

Since lack of understanding can in itself be troubling to human beings, insight into the origins of symptoms can help the self to feel more in control. For this reason, although the amelioration of symptoms through such techniques as desensitization or medication is useful in posttraumatic therapy, insight is typically a primary goal. By establishing meaningful explanations for perplexing behaviors, insight can reassure the individual that he or she is not crazy. By interpolating planned actions into automatic and unconscious sequences of behavior, it can help the individual gain more effective control over the real world, as well as over her own symptoms. And by recontextualizing disconnected or dissociated behaviors, insight can facilitate internal coherence and self-consistency. Understanding avoidance patterns, in particular, can help an individual confront situations that are not really dangerous or that are no longer a threat to the integrity of the self. A once-constricted self can feel freed. The world may become a larger, more possible place.

Understanding conditioned responses does not necessarily lead to their extinction, however. Sometimes they can best be extinguished by desensitization: repeated, carefully titrated reexposures that have a benign rather than a traumatic outcome. In psychotherapy, one role of insight is sometimes simply to help the individual seek out or tolerate such reexposures.

When mysterious presenting symptoms, such as somatic symptoms that have been shown to have no basis in physical illness or injury, are approached as memories of trauma, it is important to keep in mind that sensory and somatic memories are not necessarily cryptically encoded symbols. Although they may in some instances be dissociated from narratives with which they were once connected, they have sometimes been formed in isolation from self-referential and narrative processes. Insight, in such cases, involves placing them in a new context. Or, from another perspective, as once-isolated somatic memories are integrated, the self is organized in a new context.

Reenactment

Doctor: You see, her eyes are open.
Gentlewoman: Aye, but their sense is shut.
Doctor: What is it she does now? Look how she rubs her hands.
Lady Macbeth: Out, damned spot! Out, I say!
— Shakespeare, *Macbeth*, Act V, Scene 1

In *Macbeth*, Shakespeare, ever a shrewd observer of human nature, created a scene in which Lady Macbeth, a principal instigator of the assassination that brought her husband to the throne, reenacts her shocked response to the bloody murder. The doctor who attends her is quite familiar with such posttraumatic symptoms. The dramatization is effective because the audience, too, easily recognizes Lady Macbeth's sleepwalking as a telltale replay of an actual event rather than the fantastic fabrication of a deranged mind.

Shakespeare also exploited the relation between enactment and trauma in *Hamlet*. "The play's the thing/ Wherein we'll catch the conscience of the king," Hamlet muses as he plans to dramatize a scenario depicting the murder of his father. In this instance, of course, the enactment is not an unconscious symptom, but a deliberate ploy. Yet it is planned for the express purpose of triggering involuntary symptomatic responses in the king that might confirm Hamlet's suspicions of his guilt.

In the twentieth century, involuntary behavioral enactments are a recognized symptom of posttraumatic stress disorder. They are often clearly a form of remembering. And yet they are not necessarily perceived as such, either by the individual who reenacts or by observers, unless the traumatic context embedding them is known. In victims of chronic posttraumatic stress disorder, as in Lady Macbeth, reenactment may occur in sleep or in an altered state of consciousness, may appear completely cut off from any meaningful narrative or conscious understanding, and may be forgotten upon waking. Even when they occur in the waking state, reenactments, like flashbacks and somatic symptoms, may be disconnected from internal narratives or insight. Thus, even though they dramatically replay the traumatic event for others, the victim remains, in effect, blind and deaf to it. And unless the observer knows what is being portrayed, the reenactment may seem puzzling, even bizarre.

As a replay of trauma, reenactment is variably related to imagery and bodily experience. At the moment of reenactment, the traumatized individual, even if unconscious, may experience vivid intrusive imagery that seems to place her or him right back in the original situation. The enactment behavior is then perceived as appropriate to an actual crisis — Lady Macbeth saw the king's blood on her hands and tried over and over to wash it off.

The somatic responses associated with reenactments, such as autonomic arousal or muscular tensing, are sometimes explicable as a conditioned response to traumatic stimuli. But these are commonly elaborated by symbolic representational processes, even though symbolic representations may be so disguised that the individual has no insight into their meaning. For example, reenactment may be retained in memory as a special form of nonverbal information-processing. As such, it may reflect the information processing patterns typical of particular developmental stages or regressive reactions that reinstate stage-specific patterns. Children in what Piaget termed the sensorimotor stage, for example, apprehend and represent the world by actively engaging it. Only after language has developed can experience be encoded in the accepted and readily communicated schemas of the culture.

Eth and Pynoos (1985) describe a two-year-old boy who watched his mother murdered. A year later, after he acquired language, he vividly described the horrific event. Terr (1985) describes detailed remembrances in a fifteen-year-old girl who at age two and a half, suffered a crushed leg when a forklift fell on her. The behavior of another girl, two years old, who jabbed her finger into the "vagina" of a doll immediately on encountering it and smothered small dolls with heavier ones, also impressed Terr with the precision of enacted, though nonverbal, memories.

After the development of language, reenactment is in some instances an attempt to bridge the distressing but unarticulated gap between nonverbal or incomprehensible experiences and verbal or narrative forms. Traumatic incidents are sometimes difficult to label or schematize, not easily referable to existing modes of thought. In the absence of words, people commonly revert to gestural forms of representation. Enactments of traumatic events may involve an attempt to find a mode of communication and expression. The disruption of integration that commonly accompanies trauma may make it difficult to connect such enactments with other forms of representation, such as narrative discourse.

In other instances, reenactment may be a deliberate retreat from words. Refusing to speak of a terrible event is one way of attempting to control one's responses to it or to avoid memories associated with it. When memory and the associated emotional responses persist, however, it is not always easy to keep still and quiet. Increased autonomic arousal and the need to find some behavioral outlet for powerful, even violent feelings incites action.

The repetitive behavior that characterizes reenactments sometimes seems clearly associated with attempts at mastery. Children commonly play out repetitive scenarios of traumatic events, sometimes changing details to make the event more palatable (Eth & Pynoos, 1985; Terr, 1990, 1994). Rescue scenarios, in which the child intervenes to prevent a horrendous event, such as the shooting of a parent, are a case in point.

Narrative Constructions

One way of recovering from the disorganizing effects of trauma and reasserting control is through the construction of narratives that describe or deny the disturbing events. These narratives may be cut off from other forms of remembering, or may be to some extent integrated with them. A play scenario that reenacts a traumatic event, for example, may be accompanied by an ongoing narrative account. Such accounts may or may not be consciously self-referential; sometimes the person who invents them insists that the reenactment is just a story or that it depicts something that happened to another person.

Narratives are not necessarily communicated to others. Sometimes they remain private. Sharing stories about a trauma, however, may make it more bearable, more readily integrated into the rest of one's life. It also helps overcome the socially isolating aspects of trauma. Following the assassination of President Kennedy, for example, people shared over and over their memories of what they were doing and what they saw and how they interpreted the event. Sharing stories helped relieve tensions and overcome the socially isolating effects of the trauma. But it did not necessarily make for more accurate memories (Brown & Kulik, 1977; Neisser, 1982b).

Sharing a story invites input from others that may shape not only the structure of the narrative but also the memory underlying it. Whether others are responsible for the events in question or just attempting to cope with it themselves, a personal story may elicit dialogues or directives that modify the account. The end result is often a collective rather than an individual memory. This social transformation is not necessarily the result of any deliberate attempts at distortion; it is simply a result of the tendency of people to seek social confirmation and to conform to social expectations.

In some cases, of course, narratives are directly influenced by people who encourage or discourage particular constructions for motives of their own. These influences may be ruthlessly self-serving, as when a perpetrator of sexual assault urges or enforces secrecy in a victim, or well-meaning but misguided, as when an overzealous investigator asks leading questions of a potential courtroom witness. But they can also derive from less obvious motives. Widespread social tendencies to minimize the impact of trauma, to blame victims, and to avoid reminders of one's own helplessness — or just to "help" the victim "get over it" — also lead to explicit as well as subtle attempts to shape survivor narratives.

The effects of posttraumatic narrative on memory, like the general effects of narrative, are variable and complicated. On the one hand, an accurate narrative contributes to accurate recall by facilitating rehearsal and by organizing memory. On the other, an inaccurate narrative may distort recall. And when there is an intentional attempt to distort recall, a suggested narrative can provide confusing post-event information that greatly compromises the credibility of the victim.

The process of narrative construction imposes schematic and sequential forms of organization that constitute a kind of "removal" of memory from the immediacies of imagery and emotion that accompanied the original experience. Although this detachment is not necessarily complete or reliable — telling may itself call up images and feelings — it may serve a defensive function. Narration may help objectify and, in some sense, externalize a memory, making it easier to understand and cope with. Thus, like other forms of recollection, narration may facilitate or interfere with an accurate account of past events. It may augment or diminish a sense of personal control. It may enhance self integration or social integration or it may interfere with integration.

In any case, trauma can complicate memory in ways that compound such influences as the transformation of episodic into semantic memory or the organizing effects of schemas and scripts. In order to make sense of such effects it is necessary to consider not only the nature of memory in general but also the specific impact of trauma.

DIVERGENT NARRATIVES AND ALTERNATE SELVES

You got two very different lives you got to work with at the same time, and nobody but you can say which is the best one, or which is the real one. . . . You got to, like, control these two lives, 'specially the one on the inside before it turns inside out and you don't know whether your inside one is the real one and the outside is just faking your life to everybody. (Tyrone Morgan, in Cottle, 1980, p. 202)

At any stage of posttraumatic adaptation, recollection should be distinguished from disclosure. Clearly remembered traumas are kept secret for any number of reasons. The self may be ashamed to talk about what happened, viewing the incident as a painful reflection on personal competence and responsibility. One may feel guilty for real or imagined failings. Or the events may have produced strange sensations or reactions that cannot be communicated.

Some refusals to disclose painful events are based on attempts to protect other people from them. The self may fear traumatizing an audience or eliciting special but unwanted treatment from others, such as medical attention. Or one may fear judgmental responses from others, such as accusations or devaluations. In some instances, too, the traumatized self simply fears that other people will deny or refuse to acknowledge the significance of terrible events, producing frustration or rage in the discounted victim.

Refusal to talk about a trauma may have nothing to do with memory; sometimes it is just the hiding of a secret. Many secrets, of course, are socially orchestrated. A trauma victim may be silenced by covert or overt threats or intimidation, an expectable accompaniment to intentionally inflicted abuse. But even accounts of accidental occurrences may be silenced by other people who have their own reasons for avoiding confrontations. In either case, secrets can affect memory. They direct attention to particular events and away from others, they discourage rehearsal, and sometimes they structure divergent narrative accounts of the same event that begin to compete in memory with veridical recollections.

Posttraumatic accommodations that include hiding a secret story from an "official" one require continual vigilance; keeping the stories straight can be a demanding task, particularly if there are several audiences and variable contexts for retelling. Dissociative reactions can facilitate the sequestering of secrets by shifting the focus of attention from narratives of traumatic responses and recollections to less troubling accounts. The elaboration of divergent narratives is thus one way in which dissociative responses that are initially automatic can be intentionally exploited in posttraumatic accommodations.

Dissociative disconnections facilitate keeping the story straight, in the sense that they can facilitate consistency *within* a given story. Inconsistencies *between* stories can be quite striking, however. One function of dissociative coping is to help the individual tolerate such inconsistencies without undue anxiety. However, when inconsistencies interfere with everyday coping, the defensive response may turn out to be as maladaptive as the anxiety itself. Other people, observing such inconsistencies, may be not only intolerant but also punitive. Consequently, the individual who dissociates disparate stories is often accused of lying.

Dissociated secrets are sometimes deeply and completely hidden from the self for long periods. When they break through into consciousness, they are sometimes viewed as repressed memories that have been recovered. Yet dissociation as a cognitive mechanism is distinct from repression. Dissociation is not simply a matter of forgetting; it typically involves the disconnection or lack of integration of responses at several levels of information-processing. Many dissociated memories were once clearly in consciousness but became inaccessible after intentional attempts to exclude them from awareness. Even after they were "forgotten," the inaccessibility of such memories was not necessarily complete; it may have varied from one time or one social context to another.

Divergent narratives are sometimes used to construct dissociated identities. Again, automatic trauma responses may be incorporated into intentional defensive patterns. Trance, for example, the internal context in which dissociated identity configurations are typically elaborated (Putnam, 1989), may be an almost reflexive response to trauma in susceptible people. Nevertheless, some individuals can learn to deliberately induce trance states as a means of coping with anxiety (Waites, 1993).

TRAUMA AND PERSONAL HISTORY

At any point in life, the search for personal history is complicated not only by immediate responses to trauma, such as flashbacks or posttraumatic amnesias, but also by the way initial responses have been incorporated over time into posttraumatic accommodations. In childhood, these posttraumatic developments will be a function of the coping mechanisms available to the child at a given stage as well as of external variables, such as social support or social orchestrations of memory.

A pragmatic focus on the integrative function of memory can be a useful guide to this search. Isolated memories are like pieces of a puzzle. Unless they make sense, they cannot be incorporated into meaningful stories about significant events. When they persist in unnarrated forms, they are often experienced as symptoms rather than components of a cohesive identity. Yet the very vividness of persisting but perplexing memory fragments motivates individuals to continually try to make sense of them, to construct meaningful stories that will explain or interpret them to the self as well as to other people.

In making sense of such memories, then, it becomes evident that meaning is as important to many people as veridicality. To be sure, it *is* important to know that a remembered event is not just a fantasy. Confirming that and being validated in the confirmation is important to one's sense of reality and personal competence. Confronting the reality of a trauma is also necessary to understanding why it happened and, if possible, to avoiding repetitions. Differentiating events over which one has no control from controllable ones is a very consequential aspect of human adaptation.

But understanding the reality and significance of trauma is not merely a matter of fact-finding or pragmatic coping. In order to know oneself in the present, it is necessary to make contact with who one used to be. In this endeavor, the integration of memory is closely allied with the integration of differing versions of the self. Images and narratives, secrets and symptoms all have a part to play in self-definition. In the long run, wholeness is not just a matter of re-collecting the pieces, but of re-membering them in a unified context, an integrated self.

PART II
Evasions and Distortions

CHAPTER 7

The Subversion of Memory

Have you ever seen a foreign newspaper which passed through Russian censorship at the frontier? Words, whole clauses and sentences are blacked out so that the rest becomes unintelligible. A *Russian censorship* of that kind comes about in psychoses and produces the apparently meaningless *deliria*.

— Sigmund Freud to Wilhelm Fliess, Dec. 22, 1897, in Masson, 1985, p. 289

I began to notice what appeared to be a pattern in the omissions made by Anna Freud in the original abridged edition [of the correspondence between Freud and Fliess]. In the letters written after September 1897 (when Freud was supposed to have given up his "seduction" theory) all the case histories dealing with sexual seduction of children were excised.

— Jeffrey Masson, 1984, p. xxix

ALTERING OFFICIAL HISTORY is a time-honored form of social control. Whether the "official" who effects the change is the self, a family member, or an institutional authority, the end result is often a subversion of memory. Two radically different stories about a past event tend to create doubt and conflict. And in a conflict, the official version may triumph simply by virtue of the authoritative manner in which it is presented. The concrete, definite character of written records can seem especially authoritative.

The social programming of memory is sometimes quite systematic. Official stories are stridently and repetitively rehearsed. The effect on memory can be insidious but profound. Something repeated so often comes to be regarded as common knowledge, and when many people believe it, the lone voice of dissent is easily shouted down. Such social dynamics are a mainstay of propaganda.

Where the official story is a product not of added or changed details but of systematic deletions from an original report, the effect may be quite subtle, however. Omissions can be difficult to detect, particularly if the gaps in the story are well rationalized. If the gap is noticed at all, it may be attributed to the original author of the story rather than to the censor who changed something. And without an independent, authoritative standard, an audience or reader has no way of knowing what and how much is missing.

During the cold war, for example, much information about U.S. government surveillance and covert operations was classified, and reports that were finally obtained and inspected often contained so many deletions as to be practically indecipherable (Belfrage, 1994; Weinstein, 1990). The information lost through such deletions may never be subsequently obtainable. Important pieces of social history may be, in effect, erased forever from public memory.

Sometimes, of course, as in the case of the tapes concerning the Watergate break-in altered by Richard Nixon, the truth eventually comes to light. When disclosure occurs only after a long intervening interval, however, as was the case in Masson's (1984) uncovering of suppressed letters from the Freud-Fliess correspondence, the official but incomplete story may have had far-reaching and profound effects that cannot be easily eradicated.

Those who have a stake in official but distorted stories do not always yield to correction. In the wake of his discovery and the publication of the missing statements by Freud, for example, Masson was not hailed by the psychoanalytic establishment as a careful historian. He was, rather, drummed out of official circles by the self-styled protectors of the psychoanalytic tradition (Masson, 1984).

If official records can be so effectively suppressed and altered, it is scarcely surprising that veridical memory as unwritten history is so vulnerable to silencing. Unwanted truths are not simply a threat to the self who knows them, but to other people who do not want to be reminded. Whether the resistance to knowing arises from a wish to idealize a particular authority, as was a common motive of psychoanalysts who guarded the image of Freud, or a wish to avoid personal responsibility or punishment, as is typical of perpetrators of abuse, or simply the desire to avoid confronting terrible events, as occurs in cases of war or natural disaster, the result is often a systematic revision of history. To the extent that veridical memory persists, it is a threat that is actively opposed.

Any story long hidden can be forgotten, in the sense that it is not easily available for recall. But as individuals who have recovered memories long suppressed or dissociated can attest, what has been lost is sometimes possible to find again. Although the imperfections of memory can complicate the process of refinding, they need not be accepted at face value as a facile excuse for denying unpleasant truths.

DENIAL

Denial, whether as an intrapsychic or a social dynamic, is itself one of the most powerful distorting factors in memory. When it occurs at the time an event is originally experienced, it can distort perception. When it occurs later, it can prevent rehearsal of accurate memories or substitute a more palatable story for a painful one. When it occurs much later, it can lead to insistence that, because memory is fallible anyway, what is being recalled simply cannot be trusted.

The subversion of memory is usually selective. Denial need not be wholesale or involve a complete censorship of disturbing information; it can be restricted to a few choice details. Facts can be suppressed, too, by simply minimizing their importance. The sexual abuse of children, for example, has commonly been excused as inconsequential or even touted as beneficial (Armstrong, 1994). When facts are well established and documented, as is the prevalence of abuse in modern life (Sink, 1988), they can simply be disputed as untrue.

Where a disputed story is a matter of memory rather than of record, the personal narrative is especially vulnerable to official or authoritative distortion. Challenged to defend a memory, many people acknowledge the imperfection of their own recollections. And defending one's own version in a dispute may take so much time, energy, and, in court cases, money, that it is easier to acquiesce to a revised story than to stick to the original one. Thus, even if an original encoding or early recollection of an event has been highly veridical, later reports may be amended in memory to conform to socially orchestrated modifications.

Even well-known facts can become the target of systematic denials. Discussing modern attempts to deny the Holocaust, for example, Deborah Lipstadt (1993) describes the mix of truth and outright lies presented to confuse a naive audience, along with several current intellectual trends that contribute to the confusion. It has become fashionable in some intellectual circles, for example, to argue that texts have no fixed meanings, that there is always an alternative interpretation for any story. Such a relativistic point of view easily combines with deliberate distortion to support the idea that one of the best documented horrors of history, the Holocaust, is a debatable story rather than a historical fact.

Sometimes denial is so subtle as to be nearly unnoticeable. Details of disturbing events may be changed just slightly to render them more palatable. Sometimes only the most troublesome piece of evidence is quietly removed from view. Sometimes denial acknowledges what happened but creates a distorted explanation of why, as when victims are blamed for the disasters that befall them. Sometimes denial even denies that it is denying: "Yes, of course, child sexual abuse is rampant and awful to contemplate. But . . . " Any particular accusation made by any particular child against any particular perpetrator is then staunchly disputed as untrue (Armstrong, 1994).

In cases of intentional abuse, denial of responsibility on the part of the perpetrator is a typical part of the subordination and control of the victim. Denial of child sexual abuse, for example, is commonly a double-barreled defense: the victim is lying and, anyway, the abuse was her own fault. Or, the victim made it all up, but sexual contact with adults is something children want and, even if it happens, it's not harmful.

In some circumstances, such as sexual or physical assault, victims are also likely to be blamed for their own suffering. Such reproaches are part of a long tradition of scapegoating females for the violence commonly used to keep them "in line" and to protect male prerogatives (Waites, 1993). Females commonly internalize this tradition, blaming themselves for such uncontrollable traumas as incest, rape, and battering. In doing so, they suffer increased shame and guilt, but may, paradoxically, feel less vulnerable—if they just behave differently, perhaps a recurrence of the trauma can be prevented.

Victim-blaming and/or accusations that the victim is lying constitute explicit assaults on memory. The victim is told that her own accounts of reality are unacceptable distortions and that she will be isolated or ostracized until she revises them to bring them in line with socially approved versions of the truth.

Children, however developed their reality-testing, however veridical their memories, are especially vulnerable to deliberate intimidations. To be ostracized is not merely uncomfortable; when one is dependent on others, it can be dangerous. Safer to change one's story, to reinterpret one's memories, or, if possible, forget.

Memory, like history, sometimes reflects the simple fact that some stories have always been privileged over others. When denial is based on pressures to conform to an "official" story about an event, it helps individuals escape the isolation so often attendant on personal trauma. It offers social support to the victim in exchange for reassurance that the illusions that sustain the culture will not be shattered by unpleasant truths. Social pressures reinforce internal wishes to forget and structure rehearsal and recall to remove from view what is threatening, painful, or just unwanted. Thus, as the audience is shielded, the self is shielded, too. In the long run, denial may be such a comfortable refuge that any attempts to counter it are attacked as more dangerous than the denied events themselves.

The effects of denial on memory can be subtle and insidious. The process by which representations of past events are changed over time can be simple or convoluted. The mind may refuse to recall what it wants to forget by simply veering away from any associated idea. Or, like Freud, it can reinterpret an original experience. It can even manage to remember and forget at the same time.

When a story is intentionally silenced, the imperfection of memory is sometimes a convenient scapegoat for both the narrator and the audience. Denial tends to rationalize forgetting and distortion; who could be expected to have a clear recollection of something that never really happened? Blaming deletions or distortions on imperfections of memory can also function as a useful cover story. The claim "I can't remember" may merely mask a secret one is too intimidated to disclose. A careful investigator will refuse to take the disclaimer at face value.

Denial, it must be reiterated, does not obliterate memory; it reinterprets history. In this reinterpretive process, it changes the context in which veridical memory is embedded, shifting the focus from central facts to peripheral details, from shocked certainty to confused doubt. The end result is a distorted recollection of an original event. When this recollection is inconsistent with other recollections or with nonverbal encodings of a traumatic experience, the result can be quite confusing. A story may be presented, recanted, and reasserted, and the vacillation in itself makes it doubtful.

Sometimes, as in the case of the missing letters from Freud to Fliess, what has been censored is eventually uncovered. When that happens, one may have the feeling that a longstanding puzzle has been solved through the recovery of missing pieces whose existence was long suspected, though hidden. But it may take a very long time for the record to be corrected, and there is no guarantee that it ever will be. For many years, the version of the Freud/Fliess letters edited to conform to the wishes of Anna Freud was received wisdom among psychoanalysts. The importance of actual child sexual abuse in the development of Freudian theory remained, in effect, excluded from the canon of psychoanalytic thought.

REPRESSION

Although psychoanalytic theory for many years systematically deemphasized the effects of actual child abuse on personality development, it nevertheless called attention to the fact that remembering and forgetting are motivated developments. While Ebbinghaus (1885/1913) was plotting forgetting curves in the laboratory and experimental psychologists were focusing on the retention of nonsense syllables, psychoanalysts were attempting to decipher everyday episodic memories as cryptic encodings of meaningful events, such as intrapsychic trauma.

The fact that psychoanalysts have traditionally focused on the psychic nature of trauma has made it sometimes difficult to integrate their work with the scientific study of actual traumatic events. But psychoanalysis does not necessarily preclude such integrations. Many psychoanalysts, particularly those who emphasize the significance of relationships in personality development, have always attempted to uncover and ameliorate the effects of real traumas. From a theoretical standpoint, too, any actual trauma may be interpreted psychoanalytically in terms of the effects on intrapsychic structures. Ulman and Brothers (1988), for example, view trauma as a breach of vital self-sustaining fantasies.

One of the best-known and influential concepts of motivated forgetting is Freud's concept of repression. Yet the very popularity of this idea has led to many misunderstandings about it. Those who attack the veridicality of so-called "recovered memories," for example, often make the concept of repression a linchpin of their argument. The notion seems to be that, by invalidating the Freudian concept, one can invalidate the empirical significance of delayed recall after an intervening period of amnesia. This assumption, of course, is logically untenable. Many investigators who study trauma reactions are not psychoanalytically oriented, and in the literature on trauma reactions the concept of dissociation, which is quite distinct from the concept of repression, is given much more emphasis.

In the context of psychoanalytic theory and therapy, the concept of repression has a specific definition and set of connotations. It does not refer simply to any loss of memory, but to an intrapsychic dynamic though which certain kinds of ideas are systematically excluded from consciousness by a censoring agent, the ego. The material excluded typically involves sexual and aggressive impulses about which the individual feels conflicted. This exclusion is not necessarily either complete or permanent; the ideas that are held in check are constantly pushing for expression. Like a dammed-up river, they can break through the restraining efforts of the ego. When the "return of the repressed" is only partial, the result is a compromise formation, such as a dream image that disguises a forbidden wish. The task facing the psychoanalyst is to observe and decipher such disguised expressions. By decoding them, the affected individual can supposedly gain conscious control over powerful, emotionally significant ideas that have been split off from consciousness and can integrate them into the total personality.

Initially, the unconscious contents Freud uncovered and interpreted were considered to be *memories*; he found, over and over again, that his hysterical patients were suffering from the aftereffects of actual sexual assaults in childhood (Freud, 1896). But he eventually decided that the reports he was hearing were not historically true. He concluded that they were based instead on the patients' fantasies, particularly childhood fantasies about children's own sexual wishes and the sexual behavior of their parents. Following this change of focus, the Oedipus complex, rather than actual events, became the pivotal traumatic "reality" in psychoanalysis. Freud continued to elaborate the concept of repression as a keystone in the complex edifice of psychoanalytic theory, but repression was now generally viewed as a signpost to conflict-laden internal fantasies rather than to external events.

As psychoanalysis gained increasing prominence during the twentieth century, it became much more than a clinical theory and method. It was increasingly used to explain a wide range of phenomena in fields as diverse as literature and anthropology and was popularized by movies and the media. The concept of repression became almost a household word. But, in spite of Freud's theoretical shift in focus from memory to fantasy, popularizations of psychoanalysis tended to present a picture more in line with Freud's initial formulations. In movies like *Spellbound* and *Marnie*, for example, audiences learned that memory loss is a consequence of childhood traumas and that sudden, dramatic cures can come about through memory recovery.

Such formulaic portrayals have had a sometimes unfortunate effect on modern controversies about memory. Added to other dramatic media presentations, such as talk show appearances by individuals making extravagant claims, these stereotypical views of "recovered memories" have tended to increase simplistic thinking about complicated phenomena.

It is noteworthy, however, that, in spite of the deletions and distortions uncovered by Masson (1984) in the history of Freud's work, and in spite of the simplistic dramatizations of pop culture, an either-or perspective of memory — fantasy versus reality — tends to distort many of Freud's original insights. Whatever the limitations of psychoanalysis as an avenue to historical truth (Spence, 1982), it was one of the first psychological theories to emphasize the significance of emotion and interpersonal attachment on cognitive processes.

Even in his focus on fantasy, Freud pointed to the "kernel of truth" usually embedded in fantasies or delusions (Freud, 1940 [1938]). And although he disputed the significance of child sexual abuse in the etiology of psychopathology, he always acknowledged that such abuse sometimes actually occurs. His metaphor of himself as an archaeologist uncovering the buried past reflected his continuing recognition that the real past was, somehow, there to be recovered. Although his revised theory reflected an important shift in emphasis, it did not constitute a dismissal of the distinction between actual and imagined events. Freud was always aware, for example, that distinguishing between the real and the imaginary was a major function of the ego and that the denial of reality played an important role in the development of certain symptoms, such as fetishism. A serious failure of reality-testing resulted in psychosis. Thus, in spite of his emphasis on the role of fantasy in psychic life, Freud continued to be sensitive to the subversion of veridical memory as a source of internal conflict and as a measure of the ego's weakness.

By calling attention to the integrative function of the ego, psychoanalysis offered a valuable corrective to simplistic either-or appraisals about the nature of memory. A reported memory is not simply true or false; even when based on a real occurrence, the report is frequently a compromise formation, a complex mixture of fact and wishful thinking. Making sense of this creative construction focuses attention away from facts in themselves to an understanding of the meaning of experience.

One of the problems of psychoanalytic theory was that it was embedded in mechanistic concepts. It reflected old-fashioned tendencies to treat contents of the mind like concrete entities that can be packed away out of view and brought out intact at a later point in time. It thus fostered the reification of abstract concepts and the imaginative idea that the ego is a kind of homunculus in the mind, a puppetmaster who controls behavior. In many respects, however, psychoanalysis is no more mechanistic than other cognitive theories that treat the "memory trace" like a physical imprint that decays with disuse or can be erased. The recognition that thinking and remembering are dynamic processes involving open systems — mind and body in an ecological context — is a recent development in the psychological sciences.

In any case, the idea that the possibility of recovering lost memories stands or falls with the Freudian concept of repression misconstrues modern developments in psychoanalysis as well as modern discoveries in cognitive science. It amounts to setting up and knocking down a straw man. Recovered memories are not simply repressed memories. And repressed memories, as observed in the psychoanalytic consulting room, are not usually recovered in the sudden confrontations typical of media dramatizations.

DISSOCIATION

> My husband said he saw live wires on fire as he ran and had fear that he would be electrocuted by them. The water missed him by seconds. He saw our house go and then he said that's all he can remember. He has a mental block of it all floating by. . . . He said he lives in fear that he will remember some day. (Buffalo Creek survivor, in Erikson, 1976, pp. 158–159)

Most psychologists who specialize in the study of trauma view dissociation rather than repression as the typical dynamic in posttraumatic memory loss and recovery. Dissociation is a disconnection of ideas from ideas or of ideas from feelings that is initially based on state-dependent forms of information-processing rather than personality conflicts. Dissociation may become a habitual coping mechanism, however, and in such cases it is interwoven with individual personality dynamics.

The altered state of consciousness characteristic of a dissociative reaction may be subsequently recalled as dream-like. Or it may be altogether lost to recall until reactivated. It is commonly considered closely related to hypnotic trance states (Spiegel, 1986); yet, in contrast to externally induced hypnotic states, dissociation is frequently an automatic, immediate, self-initiated reaction. Although learning to control this reaction can be vital to recovery from trauma, control is not always easily achieved.

Some dissociative states, too, involve extreme forms of social withdrawal that make the affected individual almost impervious to external influence. These autistic trance states are quite different from the states typical of hypnotic trances (Waites, 1993).

Depersonalization and out-of-body experiences are among the most commonly reported dissociative responses to trauma. In such experiences, the mind escapes the injured or terrified body, observing it from some distant point. Or the mind flees itself, becoming unaware of what is happening or almost immediately amnesic for the traumatic events.

Dissociative reactions as a response to trauma have been studied in a variety of stressful situations, including natural disasters (Cardena & Spiegel, 1993; Koopman et al., 1994), hotel fires (Lindemann, 1944), automobile accidents (Noyes, Hoenk, Kuperman, & Slymen, 1977), war (Carlson & Rosser-Hogan, 1991), and child abuse (Frischholz, 1985). Witnessing violence can also precipitate dissociation; journalists who witnessed an execution, for example, experienced many dissociative symptoms (Freinkel, Koopman, & Spieget, 1994). Koopman and her colleagues (1994) reported that dissociative responses immediately following a traumatic event predict posttraumatic stress symptoms as measured seven months later. They interpret these symptoms as a defense against emotional pain that may lead to later problems.

Dissociation may contribute to the hypnotic-like reliving of traumas; it may be triggered by cues present during the original traumatic incident (Spiegel, Hunt, & Dondershine, 1988). Such intense reexperiencing involves an absorption in the focal experience of trauma that resembles hypnotic focusing. Alternately, the individual may compulsively focus away from the trauma, denying it access to consciousness. In this respect, the cued reactivation of trauma resembles other forms of state-dependent retrieval. It may be a major mechanism in the production of flashbacks and abreactive experiences. The retrieval of memories associated with trauma might then be available only if other conditions present at the time of the trauma, such as intense images or extreme emotional responses, were reinstated (Spiegel et al., 1988).

Spiegel (1986) notes that the experience of involuntariness may be a factor common to hypnosis and dissociation during trauma. In a study of Vietnam veterans with PTSD, subjects were found to have higher hypnotizability scores that either a normal control sample or other psychiatric patient groups. It is unclear whether the experience of trauma enhances hypnotizability or whether, in contrast, highly hypnotizable individuals are simply more susceptible to posttraumatic symptoms. It can be said, however, that hypnotizability is a capability that varies in the population (Hilgard, 1979), and there is some evidence that dissociative tendencies are hereditary (Putnam, 1989).

The relation of traumatic dissociation to the evolution of a particular character style, as occurs in dissociative disorders, is evidently a function of repeated traumatic experiences, particularly when these occur in childhood (Braun & Sachs, 1985; Frischholz, 1985). Extreme child abuse is the most commonly recognized etiological factor in dissociative identity disorder (Putnam, 1989).

Dissociation constitutes a subversion of memory to the extent that it removes from view any recollection of a particular trauma. The use of trance as a intentional coping strategy can serve as a powerful distractor not only to the self but to other people. Particularly when the trance state is accompanied by fantasizing, the dissociated individual may seem altogether out of touch with reality. The real trauma that precipitated the trance thus remains hidden from everyone. As a symptom, dissociation may thus preempt the attention of observers to the extent that the current pathology of the victim completely obscures the history of the symptoms. Those who dissociate are often accused of lying, for example, and the most severe dissociative disorder, dissociative identity, has often been viewed as a form of malingering or a factitious disorder (Goodwin, 1985).

Both dissociation as a reaction and disbelief in the reality of trauma make it easier for everyone concerned to construct a myth that everything is fine, that nothing traumatic happened (Goodwin, 1985). To complicate matters, victims of abuse, in particular, may be prone to lying, not only as a defense against pain, but as a response to the breakdown in social connectedness and the compromising of conscience that accompany familial abuse.

Sometimes both denial and dissociation lead to a simple evasive style, a blithe, hypomanic avoidance of unpleasant facts and reminders—what was traditionally called "la belle indifference" by clinicians who studied hysteria. Sometimes, however, the subversion of memory is more systematically elaborated in the development of cover stories that conceal, distort, or rationalize a traumatic event.

COVER STORIES

I heard them fighting and I knew my father was drunk and boy did he hit her. . . . So what does little Peter do? . . . I said to myself, since nobody's mentioning a word of it, I must have been dreaming the whole thing. (Peter Malone, in Cottle, 1980, pp. 79–80)

Some of the most strongly encoded and persistently stored memories evoke negative feelings or disturbing conflicts. Putting them out of mind is not easy; it requires persistent strategies of avoidance—avoiding internal contexts that might cue the memory as well as specific kinds of external cues. Among the most common strategies is a deliberate avoidance of self-referential narratives or a denial that one really experienced a particular event: "That did not happen to *me*" or "It must have been a dream."

Depersonalization, derealization, and other dissociative responses to trauma may have a dream-like quality that facilitates this interpretation. The sense of unreality is to some extent a function of the strangeness of internal responses as well as external events. It is a short step from experiencing an event in an altered state of consciousness to the narrative interpretation that the experience never happened at all in reality but was just an invention of a disordered mind.

Once formulated, the statement "This is not really happening" can become a repeated narrative in which the self takes refuge, not only at the time a trauma occurs but whenever it surfaces in memory. In this way, denial actively substitutes for accurate rehearsal. Denial may evolve from whistling in the dark to a systematic avoidance of any reminder of the disturbing event. By, in effect, "shouting down" the unwanted reality and constantly repeating the denial, one can thus continually distract oneself from what, deep down, one knows to be true.

Distraction can also be facilitated by the construction of a cover story that becomes a habitual refuge whenever the unpleasant memory is cued. The cover story may merely rationalize a remembered event: "He kept hitting her over and over because she wouldn't stop screaming." Or it may change the fundamental details of what happened: "The sound I heard was just the television turned up too loud."

Once an event has been reinterpreted, the reinterpretation can be obsessively rehearsed until it completely supplants actualities. Avoidance of the real story may, to be sure, affect variables like rehearsal that can influence basic retention. But even total avoidance of recall is not the same thing as forgetting. In many cases it is just a matter of silencing a still-remembered but disturbing story.

In some instances, the apparent forgetting is really a function of systematic dissociation; the mind has compartmentalized the traumatic memory by carefully avoiding reminders and rehearsals and by labeling it an unreal or a "not me" experience. The memory is then, in effect, encapsulated in the mind, as a foreign body is sometimes encapsulated under the skin. It remains a present danger: it may erupt like a painful abscess. But temporarily, it is controllable.

Some changes in memory that remove an original memory from consciousness do not hide it from the view of others. The denial or cover story actually preserves the record it distorts, as when an event is simultaneously rehearsed and negated: "Such and such didn't *really* happen." Or it replaces verbal narration with enactment, as when a child plays out a traumatic scenario without necessarily connecting it with her own story. Pynoos and Eth (1985), for example, describe a seven-year-old girl who, after witnessing her father strangle her mother and then pick up the body, forced her friends to play a gruesome game: "In the Mommy Game, you play dead, and I pick you up" (p. 29).

Such enactments may never be connected with consciously narrated memories. Or, if they are originally connected, the connection may be severed, so that only the enactment remains. Since the posttraumatic milieu often includes a "conspiracy of silence" or misleading explanations about disturbing events (Eth & Pynoos, 1985), behavioral enactment may be the only representative structure in which the memory is consistently preserved.

Cottle (1980) observes that, in children, much cognitive "twisting" and "untwisting" occurs on a conscious level. The desire to tell the story may strongly oppose the desire to keep it secret. Resulting cover stories may simultaneously conceal and reveal the truth. Intermittently, even the self who invents the story may be deceived by it. In some instances, conscious recollection is completely obliterated over long stretches of time.

When an invented account is substituted for a secret one, the new story must be practiced to become familiar. The very process of inventing and rehearsing may make it seemingly real and believable, even to the self. But the invention does not necessarily obliterate the original story, although critics who emphasize the significance of post-event information contend that it can. The correct story may persist in memory without distortion in spite of the carefully constructed cover story that overshadows it (Cottle, 1980).

Whatever the source of the cover-up, inconsistency in itself produces tension. It is usually easier to maintain one story than two. By constantly deflecting attention from the secret story, one may increasingly isolate it from contexts that might cue recall or make it meaningful. It may cease to compete with the cover story, so that, by virtue of familiarity as well as acceptability, the cover story is finally believed as the only true account.

Both the denial of the reality of a disturbing event and the invention of a cover story are commonly socially orchestrated by others who have a stake in the cover-up. Some evasions may be well-intentioned, as when someone decides that it is in the best interest of a victim not to talk about or be in any way reminded of the trauma. In such cases, the trauma is usually not totally denied. It is, rather, that forgetting it is an explicit goal, and efforts to achieve the goal may be carefully directed.

In other cases, the denial of trauma by others is more obviously self-serving. The fact that something bad has happened to another person shatters the illusion of safety most people rely on in everyday life (Lifton, 1967). In order to reinstate this illusion, observers may move quickly to find explanations that a terrible event did not really have to happen and that they need not fear it could happen to them. It is a short step from this rationalization that control is always possible to explicit blaming of the victim.

Finally, of course, there are instances in which both the denial of the truth and the elaboration of a cover story are intentional attempts to conceal wrongdoing or painful secrets on the part of someone. Abused children, for example, are frequently intimidated by actual threats. Parents who are trying to cover up secrets of which they are ashamed, such as alcoholism, mental illness, or a criminal history, carefully invent stories for public consumption and predict dire consequences if the truth should ever surface.

SUGGESTIBILITY AND INTIMIDATION

The subversion of memory by external agents depends to a great extent on the ignorance and/or compliance of those subverted. While people vary in their willingness to substitute a cover-up for their veridical memories, compliance can easily be effected through intimidation, especially in children. Unfortunately, those who study the effects of external influence on memory do not always sort out the effects attributable to voluntary acquiescence from those based on fearful accommodation.

The influence of social compliance on ordinary as well as on posttraumatic memory is commonly discussed in terms of the concept of *suggestibility*. Suggestibility is a hypothetical tendency that supposedly causes individuals to modify their behavior in accordance with the requests or commands of other people. It is closely associated with perceived authority (Zaragoza, 1991) and with the power differential between the one making the suggestion and the one being influenced (Ellenberger, 1970).

Extreme suggestibility is often but not always associated with hypnotic trance states (Brown, 1991). Children, not surprisingly, have been shown to be especially suggestible (Doris, 1991) and are often easily hypnotized (Hilgard, 1979). Since hypnotic susceptibility has also been found to be associated with trauma, it may be a connecting link between trauma and suggestibility. On the other hand, susceptibility to intimidation does not necessarily have anything at all to do with either hypnotic susceptibility or suggestibility. It may depend more on authoritarian attitudes in the one intimidated or the actual power of the intimidating person (Kelman & Hamilton, 1989; Milgram, 1974).

Studies of suggestibility are especially pertinent to forensic issues, particularly the credibility of witnesses. The claim that a child's testimony has been programmed by an adult, for example, has become a common defense in trials involving physical or sexual abuse (McGough, 1994). Many aspects of the investigative and/or judicial process are vulnerable to the criticism that accusations may be based on suggested rather than real events. The fact that victims, particularly children, often have difficulty articulating just what happened may encourage leading questions. Victims may readily comply with such questions when they are unsure of themselves and are impressed by the authority of the interrogator.

Studies of suggestibility in children offer contradictory perspectives on these issues (Doris, 1991). On the one hand, children have been shown to be vulnerable to post-event information concerning trauma. On the other, there are evidently limits to this vulnerability, and there are important individual differences in children. Reviewing experimental studies relevant to the credibility of child witnesses, Dent (1991) concludes that the quality of children's testimony can be influenced by many variables. Interviewing techniques (Dale, Loftus, & Rathbun, 1978), the use of misleading suggestions (Bruck et al., 1995; King & Yuille, 1987), and context reinstatement (Wilkinson, 1988) have all been found to affect the accuracy of children's reports. What children report as memory is also greatly affected by the development of expressive language skills (Leubecker, 1991) and by the child's understanding of the questions asked.

In a series of studies designed to minimize suggestibility, Dent (1991) concluded that children's recall is facilitated by suggestive questions, but that such questions also have a detrimental effect on accuracy. This robust finding is consistent with studies of the effect of post-event information on memory. However, it does not necessarily discriminate between memory as a process and suggestibility as a matter of social compliance.

Children are called on to testify in court concerning events, such as murder of a parent or child abuse, that might be expected to be associated with high levels of arousal. Hence, effects of arousal on memory may be especially pertinent to their performance. In an attempt to assess such effects, Peters (1991) examined children's eyewitness testimony about such events as a trip to the dentist, inoculations, and a simulated incident of theft and identification. He concluded that high levels of arousal can impair the eyewitness performance of children and perhaps make them more susceptible to post-event information.

Goodman (1991), in contrast, emphasizes that in her own research children have been highly resistant to abuse suggestions. She notes methodological difficulties with Peters' studies and suggests that it is not arousal as a general state but the particular emotion elicited that affects memory.

In an overview of studies of children's suggestibility, Davies (1991) points out that there is no consistent evidence that suggestibility can be viewed as a stable trait. Situational factors are major determinants of how it is exhibited.

Attacks on the credibility of victims often fail to distinguish between suggestibility and imperfections of memory. As Zaragoza (1991) emphasizes, the fact that children's testimony is influenced by suggestion does not necessarily imply any impairment in their ability to remember witnessed events. Yet, the close connection between suggestibility and memory is nevertheless evident in the tendency for people to edit and trans-form recollections to match their spoken statements.

To these observations, one might add that individual differences in competence, as well as individual differences in suggestibility, should al-ways be considered in evaluating testimony about real-life contexts. And what appears at first glance to be either a result of suggestibility or an imper-fection of memory may turn out, on closer inspection, to be mostly a matter of current motives. Among these, the freedom to speak one's mind without fear of reprisal is especially significant in many cases involving children.

One limitation of experimental studies of children's suggestibility, as of experimental studies of trauma, is that some variables cannot be ethically manipulated in the laboratory. Researchers cannot intimidate or threaten children. Yet threats and intimidation are probably among the most fre-quent sources of influence on children's real life testimony. Experimenters are also unable to fully and accurately assess the effects of attachment on children's suggestibility. Yet, the story a child — or even an adult — tells is quite often a function of whom he or she is trying to please and of a fear that, if the truth comes out, relationships will suffer.

It is worth bearing in mind, too, that suggestibility is a two-edged sword. Experimenters have usually been concerned with the effects of misleading questions and post-event information. But the suggestion to forget can be as potent an influence as the suggestion to remember. Studies of posthyp-notic amnesia (Bartis & Zamansky, 1986; Evans & Staats, 1989) offer striking examples of how subjects may temporarily lose important informa-tion when instructed to forget it. Critics contend that such forgetting is merely a matter of compliance. But the argument that the victim of posthypnotic amnesia really remembers misses the point; a temporary inability to retrieve information can produce significant gaps in a complex narrative. And memories need not be buried for decades in order to affect the performance and believability of witnesses. All that is needed to erode credibility in some cases is a momentary lapse or inconsistency. Self-doubt in the witness may engender doubt in the audience.

In child abuse cases, for example, recantation of an accusation is a common occurrence. Recantation in itself, however, does not tell us much about the accuracy of the original story. Intimidating threats are a typical part of an abuse scenario; anyone who commits a crime is likely to lie about it and try to get the victim to acquiesce in the lie. Those who work with abuse victims know, too, that the wish that the abuse had not oc-curred or loyalty to those responsible for it can be a powerful motive for changing a story (Herman, 1992).

Self-doubt can arise from internal sources as well as from external sug-gestions. Traumatic memories, particularly those related to unrepeated events, often seem dream-like or unreal. Such qualities arise from the altered states of consciousness produced by trauma as well as the lack of a familiar context in which to place the unusual event. Traumatic distortions of time, too, can make a traumatic memory seem unreal. These factors tend to erode the victim's confidence about his or her recollections of very real events.

But the most powerful factor leading to recantation is perhaps fear; the victim stands to lose something important by sticking to a veridical story. Painful retributions are not restricted to punishments. To persist in an accusation may result, instead, in isolation or ostracism. A needed parent who can, if angered, withdraw emotional as well as physical support may have been orchestrating the child's view of the world for so long that the child cannot deviate from the programmed world-views.

Studies of children's suggestibility have important implications for forensic investigations and judicial proceedings. More research involving real-life settings and such variables as the effects of specific kinds of abuse or specific attachment histories is especially needed. But such studies are unlikely to tell us much about memory as a process, or even about memory as competence. What people report should always be distinguished from what they remember.

SECRETS AND MEMORY DISTORTION

The internalization of social directives in the form of memory is, theoretically at least, distinguishable from the behavioral acquiescence that is the typical measure of suggestibility or compliance. But although suggestibility should be distinguished from memory, it is often a first step on the way to memory distortion. The subversion of memory is complete when an individual not only acquiesces to an inaccurate or distorted version of a story but believes the revision to be true.

In childhood, both suggestibility as a form of social control and memory as organized schemas of information-processing are closely tied to the patterns of reciprocal regulation between infants and caregivers. The infant's attunement to the mother's gaze and voice is an adaptive social development observable almost from birth (Brown, 1991). Normally, however, children develop autonomy as they mature. They learn to explore a world beyond the family and to exercise independent judgment about what they observe and experience. But they will throughout life remain vulnerable to external influence when they are stressed or injured or ill. And those who attempt to increase their own power and control may exploit such vulnerabilities (Herman, 1992; Lifton, 1961).

Among the dialogues children internalize are those that sustain the authority and stability of the family as a unit and preserve family myths. The evolving self embellishes these dialogues with personal experiences. An abused child, for example, may insist that suffering is inevitable or that he is a source of trouble to the family both because such messages about life have been constantly communicated to him and because his personal experience confirms them. Internal dialogues are shaped not only by explicit messages but by pointed silences. And silence may also be self-imposed when the child senses that some topic is unmentionable. As one child studied by Thomas Cottle (1980) put it, "This is a family secret; it's my job not to tell people" (p. 196).

Secret keeping can combine with the effects of traumatic memory to effectively erase a terrible event from recall. Child witnesses of homicide or suicide, for example, have intense perceptual experiences that may not be easily narrated or interpreted (Eth & Pynoos, 1985). Cottle (1980) describes the case of a sixteen-year-old girl who steadfastly maintained that her father was not really dead, in spite of the fact that he had committed suicide when she was nine. Her insistence that he had just gone away was a cover story for a very traumatic memory of overhearing his hanging himself and finding his body. "I knew he was dead. I *knew* it, but I didn't want to know it," she finally admitted (p. 227).

Cottle (1980) contends that children do not usually repress such secrets, in the sense that painful events are altogether inaccessible to recall. He discovered that, in many cases, what he thought must have been repressed was not really repressed at all, just unexpressed. Yet, in one child he observed, there was an actual gap in memory for witnessed abuse that persisted until a new traumatic experience cued recall. A young girl he calls Jacqueline was unable to remember anything about her early life until, at the age of sixteen, a child she sometimes babysat for had an accident. At that point, she said, "something sort of exploded" in her head and she remembered watching as her mother severely beat her brothers. She then began remembering other events from her previously blank childhood.

This case is instructive because it involves delayed recall in an adolescent rather than an adult. Adolescence is a time of important cognitive changes as well as important developments in identity consolidation (Erikson, 1968). Significant revisions of one's life story sometimes occur during this period. The memories accepted in this process may be forwarded as the official history of the self. And those rejected may be banished even more strictly from recall.

Over time, as children learn not only what to say but what must be left unsaid, secrets may have a powerful impact on the transformation of memory and on behavior. By the time one reaches adulthood, such secrets may have contributed to habitual styles of information processing as well as to specific cover stories. Perceptual cues associated with a secret may come to trigger automatic avoidance reactions. Habitual distractors may be employed to refocus attention whenever the unwanted memory threatens to intrude. Yet, a careful exploration of personal history can sometimes uncover a long-lost secret that was, at some point in the past, frequently rehearsed and clearly recalled. Such instances of reversible memory loss need not be attributed to some special cognitive mechanism like repression. They may, rather, involve a gradual process of evolution in which images and feelings have been disconnected from narratives and some narratives have become privileged over others.

THOUGHT REFORM AND
BRAINWASHING

The judge said—"You must not tell untrue things." On the other hand, when I told only real things, this was considered insufficient and I was not allowed to write them. I was in great psychological pain. I felt it was impossible to satisfy these people. (Father Luca, quoted in Lifton, 1961, p. 51)

The subversion of memory is not merely a random occurrence or a personal defect. It is often a systematic process achieved through methods familiar to anyone who has ever participated in a group—which includes, of course, everybody. When methods are particularly coercive, even punitive, extreme distortions can be effected. Such systematic revisions of thinking have been labeled "brainwashing" or "thought reform" and are particularly prevalent as instruments of control by totalitarian regimes.

Historical revision is important to many leaders with totalitarian agendas. Personal history as well as personal identity may be targeted for systematic transformations. Those prisoners subjected to thought reform by the Chinese communists, for example, were required to renounce the past and confess to crimes. But mere confession was not enough to satisfy their captors; the prisoner was "reeducated" until he or she could be acceptably "sincere" in deploring former behavior.

Brainwashing as a systematic form of indoctrination and control first came to widespread public attention following the Korean War. Subsequently, in movies like *The Manchurian Candidate*, it was portrayed as a horrendous tactic employed by Communist states. More recently, it has been described as a technique employed by U.S. intelligence services like the FBI and the CIA (Weinstein, 1990). Brainwashing is, of course, not really a modern invention; it has been implemented as a political tactic throughout recorded history. During the Middle Ages, for example, the Inquisition systematically hunted down and tortured "heretics," forced "confessions," and stifled intellectual as well as political dissent.

Many of the most ancient forms of thought-control involve torture. But modern despots have become more sophisticated about the uses of psychological as well as physical control tactics. Lifton (1961) has described in detail the techniques by which thought-control was managed by Communist regimes in the 1950s. The purpose of such techniques was not simply to enforce behavioral compliance in political prisoners, but rather to radically alter the identity of the person being controlled, thus internalizing the control system. According to Lifton, "The most basic feature of the thought reform environment . . . is the control of human communication" (p. 420). This is achieved through a careful control of the milieu; the individual is placed in a situation in which he is completely dependent on his captors and is deprived of information from sources that might contradict the official ones.

Brainwashing techniques include sequences of assault and leniency. The erosion of identity and autonomy is constant. Deprived of sleep or respite, the victim may begin to live in an altered state of consciousness, a hypnogogic state, in which he or she becomes highly suggestible. Dissociative tendencies are commonly heightened.

Some individuals, such as prisoners of war who may be injured and are, in any event, isolated from their own social moorings, are especially vulnerable. Yet thought-reform tactics are not restricted to times of war or the machinations of totalitarian states. Stressed, confused, or socially alienated individuals are especially at risk for manipulation by self-styled saviors who profess to offer quick solutions to their problems. A grandiose leader who seems devoid of doubt or indecisiveness may be viewed as a welcome chance to escape one's inner uncertainties (Fromm, 1941). Discussing the appeal of cults, for example, Singer (1995) points out that, because such groups offer instant, simplistic, and focused solutions to their difficulties, young people who are confused and self-doubting are likely to be especially vulnerable. Such vulnerable people are not "mentally ill" in the usual sense of that term. They are merely willing to let others take charge of their lives. By the time they reconsider this decision, they may be enmeshed in authoritarian group structures that maintain control by means of physical as well as psychological restraints.

Lifton suggests that the capacity to be manipulated by totalistic techniques is an outgrowth of the period of prolonged dependency that characterizes human childhood (1961). The infant lives in a controlled milieu in which parents and their surrogates have the power not only to satisfy physical needs, but also to define many aspects of reality and to enforce compliance with their beliefs and their standards of behavior. Authoritarian leaders exploit childhood modes of experience through deliberate forms of infantilization. An extremely totalistic environment "can literally stand reality on its head" (p. 450).

Herman (1992) notes that individuals who have been abused may also be especially vulnerable to totalistic control; in many instances, the authoritarianism of a group or cult leader is an extension of family dynamics.

The subversion of memory in authoritarian groups, whether the group consists of a family or a cult, may be accomplished by ignoring or punishing any ideas that do not match the official ones, by fostering and rewarding constant rehearsals of slogans or creeds, and by restricting input from any source that might disconfirm the cultic world-view. Singer (1995) emphasizes, however, that physical abuse is by no means necessary to produce compliance in cult members. In contrast to old-fashioned brainwashing, modern cults often focus on destabilizing a person's sense of self and offering a radically new world-view. The old identity is replaced by a "cult identity." Leaders of some modern cults even invent "past lives" for recruits (Singer, 1995). New identities based on purely fictional accounts may be constructed.

Training to think "correctly" is quite systematic. The trainee may be isolated from former associates, including family members, and is typically placed under the constant surveillance of more experienced group members, who model as well as reinforce acceptable behavior. The new identity may be marked by special changes in appearance, such as special clothing or hair styles. The indoctrinated individual may be given a new name. Physiological as well as emotional and behavioral responses may be systematically induced in members. Hyperventilation, chanting, certain kinds of dancing or other repetitive motion may effect changes in nervous system functioning that are conducive to increased suggestibility or regression to child-like patterns of thought. Dietary restrictions may impair health in ways that increase the vulnerabilty of victims. And yet such practices are not necessarily experienced as painful or coercive. They may, on the contrary, be associated with experiences labeled as blissful or transcendent.

Some of the effects of mind-control on memory are related to difficulties in concentrating or focusing attention. Memory loss is common, as well as the creation of altered or false memories (Singer, 1995). Some of these distortions may arise from stress syndromes that directly impair information-processing. Others consist of acquiescence to revised versions of history and an avoidance of thoughts, including memories, that might lead to conflict between present and past modes of living. Reality-testing may be eroded to the extent that illusory or even hallucinatory experience occurs in individuals with no previous history of psychosis. The addition of drugs to the training regimen can, of course, greatly enhance such effects. But many groups eschew drugs in favor of strictly behavioral techniques. Recovery from addiction, effected by substituting addiction to the group, may, in fact, be a stated purpose of cult activities (Singer, 1995).

A special language — buzz words and catch phrases — employed by group members may facilitate the distortion of reality and the construction of memories consistent with the group agenda. Singer (1995) points out, for example, that terms like "heavenly deception" reinterpret and rationalize behavior that might seem questionable. Denial is also observable in the general public and tends to minimize the significance of cult-orchestrated events. The Jonestown deaths, for example, have sometimes been described as suicide when, considering that they were physically as well as psychologically coerced, they are more accurately termed *murder*.

The most vulnerable victims of all of such techniques are children who have never had the opportunity to develop independent ideas or autonomous identities in the first place. Singer (1995) notes that, of the 912 members of the People's Temple who died at Jonestown, 276 were children. She describes the work of Bruce Perry, who studied a number of children between the ages of five months and twelve years who had lived under the control of David Koresh in Waco, Texas. He noted that it seemed impossible for these children to think or act independently. They could not recognize objects familiar in the outside world, such as a quarter; however, they were able to recite long quotations from Biblical scripture.

THERAPEUTIC IMPLICATIONS

Modern controversy about "repressed memories" should be evaluated in the light of how reported memory may be distorted by external pressures and intimidating threats as well as by internal dynamics. The erosion of veridical memory is seldom simply a matter of banishing the past. It is more commonly a matter of reconstructing the past to make it more acceptable to others as well as to the self. In this reconstruction, the systematic evasions and distortions of other people who feel they have some stake in a recollection can transform the retelling of personal narratives, until history has been revised to the satisfaction of everybody.

In this respect, Masson's presentation of letters by Freud that had been systematically removed from the previously published body of his work is an instructive example. The original revision of history shaped the subsequent development of psychoanalysis as a system of thought that minimized the significance of actual childhood trauma. But the eventual publication of the missing texts did not constitute a return of the repressed. It was, as is so often the case in instances of historical revision, an exposure of the suppressed.

One result of the systematic focus of psychoanalysis away from actual abuse has been a hermeneutic tradition that emphasizes that narrative truth is all an individual in psychoanalysis can discover anyway. Spence (1982) has systematically articulated the view that historical truth is not the province of psychoanalysts. The only data available to them consist of verbal statements; psychic reality is all we know or can know. It may be, however, all we need to know, since a coherent and meaningful narrative about one's past can have a profoundly therapeutic effect.

Spence's disclaimers concerning psychoanalysis could be extended to any form of psychotherapy. Even therapies that employ nonverbal modalities, such as art or play, rely heavily on narrative descriptions and verbal interpretations of what is going on.

Yet, although Spence's position is well argued, it evades rather than resolves some of the pressing practical issues facing therapists, particularly those who deal with posttraumatic problems. Insistence that no story is more likely to be true than another or that clients' narratives about the past are merely texts that have no fixed interpretation is as much a theoretical orientation as the converse position. As such, it necessarily privileges some interpretations over others; the statement that we cannot know is as consequential as the statement that we can.

The position that reality cannot be discovered in psychotherapy may be a convenient refuge from the difficulties of sorting out fact from fantasy, exploring cover-ups, and integrating dissociated knowledge structures. When attacks are mounted that accuse therapists as a group of naive or unethical practices (see Whitfield, 1995), defensive therapists can easily retreat to a longstanding tradition that emphasizes narrative rather than historical truth. They can, like Freud, point to the demonstrably powerful role of fantasy in human existence. They can insist on a stance of "therapeutic neutrality" that avoids privileging any story over another. They can even enlist experimental observations on suggestibility in this enterprise.

But clients who are used to the subversion of their memories by dismissive people are likely to be dismayed rather than reassured by such a position. There is really nothing new in the notion that trauma is just a matter of interpretation or that people should rise above terrible events and get on with their lives. There is nothing new in the accusation that children lie or exaggerate or that victims who complain are just not taking responsibility for their own suffering. There is nothing new in the denial that sexual abuse occurs and has real detrimental effects (Rush, 1980). Clients in psychotherapy, however, are often looking for something new rather than the same old denials and evasions of unpleasant facts. The difficulties in sorting out facts can be acknowledged without discouraging attempts to do so.

Any form of psychotherapy is necessarily guided by theories and orientations, including theories about how the past is represented in and affects the present. Although such orientations may remain implicit or even be verbally disavowed, they inevitably shape what happens in therapy. The assumption that child abuse is a rare occurrence, for example, leads inevitably to different emphases than the acknowledgment that it is, unfortunately, all too prevalent. The assumption that no one, not even the client who had the experience, can ever really disentangle narrative from historical truth, will lead not only to different evaluations about clients' narratives but, in some instances, to profound differences in how a client experiences and makes use of psychotherapy.

In any case, in enterprises as pragmatically organized as psychotherapy, therapeutic defensiveness merely avoids rather than resolves difficult issues and is likely to be perceived by clients as unempathic. Where the subversion of memory is a primary complaint, as when a client is troubled by conflicting versions of a story or is locked in a constant struggle to repudiate a recollection that, however strongly denied, has become obsessive, therapy that evades the question is unlikely to be very helpful.

From a practical standpoint, too, many clients expect therapy to help them confront and correct the subversion of memory for actual events, not just to supply a coherent narrative about the past. Sometimes differentiating between fact and fantasy is necessary for important and far-reaching decisions. Clients who report childhood abuse by a family member, for example, may wonder if their own children are safe with that family member. Quite apart from their feelings about the suspected perpetrator, they must confront their own responsibilities as parents.

The loss of accessible memory is itself unsettling to many people, and the motive to recover what has been lost keeps them searching. A therapist's disclaimer that we cannot really know the truth rings false to those who believe that, in fact, they *do* know, but for some strange reason cannot say.

Where records are suspect and memory incomplete, it is often tempting to search for an omnipotent other who can provide all the answers. This search is itself a legacy of infantile helplessness and dependency. Psychotherapy that shifts the focus from reliance on received truths to an exercise in independent thinking will not yield definite answers to all hard questions. But it will free the client to consider possibilities that were formerly foreclosed by the systematic subversion of memory.

Therapists have no omniscient view of the past; they can only help the client feel safe to explore it. Therapists cannot assume responsibility for clients' decisions in the present. To do so would be to exchange a therapeutic focus on client autonomy and self-care for authoritarian control. Learning to avoid the pitfalls of taking control is a commonly recognized aspect of psychotherapeutic training.

In the long run, both therapist and client must recognize that, however imperfect memory may be, it belongs to the client. Laying claim to a personal past involves confronting the fact that it *is* uniquely personal. Acquiescing to somebody else's version of it, whether the somebody else is a parent or a therapist, is an evasion of the authentic self. Merely exploring new ways of looking at things can provide important contexts for interpreting memories. Any remembered reality, however incontrovertible, must be interpreted to be useful, and such an exploration can facilitate an appreciation of how the past as received wisdom, family myth, or social appraisal has shaped one's recollections all along.

CHAPTER 8
The Self in Hiding

Remorse is memory awake,
Her companies astir,—
A presence of departed acts
At window and at door.

—Emily Dickinson

REMEMBERING AND FORGETTING are not always mutually exclusive phenomena. It is possible to remember in one way and yet forget in another.

Traumatic memories are sometimes multiply encoded in compartmentalized schemas—somatic representations, motor enactments, verbal narratives, interpersonal dialogues—that have never been integrated or that have become disconnected from one another. After one "official" narrative becomes privileged, other forms of remembering may be systematically excluded from attention. Unnoticed and unrehearsed, they may seemingly fade from memory.

This disconnection of pieces of memory from one another commonly reflects not only state-dependent learning effects of trauma on memory, but the transformations of self-referential memory as a function of social dialogues. Sometimes, though completely hidden from public view, the unspeakable is privately remembered. In other instances, it is completely disconnected from self-reflective narratives. In either case, the effect is a split between a social self and a private self. Even when not aware of this split, one may be, at some level, covertly aware of evasions and distortions and troubled by them. When that happens, the self may feel inauthentic or false, burdened by secrets, isolated by silence.

This compartmentalization of divergent narratives is a form of dissociation that can lead to marked inconsistencies in self-presentation and may compromise the credibility of the self as witness to memory. It should not be mistaken for forgetting. But it is not quite remembering, either.

ERICA

"Before my father's accident, our family was picture perfect," said Erica "My father was a school principal. My mother taught Sunday School. And my brother, Winston, was everybody's golden boy. If I had told, everybody would have been shocked, but nobody would have believed me."

Until the day she began psychotherapy, at the age of thirty, Erica had never told anyone that her brother, who was four years older, had sexually abused her from the time she was seven until he left home for college. She had never forgotten, but she had never told.

Although she had in the last few years felt increasingly burdened by this secret, she still had no intention of telling anyone other than her therapist. "I love Winston," she said. "He was never mean or rough. After our father was paralyzed in a snowmobiling accident, Winston had to be the man of the house. We all depended on him, and he was under a lot of pressure. I felt sorry for him."

But the sex had been confusing as well as exciting, and she had recently felt herself more and more disturbed remembering it. It interfered with her relationships with men, and she felt it had somehow been the real cause of a recent broken engagement.

"I have this tendency to latch onto men like a leech," she said. "I don't know how to go slow. Sex is intense, and I think the man sometimes feels pressured. Yet sometimes, although I'm really turned on, I could be having sex with just anybody.

"And I have fits sometimes. I sort of go wild and cry, even scream— about little things as well as big things. I think that was what my fiancé couldn't take anymore."

Erica had read extensively about the aftereffects of sexual abuse before she began therapy. She felt that Winston's abuse explained not only her sexual problems but also her life. Yet, as she talked more about that life, it became increasingly clear how complicated it had been. Sexual abuse had by no means been the only trauma.

"When the accident happened," she said, "we all thought my father was going to die. When we found out he would be paralyzed from the waist down, it was hard for everybody. He couldn't work at first, although he eventually went back. To make matters worse, he at one point became addicted to painkillers.

"My mother was always trying to look on the bright side and expected me and Winston to do that, too. No matter how bad I felt about anything, I couldn't talk about it. Our whole family was always busy, busy, busy proving that we were triumphing over adversity. I made straight A's. Winston was a track star. My mother went back to teaching and advanced in her career.

"Holidays were really hard," she continued. "The accident had happened over Christmas holidays. Afterwards, everybody seemed to be compulsive about making Christmas wonderful. Nobody was supposed to think or talk about what had happened. There was always this grand show as my father carved the Christmas turkey and everybody sat around the table discussing what a wonderful year we had all had.

"After my mother went back to work when I was nine, I was home by myself after school until Winston came home. I don't know which was worse, when he wanted sex with me or when he didn't. In high school, I was depressed, but I always kept up a good front. I thought about suicide, but started doing drugs—mostly pot—instead. Nobody ever knew about that either."

In therapy, Erica began to explore her memories of childhood. At first, she did not think there was much she did not remember. Her story seemed straightforward, and she narrated it coherently. The accident. Winston's sexually abusing her. Hiding from her mother. Pretending all the time.

Only gradually did she discover how much was missing from the story. During childhood, she had always had strong feelings about what was going on. But although she could talk about feelings now, she could not feel them as she talked. Instead, feelings just exploded suddenly from time to time, when she had one of her "fits."

She had forgotten, too, how hard it had been to keep the sexual secret. How awful it was in school when she realized she knew all about sexual matters her peers were just beginning to discover. How difficult it was to pretend sometimes. There was even a lengthy period when she was in fourth grade that she had almost forgotten entirely. She had missed a lot of school that year because of one ailment after another—bladder infections, intestinal upsets. At one point, the doctor had thought she might be developing an ulcer.

And although she had remembered many events from the past, Erica had also never made certain connections that began to be clear to her in therapy. She had known that her life had changed when she was seven, but she had thought about that change mostly in terms of external events. In therapy, she finally began exploring some of the psychological implications of those events.

Although her father had lived through the accident, for example, she had in some sense lost him. Even after he came home from the hospital, he was in too much distress to be emotionally available to her. As he began to recover physically, his energies were absorbed in rehabilitation and getting in shape to go back to work.

At the age of seven, Erica had suddenly gone from being Daddy's little girl to being Winston's consolation and sexual outlet. It was a shocking transition, not the kind of discontinuity a child could make much sense of. Since her father was not dead, she could not mourn him. And the sexual relationship with Winston was a disturbing substitute for the warmly supportive relationship she had previously had with her father.

In a sense, too, she lost her mother after the accident. It was not just that her mother was preoccupied with coping, although that was part of it. It was that so much had to be hidden from her; protecting mother became a fulltime job for Erica as well as for Winston.

As she explored and mourned these losses in the context of psychotherapy, Erica continually revised her appraisals of the past. Her memories for events were enriched by interpretations and reinterpretations of the meanings of events. She began to understand not only the part other people had played in her history, but how she herself had coped with stress and pain by dissociating feelings, acquiescing in cover stories, and constructing a secret life. Thus, although she had always remembered the bare bones of her story, remembering in therapy was a process of discovery for Erica. Remembering the story was one thing. Remembering the pain was something else again.

As she confronted secrets she had always known about but carefully sequestered from view, Erica encountered and gradually integrated a self in hiding. Throughout her childhood, the compulsive emphasis on how well everybody was recovering had led her to try, with varying degrees of success, to convince herself that she was really doing as well as she seemed to be. The sexual abuse was only one of her secrets. Everything negative about her life had to be hidden.

One long-lost feeling was anger. It was an especially difficult and frightening recollection. Because there was so much anger, Erica felt overwhelmed when it began to surface. And because she had always suppressed and covered up anger, she had not learned effective ways of expressing and dealing with it.

She began to feel rage toward Winston, and that was very disturbing. She needed Winston. He had been her comrade in a lonely world. How could she risk being angry toward him? Did she even have the right to be?

Erica spent long periods of therapy making excuses for Winston and trying to protect him not only from her own anger but also from the accusations against him she began to imagine were coming from the therapist. Finally, unable to fend off these negative feelings, she stopped talking to Winston altogether. It was only after she had spent considerable time confronting the negative aspects of her old relationship with him that she finally found the courage to express herself to him. When she did, she was surprised as well as relieved to discover that he, too, was in therapy. Slowly, painstakingly, she began to build a new relationship with him.

In many ways, it was even harder for Erica to confront her anger toward her mother. By the time she entered therapy, her mother was in failing health and the need to protect her had intensified. Erica decided to deal with her feelings toward her mother in the context of therapy but not to actually confront her mother about old grievances.

Anger toward her father, who had died several years before she began therapy, was perplexing as well as difficult to express. How could she blame him for anything? He had almost died in the accident and had been in pain for years afterward. So far as she could say, he had never done anything intentional to hurt her. And in spite of his distance from her and preoccupation with his own life, she still had the feeling that he had loved her very much.

Yet she was angry at him for getting hurt, for abandoning her to Winston, for not coming to her rescue when she needed him. She was even, at one point, horrified to discover that she had been angry at him for not dying. It was all so confusing and irrational. It took her a long time to sort it out.

But Erica did sort it out. When she left therapy, the bare bones of the story she had come in with had not changed much. But her memories had changed profoundly. When she came in, she reported a story. By the time she left, she had lived one.

As painful as it was to relive that story, it was also a great relief to do so. Before she relived it, she had been at the mercy of the past, weary of the cover stories she had devised to convince everybody of how well she was doing, intermittently overcome by the feelings she had left out of the story. Afterwards, she was finally able not only to remember, but to move beyond childhood. She still remembered, but the memories did not control her. It was *she* who controlled the memories.

MEMORY IN FRAGMENTS

Erica had always been aware of some ways in which she was disconnected from herself. She knew that she had lived much of her life with a burdensome secret and had developed an external facade that was, as she described it, "picture perfect" but deceptive. She had always remembered that something shameful and inexpressible had happened to her. And, from her reading, she had also come to believe that her brother's molestation of her had affected her later relationships with men. Erica knew, too, that there were times when she was "not herself." She was occasionally overcome with fits of screaming or weeping that always seemed like overreactions to little irritations. Sometimes, she even had a crying jag in which she was scarcely aware of anything at all.

Over the course of therapy, remembering became, for Erica, more a matter of connecting and reconnecting images and feelings and stories that had previously been disconnected than of dredging up dark but unrecollected secrets. In this respect, even facts sometimes functioned as cover stories. The dry account of her father's accident and the aftermath, as well as the constant rationalization of Winston's abuse, functioned for long periods in therapy to overshadow confusing sensations and emotional distress.

Previously, feelings, especially negative feelings, had not been much integrated with the narratives about the past events Erica remembered. For most of her life, feelings had been like intermittent storms that blew in from nowhere and passed, leaving her shaken and relieved but not much inclined to really reflect on the intrusion.

In therapy, she moved beyond a dry repetition of facts disconnected from feelings and began to understand what had happened to her in a more complex way. She began to recognize not only *that* but *how* her emotional outbursts were related to her traumatic history. She began to integrate feelings with narratives. She began to weave disconnected narratives into one meaningful life story.

She also began to connect always-remembered episodes that had long been disconnected from one another. Some aspects of the past, for example, though vaguely recollected, had been like isolated islands of memory. In therapy, Erica recalled with increasing clarity that strange year in fourth grade when she had been sick all the time. And as she remembered, she was surprised to discover that her body seemed to remember too. She began to fear now as then that she was developing an ulcer.

Her body, in fact, remembered a great deal that was painful to think about. Erica was sometimes intensely aware of her body. Sexual arousal, for example, was sometimes difficult for her to control. The emotional storms that shook her left her feeling physically as well as mentally exhausted. But the outward appearance of her body was part of the facade she so carefully erected. Most of the time, she tried to make sure that her body, like her life, was "picture perfect."

Yet, in spite of having always been aware of her body, sometimes hypersensitive to it, Erica had been oddly disconnected from it. During the sexual activities with Winston, for example, she had been extremely excited, but dissociated. Afterward, she had tried to calm down by distracting herself compulsively with routine activities, a coping mechanism she still used to maintain control of her feelings.

As an adult, she had also ignored her body rather punitively sometimes, having no tolerance at all for any physical illness. Like her father, she prided herself on being able to keep going no matter how bad she felt. Like her mother, she learned to not even notice.

Reconnecting with her body in therapy meant, for Erica, learning to tolerate sensations and images and emotions without either being overwhelmed by such responses or dissociatively tuning them out. Reconnecting with the self in hiding meant exposing herself in a way that at first felt terrifying. Learning to connect not only her body but herself with other people was a difficult challenge. To be emotionally involved without feeling unsafe, to be sexually aroused without feeling overwhelmed, to speak frankly but appropriately about what she really felt and thought were constant challenges.

DALTON

When Dalton was two, his mother was hospitalized for the first time with the illness from which she died six years later. After her death, his father's mother moved in and took care of him until his father remarried. Dalton was never close to the brother who was born when he was ten, shortly after the remarriage. He was never close to peers at school, either. Always shy and quiet, he easily faded into the woodwork. Yet he was a good student, and since he never got into trouble, it was easy for people to ignore him. As an adult, he was fond of saying that he did not need people.

He remembered vaguely, though, that he had been close to his mother before her death, the apple of her eye. Looking back, he saw her as a bright but fleeting moment in a miserable life. Even while ill, she had read him stories and baked cookies. He did not know she was going to die, although everyone else must have known. When she disappeared from his life, he did not cry or mourn. The world just seemed strange.

As he was growing up, his father, who traveled on business, was not around much. His grandmother, however, was always there. She was cool and efficient, a strict disciplinarian who had no tolerance for rowdiness or dirtiness. Dalton learned to stay out of her way.

A few months after his mother's death, when Dalton was eight, he found a pair of pantyhose and a handbag his grandmother had discarded in the trash. He was not sure whether or not they had belonged to his mother, but for some reason, he retrieved these articles and hid them under the bed in his room. When he was sure his grandmother was busy and not watching him, he tried on the pantyhose. Although they were too large and he knew anyway that boys were not supposed to wear such things, he felt strangely excited.

He used the handbag as a storage place for special treasures—a keychain flashlight, a plastic charm from a cereal box, an unusual rock he had found once on a picnic before his mother died. He knew his grandmother, a meticulous housekeeper, might eventually find anything he hid under the bed, so he put his secret stash in a box of old books on the back of his closet shelf. It was satisfying to think that it was always there. From time to time, he got it out and put on the pantyhose, though gradually he lost interest in the game.

Years later, when he was thirteen, Dalton took a shortcut home from school one day through a neighbor's backyard where clothing was hung to dry on a line. Suddenly he grabbed a pair of women's panties and a brassiere and stuffed them into his bookbag. At home, he found himself alone in the house and strangely excited. He undressed and put on the women's underwear and masturbated. Later, looking for a place to hide the stolen items, he remembered his secret hoardings on the back of the closet shelf and put the new treasures there where the others, long neglected, were still hidden.

Now that his grandmother no longer lived with him, it was easier to hide things. Unfortunately, however, wearing the articles of women's clothing he already owned was no longer sufficient to Dalton's needs. After he stole the undergarments from the clothesline, he began to steal other articles from other clotheslines. Eventually, he started shoplifting women's clothing from department stores. After he was caught and prosecuted for shoplifting, psychotherapy was a condition of his probation.

When he began therapy, Dalton, like Erica, seemed to remember many aspects of his past. He had long ago decided that wearing women's clothing was not a behavior he wanted to change. Stealing, however, was a problem, and he realized he needed to change enough to stay out of trouble. He was also becoming seriously involved with a woman he was thinking about marrying, and he was afraid that she would not be able to accept his transvestism.

Although Dalton did not then really want to change his compulsive behavior, he was motivated to work in therapy. Though he had not gone beyond high school, he realized he was smart enough to go back to school and wanted to prepare himself for a better job than the construction work in which he was usually employed. He also wanted to marry and have a family and a normal life.

Slowly he began to view therapy as an opportunity to explore aspects of his history that had bothered him for years. He had always resented his father, for example, for being away so much. He was still angry at his grandmother, who had sometimes beaten him severely for minor infractions. He had a litany of grievances against people who had disappointed him.

As he talked about the past, Dalton reviewed some old memories in a new light. The incident of retrieving and trying on discarded pantyhose had always seemed like a significant but isolated memory. Stealing the underwear from the clothesline as a teenager had also seemed a rather mysterious, impulsive act. "It just came out of the blue," he said. He could not even how say why it had excited him. He only knew that not just the clothing itself but the act of stealing it was such a thrill that, subsequently, he intentionally planned other thefts.

As Dalton explored the meanings of his secret life, the therapist focused on helping him connect feelings and ideas that had never been connected, as well as to reinterpret the meanings and motives of his own behavior. Feelings never named were noticed and named. The sudden mysterious absence that had been his mother's death became a terrible but acknowledged event. As he recalled her death, he began to recollect something of his life with her.

Dalton gradually began to understand that his secret hoard of keepsakes had, from the beginning, been an attempt to replace a terrible loss. He began to see, too, that his compulsion was a meaningful response to that loss and to the isolation he had lived in so much of his life. For the first time, it was safe to remember love, not just as a dissociated encounter with a garment that a woman had worn next to her skin, but as an attachment too soon broken. For the first time, too, it was safe to be sad.

One day Dalton came to therapy dressed as a woman. He announced triumphantly that no one along the way had seemed to notice. But he admitted, too, that he wanted someone to notice. And accept.

As he continued to talk about the past, however, he made an unpleasant discovery. It was all too depressing to think about. He decided he did not want to think about it after all. He began missing therapy sessions and reporting that he had shoplifted again, although he was not caught. Acknowledging the self-destructiveness of these actions, Dalton began to realize how enraged he had always been toward the people who deprived him of things he needed. After his mother's death, there had been little warmth in his life. Her death, along with his grandmother's coldness and his father's absence, had convinced him people could not be trusted. Only objects he could take forcibly and control completely could be trusted.

This sense of possession was one thing that excited him about the women's clothing he stole. It allowed him to remain in constant contact with something warm and beautiful, something he could keep forever, or, in any case, replace at will. When he put on the stolen garments he, indeed, did not need people. He was entirely self-sufficient.

Dalton knew enough about himself, however, to realize that his compulsive dressing up in women's clothing, though exciting, did not give him everything he needed. There was a part of him who wanted a real flesh-and-blood companion, someone who could really talk with him and share the reality of human contact and affection. It was this need that kept him working in therapy to find both insights about the past and present solutions to his antisocial behavior. Although he had no intention of giving up cross-dressing, he began to substitute careful shopping expeditions for shoplifting. And after a long struggle with himself, he eventually revealed his secret compulsion to his girlfriend. To his immense relief, she tried to accept it. When he ended therapy, he was uncertain about whether she would continue to do so. But he was hopeful.

KEEPSAKE CONTACTS

Dalton's therapy highlights the simple fact that symptomatic behavior does not necessarily disappear in the course of remembering the past.

Insight, in and of itself, does not always mitigate compulsive needs or change compulsive activities. But insight and understanding can sometimes help transform destructive compulsions into benign ones.

As importantly, attachments and social connections in the present can often help individuals move beyond a traumatic past. In the case of Dalton, life after the age of two had been anxious, sad, lonely, and sometimes infuriating. He could not reinvent himself through psychotherapy. But he was able to gain enough insight and control over his behavior to come out of hiding, at least with people who cared about him, and to make a less constricted life.

This case also illustrates how densely packed with meaning and memories an apparently innocuous object can be. Whether or not the handbag Dalton retrieved from the trash had belonged to his mother, he connected it with her. The key chain flashlight he kept in the handbag had been a gift from her. The unusual rock was a memento of the last picnic he remembered going on with her. The handbag, then, became an archival store of valued memories. Yet, until he talked about it in therapy, Dalton had never reflected on these objects as representations of his relationship with his mother. Although they evoked powerful emotions, he had never placed his hoardings in any narrative context.

The pantyhose, too, was a reminder of his mother, a way of reconnecting with her body. The feel of it against his skin was delicious. When he wore it, it became almost like his own skin, warmly and protectively enclosing his body. Later, in his teens, the clothing he put on acquired a more explicitly sexual significance, the focus of a masturbatory ritual that enabled him to make contact with women. It even allowed him to *be* a woman, if he so pleased. The objects he filched and hoarded thus enabled Dalton to remember and forget at the same time. What he had valued in the past was preserved intact, yet he did not have to confront what was lost.

Like ritualistic reenactments of trauma, Dalton's rituals were motivated by strong needs and feelings and reinstated important memories. But, unlike some literal reenactments, they were not just compulsive replays of events. They were, rather, complex symbolic reminders, magical undoings of trauma. And unlike veridical narrative recollections, his ritualistic enactments did not remind him of anything depressing. On the contrary, they helped him avoid depression. They preserved the pleasure and kept the pain at bay, and it was for that reason Dalton guarded them with such tenacity.

Dalton's rituals thus illustrate a process of memory development in which the literal past was simultaneously carried forward and screened from view. It was only in therapy that he was eventually able to connect concrete symbols with narrative forms and to understand their place in the larger context of his life.

THE SOCIAL CONTEXT OF SILENCE

A part of my mind knew my father was alive, another part kept telling me, no, he's dead. He has to be dead or your mother is a liar. It was like I kept telling myself, you mustn't tell anybody, you mustn't tell anybody. (Janie Sutleworth, in Cottle, 1980, p. 21)

Sometimes hiding or the compartmentalization of memories reflects an identification with other people. To be a child of particular parents means internalizing their secrets as well as their typical ways of keeping secrets. Failing to do so might threaten one's very identity. Any situation that threatens to uncover the secret is then experienced as a threat to the integrity of the self.

Traumatic experiences, even those caused by impersonal forces, are often unwanted communications because they threaten the illusion of personal control that most people have a strong wish to believe in. One reason victims are blamed is simply that they confront the rest of us with disturbing realities.

People outside the self also systematically distort aspects of the past in the service of their own agendas. Even in the absence of explicit external demands for silence, the awareness that some subjects are socially taboo or that some communications would not be believed may serve as powerful restraints.

External pressures to avoid mention of unpleasant realities may be self-serving, as when a perpetrator of abuse insists that it never happened. But they also come from well-meaning people who genuinely believe they are acting in the best interests of the person whose communication is being suppressed. Unfortunately, by protectively tip-toeing around a painful story, such well-intentioned people increase the isolation rather than the security of survivors.

Janie, quoted above, was supposedly being protected, for example. The story that her father was dead was originally orchestrated by a grandmother who advised her mother to get rid of the father and tell Janie he was dead. The child would, supposedly, be better off not knowing the truth. The cover story was also supposed to protect Janie's mother, since people might blame her mother for her father's leaving if they knew the real story.

After she saw her father and realized that the story of his death was untrue, Janie was then faced with the problem of understanding what had happened as well as the deception about it. That meant thinking long and hard about the behavior and intentions of everyone involved — who's good? who's bad? It meant integrating very disparate experiences of having had and not having had a father, of believing and disbelieving her mother, of keeping silent and trying to communicate.

At first this integrative task was so overwhelming Janie developed symptoms. Unable either to speak straightforwardly or keep silent about what was happening, she began to stammer. She began to have nightmares and screaming fits and fainting spells. Cottle (1980) concluded that her stammering, in particular, represented an identification with all three of the adults involved—both her parents and her grandmother: the child could not determine whether or not her parents were speaking to one another, and, ironically, her grandmother stammered.

In order to bridge the discontinuity that had cleaved her life in two, Janie eventually had to question and transform her identifications with her parents and the grandmother who orchestrated the false story of her father's death. Cottle (1980) felt she was symbolically reborn when the secrets were finally clarified for her.

ORCHESTRATED COVER STORIES

Other people have many ways of suggesting, if not forcibly imposing, silence. It is common, for example, to hide the suicide of a family member from children in the family. And yet, the supposed secret may be guessed at or even well-known by everyone, though never openly acknowledged by anyone. When other people provide misleading or false explanations, they do not simply reinforce the denial of terrible events; they often help orchestrate alternative narratives. Pynoos and Eth (1985), for example, describe an eight-year-old boy who saw his father lying in a pool of blood. In reality, the father's throat had been slashed. The cover story told to the boy was that his father had had a shaving accident.

Whenever the self is an unreceptive audience to a memory, it may behave like other unreceptive people. It may reinterpret the story. As a narrative, this reinterpretation of reality often leads to and blends with other distortions, including complicated stories about what is really going on.

The sense of unreality often associated with trauma is sometimes deliberately exploited by perpetrators of intentional abuse. By enforcing silence in the victim or by enacting improbable scenarios, they can cover their tracks. Child abuse, for example, may be presented as a game in which make-believe is inextricably mixed with abusive acts. Called to accounts, perpetrators can easily dismiss accusations as the product of wild imagination.

Whenever a listener does not want to hear a particular story, the privileged status of the narrator as the one who experienced the event may be challenged or ignored. Some witnesses are especially easy to challenge. Historically, even in courts of law, credibility has been powerfully associated with status; children, women, and minorities have been suspect (Armstrong, 1994; MacKinnon, 1989; McGough, 1994).

Where criminal activity is involved, as in instances of child pornography or prostitution, bizarre cover stories are supplemented by insistence that the exploited victims are criminals and will be punished for disclosing secrets. Even when silencing is well-meaning, intended to protect a vulnerable victim, the result is often a sense of social isolation as well as self-alienation.

Unspoken secrets and deceptive dialogues constitute "official" stories that, when repeated, are sometimes elaborated as family myths. The self may carry two contrasting narratives, only one of which can be spoken. Unrehearsed, even forbidden, the silenced story may fade from conscious memory. Yet the self may remain aware that the official story is, somehow, false or incomplete.

When unnarrated images or bodily feelings attest to the censored details, they may be altogether disconnected from the narrative contexts that might give them meaning. Yet they persist as enduring though mysterious memorials to painful events. The hidden story, encoded in bodily feelings or repetitive behavioral enactments, does not disappear. It is merely disconnected from verbal narrative.

Silence is usually countered, however, by powerful feelings about the secret that may be hard to disguise. One result of these conflicting motives — the wish to hide and the wish to tell — may be a cryptic representation of trauma that simultaneously reveals and conceals. Some enactments replay a traumatic memory in mime; what cannot be spoken is visually displayed. Reality, after all, can be a harsh taskmaster. Although memories are subject to severe distortion, there are limits to how much distortion can be managed by a nonpsychotic individual. It is easier to change minor details than to totally eradicate life-changing essentials.

The effect of disparate or covert narratives on memory may be to increase doubt in others as well as in the self: Which story is correct? Is there any reliable reality, or is one story as good as another? Who is the credible witness? Harsh realities, however, do not go away just because they are ignored or refuted. As Deborah Lipstadt (1993) cogently observes, "By its very nature the business of interpretation cannot be purely objective. But it is built on a certain body of irrefutable evidence: Slavery happened; so did the Black Plague and the Holocaust" (p. 21).

Some reinterpretations are based on a recognition that a disturbing event cannot be fitted into existing schemas. Others arise from an awareness that one cannot seek clarification from others; the event simply cannot be talked about with anyone else. Self-talk then reflects an awareness of having an unmentionable secret.

In such a state of social isolation, the self may not be able to avoid constructing some kind of narrative. But by labeling the experience unreal or calling it a dream, one can more easily keep quiet about it. Dreams are just fantasies. One is permitted to keep them secret, even to forget them entirely.

To accommodate reality, it is often much easier to change a story about the past than to put it completely out of mind. Self-soothing denial can leave facts intact in memory while radically altering one's recollection of feelings and meaning. "What happened was not so bad," goes the reassuring story. "Nothing is really different than before." Another way of coping with the conflict between the wish to forget and the persistence of veridical memory is through the deliberate creation of divergent narratives. The disturbing true story cannot be altogether forgotten and may even have been told on occasion. But a more palatable account is eventually constructed to replace it. By being systematically, even stridently rehearsed, the cover story becomes, in effect, privileged over the truth.

In everyday life, however, many narratives diverge only gradually as the self obsessively mulls over an originally veridical set of memories and reinterprets them. It is sometimes possible to track back to a time when the truth was accurately rendered.

CRYSTAL

As she patted an extra layer of makeup onto her cheek, Crystal realized that the bruise was still visible. If anyone at work mentioned it, she would have to invent a story about an accident. She did not really expect anyone to mention it, since her history of "accidents" was familiar to everybody. Her coworkers must know by now that Phil was hitting her. But since Crystal obviously did not want to talk about it, no one else did either.

Crystal was used to hiding. Phil's beating her was just the latest in a long line of family secrets that went back to her childhood. Growing up in a small midwestern town where her father was a respected member of the community, she had known without being explicitly told never to mention in public that he hit her mother. It did not happen too often, after all, and her mother acted as if it did not happen at all.

When she was in high school, Crystal found out that her father was having an affair with a woman who was also prominent in the community. But by that time, she was so practiced at keeping quiet about her home life that it was easy to keep this new secret, too. When her mother started drinking heavily, Crystal also kept quiet about that. She just started spending as much time as possible away from home.

Finally, when she was seventeen, she and her boyfriend, Phil, planned the biggest secret of all. They ran away one weekend and got married. And by the time Phil started hitting her, she had so much practice keeping secrets that her present life seemed a logical continuation of the past. She was such an expert at pretending that she could even fool herself. She had to be happy with Phil, didn't she? She had given up a comfortable, middle-class life to marry this man.

When Crystal entered psychotherapy at the age of thirty-six, she seemed to have an excellent memory and could give a clear account of her history. The most unpleasant events of her past — her father's outbursts — had been too often repeated to be forgotten. Yet she was vague about details and talked about her childhood as if it had happened to somebody else. Her store of memories seemed to be, in fact, a set of clichés, like the repetitive script of a soap opera.

Crystal's explanations and rationalizations were equally clichéd. Her father hit her mother because his work as a store manager was very stressful and because her mother was sometimes very argumentative and provoked him. In spite of his temper, he really loved his family, especially Crystal, who was his favorite child. And in spite of the fights, her mother really loved him. But her mother let herself go and started drinking too much. No wonder her father got fed up and started an affair.

Describing her own adult life, however, Crystal was no longer willing to excuse her husband's abuse. She had separated from him and was in therapy to help her stand by her decision to leave him and plan for her future. In therapy, she began to review her present difficulties in the light of past ones. Her life with Phil had, early on, begun to reflect certain relationship patterns she had internalized as a child. Her own marriage mirrored her parents' marriage much more obviously than she was willing to admit.

One of the most striking resemblances, of course, was the extent to which Crystal's life had become a continual cover-up. For all of her life she had been protecting what were really open secrets. Her coworkers knew she was being battered. When she began to explore her childhood, she also began to suspect that neither her father's abuse nor her mother's drinking had really been as much of a secret as the family had always pretended.

Yet, although she could readily see parallels between her father's abuse and Phil's, her tendency to emphasize contrasts made her deemphasize those parallels. Unlike her father, for example, Phil was by no means a respected member of the community. He had been into drugs and had trouble holding a job. And unlike her mother, Crystal herself was not a heavy drinker.

Crystal's need to idealize her father, in spite of his violent behavior, also functioned as a cover story for a conflict that had led directly to her involvement with Phil. She had been emotionally enmeshed with her parents. Unable to manage a gradual separation, she had finally extricated herself by literally running away from home. Because of this enmeshment, she had needed to see Phil as radically different from her father and herself as radically different from her mother.

In therapy it eventually became apparent to Crystal that her real memories of real childhood miseries were incomplete. She no longer connected them with the feelings they had aroused when she originally experienced them.

In therapy, it also gradually became apparent to Crystal that something essential was missing not only from her memories of childhood, but from her memories of her life with Phil. Although she was not hiding from the memories as narratives, she was very much in hiding from her own emotions. Much of the time she felt numb. Her feelings — fear, anger, frustration — were as well masked as the bruises on her cheeks. Which is to say that they were sometimes better concealed from Crystal than from those around her.

Once she acknowledged these hidden feelings, Crystal could make more sense of how both the feelings and her attempts to escape from them had motivated some of the most important decisions she had made, including her decision to marry Phil. In a very important sense, repeating aspects of her parents' marriage had been a way of holding onto the past while seeming to break away from it.

IN AND OUT OF THE BODY

When events are overwhelming and unusual, the remembering body and the remembering self may encode them in different modes. Vivid sensory and somatic images may remain unnarrated. Self-reflective narratives may diverge from more strictly "objective" descriptions of what is happening.

The assumption that unnarrated feelings and behaviors are simply forgotten is unwarranted. When they are repeated in symptomatic enactments or surface as dream images, they sometimes accurately replay traumatic episodes. Yet the self may not recognize these replays as a repetition of real events. And amalgamations of fantasy with reality may obscure the traumatic origin of the memories.

A simple example of this divergence of narratives is observable in instances in which an ordinarily painful physical injury goes unnoticed till after a crisis is over. At that point, it may or may not be possible to track back to the moment the injury occurred. At the time, a momentary awareness of some cue — pain or bleeding — may have been almost immediately overshadowed by a focus on external events. Similarly, the body under stress may have engaged in complex action sequences that are only vaguely, if at all, remembered. These range from self-protective behaviors like taking cover or running from a burning building to complicated attempts to rescue oneself or other people.

Some self-created transformations of traumatic experience involve interpretations of unusual sensations or perceptions. The body itself may seem unfamiliar, alien. The sense of alienation sometimes involves a feeling that the event is not a real occurrence or is not really happening to the self. The self may experience itself as a detached observer, watching from some point outside the body. Or one may observe oneself behaving like an automaton rather than a human being. Such responses are referred to clinically as "derealization" and "depersonalization" and are commonly observed in posttraumatic stress disorder.

Sometimes, however, an out-of-body experience is a transcendent experience rather than a self-alienating dissociation. When that happens, the traumatic memory, however secret, can be a positive force in an unfolding life.

CHET

One day, while playing catch with a friend, Chet ran backward into a glass patio door, cutting his arm badly. His friend's father rushed him to the emergency room. He had lost a lot of blood, and the injury to his arm required an operation. After he came home, he did not have the use of the arm for quite some time. Because of complications, he was soon in the hospital again. Most of the school year was a loss.

Chet was ten when it happened. For a long time he was in a lot of pain. But one of the most striking things he remembered about the whole experience was how, at first, there had been no pain at all. Almost as soon as he had hit the door, he had found himself outside his body, watching from above while his body was wrapped in a blanket and placed in the car.

Later, this memory was almost as significant to him as the accident itself. It convinced him that the soul really can live outside the body. His family was not religious, so he could not readily interpret his experience in the context of a belief system. But he began to think sometimes about religious beliefs. He decided that God had wanted him to live for some reason.

Sensing that other people would not believe him or that they might think him crazy, he never told anybody about the out-of-body experience. He did not find out until years later that many people had had out-of-body experiences and that such experiences were commonly associated with close calls with death.

The accident had many negative consequences in Chet's life. The arm did not heal properly. He had trouble with it for a long time, and there was an ugly scar that never really faded. But in spite of all these problems, Chet considered himself lucky to be alive. The notion that he must be alive for a purpose also stayed with him. By the time he was in high school, he had decided to devote his life to helping other people. He joined the Peace Corps and, in time, became an administrator for an social agency that did relief work with refugees from war-torn countries.

Chet's accident was, of course, by no means the only contributing factor in his positive development. A teacher who took an interest in him in high school was an inspiration as well as a valuable role model. His friend's father, who had saved his life, was for many years a dependable source of encouragement. And although his parents were sometimes dismayed by his choices in life, they were generally supportive.

As an adult, Chet did not think much about the childhood accident. But in mid-life, he took a creative writing course that required him to write about an important event in his past. For the first time, he decided to tell the story of his unusual out-of-body experience to other people. And he was surprised and gratified to learn that it was not so unusual after all.

The more he thought about the experience, the more Chet realized that a brush with death had profoundly influenced the course of his life. At the moment the accident occurred, he did not have any thought at all of dying. But later, in the hospital, he knew he might have died. It was a scary yet also exciting thought, and he never quite forgot it. He might have died, but he did not. That was the important thing.

As an adult, Chet had an unusual empathy for severely injured and dying people. He supposed it to be a legacy of his own trauma. But he always also thought of it as something more than that. It was a gift. And although he was not given to preachments or philosophizing, he valued it as such. A terrible trauma had in some mysterious way enriched his life. Whenever he reflected on that, it gave him courage to confront other difficulties.

CHAPTER 9

The Self in Pieces

"I have the feeling," Delbo says, "that the 'self' who was in the camp isn't me, isn't the person who is here, opposite you. No, it's too unbelievable. And everything that happened to this other 'self,' the one from Auschwitz, doesn't touch me now, *me*, doesn't concern me, so distinct are deep memory . . . and common memory . . . "
— Langer, *Holocaust Testimonies*, p. 5

The scaffold proved a crucial event in [Dostoevsky's] inner life. His life was "split in two," the past was ended, there began another existence, a "rebirth in a new form."
— Konstantin Mochulsky, 1967, p. 142

TRAUMA DIVIDES personal history. Since the self is to a large extent defined by its memories, disturbances in self-perception and self integration characteristic of trauma reactions complicate other effects of trauma. Major failures of integration can leave the self in pieces.

A dissociated identity configuration, however, like any identity configuration, is not a simple reaction but a complex historical development. Emergency reactions to trauma are only the beginning of a sequence that eventually results in distinct but unintegrated self-schemas. Over a lifetime, posttraumatic adaptations play as important a role in the evolution of self-defining memories as the initial trauma.

In cases of massive psychic trauma, as are characteristic of Holocaust survivors, this self-splitting is not necessarily accompanied by a loss of memory for *what* happened so much as by a sense that the horrendous events happened to a different person. Though alien, this other self is not a stranger, but rather the guardian of deep memories that persist indelibly and defy narration.

In the long run, whether or not a meaningful integration can be achieved, the evolution of the self divided by trauma is marked by a lifetime of posttraumatic accommodations and transformations. Although memory is the architect of such changes, the structures eventually created are a function of skill and competence as much as of intention. Like the phoenix rising from its ashes, the self can transcend trauma. Wholeness and integrity can replace fragmentation. But this development is not inevitable. Even saints must struggle for transcendence. Certainly, integration cannot be hurried by well-meaning exhortations to "get over it." Rather, for most survivors, it is a gradual and hard-won achievement.

When integration fails, in spite of the best efforts, fragments of the self may simply coexist as cryptic memorials to an interrupted life. The self in pieces is usually uneasy, shadowed by a loss of wholeness it can neither accept nor repair. Memory, like a shattered mirror, may be sharp and bright in places but not much use. Yet the fragments cannot be easily swept away. Like a dangerous foreign object, memory looms as an ever-present danger, and avoiding it may become the most urgent posttraumatic accommodation of all.

Sometimes two or more distinct and relatively coherent selves evolve, sharing a common body but sequestering disparate memories. When these disparate selves are on relatively friendly terms, they can cooperate to their mutual advantage. Frequently, though, there is an ongoing state of disharmony; at times, they may even be openly at war with one another.

TRANCES AND FUGUES

Not far off was a church, and the top of its gilt roof gleamed in the bright sun. He remembered that he looked with horrible intensity at this roof and at the rays which flashed from it; he could not tear himself away from the rays; it seemed that these rays were to be his new nature, that after three minutes he would somehow merge with them. (Dostoevsky, *The Idiot*, as translated in Mochulsky, 1967, p. 144)

State-dependent memory effects associated with altered states of consciousness play an important role in internal divisions and compartmentalizations. Sharp discontinuities in psychobiological processes can overwhelm the integrative function of memory. The bipolar responses that typify reactions to extreme trauma, for example, produce contrasting kinds of alterations in consciousness. State-related memories of trauma and state-related identity experiences reflect these perceived contrasts.

The altered states of consciousness characteristic of trauma reactions may be compared with those associated with normal biorhythms. Over the course of a day, arousal levels and consciousness fluctuate in predictable patterns of circadian and ultradian rhythms (Rossi, 1993). Normally, however, the boundary between sleep and waking, although not rigid, is clear enough to allow the two contrasting states to be discriminated. No matter how vividly a dream is remembered, for example, no matter how many veridical details of actual events it includes, it is usually perceived on waking to be a dream rather than reality.

Sometimes, however, sleeping and waking states are not so clearly demarcated. For instance, somnambulism, a sleep disorder in which the individual walks, talks, or engages in organized behavior while not conscious of his or her actual surroundings, is common in childhood. In fact, the class of altered states of consciousness is much larger than categories like "sleep" and "trance" or "hypnosis" would indicate. Alcohol, drugs, crowd reactions, stimulus deprivation, and extreme boredom are among the situations that can change one's level of arousal, state of awareness, and self-perception. Some such alterations are characterized by almost frenzied mood and behavior. Others involve extreme behavioral inhibition and/or a muting of awareness approaching somnolence.

Discriminations between sleep and waking may also be blurred in traumatic contexts. As a result, very real occurrences may be experienced as if in a dream. Or the traumatized individual may think and behave as if in a trance.

In traumatic states, the intentional self who ordinarily feels in conscious control of actions may seemingly be overridden by automatic reaction patterns. And when that occurs, the strangeness of external events is compounded by the strangeness of internal ones. Experiences of depersonalization or derealization, in which the individual feels self-estranged, unreal, dead, or like a machine, are common. After returning to a more normal state, memories about the self in the altered state may be experienced as distant, as if the trauma had happened to someone else (Putnam, 1989).

When an experience of trauma is rendered vague and unreal by a clouding of consciousness, the individual may wander temporarily in a fugue, an altered state of consciousness dissociated from the individual's normal waking existence. The individual in a fugue engages in organized patterns of behavior, including dialogues with other people, that may mask the fact that she is "not herself."

Fugues highlight what has been described (Braun, 1988) as a dissociative continuum; such altered states of consciousness continue for varying lengths of time and are organized by activities ranging from the simple to the complex. From this perspective, a fugue may be viewed as an extended version of a variable but normal state. Rossi (1993), for example, has described the "everyday trance" as a normal consequence of oscillations in body rhythms associated with the sleep-wake cycle. Such normal trances or fugues are observable in ordinary daydreaming or in such phenomena as "highway hypnosis." Suddenly the affected individual jumps to attention and becomes aware that, without really realizing it, he has executed some complexly organized but automatic behavior such as driving past an intended freeway exit.

The fugues precipitated by trauma, in contrast, can be characterized as trance states in which attention is refocused over an extended period and the individual cannot shift at will to consciously alert behavior. Traumatically stimulated fugues may be brief, but sometimes involve extensive, complexly organized life changes. Some individuals wander far from their native residences or even establish new lives in distant locations. Dramatic stories about lengthy posttraumatic amnesias involving identity loss often describe such posttraumatic fugue states.

Fugues are sometimes experienced or remembered as dream-like episodes that, to observers, resemble sleepwalking. Their posttraumatic origin has long been recognized in art and literature. Lady Macbeth's sleepwalking fits, in which she repetitively tried to wash her hands of the king's blood, is a famous example. The "mad scene" from the opera "Lucia di Lammermoor" also portrays the distracted heroine in a fugue-like altered state of consciousness.

In the nineteenth century, such states were considered characteristic of hysteria, a serious mental disturbance seemingly epidemic in women (Waites, 1993). They were systematically studied by psychiatrists like Janet (Ellenberger, 1970), who connected them with trauma responses and by Breuer (Breuer & Freud, 1893–1895), who connected them with what he termed a "hypnoid state." It was Freud's view of hysteria and other forms of neurosis that eventually gained ascendence in psychiatric circles, however. After that happened, the study of altered states of consciousness and the identity disorders with which such states were often associated went out of fashion.

After a long eclipse during the first part of the twentieth century, interest in posttraumatic and dissociative disorders revived. A number of social factors contributed to this development, including the Vietnam war and the Women's Movement, which focused public attention on consequences of violence against women (Waites, 1993). The renewed interest in dissociative phenomena led to valuable research and clinical findings. But the use of the term *dissociation* has not always been consistent or clear.

When inconsistent or discontinuous experiences remain disconnected in memory, they are sometimes said to be dissociated. But this term is also used to refer to the disconnection of experiences that were originally integrated. Dissociation as an outcome of complex posttraumatic coping strategies, such as the organization of a secret life, should be conceptually distinguished from basic failures of integration. It leads to different kinds of posttraumatic disturbances and presents a different set of challenges to therapeutic intervention.

Another distinction that sometimes proves useful is that between failures to integrate information-processing across different modalities, such as seeing and hearing, and the conscious construction of two discrepant narratives about the same event. Altered states produced by traumatic events affect not only the encoding and possibly the storage of images and feelings, but also the narrative organization of episodic memory and the integration of the events with self-referential memory systems. In some instances unusual sensations and perceptions remain disconnected from conscious narrative. In others, unusual perceptions of the self undergoing trauma may lead to the construction of divergent or discrepant narratives about the event or about the self.

Posttraumatic adaptations thus commonly include a mix of discontinuities and dissociations, arising both from the psychobiological effects of trauma on initial information-processing and from intentional coping strategies devised after the fact to help the individual manage residual trauma effects, including unwanted memories.

Some survivors construct two or more lives that reflect the contrasting psychobiological extremes of excitement and numbing associated with trauma reactions. When deliberate forms of coping, such as avoidance strategies and denial, are added to this mix, and when narratives are constructed about the contrasting extremes, the number of contexts associated with any given trauma multiplies. State-dependent effects on memory may multiply accordingly.

POSTTRAUMATIC AMNESIA

Posttraumatic amnesia is one of the most dramatic and popularly recognized responses to trauma. As a stereotypic plot line in books and movies, it is usually too pat an explanation to ring true. But although global psychogenic amnesias are not nearly so common as such media presentations suggest, transient, reversible psychogenic amnesias have been documented.

The existence of posttraumatic amnesia is well documented in veterans with PTSD (Cassiday & Lyons, 1992; Figley, 1985; Van Dyke et al., 1985) for example. It is also commonly reported by victims of sexual trauma. In a study of fifty-three patients with histories of sexual abuse, Herman and Schatzow (1987) found that 64 percent had experienced amnesia at some point for some or all aspects of the abuse. The earlier the abuse occurred and the more violent it was, the more likely such amnesic symptoms. Data collected by Briere and Conte (1993) substantiated these findings.

In many instances the inability to retrieve a memory at a particular point in time does not necessarily indicate that the memory is irretrievably lost. Much forgetting is simply a lack of attention to what is potentially available. Here, too, encoding-retrieval interactions are decisive. Memories that are not rehearsed are less easily retrieved than those that are. Over time, they may seem to disappear altogether from memory.

In everyday life, everyone is familiar with the vagaries of encoding-retrieval interactions. A song not heard since high school is played on the radio, transporting one back to the senior prom. A visit to a childhood home triggers a memory of a secret hiding place under the stairs. These memories were never repressed and clearly have not decayed; they were just not thought about for a long time. When an unexpected cue jogs attention, they suddenly spring into focus.

Even when a memory cannot be easily jogged, we cannot assume from the simple absence of recall that it has decayed. It may have once been strongly encoded, repeatedly rehearsed, and even retrieved at a later time before it was carefully avoided and finally disappeared from voluntary recollection.

As a result of dissociation, involuntary amnesias, or deliberate avoidance behavior, the clarity of memory for a particular trauma may vary over time. At some points it may be remembered as an episode of one's personal history. At other points it may be excluded from any conscious narrative.

The *fact* that a trauma is remembered can also be deceptive. Even when the self is cognitively aware that an event occurred, significant associated responses — powerful emotions, strange experiences of derealization or depersonalization, somatic sensations — may be deleted from recollection. Whether forgotten or remembered, however, such unintegrated responses often produce effects on adaptation that, although mysterious, cannot be ignored indefinitely.

Posttraumatic amnesia has wide-ranging effects on posttraumatic adaptations, such as identity consolidation. Traumatically induced amnesia can delete information needed to make the self as well as the past meaningful. As a psychobiological effect associated with state-dependent memory, it is complicated by deliberate posttraumatic adaptations, such as intentional avoidance of painful cues to memory.

MISMATCHED STORIES AND DIVERGENT NARRATIVES

Marilyn [van Derbur] explained to her audience . . . that as a child she had "split" into a happy "day child" and a terrified "night child." . . . Her "day child" never knew what her "night child" experienced. All memories of abuse were sequestered in the night child's mind. (Terr, 1994, p. 124)

The divided self that evolves reflects not only the nature of the trauma, but the patterning of the traumatic events. If a major discontinuity in personal history involves a one-time event, state-dependent learning effects may combine with divergent narratives to create an internal boundary between "before" and "after." If one kind of trauma has been experienced repeatedly but systematically, for example, as when sexual abuse occurs only at night, an internal split may accommodate the underlying order in the repetitions. On the other hand, if there is no predictability or order in the abuse, only a global response like chronic numbing may offer protection from it.

Not only extreme differences between historical events as sequenced in time, but radical differences in the experience of the self at different times can become the basis for internal divisions. Individual differences in coping are also important. After Marilyn van Derbur described her experiences in 1991, for example, her older sister Gwen said that she, too, had been sexually abused and had dissociated while the abuse was occurring. But she had never forgotten that it happened (Terr, 1994). Such contrasting responses to similar experiences illustrate how intimately memory is tied to personal identity as an individual achievement.

Altered states of consciousness may be wordless though intense. But they sometimes include narratives. In any case, trauma exerts variable pressures on the narrative process and the dialogues that commonly structure it.

Some trauma effects, such as increased levels of arousal and a focusing of attention, tend to increase veridicality. The presence of other observers may enhance this effect. An event observed in the presence of another person or by many spectators, such as the explosion of the Challenger spacecraft, for example, tends to evoke highly veridical memories for such details as what one was wearing that day or who was standing nearby (Terr, 1994). In other instances, the effect of trauma is to decrease veridicality.

Social validation or denial of both perception and memory plays an important role in how much distortion occurs even in early stages of information-processing. Since early encoding is based on language and social schemas, even simple narratives may be carefully edited to match the expectations of a particular audience. Such social influences, usually discussed as forms of suggestibility, may be a major source of distortion.

When social pressures shape dialogues between self and self as well as dialogues between self and other, the end result may be an internal division between a socially compliant self and a dissenting, but private, narrator. The mismatched stories and divergent narratives the remembering self creates may continue to multiply over a lifetime as unbearable but unforgettable events are constantly reconstructed in memory.

The alternative narratives the self constructs as a result of confusion, ambivalence, or conflict can give rise to a cacophony of internal voices. And the radically inconsistent modes of processing information and experiencing the self produced by trauma are a major source of mismatched stories. In extreme instances, divergent narratives about past events may make reality almost impossible for a listener to decipher.

Talk, including self-talk, is by no means the whole of memory, however. And even memories that are narrated seldom include everything remembered. Thus, even when many divergent narratives are constructed, unspeakable details may be sequestered from conscious attention and narrative organization.

Visual flashbacks and somatic images, for example, however representative of a story, however compelling to those experiencing them, are difficult to describe to outsiders and, even when clearly remembered, may remain alien to the self. Behavioral reenactments are also often difficult to decipher. When they persist in recall but remain uncommunicated, they are potential narratives, stories waiting to be told.

Even when they remain untold, vivid experiences that are not easily integrated with privileged narratives do not just fade away. They often persist in silence. Or special privileged narratives, public or private, are organized around them. "That was before," the self may say. "It's no longer important, really. I'm different now." Or, "It's silly of me after all these years to get jumpy every time there's a storm warning." Or, "The doctor says there's nothing physically wrong with me. The best way of dealing with these stomachaches is to ignore them and go on about my business." Or, "I know I've had a nightmare again, but I can't remember it. Maybe I just need medication to help me sleep." Even when a terrible event is given a narrative gloss, the story may be recounted in a detached way, as if it happened to someone else: "The accident was terrible, of course, but I never cried about it, not even at the funeral."

Much of what observers attribute to failed memory is simply an absence or even a motivated suppression of narrative. Many of the narratives that pass for memory are veridical but incomplete; they leave out images and feelings or disturbing details. As a result, the story the listener hears is not necessarily the whole story or the truest one available.

COMPULSIVE REPLAYS

Inconsistent and divergent narratives as well as other variables that contribute to memory distortion have sometimes been emphasized as evidence that victims' stories of trauma cannot be trusted. And it is undeniable that mismatched stories require cautious evaluation. But an emphasis on distortion underestimates an opposite and equally influential posttraumatic tendency, the tendency to become fixated on a trauma and to recount it repetitively. This fixation, which may consist of a monotonous though veridical replay of terrible events, can prove almost as painful to observers as to the victim caught up in it.

Compulsive repetitive enactments and stories are in some instances associated with flashbacks and seem to replay a whole episodic gestalt. To an audience, such repetitions may sound like rote recitals repeated over and over without modification. The one who plays them out may seem to be seeking an audience, yet may also seem impervious to the influence of other people. In this respect, the assumption that traumatized individuals are suggestible proves ironically unwarranted. Urging the individual in the grip of his story to cease and desist simply has no effect. The self who goes on repeating a painful story seems to be unable to move from monologue to dialogue.

Under such circumstances, even well-meaning people may get tired and tune out the story. At that point, the silence of the other becomes an important component of the failed dialogue. The repetition may then become even more insistent and strident, as if attempting to drown out the painful silence.

The responses others make to monotonous repetitions, especially the absence of any acknowledgment, send a significant message that is usually noticed by victims. Silence speaks louder than words in both confirming or denying what the self is saying, and in discrediting the self as witness to memory. In the absence of external validation, the self may lose confidence in stories even while compulsively repeating them. Yet even when they seem impervious to social influence, individuals isolated by trauma are often seeking to reestablish social dialogue.

Intimidation and enforced silence are, of course, expectable accompaniments of intentional abuse. But a refusal to talk about or listen to painful stories is not necessarily neglectful or self-serving. A refusal to acknowledge a painful story may merely be intended to distract the victim from it. Sometimes the well-meaning message from others is, "It's best for you to forget it and get on with your life."

Insistently repeated and punitive silencing, in contrast, often systematically orchestrates divergent narratives not only by driving the veridical account underground but by enforcing adherence to an official story. Sometimes the victim of such intimidation effects a compromise, replaying the secret story in disguised form. Mysterious somatic symptoms or behavioral enactments then overtly but cryptically represent the covert but unspeakable story. The self may have varying degrees of insight into these subterfuges. Like some of Cottle's (1980) subjects, one may be aware of simultaneously trying to keep a secret and trying to unburden oneself of it.

Where the self is not being actively intimidated by other people but is, in effect, the strongest source of its own silencing, there may be no insight at all into the meaning of symbolic and symptomatic forms of remembering. In any case, withdrawal of social support can help trap the traumatized individual in an obsessive but private narrative about the past that is increasingly isolating. When that happens, private internal dialogues with an imaginary audience may be created to replace the disappointing or missing social interactions.

Whether attempts at silencing are well intentioned or self-serving, then, they do not necessarily have any effect on the repetition itself. Even when an intimidated individual obediently parrots an official story, the covert story may continue to be silently but compulsively rehearsed or behaviorally enacted.

TRAUMA AND IDENTITY CONSOLIDATION

Altered states do not just affect basic processes of memory, as when a sleepwalker or the victim of an alcoholic blackout reports total amnesia for periods of organized behavior. They sometimes become the central organizing contexts around which distinct identity configurations crystallize. Depersonalization is an identity disturbance that is usually temporary, but that can subsequently interfere with the integration of traumatic experiences into a coherent self. As a transient reaction, depersonalization has been observed in one-third of research subjects who have experienced life-threatening events (Noyes & Kletti, 1976). It is also a symptom in many psychiatric and neurological conditions (Putman, 1989).

As a trauma reaction, depersonalization is sometimes assimilated to other forms of denial, such as narratives that insist that an event never really happened or that, if it did, it did not happen to the self. Such denials help relieve pressures to fit the disturbing event into existing self-schemas or to organize new ones that integrate it.

Sometimes, the identity disturbance characteristic of dissociative reactions is accompanied by a complete amnesia for self-referential information, as occurs in psychogenic amnesia or in fugue states. In extreme cases, the individual may elaborate two or more alternate identity configurations.

When the posttraumatic period is organized by many self-defining activities, such as moving to a new address, working at a new job, and even changing one's name, the relation between fugue, memory loss, and identity reconstruction is obvious. The fugue is, in effect, a way station on the road to developing an alternative identity.

If repeated traumas are managed by repeated instances of dissociation or the construction of many alternative narratives about the self, personal history becomes so disjointed that it cannot function integratively in identity consolidation. The result may be a fragmenting of identity as well as personal history. The self no longer presents a coherent, unified story about itself. Instead, several stories compete for attention.

For much of the twentieth century, the relation between altered states of consciousness, memory, and identity formation was eclipsed by orthodox psychoanalytic perspectives. It was only after the revived interest in both trauma and in altered states of consciousness that occurred during the 1970s that the early work of Janet was rediscovered (Ellenberger, 1970) and a new body of research on the subject began to emerge.

For the last two decades, much research has clarified the reciprocal interactions between memory and identity. The most serious form of disturbance, multiple personality disorder, has been found to be usually associated with extreme and repeated traumatization in childhood (Kluft, 1985; Putnam, 1989).

Certain developmental periods are especially vulnerable to disruptions of identity consolidation. Abused children who respond by dissociating may experience themselves piecemeal even in childhood. Traumatized children are also especially at risk during adolescence. As Erikson (1968) has illustrated, the integration of a coherent idea of who one is and where one is going is a major issue during that period. As the adolescent attempts to negotiate the transition between childhood and adulthood, the imagined relation between past and future has a profound impact on such life tasks as choosing a vocation or a mate.

Many adolescents become very interested in the process of constructing autobiographical memory. They recount their reflections on the past and their hopes for the future in journals and diaries. They engage in endless discussions with peers about who they have been and are and are becoming. They carefully contrive images that announce identity through dress, hair style, and makeup.

The adolescent is maturing cognitively as well as emotionally (Piaget, 1950/1981) in ways that facilitate understanding and interpreting personal history. But if trauma has delayed development or resulted in specific deficits, needed competencies are unavailable for identity consolidation. Such common legacies of trauma as difficulties in concentrating or poor impulse control can be insurmountable obstacles in coping with the increasingly complex demands of schooling and social integration.

When a trauma is a consequence of deliberate abuse, it may have been repeated over long stretches of time and have impacted adversely on several developmental periods. Repeated abuse structures expectations about the future as well as memories of the past. It affects self-concept and self-esteem. It is often accompanied by rationalizations or parental explanations that radically shape the child's view of reality: "This is happening because you are bad." Or even, "That did not really happen to you."

If the trauma has led to social withdrawal or antisocial behavior, the result may be a deficit in social skills. Such young people are especially vulnerable to those who promise instant or easy solutions. Cult leaders may appear to offer soothing liberation from confusion or salvation from conflict (Singer, 1995). Drugs or alcohol offer a ready escape and may be used as a form of self-medication and self soothing (Waites, 1993).

In adolescence, children who have been severely and repeatedly traumatized are faced with overwhelming obstacles, especially if they have used dissociation as a major coping mechanism. A child who has spent a whole life creating separate parts is unequal to the developmentally appropriate task of self integration during the teen years (Bryant, Kessler,

& Shirar, 1992). The child who has dissociated extensively may, during this time, consolidate and strengthen the boundaries between several discrete "selves."

Many less damaged people find it more natural, if still disquieting, to admit a particular gap or discontinuity in personal history and try to live with it. Some try to ignore or deny what cannot be assimilated. And some focus their attention on a narrative about the past that is not wholly false, but that, because it emphasizes the consistency rather than the confusion of the self, is less threatening.

DISSOCIATED IDENTITIES

You got two very different lives you got to work with at the same time, and nobody but you can say which is the best one, or which is the real one. (Tyrone Morgan in Cottle, 1980, p. 202)

The confused individual who displays contrasting or contradictory narratives appears inconsistent to the self as well as to others. If the inconsistency is recognized, it creates integrative pressures. The easiest accommodation may be to distort or delete some details of a troubling story, to construct a single narrative, however incomplete or distorted, and stick with it.

There is, however, another way of dealing with incongruent stories or a confusing jumble of perceptions, memories, and feelings. Some individuals maintain them in distinct compartmentalized patterns of thought or behavior. Such compartmentalized patterns are sometimes completely sequestered from conscious reflection, as when a period of time following a traumatic experience remains lost to recollection. Or they may be preserved in memory as occasionally recollected but disconnected pieces of personal history.

Dissociation makes it possible to maintain two or more different readings of the same event in this way. When the disparate reactions and behavior patterns are not integrated or are kept separate, the discomfort usually associated with inconsistency can be avoided. When this process involves coping mechanisms like self-induced trance states, "trance logic" (Orne, 1959) makes the inconsistencies and divergent narratives quite tolerable.

Dissociation leads to alternative scripts that may be played out consecutively, as when the individual vacillates between one focus or one interpretation of an event and a contradictory one. When identity configurations are organized around dissociated bodily sensations, enactments, or narratives, the resulting life story has a patchwork or piecemeal quality. If such dissociated blocks of personal history are extensive, they may become the building blocks of dissociated identities.

Children may try to defend themselves by avoidance of trauma-related cues or by suppressing communication, but the dissociative compartmentalization of identity, like identity itself, has a developmental timetable. The capacities for symbolization and narrative control characteristic of adults are only gradually acquired over the course of childhood. What adults observe is not simply a function of what happens, but of stage-specific developmental acquisitions.

The contrast between children's memory at different points in development and between child and adult memory highlights the extent to which remembering and forgetting are facilitated by the self who evaluates as well as the self who observes. The meaning of an always well remembered event may change over time. Or an event not initially experienced as a source of conflict may become, at some later point, a disturbing memory.

Sexually abused children, for example, may experience an unarticulated distress that is only later structured in narrative. At that point, the responses associated with the original experience may or may not be incorporated into the story about it. The story creates a defense against trauma that the young child was unable to achieve.

In many instances, early traumas, particularly the somatic responses they triggered, remain dissociated from later stories. The narrative itself functions to maintain a dissociation.

Other people also help orchestrate dissociated identities. They can and often do reinforce dissociation as a coping mechanism, not only by providing contrasting narratives about events, but by creating double binds that lead to conflicting responses (Waites, 1993). By interacting differently with different alter personalities, other people also reinforce the dissociation of identity. In childhood, parents are in a powerful position to do so.

When traumas are multiple, divisions may multiply. When such multiplicities occur in childhood, they can profoundly affect the consolidation of identity. Instead of a unitary self, several dissociated identity configurations may evolve.

Putnam (1989) believes that trauma contributes to the development of dissociated identities by disrupting the consolidation of self across contrasting behavioral states. Instead of an integrated personality, the traumatized child develops a series of alter personalities, which may be quite distinct in appearance and behavior. "Each time the child re-enters a specific dissociative state, additional memories, affects, and behaviors become state-dependently bound to that state, building up a 'life history' for the alter personality" (p. 54).

Alter personalities may differ in posture, speech, and mannerisms. They may even have different reactions to medications or anesthesia. Some research has shown that they are characterized by different EEG patterns, indicating that dissociated identities are mediated neurologically as well as psychologically (Putnam, 1989).

The line between organic and functional pathology in dissociated identities is not always clear. On the one hand, there may be subtle but unobserved brain disturbances caused by such aspects of early traumatization as kindling (Goddard, McIntyre, & Leech, 1969). The fact that severe dissociation is not infrequently associated with epilepsy is consistent with the speculation that neurological disturbances may be involved. On the other hand, there is no organic impairment in many cases of dissociative disorder. Observed disturbances can be traced more obviously to learned — perhaps overlearned — behavior patterns, such as learning to go into a self-induced trance state or to switch to an alter personality whenever anxiety is cued.

It has been suggested that the ability to effect the self-induced trances in which alter personalities are organized is an inherited form of hypnotic capability. In any case, there are some instances in which the parents of individuals with dissociated identities are themselves characterized by dissociated behavior patterns or the development of alter personalities. In such instances, internalizing the parent's dissociative tendencies is an expectable feature of the child's identification with the parent.

A historical perspective on the development of self-schemas, including multiple and unintegrated schemas, is especially useful when we try to make sense of dissociative disorders, of which dissociative identity disorder is the most serious. Multiple personalities strikingly illustrate the complexities of posttraumatic memory, particularly the paradox that it is possible to remember and forget at the same time. Or, from a technical point of view, that encoding-retrieval interactions vary across psychobiological states within the individual.

CONFABULATION

The dramatic variations in self-presentation characteristic of multiple personalities sometimes lead observers to conclude that such people are just putting on a show or lying. Professionals who subscribe to this interpretation insist that the disorder is factitious. And since the existence of multiplicity may only be discovered in the context of psychotherapy, some also claim that the disorder is iatrogenic, an artifact of therapeutic techniques, especially hypnosis.

This concern with credibility highlights the complexity of thought organization and memory retrieval in the dissociative disorders. Dissociative reactions, voluntary or involuntary, sometimes structure an ongoing narrative that incorporates the strangeness as well as the vividness of the occurrence: "This is just a dream; this is happening to somebody else." Such narratives may then be given an interpretative gloss or elaborated in fantasy. Paranoid fantasies, for example, may explain continuing posttraumatic symptoms, such as depersonalization or strange bodily sensations, as due to the "influence" of imagined enemies. Or the individual experiencing an out-of-body state may describe visitations to another planet.

However, most individuals who develop dissociative disorders are not out of contact with reality; dissociation as a coping mechanism may well help them to avoid psychosis. In spite of altered states of consciousness, some part of the dissociated self maintains a vigilant, survival-oriented contact with reality.

Cover stories need not depart radically from reality in order to sequester terrifying memories or structure self-reassuring narratives. A great deal of reality can be denied without introducing obviously psychotic distortions. Troublesome details of a memory may simply be deleted from awareness by persistent avoidance.

Confabulations sometimes consist of fantasy-based narratives that are quite plausible though not veridical. Such constructions are a common way that otherwise rational individuals try to fill in the gaps left by amnesias. Such constructions are typical of certain syndromes associated with organic brain damage, such as Korsakoff's syndrome. But psychogenic forms of memory loss not associated with any known organic impairment can also give rise to confabulations.

Confabulations are among the most obvious pitfalls in evaluating posttraumatic memories, particularly memories recovered after a period of delay. The addition of fantasy to memory is clear, of course, when a report is obviously delusional. Interpretations of a painful or perplexing event, for example, may invoke explanations that even sympathetic observers cannot accept — complicated plots by mysterious agents, persecutions by alien abductors, etc. But confabulations need not be extreme or preposterous and are not always associated with psychosis. Dissociated identities commonly do make up stories about themselves. Those with dissociative identity disorder may describe themselves quite differently from the way they appear to others; for example, a middle-aged female adult may present herself as a male child, or a brunette may insist she has red hair.

Such obvious fantasy elaborations, like divergent narratives, complicate the assessment of whether particular reports are veridical. But, again, either-or dichotomies obscure more than they explain. Just as an error of detail does not automatically prove that the gist of a story is incorrect, so the existence of fantasy elements in a story does not indicate that everything in the story is fantasy. Those really interested in discovering the truth cannot simply discount a particular story because it contains erroneous details. An informed evaluation takes into account the whole picture.

The existence of clear-cut confabulations in itself invites explanation. In the absence of organic impairment or psychosis, they commonly point to attempts by the mind to cope with the unbearable or to explain the inexplicable. They are thus expectable and frequently observed posttraumatic adaptations in cases where objective indices of historical truth are available.

Even psychotic delusions are sometimes organized around factual occurrences (Kaplan, 1995; Neiderland, 1974). Not everyone is able to dissociate trauma. And when an individual cannot cope, even by dissociating, posttraumatic accommodations may involve an extensive flight from reality. Delusional accounts of painful situations or attempts to rescue the beleaguered self through the construction of bizarre fantasies can then eclipse the veridical story of what has happened (Oltmanns & Maher, 1988). Still, one who looks closely may find a kernel of truth in the wildest delusions.

PARANOID REACTIONS AND
TRANSFERENCE PSYCHOSIS

One way individuals sometimes try to deal with traumatic memories is by denying disturbing thoughts or feelings in the self and attributing them to other people. "*I* am not terrified," goes the story. "*He* is." Or, "I am not terrified by what I remember from the *past*, but by what someone is doing to me in the *present*."

The latter reaction, presenting a remembered experience as a current reality, is sometimes the result of confounding flashbacks or obsessive memories with perceptions of current realities. These confused states are then explained or rationalized though fantasies about the behavior or motives of other people in one's present life; the terror triggered by memories of old injuries is thus moderated through paranoid projections. Through this process, the traumatized individual, in effect, substitutes a seemingly controllable present danger for an uncontrollable past danger.

Paranoid reactions are a common occurrence in the psychotherapy of posttraumatic disorders, particularly in individuals who have what is sometimes diagnosed as a "borderline personality structure" (Briere, 1989; Herman & van der Kolk, 1987). In many instances, such individuals have longstanding identity issues characterized by problems in maintaining boundaries between their own thoughts and feelings and those of other people. Psychotherapy with such individuals sometimes precipitates a special kind of reactive psychosis, transference psychosis, in which the client becomes confused or delusional and develops the fantasy that it is the therapy or the therapist that is dangerous, rather than the original trauma and problematic posttraumatic accommodations.

Paranoid reactions are also sometimes precipitated when a needed posttraumatic accommodation, such as a symbiotic dependency relationship, is threatened. Some traumatized individuals, particularly those who have internalized past relationships with abusive persons, reinstate these relationship experiences in psychotherapy as in life; doing so is a form of enactive remembering. When there is no insight into this development as a reenactment, the relationship with the therapist is then experienced as victimizing.

Enactive remembering can be a powerful resistance against recognizing that one is remembering. When it is accompanied by delusional narratives, such as the inference that one is being persecuted in the present, it can lead to destructive behaviors, such as attacks on the imagined persecutors. The whole problem is complicated immensely when an individual is still living in a traumatic context or is still in a relationship with an abusive partner. In such instances, the past is constantly being reflected and replayed in actual current events. Focusing on the past as a source of present anxiety and unnarrated reenactments is a difficult therapeutic challenge.

Transference psychosis is one of the most malignant developments in the psychotherapy of trauma victims (Waites, 1993). If it occurs early in the therapy, before the client has developed insight into enactment as a form of remembering, it may completely disrupt the therapeutic process. Anytime it occurs, it constitutes a therapeutic crisis.

But transference psychosis, although a hazard of psychotherapy with some clients, is not simply caused by psychotherapy and is not confined to psychotherapeutic settings. It is, rather, an interactional dynamic that commonly occurs when severely traumatized individuals with boundary problems enter into close relationships that reactivate extreme ambivalence. Childhood feelings of neediness and fear then produce alternating responses to attachment—clinging or withdrawal, idealization or devaluation. Reactions based on contrasting, unintegrated representations of attachment figures are sometimes discussed as "splitting."

Partners who cling to each other because both have been traumatized or abused are especially vulnerable to such reactions. They constantly reenact old traumas in the context of current enmeshments. The result is often a stormy but intense and sometimes tenaciously preserved relationship in which both partners vacillate between anxious attachment and angry withdrawal as they try to cope with but avoid thinking about a traumatic past.

PSYCHOSIS AND PERSONAL HISTORY

The school building became immense, smooth, unreal, and an inexpressible anguish pressed in on me. . . . Pupils and teachers were puppets revolving without cause, without objective. I recognized nothing, nobody. It was as though reality, attenuated, had slipped away from all these things and these people. (Sechehaye, *Autobiography of a Schizophrenic Girl*, 1951, pp. 25–26)

Psychosis involves a profound distortion of the relation between the self and the external world. When this disturbance is a matter of mood, as in psychotic depression, the self may feel and even believe itself to be dead, although objective features of the external world are perceived without distortion. When the disturbance involves distortions in basic information-processing or even the normal articulation of language sequences, the individual is diagnosed with a thought disorder. The most severe thought disorder is schizophrenia.

Renee, the schizophrenic girl quoted above, describes vividly what she remembers of her psychotic experience as well as her recovery from it. According to her report, it began as an unexpected and involuntary disruption of normal perception and thought. This loss of reality was quite traumatic for her. As it continued to distort her life, she struggled against it, was at first overwhelmed by it, but eventually recovered with the help of an unusually empathic psychotherapist.

There have been many theories and explanations of schizophrenia, ranging from the theory that it is primarily the result of a biological or biochemical anomaly to the idea that it is caused by distorted interpersonal relationships. Though the causes of schizophrenia are still not clearly understood, and although some would argue that it is not a unitary illness at all but a group of related syndromes which may arise from different causes, the manifestations of schizophrenia are usually as clear as they are mysterious. The individual with a severe thought disorder cannot manage a coherent life or, sometimes, even a coherent thought. Eugen Bleuler (1950), who wrote an influential book on dementia praecox, as schizophrenia was formerly called, considered a basic factor in the problem to be autistic withdrawal. The schizophrenic individual is imprisoned in a socially isolated state, out of meaningful contact with other people.

Trauma, as well as endogenous processes, such as reactions to biochemical imbalances or toxic substances, can precipitate psychogenic forms of autistic withdrawal. Whatever the precipitating factor, withdrawal cuts off dialogue with others. Sequestered with its secrets, the traumatized self may seem dead to the external world. Guessed at or unknown, the hidden trauma is most observable by others as an absence, a gap in history, or a missing piece of a puzzle.

In an extremely withdrawn state, the self and its memories are no longer guided by continual reality checks and social validation of personal narratives. As a result, delusional thinking, a special kind of fantasy-based narrative structure, may become privileged over other representations of experience (Oltmanns & Maher, 1988).

The profound distortions of perception and thinking characteristic of schizophrenia inevitably affect memory. The individual may be profoundly cut off from incoming information, lost in a private world of delusional thought, or simply lost to all thought. Even when information is taken in, it may be oddly interpreted, as when a knock at the door is incorporated into the persecutory delusion, "They have come to get me."

The psychotic experience itself can be considered an altered state of consciousness and as such might be expected to be associated with state-dependent memory effects. In any case, a period of psychosis is an important chapter in a personal life story. How the self integrates this chapter with other parts of the personal past or with the present identity impacts significantly on what gets forwarded as memory. Like other traumatic events, psychosis as self-defining memory can continually overshadow less painful memories.

Some psychoses that resemble schizophrenia in some features but are distinctly different are precipitated by trauma. A reaction labeled "hysterical psychosis," for example, was widely observed in the nineteenth century and has recently provoked renewed interest (Hollender & Hirsch, 1963; Siomopoulos, 1971; van der Hart, Witztum, & Friedman, 1993). Janet described reactive psychotic states as waking dreams or somnambulisms (Ellenberger, 1970). Breuer, who collaborated with Freud (1893–1895), wrote about them in a famous psychoanalytic patient, Anna O. He noted the importance of trance, or "hypnoid," states in such reactions.

Hysterical or reactive psychosis is characterized by a sudden and dramatic onset following a profoundly upsetting event; in this sense, as Hollender and Hirsch (1963) note, it is reactive, as some depressions are reactive. It may be characterized by hallucinations and delusions, but, in contrast to schizophrenia, any thought disorders which occur are usually circumscribed and transient (Hollender & Hirsch, 1963) and emotional responses are intense rather than flat. Duration of the psychosis is typically brief and prognosis for recovery is good (Jauch & Carpenter, 1988a,b).

Another characteristic feature of hysterical psychosis that typically distinguishes the syndrome from schizophrenia is a high degree of hypnotizability in affected individuals (Spiegel & Fink, 1979). This feature is consistent with the traumatic precipitation of the problem and with characteristic features of traumatic trance states. The comparatively short duration and good prognosis for recovery in reactive psychoses are also consistent with posttraumatic adaptations.

The hallucinations that occur in hysterical psychosis and dissociative reactions often consist of flashbacks rather than endogenous fantasy constructions (Putnam, 1989). After recovery from the psychosis, reality-testing is usually intact and the affected individual may have clear insight into the psychotic nature of previous symptoms. In this respect, hysterical psychosis is likely to be remembered as a painful period of life in which one was "crazy." There is usually no attempt to explain the abnormal experiences in terms of delusional interpretations. Schizophrenic individuals, in contrast, may have difficulty developing insight into their psychotic symptoms. They sometimes maintain delusional ideas even when in remission from floridly psychotic patterns of thought and behavior (Oltmanns & Maher, 1988).

The expectable recovery from a hysterical or reactive psychosis precipitated by trauma is, nevertheless, contingent on the developmental competencies achieved at the time of the psychosis. Reality-testing is a developmental acquisition constantly refined during childhood. Children who develop reactive psychoses may remember them differently from the way adults do and, even after recovery, may continue to confuse some psychotic experiences with reality. In children who live in abusive contexts where information input is restricted and unusual belief systems are inculcated, such as children brought up in cults sequestered from the outside world, reality-testing can be expected to be atypical even in the absence of psychosis (Singer, 1995).

Individuals who dissociate trauma may also dissociate reactive psychoses. The psychotic piece of history may then be remembered, as a dream is remembered, vaguely accessible but cut off from normal everyday life. Or it may be completely encapsulated through amnesia. When that happens, the encapsulated psychosis, since it consists of a temporary loss of reality, may become even more difficult to integrate into personality than other traumatic memories.

Finally, the class of psychotic reactions precipitated by medications or street drugs deserves mention as a sometimes terrifying episode of personal history. Even when the individual has insight into the origin and delusional nature of such psychotic responses, toxic reactions may recur later as traumatic flashbacks. Hallucinogenic drugs like LSD are notorious in this respect.

Some inexplicable responses in seemingly nonpsychotic individuals, particularly those with severe dissociative disorders, should be examined for possible origins in drug reactions. Children as well as adults experiment with hallucinogens. Some of the bizarre stories reported by individuals who were children during the 1960s make sense in the light of the prevalence of street drugs during that period. Some cults, then and now, also exploit drugs in their attempts to control the minds of initiates.

Whatever the cause of a psychotic reaction, the very experience of it is usually traumatic. And psychosis, of whatever origin, constitutes one type of trauma that may be subsequently encapsulated through dissociation. When that happens, one piece of the self, the psychotic self, may be so carefully isolated from the rest of the personality that it is not suspected by anyone unless a new trauma revives it. The possibility of precipitously uncovering an encapsulated psychotic self is another possible pitfall of psychotherapy.

In other cases, the psychotic experience, even when surmounted, becomes a focal point in identity construction, so that, forever after, the individual is defined by self and/or others as "crazy" or labeled "a schizophrenic." This possibility is especially risky when the psychotic episode occurs in childhood or adolescence.

But, though hazardous and consequential, psychotic reactions are not necessarily construed as a form of illness or a permanent liability. Those who interpret such a reaction as a religious experience, for example, may insist, even after they recover, that it was a special visitation from God or a transcendent experience. When other people accept this interpretation, the self need not hide the experience; it can become a privileged and socially rewarded narrative as well as a valuable source of psychological strength and comfort.

In any case, psychosis, like any other trauma, divides personal history. Before and after must be integrated in some kind of coherent narrative, or the self may continue to feel divided or disconnected. Even if the experience during the psychotic episode is forgotten altogether, the gap must be acknowledged and interpreted in any complete story of one's life.

PART III
The Past in the Present

CHAPTER 10

Making It Safe to Remember

A past beyond recovery seems to many unbearable.
— David Lowenthal, 1985

THE SEARCH FOR memory is motivated not only by the need for particular facts but by the general wish to revisit the past. The desire to
remember what is painful as well as what is pleasant involves human
impulses toward self-actualization as well as toward mastery. A gap in
memory is a challenge, and even carefully devised avoidance patterns are
often countered by persistent attempts to discover lost information, to
decipher cryptic messages, to integrate divergent narratives and mismatched stories.

Sometimes a chance encounter with history sets in motion a process of
intentional search. Sometimes the time just seems right to go back, reconsider, reinterpret. New discoveries call for continuing investigations as well
as continually revised interpretations. The self, always changing, discovers
new implications in even the most familiar memories. One typical context
of discovery is psychotherapy. Whether or not a therapy is focused on
memories, merely talking about oneself inevitably stirs them up. When
that happens, a deliberate foray into the past can stimulate vital insights.

Whatever prompts the quest for the past, it typically involves at some
point an explicit search for concrete and literal artifacts: oral or written
records, pictures, keepsakes. Diaries and journals, old letters, even casual
notes once jotted down as reminders can be mined as important sources
of information.

A trip into the past often involves an actual revisiting of the sites associated with personal history: childhood homes or hometowns, schools once
attended, even hospitals. An old photograph, a class reunion, a funeral
may jog memories that seemed lost forever. A misremembered fact may
start the mind puzzling about what really happened. A chance discovery

may send one to the family Bible or the attic in search of written records, or to archives and libraries.

Yet it is not just information the self is seeking, after all, but integration and meaning. And in this integration, feelings are as important as facts.

Novey (1968), discussing "the second look" at the personal past, notes that encounters with concrete artifacts are powerfully evocative because they involve sensory experiences and emotions around which early memories may have originally crystalized. By reexperiencing the literal past in the context of the present, one has an opportunity not only to rediscover the original impact of memories, but to reinterpret and reintegrate them into the present self.

Literal encounters in the present may flesh out sketchy recollections of the past and correct mistaken ones. They may confirm or discredit previous beliefs. They may enable one to discover important secrets or subversions of personal history. And they may offer new perspectives on long-known but perplexing events.

The wish to remember, however, is frequently countered by the wish to forget. This, too, is not just a matter of pleasure or pain, but involves a need for personal control. Memory is often unreliably yoked to intentions. The past may evade recollection in spite of intensive efforts and diligent searches. Or it may rise unbidden, distracting the mind from ongoing tasks, setting butterflies loose in the stomach, troubling sleep.

Not infrequently the search for personal history, at some point, evokes fear. One hesitates to go forward: better to leave skeletons in the closet and let sleeping dogs lie. This response need not sabotage the exploratory process; it can become an opportunity to explore meaning. Since, at any point in development, fear can be a major architect of memory, discovering when and why one was afraid enables the self not only to evaluate past events but to revise present responses to them. It can be liberating to discover that one no longer need be afraid of once-terrifying memories, for example, that one is no longer a helpless child but a competent and autonomous adult.

Unfortunately, however, fear is not just an irrational component of memory. Under some circumstances, it can actually be dangerous to remember. An extremely traumatic past may overwhelm present coping mechanisms. When that happens, remembering is risky, even for a mature adult.

Unfortunately, too, there are sometimes dangers based on actual threats from external sources. Those who, in the past, had a stake in subverting memory may still have power in the present. Particularly if the search for history might uncover criminal activities, it is quite likely to evoke strong defensive responses. And anyone who committed criminal acts in the past can be reasonably expected to do so again.

Because of these real and sometimes present dangers, the first order of business for those confronting a traumatic history, whether or not they do so in the context of psychotherapy, is making it safe to remember. No matter how significant the past may be as a source of current problems, no matter how necessary confronting it may seem for the integration of the self, remembering becomes dangerous if it leads to being out of control of one's life. Most people intuitively sense this. Some, to their great dismay, have experienced it forcefully, as sometimes happens when they confront past traumas too precipitously or without needed support.

INTRUSIVE RECOLLECTIONS
AND PUZZLING AMNESIAS

How one confronts the past is not always a matter of choice. It may constantly overshadow the present. It may return, unbidden, in the form of vivid images, obsessive thoughts, or incapacitating anxieties. Or, seemingly hidden from view, it may give rise to perplexing symptoms that seriously impact on present adaptations. Memories can be persistent and intrusive. Overwhelming trauma, however unspeakable, is not easily forgotten. The variable ways in which it is remembered highlight the complexity of both trauma responses and remembering as a process.

Flashbacks, vivid images that seem to replay the trauma in its original intensity, are a typical symptom in posttraumatic stress disorder. They contrast sharply with the leisurely stroll down memory lane that characterizes nostalgic reminiscence. Like a flood that sweeps everything in its path, they wash over the victim, preempting other thoughts and activities. This involuntary reliving may be so vivid that it is momentarily difficult to discriminate between past and present. Because remembering the trauma in this way is an unchosen happening rather than a controlled event, flashbacks themselves are a form of inescapable shock. Memory becomes an enemy rather than an ally in self integration.

The individual who seeks help from a therapist in controlling flashbacks usually has a clear-cut agenda: stop these memories from coming. Anything that cues the memories is likely to feel unsafe. Psychotherapy that involves talking about the trauma is experienced as a terrifying danger. And, under some circumstances this perception is correct. If the client is as overwhelmed by the memories as by the original event, psychotherapy is inevitably experienced as revictimizing. Slowing down is a priority.

However, it is not just clearly remembered traumas that present a problem in therapy. In many instances, specific traumas are not the focus of symptoms. Anxiety, nightmares, obsessive fears, somatic tensions, and other symptoms may seem as mysterious as they are irrational. When such symptoms are cryptic encodings of past trauma, their significance may only be understood after extensive exploration.

Finally, there are people who, for whatever reason, are disturbed not by what they remember, but by the fact that they cannot remember episodes or situations they feel they ought to recall. Sometimes the memory loss can be tied to a traumatic event. The victims of the Buffalo Creek flood, for example, frequently complained about memory disturbances and had a realistic awareness that these were connected with the trauma. Some memories may really be lost forever. Even potentially accessible memories may be refractory to retrieval. But such a permanent and insurmountable loss need not be taken for granted. Whatever the cause of the lack of memory for some significant episode in one's life, one need not simply capitulate to oblivion. Until one has carefully looked, who knows what might be found?

Sometimes the hasty conclusion that a memory is permanently gone results from an overly restricted view of remembering as a narrative process. As we have seen, the absence of narrative can have many sources, ranging from an original failure to encode events in words, to a deliberate silencing, to a divergence of narrative that privileges silence or a cover story over a recollection that was once well-known or openly acknowledged.

In the search for personal history, one need not naively accept every possibility that presents itself or prematurely substitute certainties for provisional considerations. There is usually no need for haste in making up one's mind. And the right to change one's mind need not be subverted by defensiveness. In the long run, only the self can decide whether the search is worthwhile. And whatever the factual status of a memory, only the self can judge its meaning.

THERAPY AS AN ADVERSARY

In recent years, because of a media focus on child abuse and an increased willingness of victims to speak out, many individuals have sought psychotherapy with the rather vague idea that something terrible, such as forgotten abuse, has happened to them. Sometimes they request a specific search for lost memories. They may even request specific techniques, like hypnosis, as an aid to the search. These are the individuals who may be most confused by current controversies about memory.

In such instances, psychotherapists are confronted with the difficult dilemma of educating the client about the complexities of memory and the limitations of psychotherapy without discounting or minimizing the client's concerns. This balancing act can be especially difficult if the client is determined to find a fast fix or tends to view the world in terms of either-or dichotomies.

The problem can be greatly compounded, too, by other people who present distorted views of the treatment process or attack it as useless or dangerous. Many people external to the psychotherapy situation simply have no realistic appraisal of what it is all about. Sometimes this misunderstanding is simply based on ignorance or lack of experience. Sometimes it is based on a fear of exploring psychological dynamics. Sometimes it is based on ulterior motives, such as the wish to scapegoat therapists who present some imagined threat to third parties.

Unfortunately, whatever the origins of mistaken views of therapy, they cannot always be corrected by offering accurate information or rational explanations. Sometimes any accurate information presented is immediately refuted or devalued. Sometimes explanations, however rational, are dismissed out of hand. Confronted with such attitudes, therapists as well as clients are placed in no-win situations; anything they say and do may be used against them.

A common misunderstanding about therapy, for example, is based on the adversarial model familiar in legal contexts. The assumption is sometimes made that psychotherapists, like attorneys, should function primarily to help clients do battle with other people. This view of psychotherapy as a battlefield inevitably places both client and therapist on the defensive against others who believe, for whatever reason, that they stand to lose by the client's therapy. Third parties may even assert that they have some right to protection from the process. In extreme cases, people who have never been actually involved in the therapy may threaten or initiate legal actions based on their beliefs that they are being harmed by it.

The situation is, of course, greatly exacerbated if either therapist or client actually enacts the fears and fantasies behind such opposition. If the therapist does attack a client's spouse or parents, defensive responses from them are expectable and realistic. And if a client moves outside the therapeutic context to attack other people in actuality, the real attack is an open invitation to a counterattack. This is especially true if lawsuits are mounted.

In spite of the complaints of clients, however, even those who have been actually abused, the psychotherapeutic context is not inherently adversarial. It is a forum in which the client can freely and safely explore all ideas, feelings, and grievances. It is a context in which subverted memories may be exposed, divergent narratives may be integrated, and internalized dialogues may be externalized.

As they facilitate this process, psychotherapists are not investigative detectives or attorneys or judges. Ideas, including veridical memories, are not evidence in any usual legal sense. Attempts by clients to obtain redress from third parties, however legitimate or even desirable, are not a part of therapy per se, and attempting to make them so erodes therapeutic boundaries. The erosion of boundaries, in turn, destroys the safety of the therapeutic context.

Nevertheless, although therapy is not inherently adversarial, the client's freedom to disagree with other people—family members, colleagues, employers, the therapist—is a legitimate therapeutic issue, and the client's autonomy is usually essential to therapeutic progress. Trouble arises when disagreement is equated with attack. Clients who are used to feeling controlled and intimidated or those who are actually dependent on parents and spouses may feel caught between their own wishes to be independent and habitual patterns of compliance. They may try to enlist the therapist as an ally in real fights.

Real fights, too, may be started by those who feel that their own control of a client is being weakened. Anything that increases the client's autonomy and freedom to think is likely to perceived as a threat by domineering people in the client's life. Authoritarian parents and abusive spouses, for example, tend to view all aspects of life in terms of a battle for control. It is not surprising that they extend this view to psychotherapy, casting clients in the role of dependent, easily led children and therapists in the role of adversaries who are trying to wrest control for themselves.

Systematic forms of intimidation, such as threats of lawsuits against clients and therapists, have sometimes made it difficult for therapists to ensure the safety of their clients in such situations. Intrusions from third parties who believe they have a vested interest in the therapy have sometimes made it difficult to maintain therapeutic boundaries and to focus on symbolic processes as distinct from destructive enactments.

Such enactments can sabotage an otherwise helpful therapy. Whenever clients or their associates initiate confrontations outside the therapy setting, the distinction between talk and action becomes crucial and the therapeutic implications of the behavior require careful clarification. Even a just and rational confrontation with other people may distract the client from more strictly therapeutic issues.

The therapist's being placed in the middle of such externalized struggles often involves the client's attempt to enact rather than make sense of an old battle. But the therapeutic focus can be lost when attention shifts from meanings to manipulations. This development is a dimension of transference and is most safely handled by being recognized as such.

TRUE AND FALSE MEMORIES

In recent years, many of these issues have been debated in the context of controversies over the accuracy of memories recovered in psychotherapy, particularly recovered memories of childhood abuse. The possibility that therapists can implant or reinforce false memories in suggestible clients has been raised as a serious challenge to clients who have, in consequence of discoveries in psychotherapy, behaved in ways that trouble other people.

In recent years, too, recovered memories have become a popular justification for decisions that have as much to do with current relationships as with past events. Some clients, citing memories of abuse, have become estranged from family members. Some have chosen to confront their assailants in public accusations. In one widely reported case, a man was convicted of murder after his daughter reported seeing him sexually assault and kill her childhood friend (Franklin & Wright, 1991).

Debates over these issues have not been confined to theoretical discussions in scientific journals. On the contrary, they have been public and well-publicized. They have tended to promote an adversarial climate that has been especially chilling for those therapists concerned with the exploration and integration of traumatic memories.

Adversarial actions have increasingly been initiated by victims as well as by accused perpetrators of child sexual abuse. Over the past few years, awareness of the prevalence of child abuse has prompted changes in law, such as changes in statutes of limitation that determine when legal actions may be instituted (Crnich & Crnich, 1992). Such changes have enabled adults to institute suits based on abuses that occurred when they were children.

Such actions have been welcomed by victims who have long felt disadvantaged under the law. They have sometimes empowered the powerless. Even so, they have sometimes impacted adversely on therapy. Even when there is no direct threat, open-minded therapeutic exploration is not easily managed in a general atmosphere of adversarial confrontation.

Sensationalized media presentations have compounded the problem by trivializing psychological issues, highlighting bizarre forms of therapy or self-help, and reinforcing the notion that complicated difficulties have simplistic causes and fast solutions. Complex issues have often been debated in sound bites rather than careful forums. Shocking exposés of therapeutic excesses have shifted the focus of public attention from the incidence of abuse to the imperfections of psychotherapy (Whitfield, 1995). Such media presentations constitute, in effect, a campaign of misinformation. Their negative impact has been undeniable. Bizarre techniques and sensational claims more easily capture public attention than more conventional or soundly based therapeutic approaches, and when such aberrations are presented as the norm, there is an understandable erosion of confidence in psychotherapy as a process.

It was perhaps inevitable that a growing public concern about abuse and posttraumatic syndromes would generate a backlash (Armstrong, 1994; Whitfield, 1995). It is clear, too, that the backlash was fueled by real excesses. The therapeutic void left by nearly a century of psychoanalytic denial of sexual abuse, for example, was filled by untrained as well as by trained therapists. Some of these were well-meaning, ethical, and genuinely helpful. But victims left vulnerable by traumatic histories also became targets for unscrupulous exploitation, and it was easy to exploit them in the name of therapy.

Several sensational trials involving child abuse dramatically highlighted such problems. Some of these involved day-care centers and allegations of organized forms of abuse involving many perpetrators (Crewdson, 1988). In the wake of these trials, there was a renewed legal focus not only on children's memory, but on techniques of obtaining evidence, particularly the use of certain diagnostic procedures by therapists and the use of leading questions by investigators (McGough, 1994).

These developments resulted in a needed review not only of theoretical issues but also of methods of gathering evidence. Unfortunately, however, there were also negative outcomes. Increased circumspection among investigators and judges combined with traditional biases against child witnesses and the growing backlash against abuse victims made it easier to discount reports of abuse. Anyone who came forward with an accusation might now be met with a reflexive cry of "Witch hunt!"

These modern trends are expectable in the light of history. The legal testimony of children has always been suspect (McGough, 1994), but it is their allegations of abuse that have traditionally been perceived as especially pernicious and have thus given rise to systematic attacks by threatened adults (Armstrong, 1994). Since the nineteenth century, there have been systematic efforts to discredit children as liars (Masson, 1984, 1986). For most of the twentieth century, the psychoanalytic contention that patients' reported memories of abuse were based on fantasies and, therefore, could not be believed as literally true lent powerful support to such efforts.

In the wake of the recently renewed controversy over recovered memories of abuse, longstanding tendencies to discount child testimony were reinforced by new assertions about the suggestibility of children, as well as by attacks on the credibility of memory. Freud's original doubts about the veracity of childhood memories were supplemented by more modern cognitive theories. The assumption that early childhood amnesia is inevitable and the known distortions of veridical memory have continued to cast doubt on children's reports of abuse.

The delayed emergence of memories in adults, which has come into more recent focus (Loftus, 1993), has been one of the most vulnerable targets of attack. As the incidence and prevalence of abuse have been publicly acknowledged, many victims have come forward to tell their stories. Increased understanding of the effects on trauma has simultaneously emerged from research on veterans and victims of natural disasters. The increased willingness of adults to come forward with long-hidden stories, even to sue accused assailants, has generated a defensive outcry against the honesty and veracity of adult victims as well as against the concept of memory recovery (Yapko, 1994). Unfortunately, therapists as well as clients have sometimes played into the backlash by misunderstanding the distinction between truth and evidence.

One effect of sensationalized presentations has been to distract attention from the complexities of memory organization to simplistic evaluations about whether a particular memory is accurate or not. Another is to replace reasoned debate about still unresolved questions with strident claims about what it is or is not possible to remember.

Some critics maintain, for example, that people do not forget traumas, or that, if they do, they cannot subsequently remember what has been forgotten (for a review, see Lindsay & Read, 1995). Critics frequently ignore or dismiss out of hand the literature on trauma. They often focus, too, on Freudian theories and terms — repression, in particular. By discrediting psychoanalytic approaches, some critics seem to imply that they have discredited all forms of psychotherapy. By pointing out problems in the concept of repression, they imply that all delayed recoveries of memory are theoretically unsupportable as well as empirically suspect. And the research literature on dissociation is often simply ignored altogether.

EVIDENCE

It is noteworthy that many of the controversies surrounding the reliability of memory seem to crystalize around issues that have long been disputed. The unreliability of eyewitness testimony, for example, might be invoked as a limitation in many kinds of judicial proceedings. But it is in the area of child abuse allegations, particularly those involving sexual abuse, that the most strident objections to eyewitness testimony have been mounted. There has been no organized outcry against the reliability of eyewitness testimony in bank robberies or convenience store holdups.

Adversarial actions and dramatic trials have sometimes had the unfortunate effect of confusing psychological issues, such as questions concerning the accuracy of memory, with issues that are strictly legal. Clients who do not understand these distinctions and those who are naive about how the law actually works may be misled into believing that, because right is on their side, justice must prevail. This attitude can be dangerous.

Anyone familiar with the legal system knows that justice may or may not prevail, and whether it does depends on many factors other than truth or the reliability of memory. For one thing, even incontrovertible truth is not evidence. In court cases, for example, the accuracy of evidence must be distinguished from the admissibility of evidence; clear and undeniable facts can be excluded from consideration if they were improperly discovered or fail to meet specified legal criteria. Moreover, in the judicial system victims, especially certain classes of victims, have always been at a disadvantage (Hoff, 1991; MacKinnon, 1989). Whatever the merits of a victim's claim, protecting the rights of the accused is still a fundamental principle in law.

This presumption that the accused is innocent until proven guilty can be especially frustrating to victims of assailants who have long histories of criminal activities. Although a proven history of offenses, which is typical of individuals given to certain forms of sexual abuse, might seem obviously relevant from the victim's perspective, it may be routinely excluded as evidence in the trial of a specific offense. Ancillary evidence of abuse, such as proof of involvement in behavior like child pornography, can also be excluded from consideration (Franklin & Wright, 1991). What is left is often just the word of the victim against the word of an accused perpetrator.

The rights of victims, in contrast to those of accused perpetrators, have only recently come to the forefront of public attention and in many instances are not well safeguarded. It may even be physically as well as psychologically dangerous for a victim to come forward. And a true story, which involves an accusation against a real criminal, may be even more dangerous than a false one.

One of the most frustrating problems confronting victims is that, once they make an accusation, they are themselves open to relentless attack. Attempts to discredit potentially damaging witnesses are a standard tactic on the part of attorneys. Rape victims have traditionally been subjected to a sometimes vicious scrutiny of every aspect of their personal lives. The recent spate of trials involving child sexual abuse has revealed the extent to which accusers, whether children or adults, remain open to such legal assaults.

Although the victim's memory is often a major focus in such cases, the appropriate role of psychological research and psychotherapy has easily been misunderstood. A courtroom is very different from a laboratory or a consulting room. In court, scientific objectivity may be perfunctorily acknowledged as a guiding principle. But when psychological research, including research on memory, is offered in testimony, the selection of findings, like the selection of any evidence, is typically determined by the adversarial motives of attorneys and their clients. In any case, a "battle of experts" tends to skew presentation of psychological data or to create the impression that there are no facts, just opinions.

Psychotherapy is in some respects even more vulnerable to misrepresentation than psychological research. Clients' statements in therapy are confidential and in any case are simply a matter of what one person tells another. For that reason, they might not ordinarily be expected to be accepted as evidence. But parties to legal disputes may decide that a client's statements in therapy are somehow relevant to their purposes. An accused person may demand access to confidential records. A client may request that the therapist testify about therapy in order to prove a point.

Fortunately, the confidentiality of psychotherapy records is still generally protected, in spite of a few successful attempts to erode the principle. But when therapy is presented as evidence, even from the client's perspective, there are serious risks for the therapist as well as the client. Most importantly, when a therapeutic context is replaced by a legal one, the therapist has no control over the safety of the situation. In the courtroom, such control is in the hands of attorneys, judges, and juries.

The therapist used to interpreting statements made in therapy from a purely therapeutic perspective may be dismayed to find them used against the client. For example, inconsistent statements made in the therapy setting, self-doubts on the part of the client, or self-incriminating statements by the client may easily be seized on to discredit the client's testimony.

In legal proceedings, psychotherapists are also more likely to be personally attacked. When psychotherapy has helped clients gain the courage to break off contact with family members or to initiate lawsuits, the instigation of such actions has sometimes been attributed to the therapist, rather than to the client's independent judgment. The methods of the therapist may be attacked as the source of reported memories of abuse, even when the memories were never lost at all but merely suppressed. In order to appear to be on the client's side, an adversary may present the client as the gullible dupe of the therapist. His or her behavior may be facilely interpreted as a function of the therapist's agenda rather than the client's goals.

When the search for truth is subordinated to the wish to win a fight at any cost, therapists are no match for trained adversaries. They may respond defensively, as if adversarial claims could be settled by amassing statistics or as if a challenge by a third party could be overcome by rational argument. Attorneys, however, are really well trained in the rules of the legal game. Consequently, the outcome of any adversarial battle is likely to depend more on the persuasiveness of attorneys than on either the weight of objective data or the opinions of therapists.

In such a climate, the vulnerability of the therapist as well as that of the client can seriously compromise any real therapeutic work. There are no longer boundaries to guarantee the safety of the therapeutic context. A situation carefully arranged by the therapist to be private and confidential and, as much as possible, relaxed and noninvasive, has been replaced by a glass house being pelted with stones.

RECANTATION

The fact that some individuals have recanted original stories of being abused has complicated all these issues. Some individuals have admitted making up stories for ulterior motives, such as revenge or the wish to please someone else. Others have retracted abuse allegations, citing their own misunderstanding or even influence by a therapist as a source of the original story. Whatever their origins, retractions have been held up as dramatic evidence of the unreliability of memory, the vulnerability of clients to therapists' suggestions, or the human capacity for deceit.

Recantation, of course, is prompted by many factors other than uncertainty of memory. In many instances it is merely a matter of silencing and intimidation. Or, when memory *is* involved, a previous subversion of memory may have led to divergent narratives that confuse present-day reports.

In the case of deliberate abuse, actual intimidation of victims by assailants is an expectable motive for recantation. Past intimidation may have contributed to divergent narratives that now lead observers to view the victim as inconsistent and unreliable, compounding the victim's self-doubt and fostering recantation. An adversarial stance that proclaims "Aha! You have changed your story; therefore your story must be false" is not in any case an avenue to truth. It is merely another source of intimidation.

Recantation of accurate as well as mistaken abuse stories is so common that those who work with victims expect it. Clients fear the consequences of telling the truth, and when faced by actual threats, their fears are a realistic dimension of the present as well as the past. Intimidation naturally results in self-protective behavior, including deliberate lying.

Posttraumatic memory is often doubtful, too, for numerous reasons, ranging from clouding of consciousness at the time of the trauma to posttraumatic amnesias and deliberate posttraumatic accommodations, such as the persistent avoidance of trauma-related cues. Divergent narratives have often been constructed in the wake of trauma, as the victim tries to account for confusing or incomprehensible experiences or to rationalize unfamiliar responses. Internalized dialogues about traumatic events have also often subverted victims' memories of what really happened and why.

The problem of recantation has long confronted those charged with evaluating the reality and extent of abuse. It is most serious in cases involving legal decisions about children, such as custody evaluations or the prosecution of alleged abusers. Ordinarily, however, it has been a less urgent problem in therapeutic contexts. Ideally, clients in therapy have time to consider ideas provisionally, need not make up their minds immediately, and are safe in changing their minds. They have the luxury of being wrong about a memory or of changing their opinions without facing negative consequences outside therapy. Even when an adult client is sure that abuse occurred in the past, there is usually no great urgency to act on that knowledge in the present. Because of the very nature of therapy, it is often the most therapeutic course to delay a momentous decision until much careful exploration has been done; Freud himself used to counsel this kind of delay.

In therapy, recantation, like everything else, is grist for the mill. The client can derive valuable insights from mistaken perceptions or revised narratives. If the recantation is based on familiar patterns of fear and silencing, it can be examined as a new version of an old story. If it is based on an accurate reappraisal and correction of a mistake, it can be viewed as a step forward in personal integration.

SAFE AND UNSAFE MEMORIES

Orchestrated attacks on psychotherapy have the potential effect of making victims even more isolated than they were in the past. And pressure to label memories *true* or *false*, coupled with the search for a quick fix or the myth of the single cause, can derail the therapeutic process. In some cases this combination precipitates destructive forms of revictimization, particularly when clients attempt to institute suits against alleged abusers.

To be sure, there are evaluative contexts in which immediate decisions about the truth or falsity of memory must be made. In cases involving allegations of child abuse or necessary decisions about child custody, psychological interviewing and testing can make valuable contributions to the investigative and decision-making process. But trained evaluators recognize and educate others concerning the limitations as well as the advantages of their techniques. They know the potential errors of measurement associated with specific tests. They understand the pitfalls in moving from group norms to inferences about individual behavior. And they are well enough informed about the complexities of memory to resist simplistic statements and accusations.

However necessary and useful in some contexts, the evaluative process is fundamentally and necessarily distinct from the therapeutic process. The therapist is, by definition, not a neutral observer or an instrument of third parties, but a caregiver who has contracted with the client to work on the client's behalf and to maintain the client's confidences.

Therapists can only protect the safety of the therapeutic context when it is carefully bounded and shielded from intrusions by third parties. Clients need to be informed in this regard. Any situation that erodes confidentially or attempts to enmesh the therapist in the client's life outside therapy tends to compromise the safety of the therapeutic context. Such situations are not always avoidable; clients' records cannot always be strictly guarded from third parties, for example. But it is always prudent for the therapist to acknowledge the implications and potential dangers of these realities.

The criticisms launched against psychotherapy in recent years, even when intimidating and destructive, should thus prompt prudence and caution in therapists. And the pressure on therapists to articulate their own special expertise and training, to explain the limits as well as the benefits of their work, has perhaps been positive. Even when rational explanations are not heeded by others, they can provide both therapist and client with needed clarifications.

One negative outcome of attacks, however, is that intimidation may lead therapists to retreat from difficult cases or compromise the effectiveness of their work. Strident attacks can subvert memory in therapy as well as in the life of the client.

An especially pernicious subversion is based on supposedly scientific arguments to the effect that clients should be discouraged from uninhibited explorations of their own minds, that therapists should dispute any reported memory that cannot be substantiated with objective, provable facts. This attitude misconstrues the basic premises of psychotherapy. In order to work effectively, psychotherapy must make the client more, not less, comfortable with exploring thoughts, even doubtful or troubling thoughts.

In a successful psychotherapy, the client's freedom to think, to believe, to decide, expands as confidence and autonomy increase. One valuable therapeutic outcome is that the client eventually moves beyond therapy to change aspects of his or her own life. At some point, this development almost inevitably involves the client's behaving in ways that arouse disapproval, fear, or outrage in others. This eventuality cannot be avoided just because, at some points, it involves risks.

In practice, this means that, even under the best circumstances, therapy will not always be safe. Even an experienced psychotherapist may view some of the client's moves toward autonomy with trepidation. And it is prudently cautious to point out and evaluate actual risks. But the right of the client to make independent decisions cannot be ethically subverted by the concerns of other people, including therapists. The ethical therapist can only offer an informed opinion and an evaluation of how such decisions may impact on the psychological well-being of the client.

In the therapeutic context, the client's priorities must always take precedence over the interests of other people. In any potential conflict of interest between the client and third parties, the therapist's expressed obligation is to the best interests of the client. The therapist is also specifically prohibited by the ethical principles of most professional organizations from violating certain boundaries. Intruding into the actual life of the client or entering into a personal relationship with the client outside the specific context of therapy is forbidden.

Sometimes a client's attempt to draw a therapist into an actual battle between the client and other people is based on a wish to view the therapist as a kind of savior. Sometimes it is just an attempt to get a therapist to say what the client cannot yet voice with confidence and authority. In any case, it is a boundary issue and a transference issue, and should be interpreted from that perspective.

Therapists who really are grandiose and willing to control the client's life are setting themselves up for attack. But even the most careful and prudent psychotherapist cannot always avoid attack. Those who work with clients who have been intimidated and abused make themselves vulnerable simply by working in the interests of the client.

COMMON MISUNDERSTANDINGS

Misunderstandings about the nature of psychotherapy and pressures to find simplistic solutions to complex problems do not, of course, arise only in adversarial situations. Even in the absence of pressures from other people, the client brings them into the therapeutic context.

The urgency and discomfort of the client's symptoms exert strong pressures on the treatment process. And many pragmatic factors, such as the availability of treatment, cost, and policies dictated by insurance carriers, impact not only on safety, but on therapeutic goals and procedures. As has been mentioned, for example, anything that erodes confidentiality is a potential threat to effective therapy. But in some situations, such as when therapy has been mandated by an external agency, erosions of confidentiality are unavoidable.

Even so, most of the threats to the client's safety and security arise from internal rather than external factors. Malignant memories, for example, can sometimes be suppressed, but not always. The emotional responses and somatic symptoms associated with such memories can often be calmed through medication, but the self in hiding is still not free to explore a wider world. And the self in pieces is still not whole. The client at odds with his or her own past may thus feel continually under siege in the present. It is scarcely surprising then that, even when there is little faith in it, the search for help goes on. Unfortunately, however, the urgency of continuing posttraumatic symptoms also produces a corresponding impatience; there is a tendency to seek a fast fix, to be beguiled by authoritarian or charismatic individuals who promise relief.

The Search for the Quick Fix

For many people, psychotherapy is a last rather than a first resort. They have sought other solutions, sometimes for years, such as avoiding trauma-related contexts, trying to talk themselves out of their anxiety, or self-medicating through alcohol or drugs. By the time they reach a given therapist, they may also have extensive experience with self-help groups, other therapies, even authoritarian cults that promised a way out. Some clients will have been hospitalized with variably helpful outcomes. Some will have experienced iatrogenic reactions that increase their distrust of any new treatment.

The client knows, then, that the quick fix is not really likely and may be relieved rather than disheartened by the therapist's acknowledgment of the seriousness of the problems and the uncertainties of treatment. Nevertheless, the urgency and discomfort of symptoms continually press the client to find some shortcut to treatment. The search for a fast fix is also usually encouraged by other people who are troubled by the client's symptoms or by third parties who want to control costs.

The search for a fast fix tends to create magical expectations about what the therapist can and should do. These magical expectations about therapy and idealizations of the therapist contrast with equally strong doubts and disillusionments. Although many clients enter treatment with high hopes, those who have been abused, especially, are at the same time hopeless about finding help. The trust they place in the therapist is likely to be fragile. Even small therapeutic mistakes or lapses in therapeutic empathy can destroy it.

It is as if the client is saying, "Help me right this minute! But I know you can't. Nobody can." Or (which is just as difficult), "Nobody else understands. But you are obviously and always wonderful!" Followed by, "I knew it! You are as imperfect and disappointing as everybody else."

Magical expectations and idealizations are treacherous if the underlying mistrust is unrecognized. The therapist cannot, of course, be perfect. Some problems can be helped a great deal, some only a little, some not at all. The best protection the therapist can offer is a realistic appraisal of the limitations of the treatment process, a continually expanded competence and knowledge base, and a commitment to caring and ethical forms of treatment.

The therapist cannot honestly make promises that cannot be kept, such as "You will get over the trauma." Or, "I will help you recover and resolve all the significant memories from your past." Or, "I have a special method or expertise other people do not know about; depend on me."

Sometimes it is necessary at the start of therapy to make the limitations of the therapeutic process clear. Too much emphasis on the imperfections of the process or the therapist, however, may merely discourage the client or increase distrust. A matter-of-fact acknowledgment of goals and limitations is usually a safer approach.

Early on, before the client is familiar with therapy as a process, the exacerbation of symptoms that occurs when conflicts begin to be explored or traumas are uncovered may be experienced as a rude awakening. If the therapist moves ahead too quickly in weakening existing defenses, such as denial and dissociation, therapy itself may be viewed as an enemy to be resisted.

At any point when therapy triggers flashbacks or other symptoms, as almost inevitably happens, the client may feel revictimized. And impatience may be intensified when memories, whether once lost or always dimly in awareness, come into focus in therapy. They may then be viewed as threats that must be eradicated as soon as possible rather than understood and integrated.

In spite of inevitable pitfalls, however, many clients experience enough relief and are able to sustain enough hope in the therapeutic enterprise that they can persist in it. The wish for a quick fix is gradually modified by a more realistic recognition of the complexities being explored. When these include a lifetime of posttraumatic accommodations, the changes being sought are often too extensive to be effected quickly. And there is usually a growing awareness as therapy progresses that there is more to confront and deal with than the specific problem or symptom for which the client originally sought help. Growing insight even in the face of ongoing discomfort thus serves as an ongoing impetus to continue treatment.

Even so, repeated clarifications of goals, limitations, and typical treatment reactions are usually in order as therapy proceeds. The client who understands that things sometimes get worse before they get better, or that the role of the therapist is quite specific and bounded, is better able to develop the patience necessary to proceed.

The Myth of the Magical Suggestion

One misunderstanding about therapy commonly raised by other people and sometimes believed by the client is that therapeutic changes are a simple matter of suggestion. The therapist is viewed as a wizard who, by simply uttering a few words, can effect radical changes in the client. Clients sometimes wish this were the case. It is part of their idealization of the therapist and has roots in the earliest infantile relations with parents perceived as magically powerful. Clients who, over a lifetime, have experienced a systematic subversion of their autonomy may also expect to be controlled by authoritarian commands, including the command to get over their symptoms. They may even want to be told what to do.

This perception of the therapeutic process as a form of authoritarian control is also encouraged by certain traditional models of therapeutic intervention, particularly those based on medical models. From this perspective, the therapist is the expert who diagnoses and prescribes; the "good" patient is the one who cooperates and follows doctors' orders. Although more client-centered models of psychotherapy have been around for many years, they have not supplanted this more authoritarian tradition. It is easy, too, to confuse the therapist's *authority* with *authoritarian* control. Therapists, as trained caregivers, do know more than their clients about some issues and procedures. As recognized professionals, they are accountable for controlling certain aspects of therapy, such as boundaries and safety.

There are also legitimate and helpful uses of suggestion. Hypnotic techniques, for example, have been stridently criticized in recent years, particularly by those who contend that false memories may be implanted by them (Loftus, 1993; Pettinati, 1988). But hypnotic interventions in psychotherapy are by no means confined to memory work. Hypnosis has long been a recognized means of helping clients achieve their own aims (Rossi, 1993). It is a technique with recognized medical uses ranging from the control of pain to the calming of anxiety (Hilgard & Hilgard, 1975). Hypnosis is usually most helpful when the client remains in control of the agenda (Rossi & Cheek, 1988). The notion of the client as obedient robot is contrary not only to the interventions of ethical therapists, but to what we know about hypnosis as a phenomenon. Hypnotic susceptibility, which is sometimes viewed as the most extreme form of suggestibility, varies in the population, however. Some individuals are not at all amenable to it (Hilgard, 1979).

The notion that therapeutic results are easily and commonly achieved through suggestion is based on the view of the client as a dependent, obedient child. But even clients who are dependent, compliant, and fearful of independent choices usually seek psychotherapy in order to move beyond their inhibitions and achieve a greater measure of autonomy. Even intimidated clients long browbeaten into compliance are often hypersensitive to control by other people and expect therapy to help them resist rather than submit to it.

The myth of the magical suggestion is, in any case, merely a myth. If therapists could effect swift and radical changes by a wave of the hand, they would never be stymied by intractable symptoms. Psychotherapy could, indeed, be a quick fix instead of a sometimes lengthy and convoluted path toward individuation.

Ironically, some of the most clear-cut evidence against the notion that people are easily manipulated by suggestions is found in studies of brainwashing and cult indoctrination. Experts in mind control employ powerful techniques, including physical manipulations such as diet control, sleep deprivation, or ritualistic practices (Lifton, 1961; Singer, 1995). They isolate the individual from normal social contexts and replace familiar relationships and routines with new ones. In some instances they employ actual threats and assaults.

It is possible for a psychotherapist, too, to employ authoritarian and manipulative techniques; grandiose and unethical therapists exist. It is even possible for a cult to be organized under the pretext of therapy (Singer, 1995). But the argument that such aberrations are typical of psychotherapy is specious. In the long run, saying that all psychotherapists are charlatans is like saying that all lawyers are shysters and all doctors are quacks. Only the most confirmed cynic really believes it.

Unfortunately, some clients come to psychotherapy with a long history of responding compliantly to the demands of other people. Traumatized individuals may also be especially susceptible to trance and sometimes self-induce trances in the therapeutic setting. In therapy, especially as transference develops, such individuals often behave as if the therapist, like domineering people from the past, is a controlling authority. Only by exploring the history and meaning of a client's submissiveness can one discover to what extent it reflects external realities, past or present, as well as hypothetical traits like "suggestibility."

The development of extreme submissiveness in a client is, in any case, no reason to avoid psychotherapy. It is, on the contrary, a serious and sometimes self-destructive problem that needs to be addressed and amelio-rated. Like any aspect of transference, the fact that it emerges in psycho-therapy does not mean that it was *caused* by therapy. Most often, it is a longstanding tendency that affected the client's relationships long before therapy and will continue to do so in the future unless corrected.

The Search for the Single Cause

The search for a fast fix is sometimes associated with the idea that complex problems have one simple cause or that current complaints are rooted in one singular event in the past. This attitude may make memory recovery the linchpin of the therapeutic process. Clients commonly say, for example, "Something bad happened to me. If I could put it out of my mind, I would be okay." Or, "Something bad *must* have happened to me. If I could remember, I would be okay."

When one especially terrible thing is known to have happened, this event easily becomes a scapegoat for all subsequent difficulties and dis-comforts in the client's life. This problem is complicated when the event produced major dislocations or posttraumatic accommodations. It is unde-niable, for example, that earthquakes or wars can change the course of life decisively and forever.

Nevertheless, it is usually simplistic and misleading to view adult prob-lems as a simple consequence of a few childhood experiences. The search for the "bad thing that happened" too easily distracts therapists as well as clients from the complexities of the personal past and of personality integration. Even terrible things that have happened to comparatively few people are part of a multifaceted life story.

It is not merely what happened, but how it has been integrated into one's life that makes the crucial difference in everyday coping. And it is not *whether* one remembers, but *how* one remembers, that makes the difference between being master of one's past or being overwhelmed by it.

The impact of early trauma on adaptation and self integration varies according to the stage of life in which the trauma occurs, the competen-cies available to the victim at that point, the way the trauma is subse-quently integrated into personal history, and how it shapes the future. By the time an adult enters psychotherapy, all of these variables will have considerably modified reactions to any particular past event. And although specific memories may be self-defining, the cornerstone of identity, the self one discovers in psychotherapy is not usually organized by one memory or even one set of memories. Even a singularly overwhelming episode is merely a chapter in a longer book.

In many instances, of course, specific traumatic memories must become a focus in therapy if the client is to integrate them and move forward. At some points a client may target traumatic events that were repeated over time, such as chronic forms of child abuse, as an explanation of a whole life history. And in some cases, the significance and duration of particular events *are* at the heart of a life story. Depending on the time period involved and the developmental stages impacted, even a single trauma can powerfully affect adaptation and identity consolidation.

The notion that one can overcome the negative effects of trauma by simply focusing on specific memories or specific traumas is, even so, simplistic. In many cases the only therapeutic approach that makes sense is one in which there are no restrictions on what can be explored and in which the client — and the therapist — can take the time for careful, painstaking work. Where the problems for which the client seeks help are woven into the total fabric of the self, effective treatment must eventually be directed to the whole person.

It is not always possible, of course, for the client to be involved in a long-term therapy. Many variables affect the feasibility of intensive treatment. The ideal of intensive, careful, long-term work may be simply out of reach. Sometimes, too, even when the therapist recognizes that long-term therapy will eventually be indicated, it makes sense to postpone it. Clients in immediate crises must direct all their time and resources to current coping. There are also unavoidable practical issues that inevitably affect treatment plans.

If a client has achieved a fairly satisfactory adaptation prior to an unusual crisis or a single trauma, therapy can sometimes focus quite specifically on immediate and practical forms of coping. Sometimes crisis intervention or short-term coping can be facilitated by an intentional attempt on the part of the therapist to help compartmentalize a trauma. In such instances, dissociation as a coping mechanism is deliberately facilitated. If the client has very limited psychological or physical resources, this may be the most feasible, even if temporary, solution.

Generally, however, it is more therapeutic to make integration rather than dissociation a keystone of the therapeutic enterprise. The more the client has, in the past, been fragmented by traumatic life events or maladaptive coping mechanisms, the more important it is for therapy to involve the whole person. A recognition of this issue has important implications for how the client's memories are integrated in the treatment process. The therapeutic focus cannot discount memories if they are part of the problem in the present. But viewing memories as simple causes of present effects is misleading. Moreover, the future as well as a past requires consideration if the client is to emerge from therapy as a whole and autonomous person.

It is also important to keep in mind that, as important as past traumatic experiences may be as a source of present anguish, symptoms such as extreme anxiety do not necessarily arise from specific traumas. Even when they have traumatic connections, symptoms usually arise from multiple causes. Many psychological symptoms for which people seek help result from conflict and pathological patterns of coping with conflict. And many posttraumatic symptoms, although originating in specific events, are shaped by complicated posttraumatic defenses and coping mechanisms.

THE STRUGGLE FOR SEPARATION

Whether related to trauma or not, many of the most intractable problems for which individuals seek help are an outgrowth of learned relationship patterns that have kept them enmeshed in interactions with other people who constantly stir up anxiety, thwart independent development, or are actually abusive. In this respect, attachment stands out clearly as the sustaining context of memory.

Relationship patterns structure attentional habits, typical modes of information processing, and the narratives and internal dialogues in which memories are embedded. And being able to move beyond malignant memories, like being able to extricate oneself from abusive relationships, often depends on histories of attachment.

People cling to memories, including memories of abuse, as a way of clinging to relationships. Starting a real fight may be an attempt at separation. But fighting can also be a way of holding on. When relationships have been abusive, this attachment pattern, however stormy, can be extremely tenacious. To move beyond the fight and really separate from abusers is terrifying.

The way memories of both relationships and specific events have been woven into personal histories affects how people enter into or extricate themselves from new relationships, including relationships with therapists. This is not to imply that used or abused people bring their problems on themselves or stay in destructive situations because of masochism. In many instances they are caught up in circumstances over which they have little or no control (Waites, 1978).

Some clients focus on a childhood trauma as a means of avoiding serious difficulties in the present, such as unresolved conflicts with parents, an unhappy sexual relationship, or a hated job. Veridical memories of abuse may be used as weapons of revenge not only against abusers themselves, but against anyone else believed to have been responsible in some way. A parent may be relentlessly blamed for the actions of another person—the other parent, a teacher, or a babysitter. Parents may even be blamed for traumatic incidents that were altogether accidental, such as a house fire, or that were necessary, such as painful medical procedures.

Disturbing incidents that did not involve intentional abuse, such as mutual sex play between siblings, may be reinterpreted as intentional abuse. Further, in some instances memories of abuse really are based on *fantasies* associated with confusing and guilt-inducing levels of sexual excitement in childhood.

These considerations do not justify a dismissive disregard of clients' memories of abuse. But they do indicate the need for a cautious evaluation of whether a memory is accurate and how it is being used in the present. Sometimes a therapist can make sense of what is going on by asking, implicitly or explicitly, "Why are you telling this story *now?*"

Sometimes a controversy that seems on the surface to be about the accuracy of memories is really about the client's freedom to disagree with controlling people and to change his or her patterns of interacting with them. As a client who has long been intimidated musters courage, this development can be even more frightening to the client and threatening to others than the recovery of specific memories.

Adversarial confrontations between adult clients who contend they were abused in childhood and family members who dispute their claims illustrate the significance of attachment as the social matrix of memory. It is not just what the client claims to remember but the use of an abuse memory as a pretext for separation from people with whom the client has been enmeshed that is at the heart of many disputes.

Because attachment patterns are so closely connected with the organization of memories, changes in attachment commonly appear in therapy in the context of memory exploration. Helping the client understand these connections can be a necessary component of personality integration. Even when an adult client is being abused in the present, however, the prudent therapist does not autocratically direct changes in the client's current interpersonal relationships. To do so would continue to erode the client's autonomy by replacing the control of others, such as the client's family, with the control of an authoritarian therapist.

The client's attempt to draw the therapist into actual fights with controlling family members is a dimension of transference. The most effective therapeutic response to such an attempt is usually interpretation and insight. Containing the fight within the therapy rather than externalizing it offers the best means for understanding it. Understanding, to be sure, may be a prelude to action, but considered and informed action is more likely to be effective than impulsive acting out.

Similarly, the therapist's attempt to enter into or even orchestrate actions external to the therapeutic context is often a dimension of counter-transference. Here, too, the most effective therapeutic response is insight. The therapist needs to discriminate fantasies about rescuing the client or providing magical forms of help from useful therapeutic interventions.

Any directives given by a therapist to a client should be evaluated from this perspective. Carefully considered directive action does have a place in psychotherapy. Sometimes the most helpful intervention a therapist can make is to offer pragmatic advice. It is sometimes even necessary for the therapist to intervene forcefully when a client becomes a danger to self or others. But such pragmatic interventions are quite different from attempts to control the client's life or to influence major life decisions. In any case, directive actions on the part of the therapist require not only cautious evaluation but a realistic appraisal of how they may impact on the therapy as a whole.

The therapist who treats children, of course, is constrained by special laws that may modify a strictly therapeutic agenda. The special vulnerability of children requires their actual protection, and therapists who treat children cannot always avoid special directive actions; protecting children may require forms of guidance and restraint or requests for outside interventions that would be inappropriate with adult clients. In the treatment of both children and adults, however, therapists' directive interventions are not only mandated but limited by law. Freedom to think, to move toward independence, and to exercise initiative remain at the heart of effective psychotherapy.

MEMORY AND TRANSFERENCE

Transference, the tendency of the client to relate to the therapist on the basis of early patterns of attachment, is one of the most dramatic forms of remembering that emerges in psychotherapy. Although it is connected to episodic memories, this connection may not be immediately obvious. By highlighting the present, particularly the present relationship with the therapist, transference seems to screen the past from view. It is up to the therapist, by recognizing repetitions and transference enactments, to interpret to the client how the past is infiltrating the present. It is often at this point that the client can achieve meaningful integrations.

In this respect, transference is one of the most valuable aids both to memory recovery in therapy and to personality integration. But as valuable as it is, it can pose serious difficulties. The very experience of transference, particularly when it involves a repetition of disturbing memories, can be frightening to the client. On the other hand, when transference feels more positive, the client may resist exploring anything unpleasant, such as a past trauma.

One response by clients to unpleasant transference developments is a struggle against them. This struggle, too, commonly reflects an earlier struggle in the life of the child. A client whose parents were controlling or authoritarian may react with defiance. A client who overidealized people who later proved disappointing may show a cynical distrust of everyone, including the therapist.

Although transference, as a pattern of relationship, reflects the child's relationships with parents, it cannot be taken as a simple undistorted picture of what happened to the client. Traumatized children may blame parents for events over which parents have no control, such as losses caused by natural disasters or pain caused by necessary medical procedures. When a loved one dies, that person may be blamed for abandoning the survivor. Although many such responses are recognized as irrational, the strong emotions they invoke should never be underestimated. Since transference configurations are organized around feelings as well as thoughts, such reactions can be a major source of difficulties in therapy.

A very traumatic or stormy history can be expected to produce stormy transference effects in psychotherapy. When that history includes extensive posttraumatic accommodations or symptoms, the chances of therapy being experienced as revictimizing are increased. If the treatment is so painful, thinks the client, maybe it would be better just to avoid it. This attitude is certainly understandable and should always be respected. Where the danger of stirring up overwhelming issues is great and/or the client's strengths for coping with them are doubtful, avoiding psychotherapy might seem to be obviously indicated.

Psychotherapists, even those who emphasized the psychic rather than the actual origins of trauma, have traditionally warned against exploring the depths with certain clients. Those with a biological orientation also tend to deemphasize explorations, attempting instead to relieve symptoms through medication. A focus on symptom relief can indeed be the therapy of choice for some clients. It is certainly the fastest and simplest approach and may be indicated at some points even for those clients treated with other therapeutic modalities. Unfortunately, however, treatment cannot always be easily avoided just because of the possibility of iatrogenic reactions or stormy transference developments. And even when they work temporarily, fast and simple solutions do not always solve the problems for which help is sought.

The problem, of course, is that, although flashbacks, painful transference reactions, and other symptoms may be triggered by psychotherapy, they were not initially caused by psychotherapy, but by real and consequential events in the client's life. If those events were episodes extended in time, they cannot be forgotten without losing a piece of personal history. If the events were repetitive occurrences, they may have shaped development and personality integration over a lifetime. And if the consequences of the events must be coped with in the present, troublesome memories are constantly being cued in daily life. However memory is approached in therapy, making it safe to remember is an ongoing aspect of the process. In any case, the safety of the self is always a priority.

CHAPTER 11

Recollection: Picking Up the Pieces

From perfect grief there need not be
Wisdom or even memory
One thing then learnt remains to me,
The woodspurge has a cup of three.

—Dante Gabriel Rossetti, *The Woodspurge*

REVISITING THE PAST can be a pleasant exercise in nostalgia, a compulsive ritual, or a chaotic happening. Bidden or unbidden, significant or trivial, meaningful or enigmatic, particular episodic memories constantly flit into and out of awareness. As they do, the self is a willing or reluctant audience. And every new encounter offers an opportunity for evaluation, revision, and reinterpretation.

Some memories are inexpressible. Some are almost inextricable from bodily responses: one may smile or wince to recall them. Many have a definite feeling tone, even when they do not evoke the intensity of emotion initially associated with them. Trauma is cumulative, and in remembering a particular trauma, images easily meld with one another.

For Carrie, for example, an old childhood trauma of being sexually abused by her father was revived and intensified by the traumatic experience of being robbed while she was a clerk in a convenience store. "The man held a gun to my head," she said. "It all happened fast, almost before I knew it. Sometimes, even now, when I haven't thought about it for a long time, I walk into a store and it all comes flooding back again. Yet whenever I deliberately *try* to think about it, it seems like a dream. At night sometimes I *do* dream about it, but the dreams are no longer like the holdup. Sometimes the man with the gun is in them but completely harmless things are going on. Or sometimes in my dreams, the man with a gun is my father, and he does the kind of stuff he did to me when I was a kid.

Sometimes I just wake up scared or with a stomachache and know I must have been having a nightmare."

Carrie's symptoms illustrate the some of complexities involved in deciphering posttraumatic memories. Dreams and intrusive images cannot just be taken as veridical replays of traumas, for example. Yet they are not necessarily totally fantastic fabrications. Even the most bizarre dreams may serve as clues to real events; this is especially true of recurring nightmares.

For several weeks after the robbery, Carrie had intrusive flashbacks of the experience. Her dreams vividly repeated the experience. Over time, though, flashbacks became less frequent; increasingly, when images of the holdup recurred, they were amalgamated with images of earlier traumas. For a long time, Carrie fought to avoid thinking about these aspects of her past. It was only after she began therapy and finally confronted the perplexing mix of memory and fantasy that she was able to make sense of her anxiety attacks and her ongoing sense of helplessness.

Repetitive reexperiencing, a typical consequence of trauma, is a retraumatizing disruption of life. Uncontrollable experiences of memory, whether intrusions or gaps, often lead to attempts to reestablish control. At that point, the experience of recollection may become a curious composite of remembering and avoiding.

At any point in the construction of personal history, the conflict between the wish to remember and the wish to forget can subvert memory. Particular recollections, seemingly clear and consistent, can become clouded and suspect. Repeated recollections can lead to revised and re-revised narratives. Unnarrated encodings may evoke visceral and reflexive responses that make no sense. The past surveyed may appear as a disconnected but tantalizing array of fragments, like the unconnected pieces of a jigsaw puzzle.

Every time a memory is brought into focus, the new retrieval context is added to the welter of contexts in which the memory is embedded. This is particularly true when the retrieval itself is vivid—when one tells a story to an important audience, for example, or repeats it as testimony in court. The social reinforcement of any recollection affects how and how strongly it will compete in memory with previous versions. Affirmation validates the self as a credible witness. Censure tends to create self-doubt and, sometimes, a revision of one's report.

Attempts to create coherence and consistency, to make sense out of puzzling accounts or to resolve discrepancies between mismatched stories create new narratives about old events. Self-relevant memories are commonly embedded in particular social contexts—family stories and cultural histories—that may assume a mythical status in an individual life. Once created, a mythical story may seem more vivid in recollection than the original. When a story is amended or a new narrative is constructed, earlier, less distorted accounts do not necessarily fade from memory. If they have a long history, especially if they were often repeated during some period, they persist as divergent, often covert narratives.

When inconsistent memories, mismatched stories, and divergent narratives exist side by side, the self may capitulate to the inconsistencies. But integration is a powerful motive in the lives of most people. Confronting memory in the context of this motive to achieve wholeness means taking an active rather than passive stance in regard to one's memories. It means intentionally picking up the pieces and painstakingly assembling them into a whole.

Thus, as development unfolds from childhood through age, the experience of memory is intimately interwoven with the integration of the self. In this ongoing process of integration, the search for memory is an active and sometimes urgent process. It involves constantly creating a new set of recollections as the self struggles to find what has been lost, to assimilate what has been found, and to organize a sometimes fragmentary history into a consistent whole.

REMEMBERING IN
THE THERAPEUTIC CONTEXT

Remembering more of the past and remembering it differently is one of the usual outcomes of psychotherapy. Even when the focus of therapy is on something else, people remember because they need to remember, because they cannot talk about themselves without consulting memory, and because every dialogue with another human being involves the matching of memories.

Helping people remember adaptively is also one of the explicit and pragmatic uses of psychotherapy. Problems with remembering or forgetting are a common presenting symptom for which people seek help. In recent years, in the wake of increased public awareness of the effects of trauma and of the prevalence of child abuse, memory issues have become even more prominent as motives for help-seeking.

Troublesome memory symptoms vary, not only from one individual to another, but within the same individual. Some memories are irritating simply because they are inconsistent with preferred views of the self or of other people. Others, such as those that replay traumatic events, may be experienced as noxious or shocking intrusions. Some memory fragments cannot be fitted into a coherent or meaningful narrative. Missing memories may leave gaps in a story, noticed or unnoticed, that perplex, tease, anger, or are just accepted with equanimity.

Memory sometimes assumes control over behavior in detrimental or destructive ways. Compulsive repetitions may replay stereotyped renditions of the past over and over without variation. Memory lapses, ranging

from transient fugues to lengthy dissociative episodes, may disrupt organized activities.

In addition to the memory issues that originally lead a client to seek
therapy, memories that arise in the context of psychotherapy pose problems as well as solutions to problems. The veridicality of such memories
has long been controversial and has recently become even more so. Freud,
who originally compared himself to an archaeologist unearthing historical
artifacts, vacillated in his attitude toward the factual status of his patients'
reported recollections. Those who came after him often exchanged a
search for historical events for a focus on interactions between the therapist and the client in the here and now.

In recent years, the problems inherent in assessing the veridicality of
memories revived in therapy have been cogently reviewed by Spence
(1982). Acknowledging the work of experimental psychologists like Loftus,
he has reminded his colleagues of all the distorting factors that can arise in
the construction and reconstruction of memory. Reviewing Freud's own
vacillations, Spence has concluded that the image of the psychoanalyst as
archaeologist is fundamentally misleading. He contends that all we know
on earth or need to know is narrative truth. Narrative truth is nevertheless
sufficient for therapeutic purposes.

In spite of Freud's repudiation of the seduction theory and the subsequent ascendence of the hermeneutic orientation in psychoanalysis, many
psychoanalysts and psychotherapists (Blum, 1980; Wetzler, 1985) have
continued to search for the historical reality behind even the most elliptical and distorted memories. The psychotherapeutic task, from this perspective, is not just the interpretation of fantasy, but the reconstruction of
history. Meaning cannot be divorced from reality. And just because the
task is difficult, it need not be abandoned.

In nonanalytic therapies, of course, the focus has always been on reality,
though not necessarily on remembered reality. Behavioral techniques effect adaptive connections between real stimuli and actual responses.
Cognitive interventions encourage rational interpretations and plans. Interpersonal and family therapies focus on actual communications and
transactions.

From the client's perspective, whatever the therapeutic focus, it is not
just the recovery of memories, but the relation between self and memory
that usually makes the difference. The self needs to be in control of memory not only to achieve meaning, but to meet the practical demands of
everyday life. Such practical issues are sometimes a therapeutic priority.

Although integration is the typical goal of intensive treatment, therapeutic techniques that attempt to isolate memories from awareness can
also sometimes be helpful. Techniques involving the controlled use of
dissociation can facilitate temporary "vacations" from disruptive memo-

ries. Medications that calm disruptive intrusions of noxious memories can be valuable.

Still, to be severed from memory in any extensive way is to be alienated from oneself. Temporary palliatives, however helpful, are only a stopgap measure, and the self in hiding or in pieces often asks more. For many people, nothing else will do but to pick up the pieces of the past, one by one, and put them together again.

PITFALLS

In spite of the best intentions, integrating memories in the therapeutic context can pose hazards. Concerns about veridicality oversimplify the issues. Whether memories are true or false—in most cases they are a mix—ambivalence toward remembering is a dynamic in most therapies. In therapy as in life, the wish to remember is not constant and unyielding. Uncomfortable veridical memories are not merely a common reason for entering psychotherapy; they may be a reason for exiting.

Whenever the self encounters unwelcome memories, the pressure to avoid or amend them conflicts with the wish to find and hold onto the truth. This conflict in itself can create so much internal tension that the self gives up the effort or capitulates to someone else's story. One of the ongoing challenges to the psychotherapist is simultaneously facilitating and titrating the emergence of memories, enabling the client to feel in control rather than overpowered.

Another therapeutic task is untangling the web of experiences and connections that may be tagged by any particular statement. Even a seemingly single and whole recollection *has* rather than *is* a history. Even what seems on the surface to be a simple recollection of a single brief episode often turns out, on close examination, to be a composite. Tracking the history of the memory can sometimes reveal how, at crucial points in a client's life, the composite was repeatedly elaborated and reconstructed.

The disparate components of autobiographical memories—images, words, feelings—are variably integrated in any recollection. The process of integration is complicated by narrative conventions as well as by dialogues between the one remembering and other people. In an initial confrontation with a piece of the past, images, emotional responses, postural and gestural responses may be jumbled together with narratives. Responses may conflict. Images may fail to match up with narratives. Multiple narratives may diverge. But the very process of trying to communicate the memory introduces coherence into what may have once been a chaotic mix.

This does not imply that the story that emerges at any given point is untrue, just that, when it comes to memory, truth is seldom an absolute.

The degree to which the memory is completely true can change from moment to moment, day to day, year to year. Pragmatically, the most meaningful questions may be, "Was it true enough to be useful then? What about now? Why?" The answer to these questions depends on the person asking and the task at hand.

Throughout therapy, an ongoing and essential task is helping the client put the pieces together. No matter how true or significant, recollections that cannot be assimilated are useless, even dangerous. Even a coherent and true story that is merely added on rather than integrated tends to add to the number of divergent narratives in the client's repertoire. Adding on stories rather than integrating them is often merely a indication of the client's compliance in therapy and runs counter to therapeutic goals of facilitating autonomy.

It should go without saying, of course, that the substitution of the therapist's stories for those of the client is counterproductive. Interpretation is a major role of a psychotherapist, but interpretation must be carefully distinguished from control and domination. During an intensive therapy, therapist and client will usually consider many stories, trying on hypotheses, making connections, fitting fragments together. But this process of trying on interpretations to discover a meaningful and logical fit is quite different from imposing one's ideas in an authoritarian way. Any interpretation is provisional. Ultimately, only the client can decide what is plausible, true, or meaningful.

Sometimes it is necessary to educate a compliant client about provisional and exploratory thinking. Clients who have never learned to think for themselves or who have been punished for doing so may need to learn basic modes of evaluating ideas as ideas. Sometimes, too, this lesson must include learning to delay judgment about facts. The importance of delaying action, particularly very consequential actions, until facts and meanings have been carefully considered deserves special emphasis.

The danger that compliant clients may accept as absolute truth some tentative and provisional hypothesis on the part of the therapist should be constantly monitored. In clients who have over a lifetime accommodated to authoritarian forms of control, this tendency can sabotage a therapy. The problem is compounded when a client, for whatever reason, *needs* to fail in therapy. At that point, the therapist may be set up as just another controlling authority the client needs to defy or escape from.

Less defiant clients, in contrast, may simply accept a therapist's interpretation without questioning it. Very disturbed clients may seize on an interpretation, including a reconstruction of memory, as a cover story that explains every problem in their life. Even a true and very significant story cannot explain a whole life. The tendency to use a painful self-defining memory as a scapegoat can distract both client and therapist from the complexities of personality integration.

Whenever memories overwhelm the one remembering, coping with this emergency response becomes a priority. At some points, even in an intensive psychotherapy that focuses on integrating memories, the most urgent task is to help the client forget, at least temporarily.

The pitfalls of psychotherapy can be compared with those of other consequential interventions, including medical interventions, that must be evaluated for risk factors but that should not necessarily be avoided just because they are risky. In many instances, intensive psychotherapy is the most sensible approach to difficult problems. Prudent therapists, nevertheless, will be sensitive to the pitfalls and strive to avoid them. It is not necessary to become unduly defensive in this regard, just vigilant, careful, and informed.

A corollary of these considerations is that, in matters of remembering, individuals must have their own timetable. Readiness to remember is as important as the ability to remember. In the long run, it is not the therapist's interpretation, but the client's comprehension that makes the difference between memories that injure and those that, even though painful, contribute to healing.

DECODING THE BODY

Somatic responses are basic building blocks of memory, particularly traumatic memory. The increased level of arousal associated with emergency reactions triggers the release of powerful hormones and neurotransmitters, as well as postural changes and behavioral responses (Waites, 1993). The body in the grip of these is action-oriented. Thinking may only come later. At that point, the original somatic responses may or may not be woven into the story of what happened.

These somatic responses are visceral encodings of the traumatic experience. Although they may not be connected with specific narratives, they reproduce states of arousal and behavioral responses that were conditioned at the time the trauma occurred. Often, such somatic responses include reflexive avoidance behaviors. They are commonly but not necessarily associated with perceived anxiety. When these anxious responses are not connected with any meaningful narrative, the individual does not know where the fear comes from, just that it is strong and interferes with volitional behavior.

Aspects of memory that do not lend themselves to narrative are harder to understand and integrate than those which can be labeled and recounted. They may be especially disturbing just because they are puzzling. Similarly, when the body enacts a memory without an accompanying narrative explanation, it may appear odd, crazy even to the self as well as to other people.

A woman consulted a psychotherapist, for example, because her husband, a Vietnam veteran, was hitting her in his sleep. From his vocalizations, she inferred that he was mistaking her for a wartime enemy. Yet, on waking, he himself had no memory of his attack. Her bruises were real enough, though, and his repetitive violence terrified her.

In evaluating somatic responses and behavioral enactments, a plausible narrative based on documented events is very helpful. Even in the absence of such corroboration, one can sometimes make plausible inferences. The wife described above, knowing her husband's combat history, made such an inference. She decided his behavior must be an aftereffect of combat and, therefore, an understandable response rather than a sign he was crazy. This inference, which was shared by her therapist, served as a useful hypothesis in planning intervention. The husband was referred for evaluation, eventually diagnosed as suffering from posttraumatic stress disorder, and appropriately treated.

One cannot simply leap to accurate inferences about past events on the basis of somatic and behavioral symptoms, however. Dreamers may lash out in nightmares that are altogether fantastic. Delusional people attack others on the basis of imagined insults. The documentation of a traumatic history is suggestive, but it does not lead to simple cause-effect explanations.

Plausibility, then, is very useful in establishing leads for further exploration and in helping make sense of a cryptic story. But it must not be mistaken for proof. There is no way to determine whether the content of the waking dream in which the man attacked his wife was a veridical memory, a fantasy about combat, or a mixture of both. He was never able to recollect consciously what he had dreamed or to form any meaningful narrative about it.

Caution is similarly in order in evaluating somatic symptoms. A stomachache in the present may seem to be connected with a memory of an actual event in childhood. If it arises every time the event is mentioned, the stomachache may be tentatively viewed as a visceral encoding of a disturbing memory. But as a definite link to a specific episodic memory, the stomachache is inconclusive. The connecting thread between past and present is the anxiety aroused on both occasions. The source of that anxiety may have been something as observably "real" as a specific threat or as uncertain as a fantasied danger. Or the client may get stomachaches in connection with any strong anxiety. Decoding the stomachache requires a look at many possible connections.

Considering many possible connections, of course, is very different from dismissing the stomachache or assuming that it provides no useful information about actual events. The cues that repetitively evoke a somatic symptom require careful examination. Sometimes the associations to the somatic symptom are specific and consistent enough to warrant useful inferences about past events. Again, plausibility may not be proof. But a plausible connection is a good start toward establishing other connections, and when many such connections have been established the result may be a convincing as well as plausible reconstruction of past events.

Corroboration

These considerations highlight the pragmatic dimension of remembering in psychotherapy. The task facing the Vietnam veteran, his wife, and all therapists involved, for example, was ameliorating a destructive symptom. No one was on trial here. Although proving beyond doubt that his attack on his wife was stimulated by a veridical memory of combat was impossible, the hypothesis that this was the case was an effective guide to treatment.

Such a pragmatic focus does not imply that truth is unimportant or that seeking facts is unnecessary. The more information available to therapist and client, the greater the opportunity for making plausible inferences. But psychotherapists are not investigative agents. They cannot seek out evidence or conduct inquiries into the facts of a case. Such behavior is not just beyond the scope of therapists' training and competence; it would, if engaged in, erode the necessary boundaries of the therapeutic context.

Exceptions to this rule, which may occur if a client is a dependent child or unable to act in her own interests, do not invalidate it. Sometimes a therapist finds it necessary to ask interventions from investigative agencies or courts and some therapists, of course, are employed by such agencies. Yet, strictly speaking, the therapeutic context is one in which evidence consists only of what the client says and does.

In attempting to validate their own memories, clients frequently seek corroborating evidence on their own. And when it might be helpful, therapists can suggest that the client do so. In the matter of somatic memories, for example, it is especially important to seek medical evaluations. What might be mistaken for a psychogenic symptom, say a bodily memory of trauma, may on careful investigation turn out to be a symptom of physical disease or injury. Some ritualistic behaviors are symptomatic of underlying neurological conditions. Any severe somatic complaint calls for a medical evaluation.

When a client has a known history of trauma or abuse, it is tempting to infer that reported somatic symptoms are bodily memories of that history. Somatic symptoms for which no underlying physical cause can be found are a common sequel to severe abuse (Waites, 1993). But jumping to premature conclusions can delay a clear understanding of what really happened and is happening. Some symptoms simply point to unhealed physical injuries, a possibility that only medical evaluation can rule out. Evaluations can usually be handled by the family physician who already knows the client's history. If not, referrals to specialists are in order.

In many cases, of course, medical evaluations will have preceded the client's seeking psychotherapy. A physician, finding no physical cause for a symptom, may have made the referral. Or the client may have had years of unhelpful medical interventions for a painful physical complaint. Some clients, too, will have iatrogenic symptoms, problems caused by medical interventions such as shock treatment or psychotropic medication. And since posttraumatic stress disorder is a frequent though often unrecognized response to painful medical interventions, the very symptoms for which the client seeks therapy may be a consequence of necessary medical treatments. For these reasons, sensitivity and empathy are especially important in medically evaluating the symptoms of traumatized individuals (Waites, 1993).

Medical conditions that are unrelated to the issues for which the client seeks psychotherapy can also impact significantly on therapy. Sometimes, for example, a traumatic history makes it hard for a client to focus on or take care of the body. When that is the case, it is all the more important for the therapist to encourage such care.

Some clients, particularly those who have been blamed for their physical symptoms or diagnosed as suffering from a psychological rather than a physical disorder, are quick to jump to the conclusion that any somatic complaint is their fault or is merely "in my head." It is then especially important that the therapist be attentive to the possibility of real disease or injury.

The dichotomy between mind and body is, of course, simplistic. Mind and body are always connected, and any health problem has psychological ramifications. Once any associated medical condition has been ruled out or treated, symptoms that seem plausibly related to psychological issues can be more confidently approached from a psychological perspective. The mystery that remains may still require painstaking efforts to unravel.

Symptoms as a Distractor

Most of the somatic symptoms presented by clients, particularly by clients who establish real commitment to the therapeutic process, are a source of suffering the client is honestly trying to overcome. And sometimes somatic symptoms can be valuable clues to lost pieces of the past. But the relation of current symptoms to past events, even very significant and consequential past events, is usually complicated.

At any point in the construction or reconstruction of memory, somatic responses can function as a distractor. At the time a trauma occurs, the individual may intentionally focus on what is happening to the body instead of what is happening outside it. Later, in the grip of anxious memories, the body is often tense or uncomfortable or ill. When these feelings are disconnected from meaningful narratives, the illness is a mystery. But, even though inexplicable, the somatic complaint itself may become the focus of obsessive ruminations and may be used as an escape from thinking about disturbing events, unresolved conflicts, or pressing responsibilities.

At any point, too, the recurrence of an old symptom may result not primarily from remembering an original trauma, but from experiencing a new one. Many psychogenic physical complaints are more closely tied to what is happening in the present than to what happened in the past. A man about to be laid off from his job may develop headaches or back problems. A woman who has recently been raped may experience a recurrence of an irritable bowel syndrome that had been previously under control.

The anxiety triggered by the current stress may, of course, be related in some way to old memories and the form the symptom takes may clearly derive from an old trauma. A client who once narrowly escaped drowning, for example, may develop symptoms of feeling suffocated. But when somatic symptoms are current responses to anxiety rather than simple replays of childhood events, they cannot be resolved by simply focusing on the past. It is necessary to ask "Why is this coming up *now?*"

Sometimes, an individual confronted by a present crisis would just rather focus on a past one. Even a veridical traumatic memory or a very real physical symptom may be used for avoidance.

A woman entered therapy, for example, complaining of aches and pains her physician had said were psychologically caused. These changed from day to day, but she began to be more and more preoccupied with her body and the fear that she had a serious, though undiagnosed disease. She was vaguely aware that her husband was becoming more distant and feared her marriage might be in trouble. But whenever that fear emerged, a physical symptom preempted her attention. In therapy, as in life, she avoided talking about her present problems and became more and more distracted by childhood vexations and traumas. Only when her husband filed for divorce did she begin to focus on what was happening to her in the here and now.

The client who is taking refuge in somatic symptoms is not wholeheartedly trying to get over the problem. Whatever the origin of the symptom, it is too useful to give up. When there are secondary gains, such as monetary compensation or leaves from work, these can seriously compromise treatment.

Nevertheless, an empathic therapist does not take a dismissive attitude toward physical symptoms even when the client may be using them for ulterior motives. Many clients, particularly those with a history of trauma, have always had their physical complaints ignored or dismissed. Their preoccupation with physical symptoms is an attempt to pay attention to and to get others to pay attention to real pains and injuries. Even if they take refuge in these injuries, they do so out of a sense of outrage or helplessness or hopelessness that needs to be acknowledged before it can be alleviated.

Because victims of intentional abuse, especially, have so often been told that they are exaggerating their pain or that they should just "get over it," and because they have so often been treated dismissively in the health-care system, it is especially important for psychotherapists to take their physical complaints seriously. Although the woman just discussed had to focus eventually on her crumbling marriage, for example, she could not really understand her own part in it without exploring her traumatic history.

SCREEN MEMORIES

> I see a rectangular, rather steeply sloping piece of meadow-land, green and thickly grown.... Three children are playing in the grass. We are picking the yellow flowers.... The little girl has the best bunch; and, as though by mutual agreement, we—the two boys—fall on her and snatch away her flowers. (Freud, *Screen Memories*, 1899, p. 311)

Early in his work, Freud (1899) described a special class of memories called *screen memories*. These consisted of vivid recollections of events in childhood that often seemed of no obvious significance to the individual and that, through analysis, could sometimes be shown to involve patent distortions. Screen memories, according to Freud, were not simply veridical accounts of historical truths; in contrast, they were created to distract the self from important but disturbing fantasies.

Analyzing the memory reported above, for example, Freud described how other memories and fantasies from young adulthood combined to give a special vividness to the earlier scene of children picking dandelions. The yellowness of the dandelions was amalgamated in memory with the yellowness of a dress worn years later by a young woman to whom the young man, now grown up, was attracted. The seemingly innocuous image of picking and stealing flowers was related to a less innocuous fantasy that became important later, the fantasy of deflowering a woman.

According to Freud, screen memories, although not necessarily untrue, are a retreat from unpleasant or forbidden ideas. Even when such memories contain veridical details, there is more to the story than meets the eye. In order to decipher them, we must look beyond reality to some connecting link between an innocuous idea and a more disturbing but hidden one. Modern psychoanalysts emphasize that earlier events may serve as screens for later ones and vice versa. As Wetzler (1985) emphasizes, a new trauma may reactivate an old conflict. The earlier event then becomes a screen for the later conflict.

Freud (1940 [1938]) described how enactments as well as ideas can serve a screening function. For example, in order to distract himself from the disturbing fantasy that the female is missing a penis, the fetishist focuses on something that is *not* missing, such as another body part or an article of clothing. This fetish, like a screen memory, simultaneously conceals and reveals a constellation of ideas associated with sexual conflict.

Transference and enactments in transference can be considered a special case of screening (Blum, 1980; Wetzler, 1985). Past traumas and conflicts are experienced with a special urgency in the here and now, and provide opportunities for reconstructing a picture of what happened developmentally.

Although many psychoanalysts question the historical accuracy of such reconstructions and emphasize that narrative truth is what matters for personality integration (Spence, 1982), others have always attempted to discover the realities underlying patients' reports (Blum, 1980; Greenacre, 1975; Novey, 1968; Schmideberg, 1953). Freud himself vacillated in this regard. On the one hand, he compared himself with an archaeologist in search of historical facts; on the other, particularly after he repudiated the seduction theory, he focused on the symbolic in his interpretations.

Freud's analysis of screen memories is in any case a powerful demonstration of how the mind engages in combinatorial play to create composites of memory and fantasy. It provides a useful theoretical approach to interpreting vivid but seemingly inconsequential memories as well as other cognitive constructions. Unconsciously as well as consciously, human beings constantly engage in symbolic elaborations of actual experiences. The reality versus fantasy dichotomy fails to do justice to these cognitive complexities. Analogical thinking and symbolic play can transform even the most accurate observations.

Unfortunately, however, an emphasis on fantasy as a dimension of memory easily lends itself to a dismissive stance regarding the historical accuracy of reported recollections. Symbolic, even cryptic encodings of past events hide not only significant conflicts and fantasies, but also significant though unspeakable memories.

Although it has been argued (Spence, 1982) that the therapeutic situation offers no way of discriminating between narrative and historical truth, as Wetzler (1985) points out, "There are vast differences between the effects of a real trauma, a diverse spectrum of real experiences interacting with pre-existing fantasies, and fantasies without any actual basis" (p. 194). The difficulties in sorting out these distinctions should not preclude conscientious therapeutic attempts to do so.

After all, unless there is independent disconfirming information, the assumption that a particular recollection is merely a screen memory or cover story is as much a hypothesis as the assumption that it speaks the unvarnished truth. The possibility that the story, even if true, has been amended by fantasy and contains distorted details should always be considered. But assuming that it is a cover for something else can be as much of a distractor from actualities as a deliberate distortion. And to the extent that the memory really does reflect historical facts, dismissing it as untrue may undermine the client's confidence in the therapeutic process.

Freud's theoretical assumptions about screen memories, then, need not prompt therapists to dismiss out of hand the possibility that what a client is reporting is, although distorted in some particulars, essentially true. Being too quick to focus on the symbolic at the expense of the literal can lead therapist and client astray. Even when an actual memory serves as a screen for important fantasies, the implications of it in actuality may have been crucial for the client's development and integration.

Certain theoretical presumptions, such as the notion that vivid details in memories indicate that screening is involved, can be especially misleading. Vivid sensory experiences are not necessarily cryptic encodings of forbidden fantasies or intrapsychic conflicts and do not necessarily derive from complicated defensive processes. Psychoanalytic assumptions that they are do not tally with modern research on trauma.

For example, Freud (1899) considered that memories in which the self observes itself cannot be reproducing an original occurrence, since the self in the midst of the original event would have been attending to external impressions. But depersonalization and self-observing—even out-of-body experiences—are quite common in traumatic states. Thus, a memory in which the self observes itself is not necessarily a later reworking of an original memory. It may be, rather, a recollection of a dissociative episode.

The assumption is also sometimes made that the very vividness and clarity of so-called screen memories make them suspect. Why should an innocuous memory be experienced so intensely? But this assumption, too, ignores the special dimensions of information-processing characteristic of traumatic states.

There is no research support for the notion that vividness is in itself an indication that the reported memory is a fantasy. Nor is there support for the notion that when incidental details are emphasized in a narrative about the past, these details merely hide intrapsychic conflicts or fantasies. Sometimes, particularly during a traumatic event, the shocked self is immobilized or unselective in gathering information. Whatever captures attention becomes vividly focused in observation and may, in consequence, become permanently fixed in memory.

MEMORY TAGS

All these years afterward . . . I remembered how small details had been indelibly fixed by shock, how yellow the sunlight was on the butter balls I rolled between two wooden paddles. (Jane Hillyer in Geller & Harris, 1994, p. 235)

Trauma has characteristic effects on perception. Normally smooth processes of scanning may become erratic. Behavioral freezing may fixate one's focus on discrete but incidental details. Or agitation may produce the opposite—a lack of focus in which details are blurred or lost entirely.

As a result of these special effects on information-processing, some vivid yet seemingly irrelevant details may come to serve as tags for traumatic memories. These tags, however seemingly incidental, may be strongly connected to conditioned somatic and emotional responses. In posttraumatic stress disorder, for example, vivid sensory images may function as visual, auditory, or olfactory cues that trigger flashbacks (McCaffrey et al., 1993; van der Kolk & Greenberg, 1987).

Such immediate sensory and visceral encodings are essentially prior to narrative. Yet they can eventually serve as memory tags for narrated stories. They facilitate the recollection of the story itself while at the same time focusing attention on some aspects of it at the expense of others.

Some memories remain as private as they are vivid because they were initially shaped by unusual modes of information processing. They persist in the individual like nodal points around which important self-defining memories crystalize. And yet, in spite of their urgency and enduring relevance to the individual, they cannot be easily communicated. Events that are different from anything ever encountered before may be hard to express even to oneself. When no meaningful narrative can be constructed, it is easy to capitulate to silence.

Sometimes, in subsequent recollecting or retelling, the emphasis placed on a small but incidental detail lends a cryptic quality to the story. It may distract the audience as well as the narrator from more disturbing details. The significance of the story may be discounted, too, especially if seemingly more important details are left out. Why would anyone remember what kind of shoes an assailant was wearing instead of, say, more definitive identifying characteristics? Why would anyone know what kind of rug was on the floor when child abuse occurred, but be unsure of what house the incident occurred in?

Although the creation of such memory tags may be based on special mechanisms of information-processing, the tags, once created, can also function as intentionally focused distractors to the mind trying to defend itself. Victims of incestuous abuse, for example, often describe how they deliberately focused on some peripheral detail that caught their attention—the design in the wallpaper, the sound of traffic outside a window (Courtois, 1988). As attention narrows and the trivial detail becomes a point of deliberate focus, the self may actually induce an altered state of consciousness, a trance that makes possible a psychological escape from what is physically inescapable (Waites, 1993).

When information about the actuality of an event is filtered out of perception, the interaction between self and world is changed in ways that may have powerful effects on memory. Subsequent rehearsals or retrievals of the event will include the original perceptual emphases or distortions. Some seemingly trivial details that have no intrinsic connection with a trauma, for example, may come to represent it ever after by virtue of an accidental contiguity that becomes permanently stored in memory.

Just because such trivial details *are* accidental, they are useful for simultaneously encoding and deflecting attention from traumatic experience. The mind may veer away from more essential and horrific details to take refuge in the incidental and innocuous. Over time, such seemingly trivial details can altogether replace more significant ones in any recounting of the event. When that happens, the odd detail stands as a cryptic code.

Intentional uses of memory tags and selective focusing, in contrast to more automatic modes of information-processing, may over time organize what Freud would have interpreted as screen memories. But, again, it must be emphasized that intentionally focusing on a distractor does not in itself negate the reality of what is being avoided or the possibility that some encodings of it have been veridical.

Once fixation on an incidental detail replaces a focus on more central and salient details of an event, the traumatized individual may be protected from stimulus overload. But the defenses themselves can lead to problems. By leaving important pieces of reality unassimilated, the self can become, in effect, cut off from internal as well as external information that might be vital for future coping. Avoidance can be temporarily soothing, but when real problems remain unsolved it increases one's sense of helplessness and incompetence. Moreover, failing to cope with traumatic realities can leave one vulnerable to repetitions of traumatic events.

ENACTMENTS

One way in which memories are somatically encoded and subsequently repeated is through enactive behavior (Eth & Pynoos, 1985; Terr, 1990, 1994). Enactments are representational or symbolic to varying degrees and may or may not be accompanied by narratives. They may occur in the waking state or while the individual is in an altered state of consciousness, a trance or fugue state.

Children commonly enact pleasant as well as unpleasant remembered events. A memory of going to the circus may be revisited for weeks in play scenarios. An inoculation by the doctor may be reenacted with a toy doctor set. A warning by a parent may be repeated to a doll. This form of remembering illustrates the close relationship between thinking and behavior in childhood, and the extent to which a child's identification with an adult is an enactive process of personality transformation. Attachment is often an important dimension of enactment.

Many reenactments consist of compulsive repetitions of traumatic events. Like the experience of flashbacks, the reenactment of traumatic memories commonly reinstates the intense states of arousal or numbing responses that accompanied the original trauma. In adults as well as children, such reenactments reveal the pressing need to discharge tensions and emotions and to master overwhelming experiences. Reenactments that occur in altered states of consciousness, such as trance or sleep, may, like narrative memories associated with such states, be inaccessible in the normal waking state.

Waking reenactments may gradually be modified by posttraumatic accommodations that change remembered events or enable the individual to reinstate control and mastery. A terrible story may gradually come to be replayed with a happier ending: rescue replaces helplessness, hurtful people are punished, or the self copes adaptively rather than being overwhelmed. Such revisions of traumatic memory may be a way of "metabolizing" trauma. They are in some ways comparable to the evolution of posttraumatic dreams from literal replays to symbolic constructions.

Childhood enactments are an example of how somatic and behavioral forms of remembering may precede and be variably integrated with language. Terr (1985, 1990), for example, describes how enactments may provide a key to past trauma that occurred even before a child developed language. Eth and Pynoos (1985) provide similar examples.

Sometimes, a seemingly meaningless act turns out, on close inspection, to be a destructive consequence of an earlier trauma. Seemingly random acts of violence, although not replays of specific scenarios, can discharge overwhelming tensions evoked by traumatic memories. Frederick (1985), for example, reports on a sniper incident in a Los Angeles schoolyard in which the assailant was suffering from PTSD as a result of the deaths of his parents and siblings in the Jonestown massacre.

In the immediate aftermath of trauma, literal reenactments are often compulsive, monotonous replays unmodified by fantasies; narrative and fantasy may be unavailable to the victim. The evolution of remembering from literal replays to symbolic transformations is a common aspect of recovery. Some forms of psychotherapy explicitly attempt to orchestrate such transformations (Waites, 1993).

ANNIVERSARY REACTIONS

One kind of symptom that commonly includes somatic and enactive components and is often associated with a traumatic history is the anniversary reaction. Clients themselves may recognize that a particular symptom occurs or is intensified on the anniversary of a significant event. But in many instances, the connection is not obvious until there is a specific search for it.

Anniversary reactions are frequently observed as an aspect of grief and mourning (Haig, 1990). In the first few months of grieving, in particular, persistent recall of memories may become especially vivid at special times, such as holidays.

The loss of a significant person through death, in fact, is a major trauma that may evoke all the symptoms of traumatic stress, including alterations in HPA axis functioning and immune functioning (Haig, 1990; van der Kolk & Greenberg, 1987). Stress reactions precipitated by bereavement may also elicit or intensify previous trauma reactions. Such reactions are an aspect of separation trauma in animals as well as in humans. The recurrence of symptoms on the anniversary of the traumatic event seems to be a special form of flashback.

Many traumatic situations, in fact, involve a double trauma — physical injury *and* psychological loss. The destruction caused by war or natural disasters frequently involves not only personal injuries but the injuries or deaths of loved ones and the loss of home or property. Individual acts of violence evoke grief as well as fear and pain. Grief reactions, like other aspects of trauma, may be dissociated.

In cases of child abuse, for example, repeated physical assaults may lead to forms of ambivalent attachment or intermittent detachment that would normally precipitate grief reactions. When grief is dissociated, as commonly occurs in such situations, normal processes of mourning are sidestepped or attenuated. They may later come to the surface suddenly and without warning, triggered by some external cue that recalls either the trauma itself or a significant feature of the disrupted attachment. Sometimes they are evoked by the process of remembering in psychotherapy.

Normally, in cases of bereavement, the social ritualization of mourning facilitates emotional catharsis and preserves social integration. Haig (1990) notes that, for individuals who are "frozen" in grief, the rituals of mourning may serve a restorative function by triggering normal grief. Anniversary dates may be incorporated into such rituals. Regular visits to the grave of the deceased, ceremonies on the anniversary of the death or interment, or private forms of memorial, such as family gatherings, help provide a shared way of responding to loss as well as an opportunity to experience renewed social connection with the living.

Many symptomatic anniversary reactions also commemorate losses of important relationships. In this respect, such reactions may be compared to the social rituals of mourning. But unlike effective mourning, which allows the bereaved individual to sort out, work through, and let go of the past, symptomatic anniversary reactions often persist as compulsive repetitions that may not be recognized as repetitions. They point strongly to the possibility that a past trauma has not been assimilated or that the work of mourning is incomplete.

When loss has been experienced in a dissociated or socially isolated state, for example, anniversary reactions may persist as cryptic encodings of trauma rather than socially meaningful memorials. The individual may discover with some surprise that a somatic symptom or enactive ritual marks an important anniversary date.

Anniversary reactions also illustrate how a single traumatic event can have multiple, disconnected codings and can function as a cover story. It may require considerable detective work to uncover a connection between a current mysterious symptom and a significant date in the past. One may discover with surprise that one gets sick every year around the time a parent died. Or that a cyclically recurring anxiety reaction tends to occur on the anniversary of a traumatic hospitalization. Or that a recurring depression commemorates a disaster or an assault.

Blum (1980) discusses how anniversary reactions represent attempts to repair and assimilate past traumas. The anniversary of a significant loss, such as loss of a parent in childhood, may heighten an awareness of the division between before and after. By reinstating the event in current symptoms as well as cognitive recollections, the individual is attempting to bridge discontinuities and master previous failures of self integration.

In psychotherapy, the reconstruction of memories associated with anniversary reactions is a complex process. The repetitions and revisions involved are not necessarily just the simple encodings of an original event, but the cumulative repetitions and revisions of memories over the years. When such reactions date from childhood, the repetitions involved may have been shaped by specific developmental tasks and acquisitions, such as the intensification of separation issues during adolescence.

Anniversary reactions that do not lead to mastery and integration can be retraumatizing. When the repetition involves physical illness or a serious psychological disturbance, such as psychosis, traumas associated with the anniversary reaction may have accumulated. The discovery and decoding of anniversary reactions can provide useful opportunities for linking somatic symptoms and unverbalized feelings with meaningful narratives. Once one has recognized that the present reaction is a reinstatement of past experiences, one can focus intentionally on making sense of what has been a distressing and perplexing set of symptoms.

Sometimes, however, the fact that particular symptoms occur on anniversary dates is recognized, but the symptoms themselves remain refractory to control. Knowing the historical origin of the symptom, in other words, does not necessarily provide relief from it. Relief requires establishing emotional as well as cognitive connections between what happened in the past and what is happening now.

Like somatic symptoms, anniversary reactions in psychotherapy can be shaped by the unfolding of transference. In this respect, the connection between attachment and remembering is especially striking. A symptom that becomes prominent during a particular therapeutic crisis, for example, may be revived with new intensity on the anniversary of that crisis.

The loss of a significant relationship in childhood may come to be commemorated not only on the anniversary of the original loss, but whenever the therapist leaves town.

ARTIFACTS

In the psychotherapy of posttraumatic disturbances, many symptoms, including intruding flashbacks, are cued by concrete reminders of the past. The reminder may be highly significant, as when the sight of an approaching storm reminds one of a destructive hurricane. Or it may consist of a representative symbol, such as a gift or valued memento from a lost relationship. Sometimes a strong response is evoked by a seemingly trivial stimulus that was only incidentally associated with a significant past event.

During a traumatic event, strong emotional as well as behavioral responses may be conditioned to incidental as well as central sensory aspects of the situation. The shaving lotion worn by a rapist may ever after trigger flashbacks in a victim. Or the very sight of a nurse may revive terror associated a painful medical procedure.

Many artifacts, including those associated with painful memories, are preserved intentionally as keepsakes. Because they are not merely things but symbolic objects with representational functions, revisiting them is not just a matter of confronting veridical memories but of integrating the meanings and motives with which memories are associated. Concrete objects are associated with people. Reencounters with objects are reencounters with images and voices, with narratives and dialogues.

The role of enduring objects and places in the search for memory is especially vital when much has been lost. In many instances, an artifact is all that is actually left of an important piece of history, the only surviving physical representation of a significant relationship.

Sometimes, artifacts are preserved out of sight; their existence remains in memory, but their meaning is not revisited and explored. Hidden away, they remain as permanent links to the past. Because contact with them is avoided, they cannot facilitate the integration of past and present. In psychotherapy, the careful avoidance of concrete reminders can be an important clue to their significance.

Volkan (1981) has described a class of artifacts he terms "linking objects" that are preserved as a means of simultaneously holding onto and avoiding the past. An object that once belonged to a dead loved one, for example, may be carefully hidden away. Instead of facilitating the work of mourning by helping the bereaved survivor revisit and work through the lost relationship, the linking object is a way of maintaining a connection with the dead without consciously assimilating the significance of the loss.

Over time, the meaning of artifacts, like the memories with which the artifacts were once connected, may get lost. In the absence of human testimony to explain them or connect them with past events, isolated objects or records may be embedded in a puzzling silence. Yet mute stones speak. If one listens carefully, familiar voices may emerge from silence.

Concrete reminders can arouse as much ambivalence as memories. Sometimes people avoid revisiting places or confronting objects because they fear the memories evoked might be unbearable. Going back to the scene of a terrible trauma, for example, can precipitate flashbacks or confront a survivor with excruciating losses. Even pictures of certain objects and places may trigger such reactions.

On the other hand, a deliberate confrontation with artifacts can be liberating, helping free the self from their power and laying old ghosts to rest. When an adult revisits childhood places, for example, there is usually a striking recognition of how much one's perspective has changed. Even things that have remained "the same" are not really the same. It is not just the self who has changed; the world has changed, too. Recognition of this fact can be valuable in coming to terms with the past.

Confronting the truism "You can't go home again" may be experienced as a blessing or a curse; either way, the self is forced to assimilate reality. In some cases, that sets in motion delayed processes of mourning.

RECORDS AND TEXTS

Written texts and documents can serve as important reminders and testimony to facts. Sometimes clients bring such records to therapy to help stimulate or clarify material that is emerging. The creation of written narrative is one way of organizing incoherent or confusing or disjointed recollections. Keeping a journal as an ongoing part of therapy can help organize thoughts and feelings and stimulate new insights.

The construction of autobiographical memory itself is sometimes compared to the writing of a text. Spence (1982) emphasizes the collaborative nature of this narrative enterprise. Consulting memory, the self in the present confronts the work of several authors, other selves — the self when younger, the self when angry, etc. — as well as other people who have shaped any particular story.

But the comparison of memory to the interpretation of a text, although sometimes useful, has important limitations. Many important autobiographical memories are not initially organized in narrative forms; some are intrinsically difficult to verbalize. Even when a memory is forwarded as an organized text, it may function to conceal as well as to reveal important episodes in personal history.

In this respect, the supposed objectivity of written records can be as misleading as the most casual memories. The assumption that what is

written down must be more accurate than what is not overlooks the deliberate uses of written texts for purposes of distorting and concealing reality.
The problem is not just that documents may be forged or that parts of
tapes may be deleted or even that seemingly detailed records are incomplete. It is, rather, that the creation of texts, like the creation of memories,
is inevitably a selective process. This selectivity is biased by the purposes
for which particular texts are intended. Scientific records dryly report facts
judged to be objective and pertinent. Individual items of information may
be obscured by statistical averages. Clinical reports or legal briefs may
focus on specific details but may supply so many interpretations that basic
facts are obscured.

Even photographs or tape recordings can be contrived to conceal as
well as reveal. In some cases, as in the edited Nixon tapes, important
information may be deliberately deleted. In other cases, technical processes can create a new version of reality, as in the case of composite
photographs.

In any case, documents are usually organized to communicate with
specific audiences. When an audience for whom they were not ordinarily
intended evaluates them, what is left out may turn out to be as significant
or potentially interesting as what is included.

In considering autobiographical records, of course, bias is not simply a
distracting inconvenience, but a major point of interest. Diaries, journals,
autobiographies, and letters are fascinating precisely *because* they are personally biased. Authors of such texts are often consciously attempting to
present the self in a favorable light. Their relationship with the imagined
audience, including the imagined self, is intensely personal and their discourse reflects deliberate intentions to persuade, excuse, and impress, as
well as to communicate (Waites, 1995).

In psychotherapy, the biases in such personal records are as important
as factual accounts in providing information about the self. The search for
personal history involves attempts not just to find out what happened in
the past, but also to meet the self or selves who used to be. If the self has
been in hiding or has been fragmented by unassimilated events, the events
are only part of the story. It is only by recognizing the impact of the
events, including the discontinuities, evasions, and distortions with which
they were associated at particular points in development, that the self can
integrate the past in the present.

The imperfections of texts and records, then, like the imperfections
of memory, are not merely roadblocks to understanding one's history.
They may be signposts to personal development. This is one respect
in which Freud's concept of screen memories continues to be useful.
Anything that conceals or distorts a memory may provide information
both about motives to conceal and about coping mechanisms and defenses.

VOICES AND DIALOGUES

In contrast to somatic symptoms, behavioral enactments, and artifacts, narrations about the past, spoken or written, often affirm the coherence as well as the persistence of memory. But even narratives that describe vivid memories are usually composites of events and interpretations. Further, the self who presents them does not necessarily speak with one voice. Nor is the voice that speaks necessarily the authentic voice of the self. Many stories are received from other people. And many individual reports turn out, on careful examination, to be based on internalized dialogues.

Clients may or may not be aware, however, that they speak in more than one voice or that a communication to the therapist is based on an old dialogue, such as an interaction with a parent. The psychotherapist, by acknowledging multiple voices and internalized dialogues, can help the client become aware of, reflect on, and integrate them.

The most striking examples of multiple voices occur in severe dissociative disorders. A client with dissociative identity disorder may present alter personalities whose voices are quite distinct, not only in terms of spoken content, but in terms of sound quality and intonation patterns (Putnam, 1989). The voice of an alter personality can occasionally be traced to the internalization of an originally external voice, such as the voice of an abusive family member. More commonly, though, it is a composite construction based on the evolution of a distinct but dissociated self-presentation (Waites, 1993).

In dissociative identity disorder, conflicting voices may converse with or argue with each other, sometimes quite stridently. When they do so internally, the individual may complain of hearing voices. Yet these invisible voices are different from those characteristic of schizophrenia. They are experienced as coming from inside rather than outside, and other people are not expected to be able to hear them. In many instances, the internal voices are recognized as alternate personalities with particular names and histories.

While psychotherapists will recognize that the alternate personalities represent the dissociative fragmentation of the self, the client usually resists this interpretation, at least at first, and argues strongly that they are really different people. This attitude provides a clue to the formation of alter personalities. Experiences, such as severe childhood traumas, that cannot be assimilated into a coherent self-structure are sometimes isolated as "not me" and subsequently elaborated into a distinct pattern of behavior, an alter personality (Bryant et al., 1992; Kluft, 1985).

Alter personalities over time evolve specific histories and develop adaptations that often mask the inconsistencies among them, at least superficially. One alter may go to work every day. Another may party on weekends. One may develop a friendship or romantic relationship not shared by others. Or one alter may develop a particular set of skills, such as drawing or dancing, that others do not share.

Because they evolve distinct histories, alter personalities usually have distinct and compartmentalized memories. Many of these are organized around specific traumas. Extreme forms of child abuse are typical of the histories of such individuals (Braun & Sachs, 1985; Frischholz, 1985; Wilbur, 1985), and an alter personality may have been organized specifically to cope with a particular trauma (Putnam, 1989).

The disjunctions in memory systems characteristic of dissociated identities create experiences of "losing time." While one alter is "out" and engaging in organized activities, other alters will have typically "gone away." As a result of this dissociative pattern, the alter or alters who retreated often remain unaware of what happened during the span of time when another alter was in control.

Although dissociated identities are the most clear-cut examples of how one individual may come to speak with multiple voices, many individuals, including those who do not use dissociation as a coping mechanism, discover in the course of therapy that the voice of the self is by no means unitary or authentic. The therapist can facilitate this discovery by asking, implicitly or explicitly, "Where did that statement come from?" or "Who first said that?"

Sometimes the answer to such questions occurs to the client with no prompting. "I'm talking like my mother now," she says. Or, "This used to be an argument between me and my father."

The development of transference facilitates the examination of multiple voices and internalized dialogues by re-externalizing conversations between the self and the therapist as a representative other. This re-externalization is not simply created by the therapist, although it may be encouraged. Even—perhaps especially—when the therapist is silent, the client tends to fill in the therapist's part of the dialogue with lines scripted from the past. This process is usually labeled *projection*; it occurs in everyday life as well as in psychotherapy and is one of the most important ways attachment histories structure remembering in the present.

One of the ways clients can observe, interpret, and come to terms with their memories in the course of psychotherapy is through the careful examination of projections. In this process, internalized voices are confronted, old scripts are reconsidered, and new patterns of dialogue are tried out. The role of the therapist in this process is not only to function as an available opportunity for projection and externalization, but to clarify what is happening and to help the client extricate past from present.

SILENCE IN PSYCHOTHERAPY

In the process of exploring the past through externalizations in the present, some therapeutic approaches, notably psychoanalysis, have traditionally cast the therapist as a mostly silent partner. This silence is often rationalized as therapeutic neutrality. The psychoanalyst is supposedly like a blank screen available to receive the projections of the patient. From this perspective, when the client attributes an old script to the therapist, the therapist's silence neither confirms nor disputes the attribution in actuality, and any distortion involved should eventually become obvious to the client. At some point, the analytic therapist does offer an interpretation, pointing out, clarifying, and explaining the distortions.

Silence can be a problematic response in the psychotherapy of trauma victims, however. Too often, silence, whether imposed by other people or simply a dimension of the unspeakable, has been a significant aspect of a traumatic history. In psychotherapy, the silence of the therapist may be perceived as a repetition of the actual trauma of social betrayal or isolation. Or it may reinstate a dissociative disconnection between narrated and unnarrated realities. When the client experiences the therapist's silence as intimidating rather than accepting, it can have a chilling effect on the therapy.

This is scarcely surprising. Silence from others, after all, is one of the most common ways silence is imposed on the self. It subverts memory by withholding confirmation that other people share a given perception or recollection. It suggests that some things are better not talked about at all. If accompanied by an aloof withdrawal, silence is often experienced as punitive.

At every point in every psychotherapy, the therapist, vocal or silent, is not merely a locus of projections, but a party to an actual dialogue. What the therapist actually says or does not say is an important communication. It is only by contrasting the actual dialogue with the therapist with previous patterns of dialogue that many clients are eventually able to move beyond the past and learn more adaptive patterns of interaction.

Words, too, can evoke past traumas, of course. What a therapist says is also subject to misunderstanding and may precipitate anxieties that trigger traumatic reactions or defenses. Whenever a response from the therapist actually echoes a response from someone else, it may be especially difficult for the client to make important discriminations between voices from the past and those in the present.

For this reason, it is sometimes important for the therapist to be explicit in helping clients discriminate present communications from past ones. A therapist may need to point out, for example, that a tentative interpretation is not the same thing as a directive order or that inferences, however plausible, are not the same as proven facts. It is sometimes necessary, too, to remind the client that the therapist is not an omnipotent authority or a mind reader.

In practice, therapeutic silence is sometimes rationalized by the assumption that the client will discover and correct distortions on his or her own. For some clients, this is the case. Clients who are extremely confused, however, need help making realistic discriminations. For many, particularly those who interpret the silence as disapproving or punitive, anxiety and an increasing sense of isolation from the therapist merely inhibit the development of insight. Consequently, whenever the client does not recognize the distinction between the therapist and other parties to a dialogue, the therapist must clarify it. Silence is not the only way therapists actually echo voices from the past, of course. The possibility that any given communication by the therapist may be experienced as a repetition of an old dialogue requires constant monitoring.

TRANSFERENCE AS MEMORY

Understanding a traumatic history requires more than a constant recitation of terrible memories. It requires making meaningful connections, breaking cycles of avoidance or destructive enactments, and consciously envisioning a different future.

In psychotherapy, one way the past infiltrates the present is in the evolution of transference. At some points, symptoms and enactments as well as narratives based on past experiences are likely to arise in response to fantasies about the therapist or about the relationship between client and therapist. The tendency of the therapeutic dialogue to stimulate old interactional patterns highlights the extent to which attachment continually functions as the social matrix of memory.

Recognized and interpreted, transference can be one of the most useful routes to understanding personal history. But the significance of transference communications and enactments as memories may be masked, and the client may resist recognizing that the current attachment reflects an old pattern.

One reason this sometimes happens is that the client is attempting to master an old trauma; the current fantasy is that, although one originally felt helpless and abandoned by other people, the therapist will change all that and give the story a happier ending. This wish for a positive outcome is not, of course, altogether misguided. It provides a powerful impetus for staying in therapy. But it can lead the client to insist prematurely that everything is changed now and the past is no longer a problem.

Though often unrecognized and misperceived, transference makes the past real and vivid in the present. It offers, therefore, an opportunity to change old response patterns and to effect new outcomes. But these changes are not magical and do not simply come about because the therapist is a wonderful or omnipotent replacement for parents who were originally disappointing. Before old patterns can be changed, they must be recognized. The past must be disentangled from the present. The client must understand that circumstances have really changed. And, importantly, the self must become the one in control.

It follows that it is very difficult to discriminate past from present when the client is still living in an abusive context or is caught up in a present crisis. As long as new traumas are constantly being created, it is difficult to move beyond old ones.

When old injuries and disappointments are replayed in the context of therapy, it can be experienced as revictimizing. The client, feeling hopeless, may then insist that the frustrations and disappointments experienced in therapy are merely proof that nothing will ever change for the better. The therapist may even become a scapegoat. With clients who have experienced severe and repeated injuries, dealing with transference is a constant, sometimes exhausting therapeutic challenge. Transference nevertheless offers one of the most valuable opportunities for exploring the past and revising one's relation to it.

INTEGRATING RECOLLECTIONS

Effective psychotherapy is much more than a replay of old dialogues. It is an encounter with new forms of dialogue. As the self is transformed, multiple voices learn to speak more harmoniously, if not in unison. Subverted memories are exposed, evaluated, and integrated. The repertory of self-defining memories is expanded to include a new relationship with the therapist and new relationship patterns that make social interactions something more than familiar echoes.

Eventually, as memories are explored, revised, and integrated, one's life story is amended not just by confrontations with the past, but by increased control in the present. By understanding and integrating history, the self can finally be liberated from repeating it.

Whether one searches out personal history as an individual odyssey or embarks on this journey in an organized setting like psychotherapy, the processes of recollecting and integrating experiences occur in tandem. Amassing a vast array of pieces may provide the illusion that one has recovered history, but in order to benefit from such activities something more must be added. The pieces must be assembled in some meaningful pattern. The past must be reinterpreted in the light of the present.

This process of integration involves the ongoing construction and reconstruction of the self not only as a unified context of remembering but also as an evolving agent of personal destiny. The past recollected and integrated becomes most meaningful as a guidepost to the future.

The obstacles to integration include not only the massive quantities of memories potentially available and the lack of connections between some of them, but the subversions of memories that have typically, over time, created many gaps and inconsistencies. When personal history has been especially discontinuous, isolated items of information, mismatched stories, and divergent narratives may comprise a vast but perplexing array of information that seemingly defies meaningful organization. Trauma further complicates the process of recollection by creating disconnections and discontinuities of experience and motivating persistent tendencies to avoid or escape. Posttraumatic remembering, like the events remembered, is commonly experienced as a danger.

The tendencies of confrontations with trauma to produce uncontrolled forms of remembering is also a constant hazard. Replacing compulsive, intrusive recollections and enactments with controlled access to memories is a basic challenge in posttraumatic therapy. Ideally, the individual is eventually able to recall without being overwhelmed. Ideally, too, one acquires the ability to resist recall when it is distracting or harmful, as when one is trying to fall asleep at night.

The task of recollecting and integrating memories can seem formidable. It can take a long time. In the sense that the self is an ongoing construction rather than a finished product, it is a process that continues over a lifetime.

One cannot necessarily hurry the process. Although a sense of urgency is a common legacy of trauma, the past will always be there. And although the self may be transient, bounded by birth and death, any moment of recollection confirms that, against all odds, the self has survived memory. This very persistence in the face of great pain and many obstacles can provide the necessary fortitude to continue the ongoing search.

CHAPTER 12
Integration:
Putting the Pieces Together

We look before and after,
And pine for what is not;
Our sincerest laughter
With some pain is fraught;
Our sweetest songs are those that tell of saddest thought.
— Shelley, "To a Skylark"

Don't tell Polly," said April. "She couldn't take it. She doesn't remember any of it."

April is an alter personality who shares a body with Polly, a young woman in her twenties. It is an odd arrangement that dissociated identities manage with varying degrees of finesse. Polly, the host personality in the system, as the identity who usually presents in psychotherapy is called, has always known that sometimes she "loses time." That is, she comes to herself after minutes or hours and is unaware of what went on in the interim.

Polly has always known, too, that sometimes while in such a dissociated state she does things like talking to people, running errands, or shopping as if she were perfectly normal. Once she came to herself in a state park miles from her home and found that she had just agreed to go on a camping trip with a man she had never met before. Once she suddenly quit a good job; she still has no recollection of how and why she did so.

Most of the time, however, in spite of her memory lapses, Polly does not get into serious trouble. She has completed college and now works as a buyer in a department store. She has a boyfriend who accepts her "quirks." She came for psychotherapy because one day recently she failed to show up for an important meeting at work and is afraid her job might be in jeopardy. She also worries that, if something is not done, her hopes for marriage may fall through.

At the point when April warns the therapist against telling Polly secrets about the past, Polly has been in therapy for several months. She knows about the existence of April and several other split-off parts of herself. She nevertheless still has trouble believing that alter personalities just take charge of her life from time to time without consulting her at all.

On the other hand, Polly cannot really deny the evidence for the truth of her multiplicity. She trusts her boyfriend, who seems to know her alters and reports to her about their behavior. She believes, too, that her boss, who does not know about Polly's multiplicity, is telling the truth about behavior Polly cannot remember.

April, on the other hand, has a good memory for many events Polly has forgotten. She knows, too, about other alters in the personality system. She is mischievous and sometimes impatient; she was the one who decided to skip the important meeting at work. But she also thinks of herself as a kind of caretaker who performs many needed activities, helping with chores Polly despises, keeping other alters in line, etc.

Other alter personalities in the system include Sally, a small, frightened child, and Roxanne, a self-indulgent adult who steadfastly denies that she was ever a child at all. Fragments with a less extensive history than the other alters are Jake, a teenage boy, and Rob, an adult male who does chores like yard work or fixing the plumbing. The male alters are an especially odd development, since their assumptions about having a male body are clearly delusional. But cross-sex alters are, in fact, typical of multiple personalities (Putnam, 1989). In Polly's case, the delusions involved are quite circumscribed. None of the alters in her system are psychotic; all are in touch with reality, though some are socially isolated.

How can the unity of personality become so fragmented that an individual seems to be living several different lives? Can the fragments be united into some consistent whole? How does personality integration come about in the first place? These questions have puzzled psychiatrists and psychotherapists for many years. One of the first to approach them systematically was Pierre Janet (Ellenberger, 1970; van der Hart, Brown, & van der Kolk, 1989; van der Kolk & van der Hart, 1989). Janet (1859–1947) was a French psychiatrist who spent his life studying and writing about dissociative phenomena. He recognized the significance of unconscious and automatic adaptations and described the problems that can arise when memory systems become disconnected from self-awareness. Although his work was for many years eclipsed by that of Freud, it has recently received considerable attention from those concerned with the diagnosis and treatment of dissociative disorders.

Janet believed that dissociated spheres of consciousness can be organized around intensely exciting experiences and emphasized the role of trauma in the evolution of multiple personality disorder. He also recognized that an inability to tell a traumatic story because it is too disturbing to confront plays an important role in splitting the memory off from consciousness (van der Kolk & van der Hart, 1989). Unable to assimilate trauma in a coherent self, the affected individual becomes fixated on the trauma and reenacts it over and over. Effective treatment involves connecting or reconnecting the dissociated patient with a coherent narrative about the traumatic past.

Many of the cases Janet discussed involved traumatic grief that had been dissociated and thus could not be worked through. He employed hypnosis in the treatment of such pathological grief reactions. By uncovering and resolving traumatic memories, his interventions enabled normal processes of mourning to proceed.

Pathological grief reactions are, in fact, a common posttraumatic response. Whether they are based on physical losses, such as the sudden death of a loved one in a natural disaster, or on psychological responses, such as the effects of intentional abuse on attachment, they are often woven into complex but dissociated trauma responses. In the grip of such reactions, the dissociated individual reenacts traumas and losses that may be scarcely acknowledged in the ordinary waking state.

In the nineteenth century, when Janet was developing his theories, another case involving traumatic grief became one of the starting points for the development of psychoanalysis. Josef Breuer reported on the case of Anna O., a young woman suffering from "hysteria" (Breuer & Freud, 1893–1895). Following the death of her father, Anna O. exhibited extreme alterations in self-presentation and mood, accompanied by amnesias. Breuer attempted to uncover memories and the meaning of her symptoms through hypnotic interventions. In attempting to understand the origins of his patient's symptoms, he theorized that hysteria arises as a result of a spontaneous dissociative reaction he termed a "hypnoid state."

Breuer's work, like that of Janet, was overshadowed by the growing ascendence of psychoanalysis, and his concept of the "hypnoid state" as a central dynamic in symptom formation was eventually eclipsed by Freud's concept of "repression." Even when the role of dissociation in traumatic symptoms was rediscovered in the last half of the twentieth century, misunderstandings and controversies about the nature of dissociation, particularly the relation between dissociation and hypnosis, sometimes confused the issues. The ensuing debates have been especially pertinent in evaluating the accuracy of memories recovered in psychotherapy.

For example, some critics have contended that dissociated identity disorder is iatrogenic, that is, a consequence of treatment interventions. Symptoms of the disorder as well as memories recovered in treatment have sometimes been attributed to hypnotic suggestions by therapists. Other critics have implied that "suggestibility," a phenomenon sometimes

associated with hypnosis, is such a ubiquitous response pattern that anything anyone might say in psychotherapy may be influenced by it.

Attacks on the credibility of material that emerges in therapy on the
grounds that the client may have been in some manner hypnotized or
manipulated by suggestion tend to target recovered memories of abuse
indiscriminately. Rational arguments are unlikely to dispel such criticisms.
It is impossible to rationally prove or disprove assertions that involve unrestricted definitions or are based on inferences by people who have not
actually observed the clinical phenomena they are discussing.

Like many aspects of recent debates about recovered memories, this
one has a long history. From the beginning, Freud's critics attributed his
discoveries and treatment successes to "suggestion." And it is undeniable
that transference, a usual development in dynamic psychotherapy, makes
individuals very sensitive to anything the therapist says or does (Roustang,
1976). But even the fact that some people are highly suggestible does not
imply that the suggestions influencing them have been originally created
in therapy. Many suggestible people have been controlled by other people
for years before entering therapy, and many have habitually exploited
self-induced trance as a defense against anxiety.

It is also misleading to equate trance with suggestibility. Some individuals enter autistic trance states in which they are relatively impervious to
outside influence (Waites, 1993). Even when hypnotized, people are not
automatons who obey without question. Brainwashing, which is a deliberate attempt to program such obedience, requires methodical interventions, usually over a period of time, that often include physical assault as
well as psychological intimidation (Lifton, 1961).

Although certain cult activities may deliberately program dissociative
identity developments (Singer, 1995), this programming usually involves
isolating the controlled individual from normal social influences and induc-
ing altered states of consciousness through such techniques as repetitive
chanting in a group setting, radical changes in diet and living arrangements, and occasionally drugs. None of these techniques are recognized as
mainstream forms of psychotherapy. The existence of unusual therapies
or autocratic therapists does not imply that the effects of most therapy can
be attributed to suggestion or that dissociative disorders are of iatrogenic
origin.

The histories of individuals with severe dissociative disorders also indicate that their symptoms are not simply iatrogenic. Dissociated identity
disorder, as typically observed by clinicians, usually dates back to the client's childhood (Putnam, 1989). The most commonly observed antecedents are extreme and repetitive childhood trauma (Kluft, 1985; Putnam,
1989). An ability to enter into self-induced trance states, which may involve inherited capabilities, does seem to play an important role in the
development of the problem. But this is an ability most dissociated identities seem to discover on their own, without outside direction.

The case of Polly, the dissociated identity described above, is illustrative. Polly began dissociating spontaneously shortly after she entered psychotherapy. Because of Polly's reported history, the therapist was alert to the possibility that she might be multiple, but she employed no specific techniques to elicit the emergence of alters. When they began to emerge, however, the therapist attempted to communicate with and get to know them rather than dismissing them as artifacts of the treatment process.

The alters provided valuable information about Polly's history, much of which was quite credible and some of which was a matter of record. Until the age of twelve, Polly had lived with a psychotic mother who abused her severely, sometimes in bizarre ways. Although, at the beginning of treatment, Polly did not remember much about the specifics of this abuse, she had vague memories that her mother had had crazy fits and that she herself had often been terrified of her mother.

April, in contrast, remembered a great deal. She recalled, for example, the time her mother locked her in her room all weekend with nothing to eat. She remembered the time her mother, claiming to be obeying the voice of God, branded her on the stomach with a metal necklace, a cross heated on the stove. The list of horrors April remembered clearly goes on and on.

When Polly was twelve, her mother locked her outside the house in sub-zero weather and a neighbor called protective services. Her mother was hospitalized, and Polly was sent to live with her mother's sister. In exchange for keeping house for her Aunt Lydia, she was given room and board and a modest allowance. "It was like dying and going to heaven," she said.

Although Polly was quite intelligent, she had never done well in school before, but under Aunt Lydia's influence she began to blossom. She made up her mind to go to college and make something of herself. And eventually she did.

In Polly's childhood, a mixture of automatic responses and deliberate attempts to deal with overwhelming events contributed to the evolution of a system of alter personalities. This system introduced order into the chaos of her early life. It supplied meaningful narratives to confusing experiences and a coherent structure to uncontrollable fragmentations. But although the dissociation of distinctly structured alter personalities enabled Polly to avoid becoming as disorganized and out of touch with reality as her psychotic mother, the solution she had found produced a new set of problems.

One approach to the new problems was denial. Polly herself often tried to cope with the difficulties and embarrassments resulting from her multiplicity by simply refusing to acknowledge it. One possible therapeutic approach might have been to suppress her symptoms or contain them more adaptively, say, by attempting to get alters to emerge only in restricted contexts.

Polly herself, with the unacknowledged but needed help of April, had attempted this solution. Yet, it did not work; the alters were too much in conflict with one another to cooperate adaptively. Roxanne, especially, tended to rebel against any attempt to restrain her.

Even before she recognized her multiplicity, Polly sensed that, to achieve the goals she envisioned for herself, she needed to confront her past as well as her symptoms. Only by carefully exploring the antecedents of fragmentation and dissociative reactions was she eventually able to replace uncontrolled coping mechanisms with more controlled ones.

This decision to confront the past meant, for both the therapist and Polly, that the split-off parts of herself would have to be addressed rather than merely suppressed. Although their emergence initially seemed to involve increased fragmentation, it was a necessary step toward eventual integration.

POLLY AND COMPANY

After Polly began exhibiting her habitual dissociative reactions in psychotherapy, it was possible, with the help of the therapist, for her to learn to pay attention to them and, gradually, change them. It is this change in her symptoms from spontaneous reactions to controlled ones, rather than the dissociation in itself, that was attributable to therapy. Without therapy, she might have continued to dissociate spontaneously, as she had done for years, without insight or control.

Initially, the dissociative responses that on the surface seemed so pathological had been an adaptive coping mechanism that had helped Polly avoid becoming psychotic. Caught between the need to escape intolerable experiences and the need to maintain a self-protective vigilance, she split herself into parts. Polly, overwhelmed by her mother's abuse, went away while April, numb but vigilant, stood guard and tried to evade or minimize the abusive behavior.

Other alters in the personality system had similar histories, often having been created in response to particular traumas. Sally and several other child alters were like regressed identity configurations, permanently trapped in childhood experiences that were still viewed and interpreted from a child's perspective. The alters were not only distinct; they were often in conflict. Sally, for example, was a scapegoat, blamed and sometimes punished for imagined badness as well as real mistakes.

Initially in therapy, it was April who remembered the abuse in detail. She explained that remembering is her "job," just as keeping the truth from Polly is her job. The child alter Sally, in contrast, did not simply remember the abuse. She relived it vividly on an ongoing basis. She accepted without question her mother's evaluation of her as a bad little girl deserving punishment. Having internalized this idea about herself, she acquiesced readily when punitive alter personalities, such as April and Roxanne, mistreated her.

In spite of her compliance with abuse, however, Sally attempted to protect herself through dissociation. Like a child trying to separate from an abusive parent, she insisted that she was psychologically separate from April and Roxanne and other alters in the system. But it was not a normal form of separation. The illusion that she was separate did not save Sally from being punished by the body that, after all, belonged to her as well as to the other alters.

The punitive alters illustrated a different aspect of how Polly had internalized her mother's behavior. When they punished Sally, they were behaving as the mother had behaved. Sometimes they actually repeated the mother's words. But they did not experience the pain Sally experienced.

The tendency of victims to reenact abuse originally initiated by others is called identification with the aggressor (Ferenzci, 1932; Freud, 1966). It is a particularly dangerous form of remembering, especially if the origin in someone else's abusive behavior is not recognized. When both aspects of the abuse scenario are dissociated in different alter personalities, as occurred in the case of Polly, identification with the aggressor can even lead one alter to attempt to kill another.

Identification, whether it involves self-destructive acts or not, is not just a form of remembering. It is a way of holding onto another person. To give up the enactive identification means confronting a painful loss.

Dissociation enables the self to avoid experiencing loss, however. Polly, in flight from conflicting identifications, denied the attachments they represented. She tried to detach herself completely from her childhood and from the mother who had tortured her by declaring herself different from both the abused child Sally and the alters mistreating her. In her everyday life, she was no longer in contact with her mother and insisted that she did not care to be. Nevertheless, in her enactive but dissociative remembering, Polly held on tightly to her mother. Anyone who observed her closely could see how enmeshed she still was in her relationship with an abusive parent.

In therapy, Polly could recognize her enactive remembering as an identification only after it was repeatedly pointed out to her. Even then, she had a hard time replacing it with narrative memory. Accepting that terrible abuse had really happened to her was an overwhelming acknowledgment. Long after she intellectually knew it to be true, she continued to deny it.

In the case of Polly, personality integration in psychotherapy involved dissolving rigid boundaries between memory systems and identity configurations that had been created over the years to effect the illusion that the client was really several different people rather than one tortured person. It meant that dissociated identity configurations had to learn to share memories, including very painful memories, rather than parceling them out to separate and distinct alters. All parts of the self had to learn to tolerate ambivalence and experience conflict as an intrapsychic development rather than just a quarrel among dissociated and externalized identities.

When dissociated identifications have enabled the self to avoid grieving losses, the recognition of sad realities can be overwhelming. Cumulative losses associated with repeated and severe traumas can, when finally recognized, precipitate depressive reactions. For this reason, the process of integration must proceed with special caution in the case of severely dissociated identities.

In Polly's case, the depression she experienced as integration proceeded was at some points as painful as the original abuse had been. On occasion, she even considered suicide. Ironically, by that time killing herself was no longer a matter of dissociated enactments based on destructive identifications. It was, rather, a desperate attempt to escape the pain from which she was no longer shielded by dissociation.

Fortunately, Polly eventually moved beyond that pain, too, and grieved her losses. She was able to do so because she could remember good things as well as bad and because her prospects for the future were promising. Still, although she had made considerable progress, she had not altogether renounced her tendencies to dissociate. When remembering threatened to overwhelm her, she could still take time out. The difference was that she had developed control over what had once been an automatic reaction.

In dissociated identities like Polly, the process of personality integration in psychotherapy is usually long and arduous. During some periods, every step forward may be followed by one or two steps backward. And even successful integration can be hazardous, since it commonly precipitates depressive reactions that dissociation had allowed the client to avoid.

THE TRANSFERENCE BRIDGE

For Polly, the process of integration was facilitated by her evolving relationship with the therapist. The way alters interacted with the therapist and with one another was shaped by the unfolding transference. Increasingly, Polly learned to communicate with the split-off aspects of herself by using the therapist as a mediator.

Transference itself is a form of remembering, although it is often not recognized as such. Originally conceptualized by Freud but almost universally observed by therapists with many differing orientations, it is usually conceptualized as the repetition in the therapeutic context of behavior patterns originally developed in childhood.

Transference, as an interpersonal dynamic, illustrates dramatically the extent to which attachment is the social matrix of memory. It reflects the narrative conventions and dialogues typical of families and cultures. It organizes dialogues in the present that echo dialogues from the past. It selects from a vast array of remembered facts or preserved artifacts those that connect the self not only with significant events, but with significant people.

Transference, like reenactment, repeats old patterns of behavior in a new context. When this happens in a therapeutic context, there is an opportunity for the therapist, who is trained to recognize and interpret transference, to point it out and help the client gain insight into the habitual patterns. In this respect, transference can become a valuable bridge to personality integration.

Thus, although transference may seem to change the focus of therapy from past conflicts and traumas to present ones or to distract the client from therapeutic goals, it is one of the most valuable aids to the therapeutic enterprise. The past can only be recollected and understood in the present. Old patterns can only be confronted and changed in the here and now.

Interpreting transference requires tact, skill, and training on the part of the therapist. It also requires a sensitivity to countertransference, the therapist's own patterns of remembering and repeating.

In psychotherapy, the client's developing attachment to the therapist may stimulate a flood of memories. At some points, however, particularly when it is experienced intensely, transference tends to obscure rather than clarify the meaning of these. The client, particularly early in treatment, wants very much to perceive both the attachment to the therapist and the memories stimulated by it as a new relationship in the here and now, rather than simply a new edition of an old story.

Moved by a wish to escape the past by insisting that everything has changed, the client may staunchly deny that any aspect of a current interaction with the therapist is a repetition. When history is being repeated not only in the context of therapy, but in interactions with people outside therapy, failure to recognize the origins in transference can be quite destructive.

It is common, for example, for a client to insist that she has learned to avoid the kinds of people who abused her in the past, only to find, with dismay, that she is again enmeshed with an abusive partner. She may continue to insist that the present enmeshment is different from past ones in spite of clear evidence to the contrary.

One development that may complicate transference is the tendency of some clients to enact contrasting feelings and interaction patterns by swinging from one extreme reaction to another. A client may insist, for example, that, in contrast to hurtful people, the therapist is wonderful. Any disruption of this idealizing transference pattern, even slight lapses in empathy on the part of the therapist, may precipitate rage or detachment. Sometimes such disruptions occur not because of anything the therapist has done, but because the client is finding it difficult to avoid a disturbing memory.

When memories create conflicts or anxiety or anger, the therapist may be blamed simply because those unpleasant feelings exist. When remembering causes pain, the therapist may be blamed for not controlling the pain. And whenever the client feels out of control of memories, the therapist may be blamed for the loss of control.

TOLERATING AMBIVALENCE

By examining and learning to understand the contrasting reactions that occur in therapy, the client is able to integrate conflicting images of the same person and to moderate inconsistent behaviors, such as swings between idealization and devaluation of other people. By learning to accept the fact that people can change their moods and their minds without changing their identities, severely dissociated individuals can also move toward integration.

Polly, for example, eventually learned to tolerate the fact that she had loved as well as hated her mother. This recognition enabled her to accept the valued features of her mother she had internalized without dissociating them in an alter who was "not me." It saddened her to realize how the same person she had loved could hurt her. But painful as it was to accept that, it enabled her to tolerate her own imperfections and take responsibility for her own destructive behavior without feeling totally bad.

Instead of parceling out her feelings and inconsistent behaviors among a group of different alter personalities, Polly gradually learned to own them all as aspects of a unified self. The transference bridge facilitated this development by enabling her to repeat old response patterns but to experience them differently. Unlike the psychotic mother, who had encouraged Polly's fragmentation and treated her as if she were different people at different times, the therapist constantly emphasized Polly's integrity and wholeness. Unlike the mother, who punished imperfections, the therapist reacted to them matter of factly, as unavoidable but manageable aspects of the human condition.

FEAR OF INTEGRATION

To individuals who have coped with traumas, even single, unrepeated traumas, through dissociation, the prospect of personality integration can be terrifying. It means thinking about the unthinkable and feeling the unbearable. For individuals who have developed multiple identities, there is also the fear that some important identity configuration might be lost altogether in the process of integration.

This fear is sometimes based on the notion that the separate parts of the self really are different people who can die. Yet, even a distinct and complexly elaborated alter personality is not a separate person; it is, rather, a part of a whole. Integration will necessarily change the way alters experience themselves, but it will not necessarily involve the disappearance of the memories, habits, and skills that typify particular alters.

In the case of Polly, for example, the alter personality Roxanne was more cut off from childhood memories than most other alters. Integration meant changing Roxanne from a dissociated configuration of thinking and behavior to a part of Polly who shared Polly's body and Polly's memories of the past. Before this happened, Roxanne equated the prospect of integration with death. Yet the shift in self-perception that integration involved did not destroy Roxanne, but transformed her.

Roxanne, after all, was not merely a fantasy construction who could disappear or be replaced by "reality." Like any identity configuration, her creation had involved fantasies, but over the years, she had accumulated much real history that Polly would always need to remember in order to feel whole. This real history, in fact, involved some of the most successful achievements of Polly's life.

Initially in therapy, Roxanne appeared as a self-indulgent adult who considered herself superior to other alters in Polly's personality system. Since she did not remember childhood at all, she seemed to represent a happy escape from it.

But it soon became apparent that Roxannne was more than an escape. Cut off from the feelings of guilt and shame associated with the early abuse, she was, in effect, an attempt to rescue Polly's self-esteem. She did that job well. It was Roxanne who boldly ventured into activities, such as accepting leadership positions in certain organizations she belonged to in college. Even though she could be capricious, even self-destructive on occasion, it was Roxanne who often impressed Polly's coworkers and bosses with her interpersonal skills and savvy.

Roxanne's achievements were thus genuine and often reflected very positively on Polly. In this respect, her function in rescuing Polly's self-esteem was too valuable to forego. In the process of integration, Roxanne's contributions and memories needed to be acknowledged as a vital part of Polly.

Similarly, other alters, even the child Sally, had needed memories and talents and skills. In the process of integration, is was necessary for these to be acknowledged and valued. Sally had to be reassured that her growing up and blending with Polly would mean transformation rather than annihilation.

Helping Sally and other alters to understand this was difficult, however. Although integration did not really mean that any alter had to die, the fear of death that had contributed to the original dissociations had to be faced. By splitting off certain experiences as "not me," Polly had convinced herself that different alters were really different people. When they began to recognize themselves as part of Polly, they were as scared as they had been when the splitting first occurred. Understanding that nobody had really died then was closely tied to accepting that nobody was really going to die now.

Even less severely dissociated individuals fear integration. The process of taking back parts of the self one has tried to push away or split off can arouse intense anxiety; at some points, the individual may even decide that dissociation is, after all, preferable to integration.

Yet most dissociated individuals who seek therapy are also confronted with the negative implications of continued fragmentation. However seemingly well adapted in some areas of life, they experience a variety of social problems and sometimes are even put at risk by their dissociative patterns. Polly's alter personality Roxanne, for example, sometimes became quickly involved with men she did not know in ways that might have endangered her.

In the long run, wholeness is such a vital need that, even while resisting it, fragmented people like Polly struggle heroically to achieve it. As they do so, they provide valuable insights not only about their own specific problems, but about the integrative process generally.

Wholeness, of course, is more often an ideal towards which one moves than a finished product. And although psychotherapy can facilitate integration, no one, in or out of therapy, attains perfection. Life, as an ongoing process of transformation, keeps confronting us with new and complex experiences that must be assimilated as well as new conflicts and roadblocks to integration.

Psychotherapy, even so, can help people not only to achieve specific integrations, but to master some of the fears and unhelpful coping mechanisms that have habitually impeded integration. By learning alternatives to uncontrolled dissociation, one moves closer to the ideal of wholeness.

THE INTEGRATIVE PROCESS

Although many clients cope with traumatic experiences and memories through dissociation, few will do so as extensively as Polly. Most clients have not been so severely fragmented. Even when the past is very painful, there are many ways of avoiding it. Some simply deny what they do not want to confront. Others take refuge in addictions that numb the pain or compulsions that constantly deflect attention from troubling ideas or feelings.

In therapy, whatever defenses are employed will usually be intensified as anxiety mounts or as traumatic memories begin to surface. The unfolding of transference will usually cast such defensive reactions in sharp relief.

Not only the traumatic past but the posttraumatic accommodations that enabled the client to survive it become a vivid part of the present.

In therapy as in life, the relationship between memory and self integration is reciprocal. Self-integration is an ongoing dimension of memory organization in human beings. And whenever integration fails, for whatever reason, memory is usually enlisted in efforts to restore it.

However the quest for personal history is organized, it can be expected to lead to unexpected insights, forgotten experiences, and changed interpretations as well as familiar memories. Any of these may stimulate further searches and reconstructions. For some, the search will be a lifelong process. Whether people make such efforts on their own or in the context of psychotherapy, the process of connecting a disparate array of materials in a coherent story can be a formidable challenge. Yet the construction of narrative can in itself have an integrative effect.

Whenever memories are fragmented or decontextualized, it may be helpful to reinstate contexts by confronting actual reminders of the past. Such reinstatements can sometimes be orchestrated in a therapeutic setting, but are often most practically managed by the client as an adjunct to psychotherapy. Going back to an old school may revive more detailed recollections concerning the vivid but isolated image of a playground swing. Listening to music popular during a particular period of one's life may bring to mind many relevant recollections.

Sometimes important pieces of a longstanding puzzle are discovered only by accident. A client in therapy announced one day, for example, that she had just found some information that helped her make sense of certain mysterious but fragmentary childhood memories. Her mother had been depressed for years and the depression had affected how she had mothered the client. But the factors contributing to her depression had never been talked about. It was only when the client began going through some important papers following her mother's death that she discovered that her mother had been coping with the loss of several important relationships at the time the client was born and, having moved far from her family of origin to a different country, had felt extremely isolated.

Within psychotherapy, context reinstatement often occurs incidentally as an aspect of the evolving transference. A client may report, for example, that the rug in the therapist's office is very like the rug in a childhood home. Or that the tree in front of the office reminds him of one he used to climb. Or that the sound of an ambulance going by as he entered the building brought a rush of old memories.

Transference itself is a kind of context reinstatement, in the sense that it reestablishes old patterns of relating and feeling. This facet of transference is a vital link to memory. It illustrates how attachment continually contextualizes and integrates the past in the present.

REGRESSION

Even in comparatively well integrated clients, the recontextualization of old memories in psychotherapy and the development of attachment to the therapist may precipitate regressive reactions. As therapy proceeds, earlier modes of reacting and remembering begin to compete with more mature adaptations. Coherent cover stories become fragmented or doubtful. Narrative remembering is increasingly replaced by enactments or somatic reactions. Adult autonomy is increasingly eroded by child-like dependency or the stormy ambivalent attachments typical of traumatized children. Regression is an expectable development, too, when the client experiences a crisis in the present or an actual reinstatement of old conflicts and anxieties.

At some points, the client may seem so involved in the past that the present is almost completely overshadowed. Though it can be challenging for the therapist and troubling for the client, such a development is not always counterproductive. Regression, for example, is one of the factors that contributes to the emergence of memories and to revised interpretations of recollections. In bringing to the surface many memories and fantasies, regression can thus provide valuable information. But although memories may be unusually vivid in states of regression, they are also often less organized. It may also be difficult to sort out fact from fantasy. This is especially a problem if the regressed individual is uncommunicative or seemingly out of contact with reality.

Regressions sometimes disconnect components of memory that have been previously connected. Vivid images or somatic sensations may suddenly arise in the absence of comprehensible narratives. A story that seemed straightforward and coherent may suddenly become confusing. A previously unified self may suddenly split into disconnected fragments.

Intense regressive episodes are often quite uncomfortable for the client, who feels out of control, infantilized, even overwhelmed. They can be frightening to the therapist, particularly if they occur early in therapy, before much is known about the client's behavior patterns. At any point, in order to be helpful rather than harmful, they require skilled and empathic management.

Some of the most dangerous and controversial psychotherapeutic techniques involve deliberately stimulating regressions through the use of hypnosis or drugs. In certain cases, in the hands of a skillful and prudent therapist, such techniques may be useful. But a regressive episode is not a magical quick fix. Unless carefully controlled and followed by working through and integration, it can do more harm than good.

Regressive experiences do not validate memories. But sometimes a regressive episode is a first step on the way to coherence. It may enable both client and therapist to form valuable hypotheses and inferences. The wealth of material produced, even if disorganized, may make it possible to compare and contrast disparate stories about the same significant event and to sort out the mix of ideas, feelings, and images associated with it. Focusing on the contrast between the past experienced regressively and the present regained and assimilated can provide important insights.

Uncontrolled regressions are one type of negative therapeutic reaction; the client gets stuck in the past, gets worse instead of better, or precipitously leaves treatment. Uncontrolled regressions are sometimes cited as cautionary tales by those critical of therapy as a process. Therapy, they then contend, is a dangerous undertaking that is better avoided.

In most instances, however, uncontrolled regressions, even when precipitated by psychotherapy, are not caused by therapy. The tendency to regress suddenly and extremely may be a longstanding problem in the client's life, perhaps the problem for which treatment was sought. Or a regressive episode in therapy may be the latest instance of a recurrent pattern of alternately confronting and avoiding the past. It may even be an attempt to defeat the therapy and prove that the client is beyond help.

In the therapeutic context, regression and transference are closely allied, so that many regressions make sense when evaluated from a transference perspective. Sometimes the client begins to cling to the therapist like a sick or abused child clinging to a disappointing parent, demanding help, but unable to develop insight and progress in treatment. Or regression may be stimulated by a real or imagined mistake on the part of the therapist. Instead of recognizing this response as a repetitive pattern and discussing the real issue, the client may take the regression as proof that therapy is not really helping.

Any stress in the present can precipitate regression in a vulnerable individual. Sometimes, too, a regressive retreat into the past is an attempt to escape being overwhelmed by present troubles. From the perspective of the integrative process, regressions and dissociative reactions enable the client to compare and contrast how different forms and contents of memories may have affected personality development. In this respect, regression, like dissociation, is a sometimes frightening but frequently constructive prelude to integration.

DOLORES

Dolores entered therapy saying that her parents had recently separated after a neighbor accused her father of molestation. Although he had staunchly denied the accusation and was not prosecuted, her mother had found a cache of pornographic photographs that convinced her of his guilt. The accusation and the aftermath precipitated an uproar in the extended family. Her father's relatives staunchly defended him. Her mother's relatives acknowledged that he might be guilty but minimized the importance of the accusation. They strongly disapproved of divorce and urged the mother to stay in her marriage.

From the beginning of therapy, Dolores was preoccupied with the thought that her father might have sexually abused her when she was a child. Yet she had no definite memories of being abused. She was feeling anxious and crazy all the time these days, she said, and wanted the therapist to help her uncover the truth.

Almost as soon as Dolores began talking about herself, she began to experience transient dissociative episodes in which she saw perplexing images: a couch in the attic, a shadowy figure hovering above her. She developed a fear of being in her house alone. She also developed somatic symptoms that were disconnected from comprehensible narratives: nausea, choking sensations, and a facial tic.

Given the accusation against her father and what she was currently reading about the effects of early abuse, Dolores believed that these symptoms indicated that, as she had feared, her father must have molested her. Yet, in spite of the troubling images, she seemed unable to uncover anything that she could call a "real" episodic memory of abuse. The therapist listened empathically but did not interpret the symptoms that were developing as necessarily indicative of early abuse. She explained to Dolores that, although the images and physical sensations were certainly suggestive, their meaning required careful exploration.

Dolores then began going into spontaneous trance states in the therapy session. In these states, she constructed narratives about her father's molesting her that seemed to go with her visual images and somatic symptoms. The therapist continued to listen attentively and supportively, but did not confirm that these narratives were necessarily veridical memories.

As the client began to elaborate fantasies that were implausible and, in some cases, seemingly impossible representations of reality, the therapist realized that the trance states were leading away from rather than toward adaptive coping. It was clear, too, that when the client emerged from the trance state she seemed disconnected from the material she had produced while in it. And she was beginning to talk in a detached way about her belief that she had been abused, as if it offered a pat explanation for a chaotic and increasingly hopeless life.

The therapist decided that the client's spontaneous regressions were not, at the moment, helpful. However veridical the memories emerging, however significant the possibility that Dolores had been sexually abused, regression was seriously interfering with her everyday coping. At that point, it made sense to the therapist to focus on present reality rather than to be led farther and farther away from it.

The present reality was that the client was being constantly badgered by her father to side with him against her mother, that her mother was calling on her constantly for care and support, that her sister had stopped speaking to anyone in the family, that her husband was dismayed and angry, and that her children were developing school problems.

Focusing on these current problems enabled Dolores to examine long-standing family conflicts and the coping mechanisms typical of family members individually and as a group. Only after she had achieved more stability in her everyday life was she able to return to questions about specific memories for past events. By then, she realized that meanings she had discovered were as significant as memories. She connected her anxieties both to patterns of coping and interaction, present as well as past, and to specific events.

As therapy continued, Dolores also began to realize that the aspects of her past she clearly remembered were as vital to her development as those she did not. Although she had earlier had no specific memories of her father abusing her, for example, she had always been aware of his jealous possessiveness toward her and his controlling behavior. Not only in childhood, but even after she grew up, he had told her what to eat, how to dress, what friends to choose, even what to think. Feeling controlled by her father yet unable to trust him had had a profound effect on her development.

Her relationship with her mother had also long been a source of anxiety and anger. Before the separation, her mother had been alternately very dependent on her father and very angry at everyone in the family, including Dolores. The client had felt emotionally abandoned by both her parents, and her sister's recent withdrawal intensified her present feelings of isolation. She had much to mourn as well as much to remember.

Exploring these issues, Dolores decided to confront her family members not with accusations of abuse, but with communications about her current needs and feelings and her wishes to change the way she had been relating to them. She refused both her father's pleas for support and her mother's demands for caretaking. She made a sincere, though futile, effort to communicate with her sister. She did not cut her present family off from contact with her family of origin, but she did begin to extricate herself, her husband, and her children from being enmeshed with them.

Eventually, feeling more in control of the present, Dolores reconsidered the past. Confronting clear but fragmentary memories in the context of her present understanding of family interactions, she decided that her father must have sexually abused her. But she recognized this inference as part of a larger picture. Although she continued occasionally to enter spontaneous trance states, she began integrating the images and sensations she experienced in these states with her normal waking existence.

The therapist continued to listen empathically, to point out connections and repetitive patterns in what the client was saying and doing, and to encourage Dolores to make her own interpretations. The therapist agreed that the inference Dolores had been molested by her father was plausible, but did not focus on it as the cause of all her problems.

One day Dolores announced that her father had been arrested in another state for child sexual abuse and that this time he would probably be prosecuted. She felt that her own memories and reconstructions had been validated. Yet she was also saddened by this development. She could not merely hate her father; she saw him now as a complicated person and her relationship with him as a complex development. She viewed his abusive behavior as a destructive but compulsive symptom, but, important as this behavior was, she realized that it was not an explanation for everything in her life or in his own.

Eventually, developing a sense of herself as a separate and autonomous person was the most positive outcome of psychotherapy for Dolores. By the time she terminated therapy, she did not need anyone else, including the therapist, to define who she was or tell her what she did or did not remember. Nor was she swayed any longer by family members who told her that she was overreacting, making up stories, and being disloyal.

CHAPTER 13
Letting Go

Set up no stone to his memory.
Just let the rose bloom each year for his sake.
For it is Orpheus. His metamorphosis
in this one and in this.

— Rainer Maria Rilke, *Sonnets to Orpheus*
(M. D. Herter Norton, Trans.)

THERE IS A TIME to search for the past, even to be immersed in it. But there is also a time to let go. This is true of life-transforming events as well as of more trivial ones.

Letting go does not mean uncontrollable forgetting, but, rather, a shifting of perspectives. More and more, attention is turned toward the here and now or to prospective visions of the future. Once the past recalled has been integrated into the fabric of one's life, attention can focus on it as needed.

Just as the decision to take up the search or to confront any particular memory is a matter of individual readiness, so is the decision to move on; only the self can decide when the time has come to let go. This decision often evolves in a natural, almost imperceptible way as a consequence of integrative processes that, however deliberate, have an unconscious dimension. Becoming more comfortable with who one was and is makes it possible to relax and shift focus. Learning that the past will always be there and that the self is safe from getting lost makes it possible to explore new territory.

Letting go is not inevitable, of course. Nor is it always an easy and natural process. For those recovering from severe traumas, it can seem an unattainable goal, and minimizing the difficulties involved only compounds them. Some wounds cannot be healed. Some life events can permanently overwhelm capacities for integration. Acknowledging terrible truths may be the only way to go on living with them.

A recognition that there are limits to recovery does not mean that one must give up or languish in despondency, however. Even in worst-case scenarios, hope is better medicine than despair.

In any case, the process of letting go cannot be hurried by clichéd preachments or magically summoned by quick-fix formulas. It cannot be forced at any point. Whether it evolves as a steady forward progression or as a stormy series of advances and retreats, it will depend on internal developments rather than external manipulations.

GETTING STUCK

Some people hesitate to explore the past at all for fear of getting stuck there. And this fear is not always unwarranted. The past can be a nostalgic retreat or a puzzle to solve. But it can also be a trap, like quicksand.

Individuals confronting trauma are especially at risk for getting stuck. Immobilization is a typical aspect of the trauma response. At the time of trauma, behavioral freezing sometimes makes it, literally, impossible to move. Afterward, psychological fixation on the trauma as a whole or on some isolated feature of it is common.

The hypervigilance that typically occurs in the immediate aftermath of trauma and often becomes chronic in posttraumatic stress disorder is an important dimension of fixation on the past. It is likely to be precipitated at any point when memories of trauma are reinstated, including confrontations in psychotherapy. The adaptive dimension of this vigilance is obvious: the self is attempting to make sure the experience of being out of control never recurs. But the price of compulsive vigilance can be exhaustion, as well as an inability to move on.

As an acute symptom, hypervigilance can be treated by specific techniques that involve focusing away from the trauma or, when the symptom is especially refractory and interferes with coping, by medication. These are temporary palliatives, however. Eventually, integrating memories and mourning losses is a more lasting and reliable way of moderating such symptoms.

Fixations are also related to the flashbacks and compulsive enactments that are characteristic of posttraumatic stress disorder. They are commonly incorporated into posttraumatic accommodations, such as intentional avoidance or interpersonal isolation, that keep the traumatized individual tied to the past even when he is not thinking about it.

Compulsive enactments are a way of constantly reinstating past events without necessarily confronting the significance of the events or narrating any story about them. Dissociated enactments enable individuals to remember and forget at the same time, to hold onto the past while seeming to let go. This is one reason why an apparent absence of involvement with traumatic memories can be so deceptive. At the same time the individual seems to have recovered, enactments, somatic symptoms, or compulsive patterns of interaction may be constantly reinstating the trauma.

Sometimes getting stuck involves obsessive rumination. Although no outward behavioral sign may betray a preoccupation with past injuries, the mind may be, nevertheless, always thinking about them. Whether this rumination is a matter of replaying the actualities of painful events or elaborating fantasies, such as imagined triumphs or revenge scenarios, the trauma is never far from consciousness. It can be a worrisome distractor from daily tasks. It can interfere with the ability to fall asleep. In this respect, obsessive rumination can be as disruptive to ongoing life as intrusive flashbacks or the inability to remember.

Both hypervigilance and obsessive rumination are sometimes associated with superstitious thinking. It is as if thinking about an event might magically prevent it from happening again. Superstition is impervious alike to logical argument and to disconfirming evidence. If a feared event does not recur, that fact can be taken as proof that by thinking about it one has warded it off. And if it does recur, one can pretend that one is, after all, a prophet with special powers who need not fear the future.

Obsessive preoccupation with memories is especially characteristic of ambivalent attachments and often represents an attempt to hold on to old relationships. Unable to let go of a needed but feared or hated relationship, the self engages in constant internal dialogues or replays remembered interactions over and over. Scenes from the past, sometimes very painful ones, are held constantly in view, like pictures at a grim but arresting exhibition. This pattern is characteristic of pathological mourning.

Denial of loss and an avoidance of mourning is, in fact, one of the most common reasons individuals get stuck in the past. What is always present in the mind, however painfully, need not be accepted as lost and, thus, need not be grieved. Through dissociation, it is even possible to intellectually acknowledge that a loss has occurred while continuing to behave as if it has not. In such instances, although the fact of loss is acknowledged, enactments may continually deny it.

Ruminating about the past is not only a way of remaining tied to it, but a convenient distractor from present worries. For individuals with a traumatic history, the tendency to focus on old injuries can be stimulated by any new stress and may involve state-dependent effects on memory. When it precipitates regressions, a present crisis may be altogether overshadowed by a past one.

Finally, there are those who are trapped in the past by guilt. Either they hold themselves responsible for bad things happening and continually seek punishment, or they simply feel that they have no right to enjoy life when others have suffered or died. Confronting and dealing with such guilt can be a long and hazardous process, particularly if the need for punishments leads to actual self-injury. The need to be punished may even make it impossible for the individual to make use of therapy. Any sign of recovery becomes a threat that is avoided by a renewed enmeshment in old pain.

To be stuck in the past in any way is to be cut off from the present and in danger of losing the future. When this danger becomes evident, it is as pressing an issue as any other roadblock to self integration.

FORGIVENESS

One traditional approach to the problem of being unable to move past old grievances is the admonition to "forgive and forget." This cliché implicitly acknowledges the dangers of getting stuck in traumatic memories. In many systems of religious thought, for example, forgiveness is considered to be not only an indication that recovery from an injury has already occurred, but an attitude that is in itself healing.

For individuals who value forgiveness, intractable anger, revenge fantasies, and loss of faith may be among the most distressing legacies of trauma. The wish to be able to forgive expresses a need to recover vital beliefs and values. For such people, forgiveness may be an explicitly stated goal and being able to forgive a significant sign of recovery.

The exhortation to forgive adds a moral dimension to trauma that does not necessarily have a healing effect, however. Sometimes it merely adds insult to injury. As an aspect of denial, it asks victims to hurry up and get over traumas that other people would prefer not to think about. Or it simultaneously acknowledges the existence of trauma and minimizes negative effects.

For victims, like other people, facile forms of forgiveness may be a way of denying the pain of old injuries. "That's all over" may be a matter of wishful thinking rather than a description of reality. If things really have changed for the better, it may still be helpful to review how the past affected one's life. Facing such realities does not necessarily lead to holding on to grudges; sometimes it is an avenue to genuine forgiveness.

Frequently, of course, counseling forgiveness, like offering a quick and easy apology, is merely an attempt to free someone responsible for an injury from accountability. The focus of attention is intentionally shifted from what someone else has done and might be expected to make amends for to the victim's complaint about it, the implication now being that the complaint is the most important problem. In this respect, the urge to forgive is sometimes a short step from blaming the victim. It implies that the victim's complaint is a cause rather than a consequence of distress; if she would just forgive and forget, she would feel better.

Confusing causes with consequences is, of course, a problem that often creates misunderstandings about the effects of trauma. Forgiveness *is*, for many individuals, correlated with recovery. But the correlation does not in itself indicate anything about causation. Although forgiveness may facilitate letting go, it may only occur after wounds have healed enough to fade into the background of one's thoughts.

Some people neither feel the need to forgive nor are able to do so. To judge them as morally defective or psychologically disordered would be, again, to add insult to injury. Those constantly enmeshed in the past by anger and revenge fantasies will probably be well advised to look closely at the negative consequences of that enmeshment, but this appraisal can be matter of fact, informed by a practical rather than a moralizing perspective.

Refusing to forgive or forget may also be a positive adaptation, particularly if this attitude motivates people to protect themselves or others from avoidable repetitions of trauma. It may stimulate attempts to educate other people. It may lead to needed social reforms, such as laws that hold individuals or groups accountable for injury or neglect. It may facilitate increased public awareness about certain forms of victimization and victims' rights.

In any case, forgiveness, like other aspects of recovery from trauma, is a matter of personal values that cannot be imposed from without. And even people who value and strive for forgiveness cannot hurry the process. It is, rather, a development that occurs, if at all, in conjunction with other aspects of recovery and self integration. It is most suspect when it increases vulnerability to future injury and most helpful when it is coupled with realistic self-protectiveness.

ENVISIONING THE FUTURE

Individuals who are stuck sometimes get unstuck by themselves. Being unable to do so is one of the most frequent reasons why people seek the help of therapists. Remembering and making sense of the past is not enough for them; they want to secure the future without being enslaved by hypervigilance, obsessive rumination, or compulsive behavior.

Getting unstuck is also a typical outcome of confronting and working through memories in psychotherapy. Once the past is known and familiar, it often becomes possible to put it out of mind without fear of losing all access to it. Prior to achieving this long-term outcome, temporary palliatives are sometimes in order. At any point, losing perspective on the present can be dangerous and increase the client's vulnerability.

Whenever remembering precipitates a crisis or stands in the way of integrative work, the therapeutic focus may need to shift to helping the client forget temporarily. Talking specifically about present situations and events can sometimes effect this shift. When the past continues to be too much present, practiced strategies for refocusing or stopping thoughts may be useful. These include meditative or self-hypnotic techniques that, in effect, substitute controlled forms of dissociation for uncontrolled ones.

Intentional focusing on some action in the present can also be a useful exercise. Even simple actions can serve as useful distractors; for those quite overwhelmed by the past, simple actions may be the only ones manageable. This focusing on action is a kind of bootstrap operation; action and attention reciprocally regulate one another and small experiences of feeling in control can serve as incentives for further attempts at mastery. Intentional distraction can also be helpful in controlling obsessive thoughts.

Simplistic as they seem, such palliatives have a legitimate place in psychotherapy as in life. Intensive psychotherapeutic work need not—should not—involve constant, unmitigated states of anxiety or tension. Temporary escapes from reality are an important dimension of adaptive coping, and those who cannot manage such escapes through their own efforts can sometimes be taught. This is one way in which relaxation techniques, imaginative imaging, or hypnotic interventions can be helpful.

Unfortunately, the uses of imagination in psychotherapy have sometimes been misunderstood, even directly opposed, by critics who warn that fantasy may contaminate memory. Such warnings misconstrue what psychotherapy is all about. To warn people away from their own creative thoughts is to collude in the constriction of the self in a way that may be as destructive as the subversion of veridical memory.

To be sure, therapeutic play has its dangers in some clients, and training and skill on the part of the therapist are always in order. Play may stimulate enactments. In a carefully guided therapy, this development can in itself be a means of reviving significant memories as a step toward integration. The move from literal repetitions to symbolic constructions is often a positive development in posttraumatic therapy (Waites, 1993).

Problems can arise, of course, whenever one is too quick to interpret a symbolic construction as a literal memory. But therapists trained to understand the complexities of symbolic thinking are unlikely to accept just any idea that comes up at face value. Historical reconstruction always requires a careful matching of known facts with plausible hypotheses. In effective psychotherapy, any particular idea, whether labeled as a memory or a fabrication, must be considered in the context of everything else the client has talked about.

The adaptive uses of imagination include freeing oneself to move beyond the confines of memory. The normal play of the mind is often distorted or disrupted by trauma. On their own, many individuals intuitively recognize this loss and attempt to reconnect with their own creativity. Getting in touch again with the capacity to play and think imaginatively is also a reason some people seek therapy. In therapeutic contexts, the ability to move beyond literal replays of the past to symbolic constructions is a positive achievement that often points to recovery from trauma (Waites, 1993).

Adaptive memory is not merely an end, but a beginning. By integrating memory with fantasy, we arrive not only where we started, but where we are going.

HOMECOMING

Exiting from the freeway, Miranda knew her way around town as surely as if she had been gone three weeks instead of thirty years. With an intuition that never played her false, she drove straight to familiar places. Some landmarks had scarcely changed at all. The school with its swings and monkey bars, the Methodist church with its picturesque steeple and bell seemed to have been suspended in time. Downtown, though, was a curious mix of old and new. The five-and-dime stood empty. A few blocks away, a shopping center was going up.

She turned down a side street and was shocked. The house she had lived in had vanished completely, replaced by nothing but a weedy vacant lot.

Something else was unsettling, too. Even things that were still in place had shrunk, and all the buildings she passed seemed closer together than she remembered. The park, once a far journey from home, was now just a hop from what had once been her backyard. The mansion next door was now just a cottage. And the vast expanse that had surrounded the house was just an ordinary suburban lot. Though these distortions were unnerving, there was no mistaking essentials. After thirty years, Miranda could still trust the mental map she had made at seven. The photos she took on this visit matched the pictures in her mind and suddenly called up others she felt certain belonged to her past.

So she could trust her memories. And if she could trust her mental map and these images, surely she could trust other recollections that could no longer be easily tested. Surely the mind that had led her unerringly to familiar places was right about what had happened to her in those places.

And yet . . . what about the misses and the gaps? The birthday party transposed to a different house? The grandmotherly housekeeper who seemed to have left no picture? The tenant she has been told used to live in the attic?

Miranda stared at the vacant lot feeling frustrated and somewhat foolish. If only the house were there. After years of avoiding and protesting and finally confronting, she had come here hoping to make peace with the past. But like the man said, you can't go home again.

As she turned to leave, she knew she would never come back.

But on a sudden impulse, she looked around for one last time, and suddenly she could see it, as real as the house next door and the school down the road. She felt herself walking up the steps and through the door as if she still lived there.

In a large front room, a slipcovered sofa faced a fireplace. In the flickering light, her shadow danced against a wall. There was another shadow, too. If Miranda looked toward the fire, she would see who was there with her. But there was no hurry. As she watched the shadows, she felt a drowsy lethargy. No hurry at all.

Then, after ages of watching the shadows, she turned at last toward the fire and saw what she had come to see. There was still no hurry. She looked a long time.

Finally, she walked away. Out of the house, down the walk, through the wrought iron gate to the street. The sun still stood high in the summer sky. With luck, she could beat the rush hour traffic. She did not look back as she drove away. The house would always be there after all. But it was time to go home.

References

Ackerman, B. P. (1981). Encoding specificity in the recall of pictures and words in children and adults. *Journal of Experimental Child Psychology, 31,* 193–211.

Ainsworth, M. D. S. (1973). The development of mother-infant attachment in B. Caldwell & H. Ricciuti (Eds.), *Review of Child Development Research* (3). Chicago: University of Chicago Press.

Ainsworth, M. D. S., Blehar, M. C., Waters, E., & Wall, S. (1978). *Patterns of attachment: A psychological study of the strange situation.* Hillsdale, NJ: Erlbaum.

Alkon, D. L. (1992). *Memory's voice: Deciphering the mind-brain code.* New York: HarperCollins.

American Psychiatric Association (1994). *Diagnostic and statistical manual of mental disorders: Fourth edition (DSM-IV).* Washington, DC: American Psychiatric Association.

Angelou, M. (1970). *I know why the caged bird sings.* New York: Random House.

Antrobus, J. (1990). The neurocognition of sleep mentation: Rapid eye movements, visual imagery, and dreaming. In R. R. Bootzin, J. F. Kihlstrom, & D. L. Schacter (Eds.), *Sleep and cognition* (pp. 1–24). Washington, DC: American Psychological Association.

Archibald, H. C., & Tuddenham, R. D. (1965). Persistent stress reaction after combat. *Archives of General Psychiatry, 12,* 475–481.

Armstrong, L. (1994). *Rocking the cradle of sexual politics.* New York: Addison-Wesley.

Astington, J. W. (1993). *The child's discovery of the mind.* Cambridge, MA: Harvard University Press.

Atkinson, R. C., & Shriffrin, R. M. (1968). Human memory: A proposed system and its control processes. In K. W. Spence & J. R. Spence (Eds.), *The psychology of learning and motivation: Advances in research and theory, 2,* 89–195. New York: Academic Press.

Axelrod, J., & Reisine, T. D. (1984) Stress hormones: Their interaction and regulation. *Science, 224,* 452–459.

Baddeley, A. D. (1990). *Human memory: Theory and practice.* Boston: Allyn & Bacon.

Badia, P. (1990). Memories in sleep: Old and new. In R. R. Bootzin, J. F. Kihlstrom, & D. L. Schacter (Eds.), *Sleep and cognition* (pp. 67–76). Washington, DC: American Psychological Association.

Bakhtin, M. (1929/1973). *Problems of Dostoevsky's poetics (2nd ed.)* (R. W. Rotsel, Trans.). Ann Arbor, MI: Ardis.

Barclay, C. R., & DeCooke, P. A. (1988). Ordinary everyday memories: Some of the things of which selves are made. In U. Neisser & E. Winograd (Eds.), *Remembering reconsidered: Eecological and traditional approaches to the study of memory* (pp. 91–125). New York: Cambridge University Press.

Barsalou, L. W. (1988). The content and organization of autobiographical memories. In U. Neisser & E. Winograd (Eds.), *Remembering reconsidered: Ecological and traditional approaches to the study of memory* (pp. 193–243). New York: Cambridge University Press.

Bartis, S. P., & Zamansky, H. S. (1986). Dissociation in posthypnotic amnesia: Knowing without knowing. *Journal of Clinical Hypnosis, 29*(2), 103–108.

Bartlett, F. C. (1932/1995). *Remembering: A study in experimental and social psychology.* New York: Cambridge University Press.

Bauer, P. A., & Hertsgaard, L. A. (1993). Increasing steps in recall of events: Factors facilitating immediate and long-term memory in 13.5- and 16.5-month-old children. *Child Development, 64,* 1204–1223.

Beahrs, J. O. (1982). *Unity and multiplicity: Multilevel consciousness of self in hypnosis, psychiatric disorder, and mental health.* New York: Brunner/Mazel.

Bekerian, D. A., & Bowers, J. M. (1983). Eyewitness testimony: Were we misled? *Journal of Experimental Psychology: Learning, Memory, and Cognition, 9,* 139–145.

Belfrage, S. (1994). *Un-American activities: A memoir of the fifties.* New York: HarperCollins.

Bell, C. (1992). *Ritual theory, ritual practice.* New York: Oxford University Press.

Blaney, P. H. (1986). Affect and memory: A review. *Psychological Bulletin, 99,* 229–246.

Bleuler, E. (1950). *Dementia praecox: or, the group of schizophrenias.* New York: International Universities Press.

Bloom, L. (1993). *The transition from infancy to language: Acquiring the power of expression.* New York: Cambridge University Press.

Blum, H. P. (1980). The value of reconstruction in adult psychoanalysis. *International Journal of Psycho-Analysis, 61,* 39–52.

Bower, G. H. (1981). Mood and memory. *American Psychologist, 36,* 129–148.

Bowers, K. S., & Hilgard, E. R. (1988). Some complexities in understanding memory. In H. M. Pettinati (Ed.), *Hypnosis and memory* (pp. 3–18). New York: Guilford.

Bowlby, J. (1982). *Attachment (2nd edition).* New York: Basic.

Brainerd, C. J., Kingma, J., & Howe, M. L. (1985). On the development of forgetting. *Child Development, 56,* 1103–1119.

Braun, B. G. (1988). The BASK model of dissociation. *Dissociation, 1*(1), 4–23.

Braun, B. G., & Sachs, R. G. (1985). The development of multiple personality disorder: Predisposing, precipitating, and perpetuating factors. In R. P. Kluft (Ed.), *Childhood antecedents of multiple personality* (pp. 37–64). Washington, DC: American Psychiatric Press.

Bremner, J. D., Randall, P., Scott, T. M., Bronen, R. A., Seibyl, J. P., Southwick, S. M., Delaney, R. C., McCarthy, G., Charney, D. S., & Innis, R. B. (1995). MRI-based measurement of hippocampal volume in patients with combat-related posttraumatic stress disorder. *American Journal of Psychiatry, 152*(7), 973–981.

Bremner, J. D., Scott, T. M., Delaney, R. C., Southwick, S. M., Mason, J. W., Johnson, D. R., Innis, R. B., McCarthy, G., & Charney, D. S. (1993). Deficits in short-term memory in posttraumatic stress disorder. *American Journal of Psychiatry, 150*(7), 1015–1019.

Bretherton, I. (1984). Representing the social world in symbolic play: Reality and fantasy. In I. Bretherton (Ed.), *Symbolic play: The development of social understanding* (pp. 1–41). New York: Academic Press.

Breuer, J., & Freud, S. (1893–1895). Studies on hysteria. In Strachey, J. (Ed. and Trans.), *The standard edition of the complete psychological works of Sigmund Freud* (Vol. 2). New York: Norton.

Brewer, W. F. (1988) Memory for randomly sampled autobiographical events. In U. Neisser & E. Winograd (Eds.), *Remembering reconsidered: Ecological and traditional approaches to the study of memory* (pp. 21–90). New York: Cambridge University Press.

Briere, J. (1989). *Therapy for adults molested as children: beyond survival.* New York: Springer.

Briere, J., & Conte, J. (1993). Self-reported amnesia for abuse in adults molested as children. *Journal of Traumatic Stress, 6* (1), 21–31.

Briere, J., & Zaidi, L. Y. (1989). Sexual abuse histories and sequelae in female psychiatric emergency room patients. *American Journal of Psychiatry, 146* (12), 1602–1606.

Brown, J. M., O'Keeffe, J., Sanders, S. H., & Baker, B. (1986). Developmental changes in children's cognition to stressful and painful situations. *Journal of Pediatric Psychology, 11,* 343–357.

Brown, P. (1991). *The hypnotic brain: Hypnotherapy and social communication.* New Haven, CT: Yale University Press.

Brown, R., & Kulik, J. (1977/1982). Flashbulb memories. In U. Neisser (Ed.), *Memory observed: Remembering in natural contexts* (pp. 23–40). New York: W. H. Freeman.

Bruck, M., Ceci, S. J., Francoeur, E., & Barr, R. (1995). "I hardly cried when I got my shot!" Influencing chldren's reports about a visit to their pediatrician. *Child Development, 66,* 193–208.

Bruner, J. S. (1975). The ontogenesis of speech acts. *Journal of Child Language, 2,* 1–19.

Bryant, D., Kessler, J., & Shirar, L. (1992). *The family inside: Working with the multiple.* New York: Norton.

Burge, S. K. (1988). Post-traumatic stress disorder in victims of rape. *Journal of Traumatic Stress, 1* (2), 193–210.

Bussey, K. (1992). Lying and truthfulness: Children's definitions, standards, and evaluative reactions. *Child Development, 63,* 129–137.

Campos, J. J., & Stenberg, C. R. (1982). Perception, appraisal, and emotion: The onset of social referencing. In M. Lamb & L. Sherrod (Eds.), *Infant social cognition: Empirical data and theoretical considerations* (pp. 273–314). Hillsdale, NJ: Erlbaum.

Cannon, W. B. (1953). *Bodily changes in pain, hunger, fear and rage* (2nd ed.). Boston, MA: Charles T. Branford.

Cardena, E., & Spiegel, D. (1993). Dissociative reactions to the San Francisco Bay area earthquake of 1989. *American Journal of Psychiatry, 150* (3), 474–478.

Carlson, E. B., & Rosser-Hogan, R. (1991). Trauma experiences, posttraumatic stress, dissociation, and depression in Cambodian refugees. *American Journal of Psychiatry, 148* (11), 1548–1551.

Carmen, E. H., Ricker, P. P., & Mills, T. (1984). Victims of violence and psychiatric illness. *American Journal of Psychiatry, 141* (3), 378–383.

Cassiday, K. L., & Lyons, J. A. (1992). Recall of traumatic memories following cerebral vascular accident. *Journal of Traumatic Stress, 5* (4), 627–630.

Catherwood, D. (1993). The robustness of infant haptic memory: Testing its capacity to withstand delay and haptic interference. *Child Development, 64,* 702–710.

Ceci, S. J., Ross, D. F., & Toglia, M. P. (1987). Suggestibility of children's memory: Psycholegal implications. *Journal of Experimental Psychology: General, 116*, 38–49.

Chandler, M. J., Fritz, A. S., & Hala, S. M. (1989). Small scale deceit: Deception as a marker of 2-, 3- and 4-year-olds' early theories of mind. *Child Development, 60*, 1263–1277.

Charniak, E., & McDermott, D. (1985). *Introduction to artificial intelligence.* Reading, MA: Addison-Wesley.

Christenson, R. M., Walker, J. I., Ross, D. R., & Maltbie, A. A. (1981). Reactivation of traumatic conflicts. *American Journal of Psychiatry, 138* (7), 984–985.

Christiaansen, R. E., & Ochalek, K. (1983). Editing misleading information from memory: Evidence for the coexistence of original and postevent information. *Memory and Cognition, 11*, 467–475.

Christianson, S. A., & Loftus, E. F. (1987). Memory for traumatic events. *Applied Cognitive Psychology, 1*, 225–239.

Chu, J. A., & Dill, D. (1990). Dissociative symptoms in relation to childhood physical and sexual abuse. *American Journal of Psychiatry, 147* (7), 887–892.

Cohen, N. J. (1984). Preserved learning capacity in amnesia: Evidence for multiple memory systems. In L. R. Squire & N. Butters (Eds.), *Neuropsychology of memory* (pp. 83–103). New York: Guilford.

Cohen, N. J., & Squire, L. R. (1980). Preserved learning and retention of pattern analyzing skill in amnesics: Dissociation of knowing how and knowing that. *Science, 210*, 207–210.

Cole, D. A., & Jordan, A. E. (1995). Competence and memory: Integrating psychosocial and cognitive correlates of child depression. *Child Development, 66*, 459–473.

Cottle, T. J. (1980). *Children's secrets.* New York: Addison-Wesley.

Courtois, C. (1988). *Healing the incest wound: Adult survivors in therapy.* New York: Norton.

Crewdson, J. (1988). *By silence betrayed: Sexual abuse of children in America.* New York: HarperCollins.

Crnich, J. E., & Crnich, K. A. (1992). *Shifting the burden of proof: Suing child sexual abusers — A legal guide for survivors and their supporters.* Lake Oswego, OR: Recollex.

Daehler, M., Bukatko, D., Benson, K., & Myers, N. (1976). The effects of size and color cues on the delayed response of very young children. *Bulletin of the Psychonomic Society, 7*, 65–68.

Dale, P. S., Loftus, E. F., & Rathbun, L. (1978). The influence of the form of the question on the eyewitness testimony of pre-school children. *Journal of Psycholinguistic Research, 7*, 269–277.

Davies, G. (1991). Concluding comments. In J. Doris (Ed.), *The suggestibility of children's recollections: Implications for eyewitness testimony* (pp. 177–187). Washington, DC: American Psychological Association.

DeCasper, A., & Fifer, W. (1980). Of human bonding: Newborns prefer their mother's voices. *Science, 208*, 1174–1176.

Dempster, F. N. (1981). Memory span: Sources of individual and developmental differences. *Psychological Bulletin, 89*, 63–100.

Dent, H. R. (1991). Experimental studies of interviewing child witnesses. In J. Doris (Ed.), *The suggestibility of children's recollections: Implications for eyewitness testimony* (pp. 138–148). Washington, DC: American Psychological Association.

Derryberry, D., & Rothbart, M. K. (1984). Emotion, attention, and temperament. In C. E. Izard, J. Kagan, & R. B. Zajonc (Eds.), *Emotions, cognition, and behavior* (pp. 132–166). New York: Cambridge University Press.

Diamond, A. (1985). Development of the ability to use recall to guide action, as indicated by infants' performance on AB. *Child Development, 56*, 868–883.

Donaldson, M. (1978). *Children's minds.* New York: Norton.

Doris, J. (Ed.), (1991). *The suggestibility of children's recollections: Implications for eyewitness testimony.* Washington, DC: American Psychological Association.

Duncan, E. M., Whitney, P., & Kunen, S. (1982). Integration of visual and verbal information in children's memories. *Child Development, 53*, 1215–1223.

Ebbinghaus, H. (1885/1913). *Memory: A contribution to experimental psychology* (H. A. Ruger & C. E. Byssenine, Trans.). New York: Dover.

Ehrlich, G. (1994). *A match to the heart: One woman's story of being struck by lightning.* New York: Pantheon.

Eich, J. E. (1977). State-dependent retrieval of information in human episodic memory. In I. M. Birnbaum & E. S. Parker (Eds.), *Alcohol and human memory* (pp. 141–157). Hillsdale, NJ: Erlbaum.

Eich, J. E. (1980). The cue-dependent nature of state-dependent retrieval. *Memory and Cognition, 8*, 157–173.

Eich, J. E. (1989). Theoretical issues in state dependent memory. In H. L. Roediger, III & F. I. M. Craik (Eds.), *Varieties of memory and consciousness: Essays in honour of Endel Tulving* (pp. 331–354). Hillsdale, NJ: Erlbaum.

Ekman, P. (1992). *Telling lies: Clues to deceit in the marketplace, politics, and marriage.* New York: Norton.

Ellenberger, H. (1970). *The discovery of the unconscious: The history and evolution of dynamic psychiatry.* New York: Basic.

Emde, R. N. (1989). The infant's relationship experience: Developmental and affective aspects. In A. J. Sameroff & R. N. Emde (Eds.), *Relationship disturbances in early childhood* (pp. 33–51). New York: Basic.

Emde, R. N., & Sameroff, A. J. (1989) Understanding early relationship disturbances. In A. J. Sameroff & R. N. Emde (Eds.), *Relationship disturbances in early childhood* (pp. 3–14). New York: Basic.

Emery, V. O., Emery, P. E., Shama, D. K., Quiana, N. A., & Jassani, A. K. (1991). Predisposing variables in PTSD patients. *Journal of Traumatic Stress, 4*(3), 325–343.

Engel, S. (1995). *The stories children tell: Making sense of the narratives of childhood.* New York: W. H. Freeman.

Epstein, S. (1994). Integration of the cognitive and the psychodynmic unconscious. *American Psychologist, 49*(8), 709–724.

Erikson, E. H. (1959/1980). *Identity and the life cycle.* New York: Norton.

Erikson, E. H. (1968) *Identity: Youth and crisis.* New York: Norton.

Erikson, K. T. (1976). *Everything in its path: Destruction of community in the Buffalo Creek flood.* New York: Simon & Schuster.

Eth, S., & Pynoos, R. S. (1985). *Post-traumatic stress disorder in children.* Washington, DC: American Psychiatric Press.

Evans, F. J., & Staats, J. M. (1989). Suggested posthypnotic amnesia in four diagnostic groups of hospitalized psychiatric patients. *American Journal of Clinical Hypnosis, 32*(1), 27–34.

Farrar, M. J., & Goodman, G. S. (1992). Developmental changes in event memory. *Child Development, 63*, 173–187.

Feinman, S., & Lewis, M. (1983). Social referencing and second order effects in ten-month-old infants. *Child Development, 54*, 878–887.

Fenson, L. (1984). Developmental trends for action and speech in pretend play. In I. Bretherton (Ed.), *Symbolic play: The development of social understanding.* New York: Academic Press.

Fentress, J., & Wickham, C. (1992). *Social memory.* Cambridge: Blackwell.

Ferenzci, S. (1932). Confusion of tongues between adults and the child: The language of tenderness and the language of (sexual) passion. In J. M. Masson (1984), *The assault on truth: Freud's suppression of the seduction theory* (pp. 283–295). New York: Farrar, Straus & Giroux.

Festinger, L. (1957). *A theory of cognitive dissonance*. Evanston, IL: Row, Peterson.

Feyereisen, P. (1991). Brain pathology, lateralization, and nonverbal behavior. In R. S. Feldman & B. Rime (Eds.), *Fundamentals of nonverbal behavior* (pp. 31–70). New York: Cambridge University Press.

Figley, C. R. (Ed.), (1985). *Trauma and its wake: The study and treatment of post-traumatic stress disorder*. New York: Brunner/Mazel.

Fish-Murray, C. C., Koby, E. V., & van der Kolk, B. A. (1987). Evolving ideas: The effect of abuse on children's thought. In B. A. van der Kolk (Ed.), *Psychological trauma* (pp. 89–110). Washington, DC: American Psychiatric Press.

Flavell, J. H., Beach, D. R., & Chinsky, J. M. (1966). Spontaneous verbal rehearsal in a memory task as a function of age. *Child Development, 37*, 283–299.

Flin, R. (1991). Commentary: A grand memory for forgetting. In J. Doris (Ed.), *The suggestibility of children's recollections: Implications for eyewitness testimony* (pp. 21–23). Washington, DC: American Psychological Association.

Foa, E. B., Riggs, D. S., & Gershuny, B. S. (1995). Arousal, numbing, and intrusion: Symptom structure of PTSD following assault. *American Journal of Psychiatry, 152* (1), 116–120.

Foley, M. A., & Johnson, M. K. (1985). Confusions between memories for performed and imagined actions: A developmental comparison. *Child Development, 56*, 1145–1155.

Foley, M. A., Johnson, M. K., & Raye, C. L. (1983). Age-related changes in confusion between memories for thoughts and memories for speech. *Child Development, 54*, 51–60.

Frankel, F. H. (1993). Adult reconstruction of childhood events in the multiple personality literature. *American Journal of Psychiatry, 150* (6), 954–958.

Franklin, E., & Wright, W. (1991). *Sins of the father*. New York: Fawcett Crest.

Frederick, C. J. (1985). Children traumatized by catastrophic situations. In S. Eth & R. S. Pynoos (Eds.), *Post-traumatic stress disorder in children* (pp. 71–99). Washington, DC: American Psychiatric Press.

Freeman, M. (1993). *Rewriting the self: History, memory, narrative*. New York: Routledge.

Freinkel, A., Koopman, C., & Spiegel, D. (1994). Dissociative symptoms in media eyewitnesses of an execution. *American Journal of Psychiatry, 151* (9), 1335–1339.

Freud, A. (1966). *The writings of Anna Freud, Vol. II, 1936. The ego and the mechanisms of defense* (revised edition). New York: International Universities Press.

Freud, S. (1896). The aetiology of hysteria. In J. Strachey (Ed. and Trans.), *The standard edition of the complete psychological works of Sigmund Freud* (Vol. 3, pp. 189–221). New York: Norton.

Freud, S. (1899). Screen memories. In J. Strachey (Ed. and Trans.), *The standard edition of the complete psychological works of Sigmund Freud* (Vol. 3, pp. 303–322). New York: Norton.

Freud, S. (1920). Beyond the pleasure principle. In J. Strachey (Ed. and Trans.), *The standard edition of the complete psychological works of Sigmund Freud* (Vol. 18, pp. 3–143). New York: Norton.

Freud, S. (1940 [1938]). Splitting of the ego in the process of defense. In J. Strachey (Ed. and Trans.) *The standard edition of the complete psychological works of Sigmund Freud* (Vol. 23, pp. 271–278) New York: Norton.

Freud, S. (1985). *The complete letters of Sigmund Freud to Wilhelm Fliess, 1887–1904* (J. M. Masson, Ed. and Trans.). Cambridge, MA: Belknap.

Friedman, W. J. (1991). The development of children's memory for the time of past events. *Child Development, 62,* 139–155.

Frischholz, E. J. (1985). The relationship among dissociation, hypnosis, and child abuse in the development of multiple personality disorder. In R. P. Kluft (Ed.), *Childhood antecedents of multiple personality* (pp. 99–126). Washington, DC: American Psychiatric Press.

Fromm, E. (1941). *Escape from freedom.* New York: Farrar & Rinehart.

Gaensbauer, T. (1980) Anaclitic depression in a 3 1/2-month-old child. *American Journal of Psychiatry, 137* (7), 841–842.

Gazzaniga, M. S. (1985). *The social brain: Discovering the networks of the mind.* New York: Basic.

Geller, J. L., & Harris, M. (1994). *Women of the asylum: Voices from behind the walls, 1840–1945.* New York: Doubleday.

Gibbs, M. S. (1989). Factors in the victim that mediate between disaster and psychopathology: A review. *Journal of Traumatic Stress, 2* (4), 489–513.

Gibson, W. (1975). *The miracle worker.* New York: Bantam.

Goddard, C. V., McIntyre, D. C., & Leech, C. K. (1969). A permanent change in brain functioning resulting from daily electrical stimulation. *Experimental Neurology, 25,* 295–330.

Gomes-Schwartz, B., Horowitz, J., & Sauzier, M. (1985). Severity of emotional distress among sexually abused preschool, school age, and adolescent children. *Hospital and Community Psychiatry, 36* (5), 503–508.

Goodman, G. S. (1991). Commentary: On stress and accuracy in research on children's testimony. In J. Doris (Ed.), *The suggestibility of children's recollections: Implications for eyewitness testimony* (pp. 77–82). Washington, DC: American Psychological Association.

Goodman, G. S., & Clarke-Stewart, A. (1991). Suggestibility in children's testimony: Implications for sexual abuse investigations. In J. Doris (Ed.), *The suggestibility of children's recollections: Implications for eyewitness testimony* (pp. 92–105). Washington, DC: American Psychological Association.

Goodwin, D. W., Powell, B., Bremer, D., Hoine, H., & Stern, J. (1969). Alcohol and recall: State dependent effects in man. *Science, 163,* 1358–1360.

Goodwin, J., Attias, R., McCarty, T., Chandler, S., & Romanik, R. (1988). Reporting by adult psychiatric patients of childhood sexual abuse. *American Journal of Psychiatry, 145* (9), 1183.

Goodwin, J. (1985). Credibility problems in multiple personality disorder patients and abused children. In R. P. Kluft (Ed.), *Childhood antecedents of multiple personality* (pp. 1–19). Washington, DC: American Psychiatric Press.

Graf, P., & Masson, M. E. J. (Eds.), (1993). *Implicit memory: New directions in cognition, development, and neuropsychology.* Hillsdale, NJ: Erlbaum.

Greco, C., Rovee-Collier, C., Hayne, H., Griesler, P., & Earley, L. (1986). Ontogeny of early event memory: I. Forgetting and retrieval by 2- and 3-month-olds. *Infant Behavior and Development, 9,* 441–460.

Green, A. (1985). Children traumatized by physical abuse. In S. Eth & R. Pynoos (Eds.), *Post-traumatic stress disorder in children* (pp. 135–154). Washington, DC: American Psychiatric Press.

Greenacre, P. (1975). On reconstruction. *Journal of the American Psychoanalytical Association, 23,* 693–712.

Greenwald, A. G. (1980). The totalitarian ego: Fabrication and revision of personal history. *American Psychologist, 35,* 603–618.

Grinker, R., & Spiegel, J. (1945). *Men under stress.* Philadelphia: Blakiston.

Haig, R. A. (1990). *The anatomy of grief: Biopsychosocial and therapeutic perspectives.* Springfield, IL: Charles C. Thomas.

Halford, G. S., Mayberry, M. T., O'Hare, A. W., & Grant, P. (1994). The development of memory and processing capacity. *Child Development, 65,* 1338–1356.

Harlow, H. F., & Harlow, M. K. (1971). Psychopathology in monkeys. In H. D. Kimmel (Ed.), *Experimental psychopathology.* New York: Academic Press.

Harris, P. L., & Kavannaugh, R. D. (1993). Young children's understanding of pretense. *Monographs of the Society for Research in Child Development, Serial No. 231, 58* (1).

Hayne, H., & Rovee-Collier, C. (1995). The organization of reactivated memory in infancy. *Child Development, 66,* 893–906.

Heath, R. A. (1994). The cognitive RISC machine needs complexity. *Behavioral and Brain Sciences, 17,* 669–670.

Hellige, J. B. (1983) Hemisphere × task interaction and the study of laterality. In J. B. Hellige (Ed.), *Cerebral hemisphere asymmetry: Method, theory, and application* (pp. 411–443). New York: Praeger.

Herman, J., & van der Kolk, B. (1987). Traumatic antecedents of borderline personality disorder. In B. A. van der Kolk (Ed.), *Psychological trauma* (pp. 111–126). Washington, DC: American Psychiatric Press.

Herman, J. L. (1992). *Trauma and recovery.* New York: Basic.

Herman, J. L., & Schatzow, E. (1987). Recovery and verification of memories of childhood sexual trauma. *Psychoanalytic Psychology, 4,* 1–14.

Hermans, H. J. M., & Kempen, H. J. G. (1993) *The dialogical self: Meaning as movement.* New York: Academic Press.

Hilgard, E. R., & Hilgard, J. R. (1975). *Hypnosis in the relief of pain.* New York: Brunner/Mazel.

Hilgard, J. R. (1979). *Personality and hypnosis: A study of imaginative involvement.* Chicago: University of Chicago Press.

Hill, W. L., Borovsky, D., & Rovee-Collier, C. (1988). Continuities in infant memory development. *Developmental Psychobiology, 20,* 43–62.

Hinde, R. A. (1982). *Ethology: Its nature and relation with other sciences.* Oxford: Oxford University Press.

Hoff, J. (1991). *Law, gender, and injustice: A legal history of U.S. women.* New York: New York University Press.

Hoffman, M. L. (1984) Interaction of affect and cognition in empathy. In C. E. Izard, J. Kagan, & R. B. Zajonc (Eds.), *Emotions, cognition, and behavior* (pp. 103–131). New York: Cambridge University Press.

Hollender, M. H., & Hirsch, S. J. (1963). Hysterical psychoses. *American Journal of Psychiatry, 120,* 1066–1074.

Horne, J. A. (1988). *Why we sleep.* New York: Oxford University Press.

Horowitz, M. J. (1992). *Stress response syndromes.* Northvale, NJ: Jason Aronson.

Hudson, J., & Nelson, K. (1983). Effects of script structure on children's story recall. *Developmental Psychology, 19,* 625–635.

Hudson, J., & Nelson, K. (1986). Repeated encounters of a similar kind: Effects of familiarity on children's autobiographic memory. *Cognitive Development, 1,* 253–271.

Humphreys, M. S., Wiles, J., & Dennis, S. (1994). Toward a theory of human memory: Data structures and access processes. *Behavioral and Brain Sciences, 17,* 655–692.

Hundeide, K. (1985). The tacit background of children's judgments. In J. V. Wertsch (Ed.), *Culture, communication, and cognition: Vygotskian perspectives* (pp. 306–322). New York: Cambridge University Press.

Husain, A., & Chapel, J. L. (1983). History of incest in girls admitted to a psychiatric hospital. *American Journal of Psychiatry, 140* (5), 591–593.

Izard, C. E. (1984). Emotion-cognition relationships and human development. In C. E. Izard, J. Kagan, & R. B. Zajonc (Eds.), *Emotions, cognition, and behavior* (pp. 17–37). New York: Cambridge University Press.

Izard, C. E., Kagan, J., & Zajonc, R. B. (Eds.), (1984). *Emotions, cognitions, and behavior.* New York: Cambridge University Press.

Jacoby, L. L. (1988). Memory observed and memory unobserved. In U. Neisser & E. Winograd (Eds.), *Remembering reconsidered: Ecological and traditional approaches to the study of memory* (pp. 145–177). New York: Cambridge University Press.

James, W. (1892/1985). *Psychology: The briefer course.* Notre Dame, IN: University of Notre Dame Press.

Jauch, D. A., & Carpenter, W. T. (1988). Reactive psychosis I: Does the pre-DSM-III concept define a third psychosis? *Journal of Nervous and Mental Disease, 176* (2), 72–81.

Jauch, D. A., & Carpenter, W. T. (1988). Reactive psychosis II: Does DSM-III-R define a third psychosis? *Journal of Nervous and Mental Disease, 176* (2), 82–86.

Jaynes, J. (1976). *The origin of consciousness in the breakdown of the bicameral Mind.* Boston: Houghton Mifflin.

Johnson, M. K. (1988). Discriminating the origin of information. In T. F. Oltmanns & B. A. Maher (Eds.), *Delusional beliefs* (pp. 34–65). New York: Wiley.

Johnson, M. K., & Raye, C. L. (1981). Reality monitoring. *Psychological Review, 88,* 67–85.

Kagan, J. (1984). The idea of emotion in human development. In C. E. Izard, J. Kagan, & R. B. Zajonc (Eds.), *Emotions, cognition, and behavior* (pp. 38–72). New York: Cambridge University Press.

Kail, R. (1990). *The development of memory in children.* New York: W. H. Freeman.

Kaplan, L. J. (1995). *No voice is ever wholly lost.* New York: Simon & Schuster.

Keller, H. (1902/1988). *The story of my life.* New York: Bantam.

Kelman, H. C., & Hamilton, V. L. (1989). *Crimes of obedience: Toward a social psychology of authority and responsibility.* New Haven: Yale University Press.

Kiecolt-Glaser, J. K., Garner, W., Speicher, C., Penn, G. M., Holliday, J., & Glaser, R. (1984). Psychosocial modifiers of immunocompetence in medical students. *Psychosomatic Medicine, 46,* 7–14.

Kihlstrom, J. F. (1990). The psychological unconscious. In L. Pervin (Ed.), *Handbook of personality: Theory and research* (pp. 445–464). New York: Guilford.

Kimberly, A. L., Vaillant, G. E., Torrey, W. C., & Elder, G. H. (1995). A 50-year prospective study of the psychological sequelae of World War II combat. *American Journal of Psychiatry, 152* (4), 516–522.

King, M. A., & Yuille, J. C. (1987). Suggestibility and the child witness. In S. J. Ceci, M. P. Toglia, & D. F. Ross (Eds.), *Children's eyewitness memory* (pp. 24–35). New York: Springer-Verlag.

Kinney, L., & Kramer, M. (1984). Sleep and sleep responsivity in disturbed dreamers. *Sleep Research, 13,* 102.

Kinsbourne, M., & Hiscock, M. (1983). Asymmetries of dual-task performances. In J. B. Hellige (Ed.), *Cerebral hemisphere asymmetry: Method, theory, and application* (pp. 255–334). New York: Praeger.

Kluft, R. P. (Ed.), (1985). *Childhood antecedents of multiple personality.* Washington, DC: American Psychiatric Press.

Kohut, H. (1971). *The analysis of the self.* New York: International Universities Press.

Kolb, L. C. (1987). A neurological hypothesis explaining posttraumatic stress disorders. *American Journal of Psychiatry, 144* (8), 989–995.

Koopman, C., Classen, C., & Spiegel, D. (1994). Predictors of posttraumatic stress symptoms among survivors of the Oakland/Berkeley, Calif., firestorm. *American Journal of Psychiatry, 151* (6), 888–894.

Kramer, M. (1990). Nightmares (dream disturbances) in posttraumatic stress disorder: Implications for a theory of dreaming. In R. R. Bootzin, J. F. Kihlstrom, & D. Schacter (Eds.), *Sleep and cognition* (pp. 190–202). Washington, DC: American Psycholgocial Association.

Krasne, F. B. (1978). Extrinsic control of intrinsic neuronal plasticity: An hypothesis from work on simple systems. *Brain Research, 140,* 197–216.

Kreutzer, M. A., Leonard, C., & Flavell, J. H. (1975/1982). Prospective remembering in children. In U. Niesser (Ed.), *Memory observed: Remembering in natural contexts* (pp. 343–348). New York: W. H. Freeman.

Krystal, J. H. (1990). Animal models for posttraumatic stress disorder. In E. L. Giller (Ed.), *Biological assessment and treatment of posttraumatic stress disorder* (pp. 3–26). Washington, DC: American Psychiatric Press.

Laird, J. D., Wagener, J. J., Halal, M., & Szegda, M. (1982). Remembering what you feel: The effects of emotion on memory. *Journal of Personality and Social Psychology, 42,* 646–657.

Langer, L. L. (1991). *Holocaust testimonies: The ruins of memory.* New Haven: Yale University Press.

Lash, J. P. (1980). *Helen and teacher: The story of Helen Keller and Anne Sullivan Macy.* New York: Delta/Seymour Lawrence.

Lashley, K. S. (1929). *Brain mechanisms and intelligence: A quantitative study of injuries to the brain.* Chicago: Chicago University Press.

Lashley, K. S. (1950). In search of the engram. *Symposia of the Society of Experimental Biology, 4,* 454–482.

Laufer, R. S., Frey-Wouters, E., & Gallops, M. S. (1985). Traumatic stressors in the Vietnam War and post-traumatic stress disorder. In C. R. Figley (Ed.), *Trauma and its wake: The study and treatment of post-traumatic stress disorder* (Vol. I, pp. 73–89). New York: Brunner/Mazel.

Lee, K. A., Vaillant, G. E., Torrey, W. C., & Elder, G. H. (1995). A 50-year prospective study of the psychological sequelae of World War II combat. *American Journal of Psychiatry, 152* (4), 516–522.

Leubecker, A. W. (1991). Commentary: Development of event memories or event reports? In J. Doris (Ed.), *The suggestibility of children's recollections: Implications for eyewitness testimony* (pp. 24–26). Washington, DC: American Psychological Association.

Lifton, R. J. (1961). *Thought reform and the psychology of totalism: A study of "brainwashing" in China.* New York: Norton.

Lifton, R. J. (1967). *Death in life: Survivors of Hiroshima.* New York: Simon & Schuster.

Lifton, R. J., & Olson, E. (1976). The human meaning of total disaster: The Buffalo Creek experience. *Psychiatry, 39,* 1–18.

Lillard, A. S. (1993). Young children's conceptualization of pretense: Action or mental representational state? *Child Development, 64,* 372–386.

Lindberg, M. (1991). An interactive approach to assessing the suggestibility and testimony of eyewitnesses. In J. Doris (Ed.), *The suggestibility of children's recollections: Implications for eyewitness testimony* (pp. 47–55). Washington, DC: American Psychological Association.

Lindemann, E. (1944). Symptomatology and management of acute grief. *American Journal of Psychiatry, 101,* 141–148.

Lindsay, D. S., & Read, J. D. (1995). "Memory work" and recovered memories of childhood sexual abuse: Scientific evidence and public, professional, and personal issues. *Psychology, Public Policy, and Law, 1* (4), 846–908.

Linton, M. (1982). Transformations of memory in everyday life. In U. Neisser (Ed.), *Memory observed: Remembering in natural contexts* (pp. 77–91). New York: W. H. Freeman.

Lipstadt, D. E. (1993). *Denying the Holocaust.* New York: Free Press.

Loftus, E. F. (1993). The reality of repressed memories. *American Psychologist, 48* (5), 518–537.

Loftus, E. F., & Loftus, G. R. (1980). On the permanence of stored information in the human brain. *American Psychologist, 35,* 409–420.

Loftus, E. F., Polansky, S., & Fullilove, M. T. (1994). Memories of childhood sexual abuse: Remembering and repressing. *Psychology of Women Quarterly, 18,* 67–84.

Lowenthal, D. (1985). *The past is a foreign country.* New York: Cambridge University Press.

Luria, A. R. (1968). *The mind of a mnemonist.* New York: Avon.

Lyon, T. D., & Flavell, J. H. (1994). Young children's understanding of "remember" and "forget." *Child Development, 65,* 1357–1371.

MacKinnon, C. A. (1989). *Toward a feminist theory of the state.* Cambridge, MA: Harvard University Press.

Mahler, M. S., Pine, F., & Bergman, A. (1975). *The psychological birth of the human infant: Symbiosis and individuation.* New York: Basic.

Malatesta, C., & Haviland, J. (1982). Learning display rules: The socialization of emotion expression in infancy. *Child Development, 53,* 991–1003.

Mandler, J. M. (1984). *Stories, scripts, and scenes: Aspects of schema theory.* Hillsdale, NJ: Erlbaum.

Mans, L., Cicchetti, D., & Sroufe, L. A. (1978). Mirror reactions of Downs syndrome infants and toddlers: Cognitive underpinnings of self-recognition. *Child Development, 49,* 547–556.

Markus, H., & Sentis, K. (1980). The self in social information processing. In J. Suls (Ed.), *Social psychological perspectives on the self* (pp. 41–70). Hillsdale, NJ: Erlbaum.

Marmar, C. R., Weiss, D. S., Schlenger, W. E., Fairbank, J. A., Jordan, B. K., Kulka, R. A., & Hough, R. L. (1994). Peritraumatic dissociation and posttraumatic stress in male Vietnam theater veterans. *American Journal of Psychiatry, 151* (6), 902–907.

Masson, J. M. (1984). *The assault on truth: Freud's suppression of the seduction theory.* New York: Farrar, Straus & Giroux.

Masson, J. M. (Ed. and Trans.) (1986). *A dark science: Women, sexuality, and psychiatry in the nineteenth century.* New York: Farrar, Straus & Giroux.

Mazor, A., Gampel, Y., Enright, R. D., & Orenstein, R. (1990). Holocaust survivors: Coping with post-traumatic memories in childhood and 40 years later. *Journal of Traumatic Stress, 3,* 1–14.

McCaffrey, R. J., Lorig, T. S., Pendrey, D. L., McCutcheon, N. B., & Garrett, J. C. (1993). Odor-induced EEG changes in PTSD Vietnam veterans. *Journal of Traumatic Stress, 6* (2), 213–224.

McCann, I. L., & Pearlman, L. A. (1990). *Psychological trauma and the adult survivor: Theory, therapy, and transformation.* New York: Brunner/Mazel.

McGough, L. S. (1994). *Child witnesses: Fragile voices in the American legal system.* New Haven: Yale University Press.

Mead, G. H. (1934). *Mind, self, and society.* Chicago: University of Chicago Press.

Mehrabian, A. (1981). *Silent messages: Implicit communication of emotions and attitudes.* Belmont, CA: Wadsworth.

Mellman, T. A., Kulik-Bell, R., Ashlock, L. E., & Nolan, B. (1995). Sleep events among veterans with combat-related posttraumatic stress disorder. *American Journal of Psychiatry, 152* (1), 110–115.

Milgram, S. (1974). *Obedience to authority: An experimental view.* New York: Harper & Row.

Miller, G. A. (1956). The magical number seven, plus or minus two: Some limits on our capacity for processing information. *Psychological Review, 63,* 81–97.

Mochulsky, K. (1967). *Dostoevsky: His life and work* (M. A. Minihan, Trans.). Princeton: Princeton University Press.

Moorcroft, W. H. (1989). *Sleep, dreaming, and sleep disorders: An introduction.* New York: University Press of America.

Mullen, P. E., Martin, J. L., Anderson, J. C., Romans, S. E., & Herbison, G. P. (1993). Childhood sexual abuse and mental health in adult life. *British Journal of Psychiatry, 163,* 721–732.

Myers, N. A., Clifton, R. K., & Clarkson, M. G. (1987). When they were very young: Almost threes remember two years ago. *Infant Behavior and Development, 10,* 123–132.

Nader, K., Pynoos, R., Fairbanks, L., & Frederick, C. (1990). Children's PTSD reactions one year after a sniper attack at their school. *American Journal of Psychiatry, 147* (11), 1526–1530.

Neale, J. M. (1988). Defensive functions of manic episodes. In T. F. Oltmanns & B. A. Maher (Eds.), *Delusional beliefs* (pp. 138–156). New York: Wiley.

Neiderland, W. (1974). *The Schreber case.* New York: Quadrangle Books/New York Times.

Neisser, U. (1967). *Cognitive psychology.* New York: Appleton-Century-Crofts.

Neisser, U. (1982a). John Dean's memory: A case study. In U. Neisser (Ed.), *Memory observed: Remembering in natural contexts* (pp. 139–159). New York: W. H. Freeman.

Neisser, U. (1982b). Snapshots or benchmarks? In U. Neisser (Ed.), *Memory observed: Remembering in natural contexts* (pp. 43–48). New York: W. H. Freeman.

Neisser, U. (Ed.) (1982c). *Memory observed: Remembering in natural contexts* (pp. 189–200). New York: W. H. Freeman.

Neisser, U. (1988). What is ordinary memory the memory of? In U. Neisser & E. Winograd (Eds.), *Remembering reconsidered: Ecological and traditional approaches to the study of memory* (pp. 356–373). New York: Cambridge University Press.

Nelson, K. (1988). The ontogeny of memory for real events. In U. Neisser (Ed.), *Remembering reconsidered: Ecological and traditional approaches to the study of memory* (pp. 244–276). New York: Cambridge University Press.

Nelson, K., & Gruendel, J. (1981). Generalized event representations: Basic building blocks of cognitive development. In A. Brown & M. Lamb (Eds.), *Advances in developmental psychology* (Vol. 1). Hillsdale, NJ: Erlbaum.

Nir, Y. (1985). Post-traumatic stress disorder in children with cancer. In S. Eth & R. S. Pynoos (Eds.), *Post-traumatic stress disorder in children* (pp. 123–132). Washington, DC: American Psychiatric Press.

Novey, S. (1968). *The second look: The reconstruction of personal history in psychiatry and psychoanalysis.* Baltimore: Johns Hopkins University Press.

Noyes, R., & Kletti, R. (1976). Depersonalization in the face of life threatening danger: A description. *Psychiatry, 39,* 19–27.

Noyes, R. Hoenk, P. R., Kuperman, S., & Slymen, D. J. (1977). Depersonalization in accident victims and psychiatric patients. *Journal of Nervous and Mental Disease, 164,* 401–407.

Ochberg, F. M. (1988). *Post-traumatic therapy and victims of violence*. New York: Brunner/Mazel.

Oltmanns, T. F., & Maher, B. A. (1988). *Delusional beliefs*. New York: Wiley.

Ong, W. J. (1982). *Orality and literacy: The technologizing of the word*. London: Methuen.

Orne, M. T. (1959). The nature of hypnosis: Artifact and essence. *Journal of Abnormal and Social Psychology, 58*, 277–299.

Orr, S. P., Pitman, R. K., Lasko, N. B., & Herz, L. R. (1993). Posttraumatic stress disorder imagery in World War II and Korean combat veterans. *Journal of Abnormal Psychology, 102*, 152–159.

Owings, R. A., & Baumeister, A. A. (1979). Levels of processing, encoding strategies, and memory development. *Journal of Experimental Child Psychology, 28*, 100–118.

Parkin, A. J. (1987). *Memory and amnesia: An introduction*. Oxford, England: Basil Blackwell.

Perner, J. (1993). *Understanding the representational mind*. Cambridge, MA: MIT Press.

Perris, E. E., Myers, N. A., & Clifton, R. K. (1990). Long-term memory for a single infant experience. *Child Development, 61*, 1796–1807.

Perry, S., Difede, J., Musngi, G., Frances, A. J., & Jacobsberg, L. (1992). Predictors of posttraumatic stress disorder after burn injury. *American Journal of Psychiatry, 149* (7), 931–935.

Peters, D. P. (1991). The influence of stress and arousal on the child witness. In J. Doris (Ed.), *The suggestibility of children's recollections: Implications for eyewitness testimony* (pp. 60–76). Washington, DC: American Psychological Association.

Pettinati, H. M. (1988). *Hypnosis and memory*. New York: Guilford.

Piaget, J. (1950/1981). *The psychology of intelligence*. Totawa, NJ: Littlefield, Adams, & Co.

Piaget, J. (1962). *Play, dreams, and imitation in childhood*. New York: Norton.

Pitman, R. K., Orr, S. P., Forgue, D. F., deJong, J. B., & Claiborn, J. M. (1987). Psychophysiologic assessment of posttraumatic stress disorder imagery in Vietnam combat veterans. *Archives of General Psychiatry, 44*, 970–975.

Putnam, F. (1989). *Diagnosis and treatment of multiple personality disorder*. New York: Guilford.

Pynoos, R. S., & Eth, S. (1985). Children traumatized by witnessing acts of personal violence: Homicide, rape, or suicide behavior. In S. Eth & R. S. Pynoos (Eds.), *Post-traumatic stress disorder in children* (pp. 19–43). Washington, DC: American Psychiatric Press.

Rand, G., & Wapner, S. (1987). Postural status as a factor in memory. *Journal of Verbal Learning and Verbal Behavior, 6*, 268–271.

Reiss, D. (1989). The represented and practicing family: Contrasting visions of family continuity. In A. J. Sameroff & R. N. Emde (Eds.), *Relationship disturbances in early childhood* (pp. 191–220). New York: Basic.

Restak, R. M. (1994). *The modular brain*. New York: Simon & Schuster.

Rimé, B., & Schiaratura, L. (1991). Gesture and speech. In R. S. Feldman & B. Rime (Eds.), *Fundamentals of nonverbal behavior* (pp. 239–281). New York: Cambridge University Press.

Roberts, J. (1988). Setting the frame: Definitions, functions, and typology of rituals. In E. Imber-Black, J. Roberts, & R. Whiting (Eds.), *Rituals in families and family therapy* (pp. 3–46). New York: Norton.

Rogers, T. B. (1980). A model of the self as an aspect of the human information processing system. In N. Cantor & J. H. Kihlstrom (Eds.), *Personality, cognition, and social interaction* (pp. 193–214). Hillsdale, NJ: Erlbaum.

Rose, R. M. (1980). Endocrine responses to stressful psychological events. *Psychiatric Clinics of North America, 3*, 251–276.

Rose, S. (1992). *The making of memory: From molecules to mind.* New York: Doubleday.

Rosen, J., Reynolds, C. F., Yeager, A. L., Houck, P. R., & Hurwitz, L. F. (1991). Sleep disturbances in survivors of the Nazi Holocaust. *American Journal of Psychiatry, 148* (1), 62–66.

Rosenberg, D. (1984). The quality and content of preschool fantasy play: Correlates in concurrent social/personality function and early mother-child attachment relationships. Unpublished doctoral dissertation, University of Minnesota.

Ross, R. J., Ball, W. A., Sullivan, K. A., & Caroff, S. N. (1989). Sleep disturbance as the hallmark of posttraumatic stress disorder. *American Journal of Psychiatry, 146* (6), 697–707.

Rossi, E. L. (1993). *The psychobiology of mind-body healing: New concepts of therapeutic hypnosis, Revised edition.* New York: Norton.

Rossi, E. L., & Cheek, D. B. (1988). *Mind-body therapy: Methods of ideodynamic healing in hypnosis.* New York: Norton.

Roustang, F. (1976). *Dire mastery: Discipleship from Freud to Lacan* (N. Lukacher, Trans.). Baltimore: Johns Hopkins University Press.

Rowen, A. B., & Foy, D. W. (1993). Post-traumatic stress in child sexual abuse survivors: A literature review. *Journal of Traumatic Stress, 6* (1), 3–20.

Rubin, D. C. (Ed.) (1986). *Autobiographical memory.* New York: Cambridge University Press.

Rush, F. (1980). *The best kept secret: Sexual abuse of children.* New York: McGraw-Hill.

Saarni, C. (1989). Children's understanding of strategic control of emotional expression in social transactions. In C. Saarni & P. L. Harris (Eds.), *Children's understanding of emotion* (pp. 181–208). New York: Cambridge University Press.

Salaman, E. (1970/1982). A collection of moments. In U. Neisser (Ed.), *Memory observed: Remembering in natural contexts.* New York: W. H. Freeman.

Saltz, E., & Dixon, D. (1982). Let's pretend: The role of motoric imagery in memory for sentences and words. *Journal of Experimental Child Psychology, 34,* 77–92.

Sameroff, A. J. (1989). Principles of development and psychopathology. In A. J. Sameroff & R. N. Emde (Eds.), *Relationship disturbances in early childhood: A developmental approach* (pp. 17–32). New York: Basic.

Schachtel, E. G. (1947/1982). On memory and childhood amnesia. In U. Neisser (Ed.), *Memory observed: Remembering in natural contexts* (pp. 189–200). New York: W. H. Freeman.

Schank, R. C., & Abelson, R. P. (1977). *Scripts, plans, goals, and understanding.* Hillsdale, NJ: Erlbaum.

Schmideberg, M. (1953). Infant memories and constructions. *Psychoanalytic Quarterly, 19,* 468–481.

Schoen, L. S., Kramer, M., & Kinney, L. (1984). Auditory thresholds in the dream disturbed. *Sleep Research, 13,* 102.

Schwartz, B., & Reisberg, D. (1991). *Learning and memory.* New York: Norton.

Schwarz, E. D., Kowalski, J. M., & McNally, R. J. (1993). Malignant memories: Post-traumatic changes in memory in adults after a school shooting. *Journal of Traumatic Stress, 6* (4), 545–553.

Searleman, A., & Herrmann, D. (1994). *Memory from a broader perspective.* New York: McGraw-Hill.

Seay, B., Alexander, B. K., & Harlow, H. F. (1964). Maternal behavior of socially deprived rhesus monkeys. *Journal of Abnormal and Social Psychology, 69,* 345–354.

Sechehaye, M. (1951). *Autobiography of a schizophrenic girl* (G. Rubin-Rabson, Trans.). New York: Grune & Stratton.

Selye, H. (1956). *The stress of life.* New York: McGraw-Hill.

Shalev, A. Y., Orr, S. P., & Pitman, R. K. (1993). Psychophysiologic assessment of traumatic imagery in Israeli civilian patients with posttraumatic stress disorder. *American Journal of Psychiatry, 150* (4), 620–624.

Shanks, D. R., & St. John, M. F. (1994). Characteristics of dissociable human learning systems. *Behavioral and Brain Sciences, 17,* 367–447.

Sheingold, K., & Tenney, Y. J. (1963). Memory for a salient childhood event. In U. Neisser (1982), *Memory observed: Remembering in natural contexts* (pp. 201–212). New York: W. H. Freeman.

Shilony, E., & Grossman, F. K. (1993). Depersonalization as a defense mechanisms in survivors of trauma. *Journal of Traumatic Stress, 6* (1), 119–128.

Shopper, M. (1995). Medical procedures as a source of trauma. *Bulletin of the Menninger Clinic, 59* (2), 191–204.

Singer, J. A., & Salovey, P. (1988). Mood and memory: Evaluating the network theory of affect. *Clinical Psychology Review, 8,* 211–251.

Singer, J. A., & Salovey, P. (1993). *The remembered self: Emotion and memory in personality.* New York: Free Press.

Singer, M. T. (1995). *Cults in our midst: The hidden menace in our everyday lives.* San Francisco: Jossey-Bass.

Sink, F. (1988). Sexual abuse in the lives of children In M. B. Straus (Ed.), *Abuse and victimization across the life span* (pp. 82–106). Baltimore: Johns Hopkins University Press.

Siomopoulos, V. (1971). Hysterical psychosis: Psychopathological aspects. *British Journal of Medical Psychology, 44,* 95–100.

Slackman, E., & Nelson, K. (1984). Acquisition of an unfamiliar script in story form by young children. *Child Development, 55,* 329–340.

Solomon, Z., Mikulincer, M., & Arad, R. (1991). Monitoring and blunting: Implications for combat-related post-traumatic stress disorder. *Journal of Traumatic Stress, 4* (2), 209–220.

Southwick, S. M., Morgan, A., Nagy, L. M., Bremner, D., Nicolaou, A. L., Johnson, D. R., Rosencheck, R., & Charney, D. S. (1993). Trauma-related symptoms in veterans of Operation Desert Storm: A preliminary report. *American Journal of Psychiatry, 150* (10), 1524–1528.

Spence, D. P. (1982). *Narrative truth and historical truth.* New York: Norton.

Sperling, G. (1960). The information available in brief visual presentations. *Psychological Monographs: General and Applied, 74,* 1–29.

Sperling, G. (1963). A model for visual memory tasks. *Human Factors, 5,* 19–31.

Spiegel, D., & Fink, R. (1979). Hysterical psychosis and hypnotizability. *American Journal of Psychiatry, 136* (6), 777–781.

Spiegel, D., Hunt, T., & Dondershine, H. E. (1988). Dissociation and hypnotizability in posttraumatic stress disorder. *American Journal of Psychiatry, 145* (3), 301–305.

Spiegel, D. (1986). Dissociating damage. *American Journal of Clinical Hypnosis, 29* (2), 123–131.

Squire, L. R. (1987). *Memory and brain.* New York: Oxford University Press.

Sroufe, L. A. (1989). Relationships, self, and individual adaptation. In A. J. Sameroff & R. N. Emde (Eds.), *Relationship disturbances in early childhood* (pp. 70–94). New York: Basic.

Stenberg, C., Campos, J., & Emde, R. (1983). The facial expression of anger in seven-month-old infants. *Child Development, 54,* 178–184.

Stern, D. N. (1989). The representation of relational patterns: Developmental considerations. In A. J. Sameroff & R. N. Emde (Eds.), *Relationship disturbances in early childhood* (pp. 52–69). New York: Basic.

Stone, E. (1988). *Black sheep and kissing cousins: How our family stories shape us.* New York: Penguin.

Strichartz, A. F., & Burton, R. V. (1990). Lies and truth: A study of the development of the concept. *Child Development, 61,* 211–220.

Sullivan, H. S. (1953). *The interpersonal theory of psychiatry.* New York: Norton.

Sullivan, M., Rovee-Collier C., & Tynes, D. (1979). A conditioning analysis of infant long-term memory. *Child Development, 50,* 152–162.

Sutker, P. B., Winstead, D. K., Galina, Z. H., & Allain, A. N. (1991). Cognitive deficits and psychopathology among former prisoners of war and combat veterans of the Korean conflict. *American Journal of Psychiatry, 148* (1) 67–72.

Swanson, J. M., & Kinsbourne, M. (1979). State-dependent learning and retrieval: Methodological cautions and theoretical considerations. In J. F. Kihlstrom & F. J. Evans (Eds.), *Functional disturbances of memory* (pp. 275–299). Hillsdale, NJ: Erlbaum.

Terr, L. C. (1985). Children traumatized in small groups. In S. Eth & R. S. Pynoos (Eds.), *Post-traumatic stress disorder in children* (pp. 45–70). Washington, DC: American Psychiatric Press.

Terr, L. C. (1990). *Too scared to cry: Psychic trauma in childhood.* New York: HarperCollins.

Terr, L. C. (1994). *Unchained memories: True stories of traumatic memories lost and found.* New York: Basic.

Tonkin, E. (1992). *Narrating our past: The social construction of oral history.* New York: Cambridge University Press.

Treffert, D. A. (1989). *Extraordinary people: Understanding savant syndrome.* New York: Ballantine.

Trimble, M. R. (1985). Post-traumatic stress disorder: History of a concept. In C. R. Figley (Ed.), *Trauma and its wake: The study and treatment of post-traumatic stress disorder* (Vol. I, pp. 5–14). New York: Brunner/Mazel.

Tulving, E. (1983). *Elements of episodic memory.* Oxford: Clarendon Press.

Ulman, R. B., & Brothers, D. (1988). *The shattered self: A psychoanalytic study of trauma.* Hillsdale, NJ: Analytic Press.

van der Hart, O., Brown, P., & van der Kolk, B. A. (1989). Pierre Janet's treatment of post-traumatic stress. *Journal of Traumatic Stress, 2* (4), 379–395.

van der Hart, O., Witztum, E., & Friedman, B. (1993). From hysterical psychosis to reactive dissociative psychosis. *Journal of Traumatic Stress, 6* (1), 43–64.

van der Kolk, B. A. (1987a). The psychological consequences of overwhelming life experiences. In B. A. van der Kolk (Ed.), *Psychological trauma* (pp. 1–30). Washington, DC: American Psychiatric Press.

van der Kolk, B. A. (1987b). The separation cry and the trauma response: Developmental issues in the psychobiology of attachment and separation. In B. A. van der Kolk (Ed.), *Psychological trauma* (pp. 31–62). Washington, DC: American Psychiatric Press.

van der Kolk, B. A., & Greenberg, M. S. (1987). The psychobiology of the trauma response: Hyperarousal, constriction, and addiction to traumatic reexposure. In B. A. van der Kolk (Ed.), *Psychological trauma* (pp. 63–67). Washington, DC: American Psychiatric Press.

van der Kolk, B. A., & van der Hart, O. (1989). Pierre Janet and the breakdown of adaptation in psychological trauma. *American Journal of Psychiatry, 146* (12), 1530–1540.

van der Kolk, B. A., Brown, P., & van der Hart, O. (1989). Pierre Janet on post-traumatic stress. *Journal of Traumatic Stress, 2,* 265–278.

van der Kolk, B. A., Greenberg, M. S., Boyd, H., & Krystal, J. (1985). Inescapable shock, neurotransmitters, and addiction to trauma: Toward a psychobiology of post-traumatic stress. *Biological Psychiatry, 20,* 314–325.

Van Dyke, C., Zilberg, N. J., & McKinnon, J. A. (1985). Posttraumatic stress disorder: A thirty-year delay in a World War II veteran. *American Journal of Psychiatry, 142* (9), 1070–1073.

Van Gennep, A. (1960). *The rites of passage.* Chicago: University of Chicago Press.

Vansina, J. (1985). *Oral tradition as history.* Madison: University of Wisconsin Press.

Volkan, V. D. (1981). *Linking objects and linking phenomena.* New York: International Universities Press.

Volkan, V. D. (1988). *The need to have enemies and allies: From clinical practice to international relationships.* Northvale, NJ: Jason Aronson.

Waites, E. A. (1977–78). Female masochism and the enforced restriction of choice. *Victimology: An International Journal, 2* (3–4), 535–544.

Waites, E. A. (1993). *Trauma and survival: Post-traumatic and dissociative disorders in women.* New York: Norton.

Waites, E. A. (1995). Transference dimensions of biography. *Psychoanalytic Review, 82* (1), 107–124.

Waldfogel, S. (1948/1982). Childhood memories. In U. Neisser (Ed.), *Memory observed: Remembering in natural contexts.* New York: W. H. Freeman.

Walker, E. L. (1958). Action decrement and its relation to learning. *Psychological Review, 65,* 129–142.

Weinstein, H. M. (1990). *Psychiatry and the CIA: Victims of mind control.* Washington, DC: American Psychiatric Press.

Wellman, H. M., & Estes, D. (1986). Early understanding of mental entities: A reexamination of childhood realism. *Child Development, 57,* 910–923.

Wetzler, S. (1985). The historical truth of psychoanalytic reconstructions. *International Review of Psycho-Analysis, 12,* 187–197.

Whitfield, C. L. (1995). *Memory and abuse: Remembering and healing the effects of trauma.* Deerfield Beach, FL: Health Communications.

Wilbur, C. B. (1985). The effect of child abuse on the psyche. In R. P. Kluft (Ed.), *Childhood antecedents of multiple personality* (pp. 21–35). Washington, DC: American Psychiatric Press.

Wilkinson, J. (1988). Context effects in children's event memory. In M. Gruneberg, P. Morris, & R. Sykes (Eds.), *Practical aspects of memory: Current research and issues* (Vol. I). Chichester, England: Wiley.

Winnicott, D. W. (1971). *Playing and reality.* New York: Basic.

Wolff, P. (1969). The natural history of crying and other vocalizations in early infancy. In B. Foss (Ed.), *Determinants of infant behavior.* New York: Wiley.

Woolley, J. D., & Wellman, H. M. (1993). Origin and truth: Young children's understanding of imaginary mental representations. *Child Development, 64,* 1–17.

Yapko, M. D. (1994). *Suggestions of abuse.* New York: Simon & Schuster.

Yehuda, R., Giller, E. L., Southwick, S. M., Lowy, M. T., & Mason, J. W. (1991). Hypothalamic-pituitary-adrenal dysfunction in posttraumatic stress disorder. *Biological Psychiatry, 30,* 1031–1048.

Yehuda, R., Kahana, B., Binder-Byrnes, K., Southwick, S. M., Mason, J. W., &

Giller, E. L. (1995). Low urinary cortisol excretion in holocaust survivors with posttraumatic stress disorder. *American Journal of Psychiatry, 152* (7), 982–115.

Yehuda, R., Keefe, R. S. E., Harvey, P. D., Levengood, R. A., Gerber, D. K., Geni, J., & Siever, L. J. (1995). Learning and memory in combat veterans with posttraumatic stress disorder. *American Journal of Psychiatry, 152* (1), 137–139.

Zaidi, L. Y., & Foy, D. W. (1994). Childhood abuse experiences and combat-related PTSD. *Journal of Traumatic Stress, 7* (1), 33–41.

Zajonc, R. B., & Markus, H. (1984). Affect and cognition: The hard interface. In C. E. Izard, J. Kagan, & R. B. Zajonc (Eds.), *Emotions, cognition, and behavior.* New York: Cambridge University Press.

Zaragoza, M. S. (1991). Preschool children's susceptibility to memory impairment. In J. Doris (Ed.), *The suggestibility of children's recollections: Implications for eyewitness testimony* (pp. 27–39). Washington, DC: American Psychological Association.

Zeitlin, S. J., Kotkin, A. J., & Baker, H. C. (1982). *A celebration of American family folklore.* New York: Pantheon.

Index